COLONIAL FAMILIES

of
ANNE ARUNDEL COUNTY,
MARYLAND

Robert Barnes

Colonial Roots
Millsboro, DE
2015

Colonial Roots

Helping you grow your family tree

ISBN 978-1-68034-027-3
First printing 1995
Second printing 2003
Reprinted January 2015

CONTENTS

[page intentionally blank]

INTRODUCTION

Anne Arundel County lies on Maryland's coastal plain and is bounded on the north by Baltimore City and Baltimore County, on the west by Howard and Prince George's Counties, on the south by Calvert County, and on the west by the Chesapeake Bay.

The county was originally settled by ten Puritan families who came, at the invitation of Lord Baltimore, to Maryland from the Nansemond River in Virginia. They called their new home Providence, and soon developed communities at Herring Creek, West River, South River, Middle Neck, and Broad or Town Neck.[1] These Puritans, who were the victims of persecution in Virginia, showed their gratitude by refusing to take an Oath of Allegiance to Lord Baltimore, but they were represented at the General Assembly of 6 April 1650. That same month, an Act was passed establishing Providence into a county by the name of Annarundel.[2]

The new county was named for the Lady Anne Arundel, wife of Cecilius Calvert, Lord Baltimore.

In 1674, the southern limits of Baltimore County were declared to be "on the south side of the Patapsco River, and from the highest plantations on that side of the river, due south into the woods." However, in 1726, the General Assembly passed an Act making the Patapsco River the boundary between the two counties.[3]

Other than some adjustments of the boundary between Anne Arundel and Calvert Counties in 1777 and 1825, the last major change in the boundary lines of Anne Arundel County occurred in 1838 when Howard District was created and established as a separate county in 1851.[4]

For some time my interests in the families of Anne Arundel County centered on the Barnes and Phelps lineages. Over the years, I have worked on my Barnes and related families, and performed research on the Phelps line for my friend Samuel Phelps, Jr. In considering a publication of other families of the County, I have elaborated on some of the related

---

[1] Edward B. Matthews. "The Counties of Maryland: Their Origin, Boundaries, and Election Districts," *Maryland Geological Survey, Volume Six* (Baltimore: The Johns Hopkins Press, 1906), p. 435.
[2] *Archives of Maryland,* hereafter abbreviated as ARMD, 1:180, 183, 292.
[3] Matthews, *op. cit.,* pp. 436-438.
[4] Matthews, *op. cit.,* pp. 439-441.

families, as well as other families of interest. In expanding coverage, I have avoided those families addressed by Harry Wright Newman in his three volumes of *Anne Arundel Gentry*, except in instances in which I have new information. I treated J. D. Warfield's *Founders of Anne Arundel and Howard Counties* in a similar manner. Elise Greenup Jourdan, in her excellent series, *Early Families of Southern Maryland*,[5] has also discussed a number of Anne Arundel County families.

I have also included information from some articles on Anne Arundel County families that have appeared in issues of the *Maryland Genealogical Society Bulletin.*

A number of people contributed to this volume by sending material or by allowing material I had compiled for them to be included. They are acknowledged in the section on their particular family. At this point, I must acknowledge the vast amount of material contributed by Larry Bowling, Wanda Barnes Hall, and Carol Gehrs Mitchell on the Barnes Family, and I am indebted to the late Dr. Caleb and Ruth (Barnes) Dorsey for the material they shared with me many years ago when I was first getting started.

A variety of primary sources were used in putting together this volume of *Colonial Families of Anne Arundel County*. Some of them are described below.

Land Records were combed looking for statements that provided clues to marriages, descents of property, and places of origin. Sometimes rather complicated family relationships were unraveled on the pages of land records.

The Anne Arundel County Judgement Records (in other counties sometimes called Court Proceedings) were found to be full of information.

Probate Records - including wills, inventories, administration accounts, and final distributions of estates - are one of the staple resources of genealogical research. All categories of records were searched in order to build as complete a picture of the family as possible. This part of the research was made much easier by the many excellent volumes of probate materials abstracted, indexed, and published by Vernon L. Skinner, Jr.

---

[5] Westminster: Family Line Publications.

Depositions, sworn testimony by witnesses called deponents, were found in a variety of places. Land commissions, land records, and ejectment papers[6] are just a few of the sources for these items, which usually give the name of the deponent and his or her age. Oft times there are references to other family members. The work done by Henry C. Peden, Jr., in abstracting and publishing these early depositions helped my research greatly.

Robert Barnes
Perry Hall, Maryland
October 1996

---

[6] Ejectment Papers deal with cases involving landlords, tenants, and ownership of land. The documents in these cases, especially the depositions, often contain much helpful family history.

ANCESTRY OF
CATHERINE SUSAN BARNES, b. 14 July 1993
and
ROBERT CARROLL BARNES, b. 3 December 1995

(?) - indicates linkage to preceding generation is not proven.
Known immigrant ancestors are in boldface type.

1.   Catherine Susan Barnes, b. 14 July 1993.
1.   Robert Carroll Barnes, b. 3 December 1995.

Second Generation
2.Rev. Robert William Barnes, Jr., b. 16 March 1961, m. on 27 June
      1987:
3.Linda Bell Wentworth, b. 19 October 1963 at Brattleboro, VT.

Third Generation
4.Robert William Barnes, Sr., b. 22 March 1939, Baltimore, MD, m. 17
      April 1960:
5.Catherine Ellen Rockel, b. 25 June 1937. Robert and Catherine were
      the parents of:
            a.Robert William Barnes, Jr., b. 16 March 1961, m. Linda
                  Bell Wentworth.
            b.JoAnne Barnes, b. 13 April 1967.
            c.Nancy Lee Barnes, b. 7 August 1970.
            d.Susan Ellen Barnes, b. 21 September 1978.
6.Carroll Clemens Wentworth, b. 5 October 1927 at Brattleboro, m. 7
      July 1962:
7.Susan Million Whitney, b. 21 June 1941, New York City, NY.

Fourth Generation
8.William Cary Barnes, b. 19 May 1908, Baltimore, MD, d. 27 October
      1963, Baltimore, MD, m. 26 June 1937:
9.Marion Valentine Rigney, b. 14 February 1918. (She m. 2nd, on 25
      November 1965, Nathan Bernstein.) William and Marion
      were the parents of:
            a.Robert William Barnes (#1).
b.Ronald Lee Barnes, m. Barbara Sleeger.
            c.Nancy Louise Barnes, m. Ronald Saari.
            d.Marjorie Lee Barnes.
10.William Rudolf Rockel, b. 30 May 1890, d. 10 May 1955, Veteran of
      World War I.
11.Dorothy Elizabeth Barnes, d. February 1992. William and Dorothy
      (Barnes) Rockel were the parents of:
a.Catherine Barnes, b. 25 June 1937, m. Robert William Barnes.
            b.William Rudolf Barnes, Jr., b. 27 August 1938, m. 1st,
                  Helen (N), and 2nd, (N) (N).

c.Dorothy Mae Barnes, b. 19 April 1941.

d.Henry Barnes, b. 23 April 1943, m. Marie Josephine Roemer.

e.Robert Lawrence Barnes, b. 22 October 1947, m. 1st Sharon (N), and 2nd Gloria Pumphrey.

12.Harland Harrington Wentworth, b. 5 November 1889, East Dover, VT, d. August 1936 at Brattleboro, VT, m. 1921:

13.Corena Alice Bell, b. 6 March 1889, Jacksonville, VT, d. March 1968 at Brattleboro, VT.

14.Horace Burton Whitney, b. 8 May 1910, New York, NY, d. 25 February 1964, m. 9 May 1936 (or 1937):

15.Martha Million, b. 24 August 1910, Richmond, KY, d. 26 November 1955, Pelham, NY.

Fifth Generation

16.Cary McHenry Barnes, b. 16 April 1877, d. 14 April 1957, Baltimore, MD, m. 28 June 1905:

17.Mamie Missouri Swam, b. 1 August 1877, d. 2 September 1956.

18.George Luther Rigney, Jr., b. 9 November 1886, Baltimore Co., MD, d. 22 March 1969, m. 16 April 1917:

19.**Florence Malvina Habgood,** b. 28 November 1889, Eastbourne, England, d. 28 November 1984, Baltimore, MD, on her 95th birthday. George and Florence were the parents of:

a.Marion Valentine Rigney (#9 above).

b.Lillian Lorraine Rigney, m. Rev. George W. Pferdeort.

20.George Rockel, bur. Loudon Park Cemetery, Baltimore, MD.

21.Katherine Tantz, bur. Loudon Park Cemetery, Baltimore, MD.

22.Elmer Francis Barnes, b. 1882, d. 1951, bur. Providence Church, Gamber, Carroll Co., MD.

23.Elizabeth Heath or Heif.

24.Charles Lucien Wentworth, b. c1846.

25.Sarah Harrington, b. Barre, MA.

26.Frank P. Bell, b. 4 March 1847, Colerain, MA, d. 1925, Brattleboro, VT, m. 1 January 1873:

27.Eva Olive Tenney.

28.Miles S. Whitney, d. 23 February 1963, Buffalo, NY, m. 22 June 1907:

29.Mayme Noble Young, b. 18 March 1883, Dundee, NY, d. 3 February 1966, Snyder, NY.

30.Edwin Peyton Million, b. 15 October 1858, White Hall, KY, d. 27 June 1943, Brocksville, MI, m. 18 April 1905:

31.Nancy Ellen Hampton, b. 16 June 1877, Breathitt Co., KY, d. 22 September 1960, Washington, DC.

Sixth Generation

32.Michael Denton Barnes, d. 4 March 1915, Baltimore, MD, m. 10 Febraury 1870:

33.Christie Anne Taylor, d. 30 October 1913, Baltimore, MD.
34.John Wesley Swam, b. 28 July 1855, Baltimore, MD, d. 1937,
    Baltimore, MD, m. 21 July 1878, York Co., PA:
35.Sarah E. Sweitzer, b. November 1855, York Co., PA, d. 1937,
    Baltimore, MD.
36.George Luther Rigney, Sr., b. 5 August 1855, Baltimore Co., MD, d.
    24 August 1915, m. 25 December 1878:
37.Lydia Sophia Hoffman, b. 18 August 1860, d. February 1929.
38.Edwin Thomas Habgood, of Eastbourne, Sussex, England.
39.Mary Anne Newman, b. 15 November 1850, Tewkesbury, Glos.,
    England.
40.**Henry Rockel,** bur. Loudon Park Cemetery, Baltimore, MD.
41.**Elizabeth Habermahl,** bur. Loudon Park Cemetery, Baltimore, MD.
42.**August Tantz.**
43.**Mary Stephan.**
44.Jabez Nelson Barnes, b. 1851, d. 1939, Providence Church, Gamber,
    Carroll Co., MD.
45.Keturah Ellen Haines, b. 1861, d. 1929, Providence Church, Gamber,
    Carroll Co., MD.
46.William Heath or Heif.
47.Elizabeth (N).
50.William Harrington, b. c1820, Petersham, MA, m. 2nd, 23 October
    1849:
51.Mary Eliza Hale, b. c1830.
52.James Bell.
53-55.Unknown.
56.Burton G. Whitney, b. 21 August 1854, Clayton, NY, d. 1937,
    resident of Clayton, NY, m. November 1878:
57.Helen Charlebois.
58.Horace J. Young.
59.Emma Gallop.
60.Green B. Million.
61.Sarah Jackson.
62.James Johnson Hampton, Judge in Lee Co., KY.
63.Drusillla Cawood.

Seventh Generation
64.Samuel Barnes, b. c1803, d. 19 August 1879, m. 26 July 1833,
    Baltimore, MD:
65.Elizabeth Sampson, b. c1810, d. 29 August 1885.
66.Richard Taylor, b. c1809, Baltimore Co., MD, d. 1 April 1877, m. 22
    December 1834, Baltimore Co., MD:
67.Ellen Norris, b. c1809, d. 7 July 1870, Baltimore Co., MD.
68.William Swam, b. c1813, d. 10 October 1882.
69.Mary Anne Harris, b. c1818, Baltimore Co., MD.
70.Jacob Sweitzer, b. 10 February 1824, d. 28 April 1862, resident of
    York Co., PA.

71.Julian Bahn, d. 22 October 1905 at York Co., PA.

72.John Rigney, b. c1817, d. 15 October 1889.

73.Mary Taylor, d. 23 December 1883, age 47.

74.Daniel Hoffman, b. 8 May 1837, Baltimore Co., MD, d. 28 April
    1918. Fought in the Union Army in the Civil War, serving
    three years, first as a private in Capt. Frank H. Hardesty's
    Company, 1st Regiment of the Potomac Home Brigade, and
    later transferred to Company G of the 13th Maryland
    Infantry.

75.Mary Elizabeth Sipe, b. 1 September 1840, d. 12 December 1906.

76.John Habgood, b. c1826, Leigh, Wilts., England.

77.Jane Kinnett, bapt. 26 December 1824, Purton Stoke, England.

78.Alexander Newman, bapt. 3 June 1804, d. 29 December 1869, in
    England, m. 10 February 1834:

79.Anne Evenis, bapt. 9 February 1812, d. 30 June 1864, age 53.

80.George Rockel.

81.**Anna Margaret Moeller,** b. September 1804 in Engelrod, Hesse-
    Darmstadt, came to Baltimore, MD, after her husband d.,
    she d. 3 October 1876 and was bur. in Western Cemetery,
    Baltimore, MD.

88.Moses Barnes, b. 11 September 1810, d. 18 September 1892,
    Providence Church, Gamber, Carroll Co., MD.

89.Kezia Murray, b. 20 February 1814, d. 1 March 1901, Providence
    Church, Gamber, Carroll Co., MD.

90.Louis Francis Haines, b. 1832, d. 1924, Providence Church, Gamber,
    Carroll Co., MD.

91.Agnes Jane Shipley, b. 1839, d. 1915, Providence Church, Gamber,
    Carroll Co., MD.

100.Isaac Harrington.

101.Lydia (N).

102.Joel Hale, b. c1796 in VT, d. 25 June 1884 at West Windsor,
    Windsor Co., VT, m. 1st, 5 June 1827 [He m. 2nd, on 5 July
    1831, Pluma Taylor, b. c1808, d. 15 March 1885, age 77 at
    Bolton, CT. She is bur. at West Windsor, VT.]:

103.Chloe Taylor, b. c1803, d. at West Windsor, VT, 1 January 1829,
    age 26.

112.(Possibly) Floyd E. Whitney, b. c1825, Clayton, NY, d. 1894.

113.Cynthia M. Barrows.

114.Joseph Charlebois, b. c1833, m. 31 December 1850:

115.Helen Bertrand, b. 4 September 1838, d. 10 August 1905.

124.Major Hamilton Hampton, b. 14 April 1806, lived at Roan
    Mountain, TN.

125.Rebecca Flanery.

126.Moses Cawood, b. 6 May 1820, moved to Owsley Co., KY, in 1857,
    m. 1840 in Harlan Co., KY. Killed during the Civil War.

127.Emily Maddy, b. 15 January 1821, d. 30 April 1894.

Eighth Generation

128.William Barnes, b. 9 September 1771, Anne Arundel Co., MD.

129-131.Unknown.

132.Richard Taylor, b. 26 March 1768, Baltimore Co., MD, d. 14 July 1853.

133.Catherine Stansbury, b. c1778, d. 7 July 1827, in Baltimore Co., MD.

134-137.Unknown.

138.Caleb Harris of Baltimore Co., MD.

139.Maria Baker, b. 13 January 1794, d. 2 September 1875.

140.George Sweitzer, b. 23 March 1795, d. 23 October 1877, York Co., PA.

141.Susanna Catherine Heckman, b. 4 March 1795, d. 26 March 1882, York Co., PA.

142.John Bahn, d. 9 March 1871, York Co., PA.

143.Magdalena Swartz, b. 5 May 1800, d. 18 July 1869, York Co., PA.

144-145.Unknown.

146.George Taylor, b. c1808, d. 12 April 1860 in Baltimore Co., MD.

147.Susanna E. Tracey, b. c1812, d. 26 March 1876 in Baltimore Co., MD.

148.Henry Hoffman, b. by 1818, living in 1850 in Baltimore Co., MD.

149.Lydia Shearer, b. c1807.

150.John T. Sipes, b. 21 December 1801, d. 13 August 1882.

151.Ruth Ann Fredericks, b. 8 April 1813, d. 24 January 1883.

152.James Habgood, b. c1805, Leigh, Wilts., England.

153.Elizabeth (N), b. c1797, Wilts., England.

154.(?) Joseph Kinnett, m. 9 November 1814, Purton, Wilts., England.

155.(?) Elizabeth Matthews.

156.John Newman, m. 23 April 1797, England:

157.Mary Atwood.

158.Thomas Evenis, bapt. 29 November 1789, m. 20 October 1808, England:

159.Ann Salt.

160.John Henry Rockel, b. 9 February 1776 in Lauterbach, Hesse-Darmstadt, m. there on 2 December 1808:

161.Juliana Schilling, b. 9 September 1776 in Lauterbach, Hesse-Darmstadt.

162.Johann Heinrich Moeller.

163.Anna Barbara Delcher.

176.Moses Barnes.

177.Airey Poole.

178.Jabez Murray, b. 19 December 1771, d. 19 August 1847, bur. Sandymount Church, Carroll Co., MD.

179.Sarah Richards, b. 17 December 1782, d. 28 October 1868, bur. Sandymount Church, Carroll Co., MD.

180.Benjamin Haines, b. c1794.

181.Mary Barnes, b. c1794.

182.Frederick Shipley, b. 18 March 1807, d. 6 April 1864, bur. Mt.
    Pleasant Methodist Church, Gamber, Carroll Co., MD.
183.Ketura Poole, b. (?), d. 21 March 18--, age 34? years, 4 months, 23
    days, bur. Mt. Pleasant Methodist Church, Gamber, Carroll
    Co., MD.
204.Silas Hale, b. 28 May 1760, d. 15 March 1835, private from MA in
    the Revolutionary War, he m. 2nd, Huldah (N).
205.Sarah Pearson.
224.James Whitney, b. 1796 at Albany, NY or VT.
225.Abigail Ormsby.
226.Oliver Barrows, b. 1776, d. 1851.
227.Miriam Wilkie, b. 1781, Ashfield, MA, d. 1865, Sackett's Harbor.
248.Johnson Hampton, b. 1775, d. 1855.
249.Sarah Baker, d. 31 May 1896, age 95.
250.Silas Flannery, M.D.
252.John Cawood, b. 1786.
253.Nancy Turner, b. 1795, Harlan Co., KY, said to be the first white
    child b. in Harlan Co., KY.

Ninth Generation
256.Michael Barnes, of Anne Arundel Co., MD, took Oath of Fidelity in
    1778, d. by 1799.
257.Patience Shipley.
264.Richard Taylor, b. 6 February 1738, d. 1821 in Baltimore Co., MD.
    Refused to take the Oath of Fidelity in 1778.
265.Anna Stevenson of Baltimore Co., MD.
266.Luke Stansbury, d. by 1798, Baltimore Co., MD.
267.Catherine (N).
276.Thomas Harris, d. by 9 December 1845, Baltimore Co., MD.
280.Adam Sweitzer, b. 1 January 1771, d. 2 April 1863, York Co., PA.
281.Anna (N).
282.George Heckman, b. 16 October 1766, d. 17 April 1856, bur.
    Saddler's Church, Hopewell Township, York Co., PA.
283.Catherine (Minnich?), b. 4 May 1765, d. 20 February 1824, bur. at
    Saddler's Church.
284.**Frederick Bahn,** b. c1758 in Germany, d. 1856, York Co., PA.
285.Catherine (N).
286.Henry S(ch)wartz, b. 23 April 1774, d. 27 May 1844, York Co., PA.
287.Anna Maria Zech, b. 30 April 1778, d. 18 September 1852, York
    Co., PA.
292.(?) Edward Taylor, d. by 24 November 1829, Baltimore Co., MD, m.
    by license dated 20 January 1789:
293.(?) Ann Brown.
294.(?) Joshua Tracey, b. 1746, d. 1832.
295.(?) Catherine Stiffler, b. 18 July 1791, d. 6 November 1871.
296.Gottlieb Hoffman, served in War of 1812, d. by 25 June 1817, m. 18
    March 1805 in Baltimore Co., MD:

297. Rachel Marshal, she m. 2nd, Levi Lamotte.
298. (John) Daniel Shearer, b. 10 September 1765, bapt. 15 September 1766, St. Jacob's Church, Codorus Township, York Co., PA, d. 3 February 1856, Baltimore Co., MD, bur. St. Peter's Lutheran Church.
299. Mary Sophia Smith (dau. of George and Catherine [Gohn] Smith), b. 29 October 1768, d. 21 March 1849, bur. at St. Peter's Lutheran Church.
302. (?) Aquila Frederick, d. 1864.
303. M(?) (N), b. c1777, living in 1870.
304. Thomas Habgood, age 76 in 1851, b. South Cerny, Wilts., England. (1851 census), bapt. 15 August 1775 (parish register).
305. Sarah (N), age 76 in 1851, b. Brayon, Wilts. (1851 census).
316. Thomas Evenis.
317. Sarah (N).
320. Johann Rockel, b. c1749, d. at Lauterbach, Hesse-Darmstadt, 30 January 1807, age 59.
321. Anna Catherine Schiebelhuth, b. c1758, d. 11 January 1809.
322. Johann Heinrich Schilling.
323. Anna E. Doll.
352. Dorsey Barnes, bro. of #362 below.
353. Lydia Musgrove.
356. John Murray, b. 1747, d. 1833, Baltimore Co., MD, Captain in Baltimore County Militia during the Revolutionary War.
357. Diana (possibly Cox).
358. Richard Richards, d. 1834, Baltimore Co., MD.
359. Anne Brown.
360. Daniel Haines, d. c1846 in Carroll Co., MD, m. by license dated 24 January 1782:
361. Ann Sollers.
362. Adam Barnes, d. 1809, Baltimore Co., MD, bro. of #352 above.
363. Ruth Shipley.
364. Adam Shipley.
365. Ruth Chrisman.
366. Lloyd Poole, b. 14 March c1781, d. 22 February 1863, bur. Mt. Pleasant Methodist Church, Gamber, Carroll Co., MD.
367. Naomi Barnes, dau. of Adam Barnes (362) and Ruth Shipley (363), b. 10 June 1785, d. 12 May 1873, bur. Mt. Pleasant, member of Methodist Church for over 76 years.
408. Samuel Hale, b. 20 March 1719, d. 4/5 July 1805, in 1760 resided Leominster, Warwick Co., MA.
409. Eleanor Smith, b. 1727, d. 7 March 1794.
448. Capt. William Whitney, b. 1749, d. 1800, of VT.
454. (Possibly) John Wilkie, d. Buckland by 1 June 1805, m. 12 June 1766 at Ashfield, MA. (Russell L. Warner, *Miles Standish of the Mayflower and His Descendants for 5 Generations.*

Published by the General Society of Mayflower
Descendants, 1990.):
455.(Possibly) Elizabeth Standish, b. Mansfield, CT.
496.James Hampton, fought at King's Mountain, killed by lightning in
1784, having moved to NC.
497.Rachel Freeman.
504.Berry Cawood, b. 1747 (DAR Patriot Index says 1758), d. post 1834.
Private from VA and NC in Revolutionary War, pensioned.
505.Nancy Scott.
506.William Turner.
507.Susan Bailey.

Tenth Generation
512.Adam Barnes, d. c1779, of Anne Arundel Co., MD.
513.Honor Dorsey.
514.William Shipley, b. 1 May 1729, Anne Arundel Co., MD, m. by
November 1756:
515.Rebecca Ogg, b. 16 November 1732.
528.Thomas Taylor of Baltimore Co., MD.
529.Sarah Price.
530.Henry Stevenson of Baltimore Co., MD.
531.Jemima Merryman.
532.Thomas Stansbury, b. 24 April 1714, d. 1798, m. 2 March 1735, took
Oath of Fidelity to State of MD, 1778:
533.Hannah Gorsuch, b. 1718.
560.Andrew Sweitzer, b. by 1751, d. 1818.
561.Elizabeth Geringer, d. after 1818.
564.**Sebastian Heckman,** immigrated on *The Chance*, 1766, d. after
1792, York Co., PA.
565.Susanna (?), d. 1812 in Baltimore Co., MD.
566.(?) **Philip Simon Minnich,** b. 1728, d. c1797.
567.(?) Catherine Elizabeth (N).
572.Henry Schwartz, b. 22 July 1751, d. 1799 Shrewsbury Township,
York Co., PA.
573.Anna Magdalena Schafer.
574.Michael Zech, b. c1755, d. 21 May 1817.
575.Marie Dorothea Ehrhart, b. 13 April 1760, d. 13 May 1832, York
Co., PA.
586.John Brown, d. Baltimore Co., intestate, by 27 December 1820.
588.Bazel Tracey, living 1815.
590.Jacob Stiffler, d. by 1831, Baltimore Co., MD.
591.Anne Taylor.
592.**William Hoffman,** b. 1740 in Frankfort on the Main, d. Baltimore
Co., MD, on 16 June 1811, m. 4 June 1771 in Philadelphia,
PA:
593.Susanna Weinbach, b. 26 October 1741, d. 26 April 1803 in
Baltimore Co., MD.

594.William Marshall, d. 1809, Baltimore Co., MD.
595.Rachel Cox.
596.**Jacob Shearer,** b. c1719, d. c1791, came by 1732 on the *John and William,* m. 2nd:
597.Maria Barbara Heller or Keller, b. c1730, d. after March 1805.
598.John George Schmidt/Smith, b. 8 October 1734, d. 1806 York Co., PA.
599.Catherine Elizabeth Gohn, b. 16 September 1744, York Co., PA.
604.**John Frederick,** immigrated from Germany, settled in Baltimore Co., MD.
608.Philip Habgood of England.
609.Susannah.
704.John Barnes, d. 1800 in Baltimore Co. [Son of Adam and Honor (Dorsey) Barnes, #512-513 above.]
705.Hammutal (Shipley?).
706.John Musgrove, d. c1785, Montgomery Co., MD.
712.Jabez Murray.
713.Mary Wheeler.
716.Richard Richards, b. c1725, d. 1811, Baltimore Co., MD.
717.Sarah Hooker.
718.   (Possibly) John Brown, d. intestate by 1820.
720.Michael Haines.
721.Catherine (N).
722.Francis Sollers, d. by 1798.
723.Elizabeth Bowen.
728.Adam Shipley, d. by 1765.
729.Hammutal Tivis.
732.Peter Poole.
733.Ruth Whipps.
816.Israel Hale (Heald), b. 2 December 1687, d. 2 June 1734.
817.Rachel Butterick, d. 26 January 1746.
910.Miles Standish, b. 18 November 1709 at Preston, CT, d. after 1790, m. 1st, 2 November 1737 at Mansfield.
911.Jerusha Fuller.
1008.Stephen Cawood.
1009.Esther Berry.

Eleventh Generation

1024.James Barnes, d. c1726, Baltimore Co., MD.
1025.Ketura Shipley.
1026.John Dorsey, d. in Anne Arundel Co., MD.
1027.Honor (?).
1028.Robert Shipley, b. c1678, d. 1763 in Anne Arundel Co., MD.
1029.Elizabeth Stevens.
1030.George Ogg, Jr., b. 30 April 1696 in Anne Arundel Co., MD, living in November 1756, m. 22 August 1722:
1031.Mary Potee.

1056.Richard Taylor, d. c1726, Baltimore Co., MD.
1057.Anne Tracey, was transported to MD, c1671.
1058.Mordecai Price, d. Baltimore Co., MD.
1059.Mary Parsons.
1060.**Edward Stevenson**, d. 1714, Baltimore Co., MD.
1061.Mary (N), she m. 2nd Henry Sater.
1062.Charles Merryman, Jr., d. 1722 testate, Baltimore Co., MD.
1063.Jane Long, widow of Jos. Peake, she m. 3rd Benjamin Knight.
1064.Thomas Stansbury, b. 1678, d. 4 May 1766 in Baltimore Co., MD.
1065.Jane Hayes.
1066.Charles Gorsuch, b. 1686, d. 1748 in Baltimore Co., MD.
1067.Sarah Cole, b. 1693, d. 1758.
1120.John Sweitzer, d. by 24 February 1801, rendered Patriotic Service
   in PA during the Revolutionary War.
1121.Catherine [Blesing?].
1122.Adam Geringer.
1132.**Johann Peter Muench,** b. c1698, d. by 15 May 1761 in Berks Co.,
   PA, m. 1st 19 September 1724 at Friebach, Southern
   Palatinate, came in 1737 on the *Samuel*:
1133.**Maria Christina Barbara Oster,** d. by 1756.
1144.Andrew Schwartz, d. c1789, Shrewsbury Township, York Co., PA.
1145.Anna Margaret (N).
1146.**John David Shaffer,** d. 1769/70, York Co., PA, m. 13 March
   1743:
1147.**Anna Catherine Simon**, b. c1720, d. c1785.
1148.**Jacob Zech,** d. c1798 in Rockingham Co., VA.
1149.Anna Maria Kohler, d. c1779, Berks Co., PA.
1150.**(John) William Ehrhart,** b. 1721 at Staudernheim, N. Pfalz, came
   in 1741 on the *Friendship*, d. c1781 York Co., PA, m. 1
   December 1746:
1151.Anna Catherine Schreiner d. c1807.
1176.Teague Tracey, d. c1712 in Baltimore Co., MD, d. by 18 June 1712
   in Baltimore Co., m. 3 November 1694 in Anne Arundel
   Co., MD:
1177.Mary James.
1180.**Jacob Stiffler,** b. c1733 in Germany, d. 1807 in Bedford Co., PA.
1181.Catherine Anna Meyers.
1182.George Taylor.
1183.Mary (N).
1184.George Hoffman of Frankfort on the Main, m. by 1740:
1185.Elizabeth (N).
1190.Jacob Cox, d. Baltimore Co., MD, 1798.
1191.Kezia Peregoy.
1196.Henry Schmidt.
1197.Catherine (N).
1198.**Philip Gohn,** came on the *Thistle,* 1738.
1199.**Maria Sophia Bracher,** b. c1711/2, Hornbach, Germany.

1424.**James Murray,** d. 1704, Baltimore Co., MD.
1425.Jemima Morgan.
1426.William Wheeler.
1427.Martha West.
1432.Edward Richards.
1433.Mary (N).
1434.Samuel Hooker.
1435.Sarah (N).
1436.George Brown.
1437.Mary Stevenson.
1444.Robert Sollers.
1445.Mary Selby.
1446.John Bowen, d. by 1742, Baltimore Co., MD.
1447.Mary (N).
1456.Adam Shipley, d. c1770.
1457.Ruth (N).
1458.Robert Tevis.
1466.John Whipps.
1467.Sarah Lucretia Ogg.
1632.Israel Heald, b. 1660, d. 1738.
1633.Martha Wright, d. 1746.
1820.Israel Standish, d. Preston, CT, by 26 January 1729/30, m. 8
       February 1703/4 at Preston:
1821.Elizabeth Richardson, b. Weymouth, d. by 26 January 1729/30.
1822.Matthew Fuller.
1823.Elizabeth Broughton.
2016.John Cawood, b. c1693.
2017.Elizabeth Smallwood.
2018.(Probably) William Berry.
2019.(Probably) Esther Wakefield.

Twelfth Generation
2048-2049.Unknown.
2050.**Adam Shipley**.
2051.Lois (N).
2052.Edward Dorsey.
2053.Sarah Wyatt.
2058.Charles Stevens, b. by 1666, d. by 1703.
2059.Elizabeth (N), she m. 2nd, 1704, Thomas Browne, Jr.
2060.George Ogg, Sr., living December 1723, having m. 1691:
2061.Elizabeth Bagley.
2062.(Possibly) Francis Potee(t), d. by August 1709, Baltimore Co., MD.
2063.Lucy (N) who m. 2nd John Swinyard.
2114.**Samuel Tracey,** immigrated to MD in 1671 and was granted 700
       acres.
2115.(Possibly) Alce (N).
2116.Thomas Price of Anne Arundel and Baltimore Cos., MD.

2117.Elizabeth (Johnson?).
2118.**Thomas Parsons,** may be the Thomas who was transported 77in 1649, d. by 31 May 1684.
2119.Isabella (N), she m. 2nd Benjamin Capel, she d. by 22 December 1717.
2124.Charles Merryman, Sr., d. 1725, Baltimore Co., MD.
2125.Mary (N).
2126.Thomas Long.
2127.**Jane (N) (Waites) (Dixon)** [widow of John Dixon #4262].
2128.**Tobias Starnborough,** transported in 1658 with his parents.
2129.Sarah Raven, she m. 2nd Enoch Spinks.
2130.John Hayes.
2131.Abigail Dixon, she m. 1st Thomas Scudamore.
2132.**Charles Gorsuch,** bapt. 25 August 1642, d. 1716 in Baltimore Co., MD, he m. 2nd, 12 February 1690, Anne Hawkins.
2133.Sarah Cole, d. by 1690.
2134.**John Cole,** b. c1669, m. 2nd Dinah Hawkins.
2135.Joanna Garrett, b. c1675, d. 1714.
2264.**Johann Philip Muench,** weaver.
2266.Leonard Oster.
2294.**Nicholas Simon,** b. c1696, d. 1739, arriving 27 August 1739 on the *Samuel.*
2300.Johann Peter Erhard.
2301.Anna Margaret Becker, bapt. 1682.
2380.Jacob Cox, d. 1 November 1724.
2381.Elizabeth Merryman, she m. 2nd Samuel Smith, d. 1770.
2382.Henry Peregoy.
2398.John George Bracher.
2399.Susanna Margaretta Born, b. c1676, of Unterhof, Switzerland.
2850.**Thomas Morgan.**
2868.Thomas Hooker, b. c1660.
2869.Sarah (N), d. by 1720.
2874.Edward Stevenson, same as #1060.
2875.Mary (N), same as #1061.
2888.John Sollers.
2889.Anne (N).
2890.William Selby.
2891.Mary (N).
2892.**Jonas Bowen,** d. by 1699.
2893.Martha (N).
2912.Richard Shipley (son of Adam and Lois Shipley, #2050-2051 above).
2913.Susanna Stevens.
2932.John Whipps.
2993.Margaret Theerston.
2934.George Ogg (same as George Ogg #1030).
2935.Mary Potee (same as #1031).

3264.John Heald.
3265.Dorothy Royle.
4032.Stephen Cawood, b. c1670.
4033.Mary Cox.
4034.Thomas Smallwood, d. 1734.
4036.Dr. Samuel Berry.

Thirteenth Generation
4104.**Edward Dorsey,** came to Anne Arundel Co., MD, from VA,
    c1650, drowned by 2 August 1659.
4105.**Anne (N),** may have returned to VA after 1659.
4106.**Nicholas Wyatt,** came to VA by 1646, came to Anne Arundel Co.,
    MD, by 1651, d. by 25 September 1676.
4107.Damaris (N), widow, after 1676 m. 3rd Thomas Bland.
4116.Charles Stevens, d. c1658-1666.
4117.Susanna (possibly Norwood), who m. 2nd John Howard.
4248.**John Merryman,** came to VA prior to 1650, d. by 1680.
4249.**Audrey (N),** transported 1649 by John Merryman, she m. 2nd
    Edward Carter, of Lancaster Co., PA, by 10 November
    1680 when she and her sons William and Charles
    Merryman and her second husband conv. 50 acres to Col.
    John Carter and Capt. David Fox (Culver, "Merryman
    Family," *MD Genealogies*, II, 210).
4256.**Detmar Sternberg,** transported 1658.
4257.**Renske (N).**
4258.**Luke Raven,** came to VA c1665, in MD by 1671.
4262.**John Dixon,** immigrated c1665, d. by 27 August c1670/1.
4263.**Jane (N),** widow of (N) Waites, she m. 3rd Thomas Long.
4264.Rev. John Gorsuch, d. c1647, m. c1628:
4265.**Anne Lovelace,** d. by 1652 in VA.
4266.**Thomas Cole,** immigrated to MD c1649, probably d. by 1679.
4267.**Priscilla (N),** immigrated c1649.
4270.Dennis Garrett, murdered by Capt. John Oldton on 31 July 1691, in
    Baltimore Co., MD.
4271.Barbara (possibly Stone), she m. 2nd Thomas Broad.
4600.Johannes Erhard of Staudernheim, N. Pfaltz.
4602.Nicholas Becker.
4762.**Charles Merryman, Sr.,** d. 22 December 1725 [#2124 above].
4763.Mary (?) [#2125 above].
4764.Henry Peregoy.
4765.Amey Green.
4798.Theodore Born.
4799.Kunigunda Forster.

Fourteenth Generation
8528.Daniel Gorsuch, d. 1638, m. 30 April 1599:
8529.Alice Hall, bapt. 25 December 1574, d. c1662/3.

8530.Sir William Lovelace, d. 1648.
8531.Anne Barne, d. c1633.
8542.(?) Thomas Stone, flourished 1685.
9524.**John Merryman (same as #4248).**
9525.**Audrey (N) (same as #4249).**
9528.**Joseph Peregoy.**
9529.Sarah Mumford.

Fifteenth Generation
17056.William Gorsuch.
17057.Avice Hillson.
17058.John Hall, d. 19 November 1618.
17059.Anne Browne, d. 16 December 1619.
17060.William Lovelace, bapt. 30 September 1561, bur. 12 October
       1629.
17061.Elizabeth Aucher, bur. 3 December 1627.
17062.William Barne, b. 1568, d. 1619.
17063.Anne Sandys, b. 21 January 1570.
19058.**Edward Mumford,** transported to MD by 1667, in Baltimore Co.,
       MD, by March 1675.
19059.Ann (?).

Sixteenth Generation
34112.Humphrey Gorsuch.
34113.Eme (N).
34116.Thomas Hall.
34117.Margaret Pawthorne.
34118.John Browne, d. 29 September 1570.
34119.Christian Clarket.
34120.William Lovelace, d. 1577.
34121.Anne Lewis.
34122.Sir Edward Aucher.
34123.Mabel Wroth, b. 1542, d. 1597.
34124.Sir George Barne, b. 1525, d. 1592.
34125.Anne Gerrard.
34126.Edwin Sandys, Archbishop of York, b. c1519, d. 10 July 1588.
34127.Cecily Wilsford, d. c1610/11.

ANCESTRY OF
SAMUEL ARTHUR PHELPS, JR.

Known immigrant ancestors are in boldface type.

First Three Generations
1.Samuel Arthur Phelps, Jr., b. 24 May 1924
1.Anna Cecelia Phelps, b. 8 April 1925, m. Samuel De Amicis.

2.Samuel Arthur Phelps, Sr., b. 8 October 1899, d. 18 September 1986
3.Anna Gertrude Maskell, b. 23 June 1902 or 1904, d. 24 August 1993,
    bur. in New Cathedral Cemetery, Baltimore, MD.

4.Lewis Ellwood Phelps, b. c1859, d. 20 November 1942, Sheriff of
    Howard Co. in 1904, m. 30 March 1882 at Linthicum, MD.
5.Rosalie Nichols, b. c1862, d. 17 November 1915.
6.**Thomas Joseph Maskell**, b. 1863, Mahoneck, near County Cork
    Border, in Limerick Co., Temple Glantine Parish, Ireland.
    He d. 15 July 1922 and is bur. in New Cathedral Cemetery,
    Baltimore, MD.
7.Anna Elizabeth Cecilia Harper, b. 10 September 1869 at St. Charles
    Borromeo Parish, Pikesville, MD. (Birth record gives name
    as Anna E.; marriage record gives name as Anna C.)

Fourth Generation
8.Middleton Belt Phelps, b. c1833/8, bur. Mountain View Cemetery,
    Howard Co., MD.
9.Henrietta Sophia Vernay, b. 13 March 1832, d. 28 May 1899, bur.
    Mountain View Cemetery.
10.Benjamin Franklin Nichols, b. 28 July 1830, d. 29 December 1911, bur.
    St. Mark's Episcopal Church, 000hland, MD.
11.Mary Jane Hearn, b. 7 December 1833, d. 29 April 1900, bur. St.
    Mark's Episcopal Church, Highland, MD.
12.**Martin F. Maskell,** b. c1839 in County Cork, Ireland, d. 26 March
    1906 in Baltimore, MD.
13.Mary Mahoney, b. in Ireland and never came to MD.
14.(John Henry?) Harper.
15.Cecilia Connolly. Records of St. Charles Borrmoeo Church state she d.
    at age 34 (date not given) of spasm at childbirth. She was
    bur. in the Connolly Lot at St. Charles Borromeo Church,
    Pikesville, MD.

Fifth Generation
16.Nelson Phelps, b. c1797, m. by BAML dated 2 December 1823
    (Baltimore Co. Marriage License, names minister as
    McCormick):
17.Ann Carr, b. c1798.

18.John Verney, b. 31 October 1801, d. 1 July 1867, m. 8 March 1825,
    resident of Howard Co., MD:
19.Margaret Almira Bayly, d. 25 February 1895. She and her husband are
    bur. at Mt. Olivet Cemetery, 1930 Frederick Avenue,
    Baltimore, MD.
20.Samuel Nichols, b. c1786/7, Sergeant in Anne Arundel Militia during
    the War of 1812, m. 21 September 1815:
21.Susan Hardy, b. c1795.
22.Artemus Hearn, b. c1803/5, d. 8 June 1885, m. by license dated 20
    November 1830 in Baltimore Co., MD:
23.Elizabeth Close, b. c1811/2, d. 20 April 1858.

Sixth Generation
32.Ezekiel Phelps, d. by 10 December 1825, m. 7 May 1794 in Anne
    Arundel Co., MD:
33.Margaret Watkins, probably the Margaret b. 5 June 1767 in All
    Hallows Parish, Anne Arundel Co., MD.
36.Peter Vernay, b. c1763, d. 12 March 1824, of Harford Co., MD.
37.Mary Tate, d. 20 July 1838 in her 70th year.
38.Elisha Bayly, b. c1771, probably in VA, d. 1830 in Baltimore Co., MD,
    m. 1 September 1791, probably in VA:
39.Jennett (N), b. c1775, d. 5 November 1827 in Baltimore Co., MD, in
    her 54th year.
40.Robert Nichols, b. c1755, d. c1821.
41.Sarah Robertson.
42.George Hardy, b. 1750 in Prince George's Co., MD, d. 1805 in Anne
    Arundel Co., MD, m. 1786; took the Oath of Allegiance to
    the State of MD, and served as a private during the
    Revolutionary War.
43.Priscilla Jenkins, b. c1766, d. 17 December 1853, (*Baltimore Sun,* 20
    December 1853).
44.Isaac Hearn, b. c1771.
45.Elizabeth (N).
46.Samuel Close, d. by 30 April 1825 in Anne Arundel Co., MD, before
    1815 lived in Frederick Co., MD, m. 1796:
47.Susanna Lenhart.

Seventh Generation
64.(Possibly) Isaiah Phelps, b. 23 March 1728, living in 1778.
66.John Watkins, b. 1727.
67.Esther Belt.
72.James Vernay, in Harford Co., MD, by 1777 when he witnesed a will;
    in 1783 in Bush River Upper or Eden Hundred (1783 Tax
    List); he was signer of the Association of Freemen in 1776
    from Spesutia Upper Hundred; in 1778, as James Varney, he
    signed the Oath of Allegiance to the State of MD.

74.David Tate, d. by 22 June 1813 in Harford Co., MD., m. 15 March 1768 in St. John's Parish:
75.Elizabeth Sinclair.
80.William Nichols, d. c1784 in Anne Arundel Co., MD.
84.(Possibly) William Hardy, b. 4 April 1722, d. by 1757.
85.(Possibly) Elizabeth Lanham.
86.Enoch Jenkins, d. by 1794.
87.(Probably) (N) Conn.
88.Michael Hearn, b. c1740/50.
92.**Christian Close,** came from Gerbesburg, Switzerland, to York Co., PA, d. 1794. [His name was originally spelled Kloss.]
93.Catherine (N), d. c1813.
94.Wilhelm Lenhart, b. 22 November 1745, d. 27 October 1819.
95.Anna Maria (Rush?), b. 24 September 1751, d. 22 October 1822.

Eighth Generation
128.Walter Phelps, b. 14 September 1703, d. by March 1764, m. 9 January 1727 in All Hallows Parish, Anne Arundel Co., MD:
129.Mary Bazil, b. 13 September 1707.
132.John Watkins, b. 1689, d. 1734.
133.Mary Warman, d. 1768.
134.Benjamin Belt, b. c1682, d. 1773.
135.Elizabeth (probably Middleton), living 1724.
148.(Possibly) Dr. Samuel Tate, b. c1721, living in 1776, Harford Co., MD.
149.Ann (N), b. c1718, living in 1776, Harford Co., MD.
150.James Sinclair, d. in Baltimore Co., MD, by 5 May 1761.
151.Mary Lester, b. 19 May 1722, d. by 19 August 1771.
160.William Nichols, Sr.
161.Sarah Thornborough, widow of Richard Simmons.
168.George Hardy, d. c1758.
169.Elizabeth Droyen or Drane.
170.Richard Lanham of Prince George's Co., MD.
171.Winifred Jenkins, d. by 26 February 1772, Prince George's Co., MD.
172.Daniel Jenkins, d. c1779, Prince George's Co., MD, m. by 1734:
173.Ruth Peerce.
174.(Probably) George Conn, b. 1732, d. c1774.
175.Sarah Isaac, b. 1744.
188.**Johan Peter Lenhart,** b. 1707, d. 1774, arrived at Philadelphia, PA, on the ship *Two Brothers*, 15 September 1749.
189.**Maria Margaretha (N),** b. 1713, d. 1777.

Ninth Generation

256. Walter Phelps, b. 17 June 1680, living in March 1760, m. 1 December 1702 in All Hallows Parish, Anne Arundel Co., MD:
257. Mary Cheney.
258. Ralph Basil, under 17 in 1665, d. by 27 June 1728, m. 23 September 1697.
259. Rose Hopper, b. 12 January 1679.
264. John Watkins, bur. 27 February 1696, m. by 1691:
265. Anna Gassaway, d. by 30 March 1742, m. 2nd William Burgess, and 3rd Richard Jones.
266. Stephen Warman, b. c1670, d. 1740, m. 1st Sarah Watts (listed below). (He m. 2nd Esther Gross; 3rd Mary Parrish.)
267. Sarah Watts, bur. 13 February 1700.
268. John Belt, d. 1698, Anne Arundel Co., MD.
269. Elizabeth Tydings, she m. 2nd John Lamb.
270. (Probably) **Robert Middleton,** b. c1651, d. by April 1708.
271. (Probably) Mary Wheeler.
300. William Sinclair (Sinkler).
301. Elizabeth (N).
302. Peter Lester, d. 4 May 1723 (or August 1733).
303. Ann (N).
320. Robert Nichols.
336. William Hardy, d. 1718.
337. Elizabeth (N).
338. Anthony Drayne/Drean, d. by 1723, Prince George's Co., MD.
339. Elizabeth (possibly Pile), b. 1694.
340. **John Lanham,** Sr., b. c1658/60, transported to MD, c1678 on ship *Dover*, of London, alive in 1734.
341. Dorothy (N), alive in 1713.
342. Daniel Jenkins, d. c1703.
343. (Possibly) Elizabeth (N).
344. Daniel Jenkins, d. c1703 (as in #342).
345.   (Possibly) Elizabeth (N) (as in #343).
346. John Peerce, b. c1679, d. c1766.
347. Martina Gale.
348. Hugh Conn, m. 1st Elizabeth Todd, m. 2nd:
349. Jeane (N).
350. Richard Isaac, b. 21 January 1720/1.
351. Sarah Jacob, b. 17 May 1719.

Tenth Generation

512. **Walter Phelps,** b. c1639, bur. 5 May 1719.
513. **Elizabeth** (possibly Benson), bur. 18 August 1706.
514. Richard Cheney, Jr., b. by 1658, d. December 1704.
515. Mary (N).
516. **Ralph Bassell,** came to MD in 1658, d. by 24 June 1672.
517. Mary (N).

518.Robert Hopper. bur. 14 November 1700.

519.Mary (N), m. 2nd, Isaac Davies.

528.**John Watkins** of VA and MD, d. c1682.

530.**Nicholas Gassaway,** bapt. 11 March 1634 in St. Margaret's Parish, Westminster, England, d. 1691/2, m. 2nd, by 1672:

531.Anne Besson.

532.**Stephen Warman,** bapt. 12 August 1638, at St. Michael's Cornhill, London, came to VA c1663, m. by 1663:

533.**Dorothy (N)** (living 1663).

534.**Francis Watts** of Anne Arundel Co., MD, transported to MD c1651.

535.Sarah (N).

536.**(Probably) Humphrey Belt,** landed in Jamestown in 1635 from Gravesend, England, immigrated to MD by 1663.

538.**Richard Tydings,** d. circa February 1687.

539.Charity (N).

542.**John Wheeler,** immigrated c1659, d. by 9 January 1694/5.

543.Mary (N), b. c1629/30, living 11 November 1693.

604.(N) Lester

605.Ann (N) who d. 17 August 1716.

676.(Possibly) James Drane, Ranger and Land Proprietor of MD.

678.Francis Pile(s), c1660, d. 1727.

692.John Peerce.

693.Sarah Sprigg, she m. 2nd Enoch Combes.

694.Edward Gaile, d. by 1 February 1685, Charles Co., MD.

695.Ruth (possibly Rozer), m. 2nd William Clarkson, 3rd Edmond Goodrick.

700.Richard Isaac, d. in Prince George's Co., MD, by 28 June 1759.

701.Sarah Pottenger.

702.Benjamin Jacob, b. c1688 in Anne Arundel Co., MD, d. by 1770, m. 1711:

703.Alice Westall, b. 21 September 1693.

Eleventh Generation

1024.(N) Phelps.

1025.**Rebecca (N),** came to MD with her son Walter.

1028.**Richard Cheney, Sr.,** b. c1630, immigrated c1650, d. by c15/16 August 1688, m. 1st:

1029.**Charity (N),** immigrated c1650, d. by 9 January 1685/6.

1036.(N) Hopper, father of Charles and Robert.

1056.John Watkins, in VA by 1640, settled in Lower Norfolk Co., VA, where he d. by 1648.

1057.Frances (N), m. 2nd, by 6 August 1655, Edward Lloyd.

1060.Thomas Gassaway, of London, bur. 19 November 1658 in St. Margaret's Parish, Westminster, England, m. 2nd, 6 January 1631, at St. Mary le Strand:

1061.Ann Collingwood, sister of John Collingwood, of London.

1062.**Thomas Besson,** c1617-1679.
1063.**Hester (N),** widow of Henry Caplin.
1064.Stephen Warman, b. 24 July, bapt. 31 July 1603 in St. Peter's
   Cornhill, London, m. 2nd, by license dated 21 June 1637:
1065.Susanna Pilston.
1356.Francis Pile(s), in Calvert Co., MD, by 1671, living in 1685.
1384.John Peerce, d. by 9 May 1679 in Calvert Co., MD.
1396.**Thomas Sprigg,** d. 1704, m. 1st:
1397.Katherine Graves (widow of William Roper).
1400.**Joseph Isaac,** d. in Calvert Co., MD, by 23 February 1688/9.
1401.Margaret (N), widow of (N) Brown, by whom she had a son Joseph
   Brown.
1402.**John Pottenger,** probably the John who was bapt. 29 November
   1661 and transported to MD from Bristol in 1684, d. in
   Prince George's Co., MD, by 7 April 1735.
1403.Mary (possibly Beall, but probably not a dau. of Ninian Beall).
1404.**John Jacob,** immigrant, b. c1632, probably in England, d. October
   1726 in Anne Arundel Co., MD, m. by 1 March 1674/5:
1405.Ann Cheney.
1406.George Westall, b. by 1659, d. 1702, m. c1678/9:
1407.Sarah Wade.

Twelfth Generation
2128.William Warman, cook, resided Leadenhall St., London, bur. 7
   November 1632 at St. Michael's Cornhill, London, m. 1st:
2129.Alce (N), bur. 9 July 1625 at St. Michael's Cornhill, London.
2768.Thomas Peerce, d. by February 1675.
2760.Martha (possibly Notley).
2794.Capt. **Thomas Graves,** of VA, d. by 5 January 1635/6, arrived in
   VA in 1607 on ship *Margaret and Mary.*
2795.Katherine (N), living 20 May 1636.
2800.Richard Isaacke, bapt. 23 February 1606, m. November 1633:
2801.Elizabeth Sharpe, bapt. 24 February 1613 at Bassingthorpe,
   Lincolnshire, England.
2804.Robert Pottenger, bapt. at Lambourne, Berkshire, England, and may
   be the Robert bur. at Christ Church, Newgate, on 16
   November 1709.
2805.Sarah (N), bur. at Lambourne, 19 November 1671.
2810.**Richard Cheney.**
2811.Charity (N).
2812.**George Westall,** in MD by 1659.
2814.**Robert Wade,** in Anne Arundel Co., MD, by 9 June 1675, d. by 13
   November 1694.

Thirteenth Generation
4288.Robert Belt of Styllyngfleete, Yorkshire, England.

5536.**Thomas Pearce** of England and VA, arrived in VA aboard the *Mary and Margaret* in 1608.
5600.Edward Isaac, bapt. 22 November 1595 at Long Bennington, Linconshire, m. 6 May 1605 at Fulkbeck, Lincolnshire:
5601.Jane Chaney.
5602.William Sharpe.
5603.Elizabeth Coney.
5608.Robert Pottenger, bapt. at Lambourne, 10 December 1606, bur. at Aldbourne, Wiltshire, 8 February 1664/5, m. 6 May 1663:
5609.Cecily Sexton, bur. at Aldbourne, 9 October 1670.

Fourteenth Generation
11200.Richard Isaac, d. June 1591 at Foston or Long Bennington, Lincs.
11201.Alice or Elizabeth Sharpe.
11216.Henry Pottenger, b. at Cholsey, Berkshire, c1565, bur. at Lambourne, 10 April 1613, m. 30 April 1593:
11217.Elizabeth Absolon, bapt. at Cholsey, Berkshire, on 18 October 1561.

Fifteenth Generation
22432.Walter Pottenger, b. c1540, bur. at Cholsey, Berkshire, 14 October 1642, m. 24 May 1562:
22433.Joane Holloway, bur. at Cholsey, 1 June 1604.
22434.Richard Absolon (son of John Absolon).
22435.Joan Smyth.

SOURCE ABBREVIATIONS

(Source of entry is followed by volume and page number.)

AAAD:Anne Arundel County Administration Accounts.

AACR:*Anne Arundel County Church Records of the 17th and 18th Centuries.* By F. Edward Wright. Westminster, MD: Family Line Publications, 1989.

AADI:Anne Arundel County Distributions.

AAEJ:Anne Arundel County Ejectment Papers, MSA.

AAGE:*Anne Arundel Gentry Revised and Augmented.* By Harry Wright Newman. 2 volumes. Westminster, MD: Family Line Publications.

AAJU:Anne Arundel County Judgment Records.

AALC:Anne Arundel County Land Commissions. Abstracted by Henry C. Peden, Jr., and included in his book, *More Maryland Deponents, 1716-1799.* Westminster, MD: Family Line Publications.

AALR:Anne Arundel County Land Records. Abstracted by Rosemary B. Dodd and Patricia Bausell. 1662-1719. 3 volumes. The Anne Arundel County Genealogical Society.

AAML:Anne Arundel County Marriage Licenses, MSA.

AARP:*Revolutionary Patriots of Anne Arundel County.* By Henry C. Peden, Jr. Westminster, MD: Family Line Publications.

AAWB:Anne Arundel County Will Book.

AMG:*The* [Annapolis] *Maryland Gazette.* See Karen Green, *The Maryland Gazette, 1727-1761.* See also Robert Barnes, *Marriages and Deaths from the Maryland Gazette, 1727-1839.* Baltimore, MD: Genealogical Publishing Company.

ARMD:*The Archives of Maryland.*

BACP:Baltimore County Court Proceedings.

BALR:Baltimore County Land Records.

BAML:Baltimore County Marriage Licenses, MSA.

BAWB:Baltimore County Will Book.

BCF:*Baltimore County Families, 1659-1759.* By Robert W. Barnes. Baltimore, MD: Genealogical Publishing County, 1989.

BFD:*Abstracts of the Balance Books of the Prerogative Court of Maryland, 1751-1777.* 4 volumes. Abstracted by Debbie Moxey (Liber 1) and Vernon L. Skinner, Jr.

(Libers 2-7). Westminster, MD: Family Line
Publications.

CBE1:*The Complete Book of Emigrants, 1607-1660*. By Peter Wilson
Coldham. Baltimore, MD: Genealogical Publishing
Company.

CRLR:Carroll County Land Records.

CRML:Carroll County Marriage License.

CRWB:Carroll County Will Book.

FOUW:*Founders of Anne Arundel and Howard Counties*. By J. D.
Warfield. (1905). Reprint: Family Line Publications,
1990.

FRWB:Frederick County Will Book.

HAWB:Harford County Will Book.

INAC:*Abstracts of the Inventories and Accounts of the Prerogative Court
of Maryland, 1674-1718*. Abstracted by Vernon L.
Skinner, Jr. Westminster, MD: Family Line
Publications.

MCHP:Maryland Chancery Paper.

MCHR:Maryland Chancery Record.

MCW:*Maryland Calendar of Wills, Volumes 1-5*.

MDAD:*Abstracts of the Administration Accounts of the Prerogative Court
of Maryland, 1718-1731*. Libers 1-10. Abstracted by
Vernon L. Skinner, Jr. Westminster, MD: Family
Line Publications.

MINV:*Abstracts of the Inventories of the Prerogative Court of Maryland,
1718-1777*. Abstracted by Vernon L. Skinner, Jr.
Westminster, MD: Family Line Publications.

MOML:Montgomery County Marriage License.

MOWB:Montgomery County Will Book.

MWB:Maryland Will Book.

PCLR: Provincial Court Land Records.

QRSM:*Quaker Records of Southern Maryland, 1658-1800*. By Henry C.
Peden, Jr. Westminster, MD: Family Line
Publications.

TALR:Talbot County Land Record.

OTHER ABBREVIATIONS

a.	acre / acres
AA Co.	Anne Arundel County
adj.	adjoining / adjacent
admin.	administered / administrator
admx(s).	administratrix (administratices)
afsd.	aforesaid
AL Co.	Allegheny County
als.	alias
b.	born
BA Co.	Baltimore County
bapt.	baptized
BC	Baltimore City
bro(s).	brother(s)
bur.	buried
c	circa / about
CA Co.	Caroline County
CE Co.	Cecil County
CH Co.	Charles County
cont.	containing
conv.	conveyed
CR Co.	Carroll County
CV Co.	Calvert County
d.	died
dau(s).	daughter(s)
dec.	deceased
dep.	deposed
dist.	distributed
DO Co.	Dorchester County
dwell. plant.	dwelling plantation
e.	east
exec(s).	executor(s)
extx(s).	executrix (executrices)
FR Co.	Frederick County
HA Co.	Harford County
HO Co.	Howard County
inv.	inventoried
KE Co.	Kent County
m.	married/month
MO Co.	Montgomery County
n.	north

n.e.	northeast
nunc.	nuncupative
n.w.	northwest
PG Co.	Prince George's County
plant.	plantation
QA Co.	Queen Anne's County
s.	south / shilling(s)
sd.	said
s.e.	southeast
SM Co.	St. Mary's County
SO Co.	Somerset County
s.p.	died without issue
surv.	surveyed
s.w.	southwest
TA Co.	Talbot County
Test:	Testes (meaning witnesses)
tob.	tobacco
T.P.	Testamentary Proceedings
w.	west
WA Co.	Washington County
wit.	witness(es) / witnessed
States	U.S. Postal Service Standard Abbreviations

THE ACTON FAMILY

1.   RICHARD ACTON immigrated to MD prior to 1658.{MPL 5:415} He seems to have been in MD by 15 Nov 1651 when he surv. 100 a. called *Acton.*{MRR:192}

No record of any will, administration, or other reference to the estate of this early Richard Acton has been found.

Richard Acton has been tentatively identified as the father of five children: SARAH, m. John Marriott; JOHN, d. 1688; ELIZA, m. (N) Smith; (possibly) CATHERINE, m. (N) Kitton; and (possibly) ANN, m. (N) Baker.

2.   JOHN ACTON, son of Richard, d. in AA Co. by July 1688. He m. Margaret (N).

As John "Acteon," he was listed as a debtor on 16 Sep 1685 in the inventory of Michael Cusack of AA Co.{INAC 8:499}

On 15 July 1686, John Acton, of AA Co., and his wife Margaret conv. to William Troth 300 a. called *Acton,* patented to Richard Acton of AA Co., dec., father of sd. John, on 15 April 1671, on the n. side of the Choptank River.{TALR 5:143}

John Acton d. leaving a will dated 3 May 1688 and proved 25 July 1688. He named his sister Eliza Smith, Thomas Renolls, Sarah Maryot [Marriott], Catherine Kitton, and Ann Baker, his bro.-in-law John Marriott, and Sarah, widow of Joshua Dorsey, as well as the two children mentioned below.{MWB 6:1}

The estate of John Acton was appraised on 25 July 1688 by Lancelot Todd and Thomas Baker and valued at £90.1.4 and 4000 lbs. of tob.{INAC 10:47} John Marriott admin. the estate (date not given). {INAC 10:319}

John Acton was the father of: RICHARD; and ABIGAIL.

3.   RICHARD ACTON, son of John, m. Anne Sewell in St. Anne's Parish, AA Co., on 11 Dec 1707.{AACR:65}

Richard Acton and John Marriott wit. a deed on 11 March 1703/4. {AALR WT#2:188}

On 29 April 1707, Richard Acton conv. *Acton* to Samuel Norwood.{AALR WT#2:553}

Richard Acton, of BA Co., d. leaving a will dated 8 Oct 1740 and proved 6 May 1741. He appointed his wife Anne extx., and left her his entire estate, real and personal, also some personalty was left to his grandson Richard. He also named his grandsons Richard and Henry Young, and named his daus. Margaret and Hannah. The will was wit. by Richard Richardson, Edward Norwood, Job Lewis, and John Dye. {MWB 22:319}

An administration bond was posted on 1 Oct 1747 by the extx. Anne; she admin. the estate on 19 Oct 1748.{BCF:1-2}

Richard and Anne were the parents of: RICHARD, d. c1740; MARGARET, m. Sewell Young on 13 Jan 1736; and HANNAH.

4.   RICHARD ACTON, son of Richard and Anne, d. by 6 Nov 1740 when an administration bond was posted by George Bailey. Richard had at least one son: RICHARD (named in the will of his grandfather, Richard Acton).

THE BARNES FAMILY

1.   JAMES BARNES, progenitor of the family was in MD by 9 Aug 1698, and d. by 13 July 1726. He m., prior to the earlier date, Ketura, dau. of Adam and Lois (N) Shipley.

On 9 Aug 1698, Richard Shipley, admin. of the estate of his father, Adam Shipley, conv. to his sisters Ketura Barnes and Lois Shipley, each 100 a. of *Shipley's Choice*, on the s. side of Severn River. {AALR IH#1:82} A map of land grants on the s. side of the Severn River shows this tract lying across the road about one mile n. of Severn Crossroads, and running down to the water's edge. {Caleb Dorsey, "Original Land Grants of the South Side of Severn River," *MHM*, Dec 1958, 53:394-400}

Baltimore County Tax Lists for the Years 1701-1706 show James Barnes living in Elk Ridge Hundred (then in BA Co., later in AA Co., currently in HO Co.). In 1702, Darby Regan, Thomas Mawdey, and Joseph Hall were with him. In 1703, Regan, Hall, and Thomas Peregnay were in his household; Hall and Thomas Ottaway were with him in 1705; and in 1706 only Joseph Hall was listed in the Barnes household. {William N. Wilkins, "Baltimore County Tax Lists, 1699-1706," typescript, MHS}

On 29 Sep 1712, Richard Shipley conv. to James Barnes 103 a. of *Eve's Dowry,* being part of a larger tract called *Adam the First* (located near Oakland Mills in HO Co.). {BALR TR#A:210}

James Barnes d. by 13 July 1726 when his estate was inven. by Jno. Hammond of Charles and [Thomas?] Wainwright, and valued at £85.18.9. The inventory included a set of carpenter's tools and some shoemaker's tools, in addition to the usual furniture and farming equipment. Robert Shipley, "bro.," signed as kin, and Richard Snowden and Phi. Hammond were listed as creditors, although Hammond was reluctant to sign at first as he claimed the goods were not well appraised. The inventory was filed on 6 May 1727 by Ketura Barnes, admx. of the dec. An additional inventory was filed on 13 [Oct] 1727, totalling £0.18.9.{BAINV 4:265, 268}

Ketura Barnes admin. the estate on 11 May 1728.{MDAD 9:150} She was still living in Elk Ridge in Aug 1730 when she deeded personal property to Peter Barnes, who was to pay a debt owing to Philip Hammond.{AALR IH&TI#1:2}

James and Ketura (Shipley) Barnes were the parents of: RICHARD; ROBERT; ADAM; JAMES; PETER; JOSHUA; KETURA m. 22 Oct 1728 Richard Shipley{St. Anne's Parish, AA Co.}; SUSANNA, b. 15 May 1715, bapt. 29 July 1717{Ibid.}; and NATHAN, b. 18 June 1717, bapt. 29 July 1717.{Ibid.}

Second Generation

2.   RICHARD BARNES, son of James (1) and Ketura (Shipley) Barnes, was living on 18 Oct 1751. He m. 1st, on 28 July 1716, Sarah Stevens, dau. of Charles and sister of William Stevens; he m. 2nd, by 1740, Catherine (N).{AACR:78; AALR BB#3:24}

He conv. to his bro. Adam Barnes 150 a. of land which Adam later had surv. into the 287 a. tract *Adam's Forest*.{MPL EI#6:274}

On 25 May 1725, Richard Barnes patented *Good for Little*, 250 a. in what is now HO Co. Dr. Caleb Dorsey, in his map of HO Co. land grants, placed this tract as stretching from Meadow Ridge High School to MD Route 103. On 30 May 1730, Richard Barnes, carpenter, mortgaged the land on Elk Ridge, and *Adam the First*, to Philip Hammond.{MPL PL#6:162; AALR TI#1:257}

On 7 July 1740, Richard and his wife Catherine conv. to Peter Barnes 146 a., part of *Shipley's Search*, in exchange for 103 a. called *Eve's Dower* (part of *Adam the First*, which Richard had most likely inherited from his father James Barnes). On 31 Jan 1742, Richard and his wife Catherine conv. to Robert Shipley 146 a. *Shipley's Search*. On 8 May 1744, Richard purchased 200 a. called *Bold Venture* from Edward and Eleanor Edwards, on the upper part of Severn River. {AALR RB#1:17, 246, 383 and RB#3:459}

Richard's place in the family is confirmed by a sale he made on 15 June 1744 to his bro. Adam Barnes, of a servant boy named Thomas Broxton, and some cattle and furniture.{AALR RB#1:392}

On 6 Sep 1744, Richard, again joined by his wife Catherine, sold to James Watts all that tract called *Watts' Share*, part of a larger tract called *Bold Venture*, originally granted to Richard Kethin. On 8 Nov 1745, Richard Barnes and wife Catherine sold to Peter Barnes a tract called *Eve's Dowry* (part of *Adam the First*), 103 a., in exchange for 146 a. called *Shipley's Search*, originally patented to Robert Shipley for 543 a., and conv. by him to Peter Barnes, who in turn conv. it to the sd. Richard Barnes.{AALR RB#1:425, RB#2:162}

Richard Barnes served on the Grand Jury of November 1735 and is mentioned in a session of the August 1746 Court as a "person trading, merchandising, and using commerce at AA Co."{AAJU, Nov 1735 Court:353, IB#6:231}

The Debt Book for 1750 shows Richard Barnes owning 150 a. *Hickory Thicket,* and 100 a., part of *Bold Venture.* By 18 Oct 1751, he and his wife Catherine were in BA Co. when they sold the remainder of *Bold Venture* to Philip Hammond.{AADB 1750; AALR RB#3:459}

Richard had at least two sons, the first one definitely by his wife Sarah Stevens: BENJAMIN, b. 3 Oct 1716{St. Anne's Parish Register, AA Co.}; and RICHARD, Jr.

3.   ROBERT BARNES, son of James (1) and Ketura (Shipley) Barnes, d. 1776 in FR Co. He m. Lois Porter, dau. of Peter and Lois (Shipley) Porter on 11 Feb 1728 in St. Anne's Parish, Annapolis. {AACR:95}

On 13 June 1734, with Peter Barnes, he patented 154 a. *Brother's Level,* and on 24 Sep 1749, he patented 420 a. *Addition to Brother's Level.* In 1752, he and his wife Lois conv. 60 a. of the latter tract to Peter Barnes.{MPL EI#2:128; BY&GS#2:508; and AALR BB#1:35}

He also owned tracts called *Barnes' Purchase* (296 a. which he had patented), *His or Mine,* purchased from William Harrison, and 18 a. which he patented as *Stony Hills.*{MPL BC#9:473, BC#10:58}

In 1736, he served on the jury of the AA Co. November Court. He was a member of the Grand Jury at the June Court, 1741, and at the June Court, 1748, he appeared as a surety for Adam Shipley who was licensed to keep an ordinary. He himself was granted a license to keep an ordinary in June 1758.{AAJU IB#1:219, ISB#1; also June 1758 Court:265}

By 1770, he had moved to FR Co. where he had assigned his right to the 18 a. *Stony Hills* to John Dorsey (endorsement, dated 19 March 1770, on back of patent).{Index to Maryland Patents, MSA}

In 1773, as Robert Barnes of AA Co., he gave bond to his son Robert, Jr., to convey to him 100 a. of *Barnes' Purchase,* and *Addition to Brother's Level.* It was sold at public sale to James Brown for 200 lbs., but the assignment was not received at the death of Robert Barnes, Sr., and so in 1779 Joshua Barnes, heir-at-law, and Ezekiel and Silvanus Barnes, sons and heirs of the will of Robert Barnes, and now living in WA Co., conv. the land again. The deed was wit. by Jos. Chaplin and Richard Davis.{WALR B:91-95}

Robert Barnes d. leaving a will made 2 Dec 1775 and proved 22 Oct 1776, in which, as Robert Barnes, Sr., of *Chew's Farm,* he named as heirs daus. Rachel (and possibly her sons Joshua, Robert and Nathan), Katy (and her son Peter), and Sarah, and sons Joshua, Robert, and Nathan. To his two youngest son Sylvanus and Ezekiel he gave 1/2 part of the lot adjacent the lot where he dwelt, and known as #14, Plat of

Frederick Town, Plat #123. The will was wit. by John Phillips, Richard Davis, and Lecon Davis.{FRWB A#1:585}

Another reading of his will, by Carol Gehrs Mitchell gives this interpretation: Robert Barnes, Sr., of *Chew's Farm*, left a will written on 2 Dec 1775 and probated 22 Oct 1776. He described himself as being in a weak condition. He gave bequests of 1 s. each to his dau. Rachel, sons Joshua, Robert, Nathan, dau. Katy's son, Peter, and dau. Sarah. To his two youngest son Sylvanus and Ezekiel he gave 1/2 part of the lot adjacent the lot where he dwelt, and known as #14, Plat of Frederick Town, Plat #123. The will was wit. by John Phillips, Richard Davis, and Lecon Davis.{FRWB A#1 and GM#1:585-586, abstracted in *Western Maryland Genealogy Quarterly*, 5 (Jan 1989):20}

Robert and Lois (Porter) Barnes were the parents of: JOSHUA; NATHAN; RACHEL; ROBERT; KATY (for Katherine or Keturah?); SARAH; SILVANUS; and EZEKIEL.

4.   ADAM BARNES, son of James (1) and Ketura (Shipley) Barnes, d. testate in AA Co. in 1779. He m. c1732, Hannah, dau. of John Dorsey; she was b. 26 Aug 1709, and d. in 1789.

The late Dr. Caleb Dorsey believed that Adam Barnes was b. c1700/10 at *Shipley's Choice*, on the s. side of Severn River, near Indian Landing, but in 1712 moved with his parents into what is now HO Co. (but was then BA Co.) when his father bought 103 a. of *Eve's Dowry*.

Adam was prominent in local affairs. The Anne Arundel Judgment Records show that in Nov 1735 he was a grand-juror in the county court; in Aug 1740 he attended court for eight days as a witness for John Dorsey against Alexander Black; he appeared as a witness again in Aug 1743 and June 1748, and in Nov 1752 he was made overseer of roads for Campbell's Hundred. In June 1759, he was bail for Henry Barnes.{AAJU Court Sessions of Nov 1735:353; Nov 1752:431, and June 1759:516}

Adam and his bro. Peter were on the vestry of Christ Church Queen Caroline Parish in 1738, when Caleb and John Dorsey conv. to the church two a. of land, part of *New Year's Gift*, on which the present church now stands.{AALR RD#3:85}

In March 1745/6, he was one of the signers of a petition to Governor Bladen, from the Freeholders of MD, asking to have the allowance for jurors increased. The petition was rejected.{CMSP, The Black Books, item 511}

About 1748, Adam was one of the signers of a petition from the inhabitants of Upper AA Co., to Governor Ogle, asking that Elk Ridge be erected as a town. In June 1760, in response to a proclamation of Governor Sharpe, he was one of the subscribers from Queen Caroline

Parish and Poplar Springs Chapel, to a fund to aid the sufferers from the Boston Fire.{CMSP, The Black Books, items 567, 1029}

On 22 Oct 1764, Adam Barnes deeded to his five daus. a portion of his land as follows: Ruth Stephens was to have 105 a. of *Invasion,* Susanna Linthicum was to have 149 a. of the same tract, Patience Norwood was to have another 145 a. of *Invasion* and *Cumberland,* Sophia Pedicote was to have 131 a. of *Invasion,* and Hannah Barnes was to have 180 a. of *Invasion* and *Cumberland.* On the same day Adam deeded to his son Henry Barnes 94 a. of *Invasion.*{AALR BB#3:271, 282, 340, 342, 343, and 344}

Sometime after dividing some of his land among his daus. and his oldest son, Adam Barnes provided for his other sons as well. On 27 July 1765, he conv. to his son John 126-3/4 a. of *Invasion,* and 46 a. part of *Conclusion.* On 3 June 1775, he deeded to his son James part of *The Invasion.*{AALR BB#3:416 and IB#5:256}

On 2 March 1778, he took the Oath of Fidelity to the State of MD. {CMSP, The Red Books, No. 4, Part 3, item 150}

Adam Barnes d. leaving a will dated 19 Nov 1768 and proved 16 Feb 1779, leaving his dwell. plant. and all personal estate to his wife Hannah. Son James was to have part of *Dorsey's Grove,* and part of *Invasion.* Son Michael was to have part of *Cumberland,* and after Hannah's death his personal estate was to be divided among all his children: Henry, John, Sophia, Ruth, Susanna, James, Patience, Hannah, and Michael (the latter not yet 21). Wife Hannah and son James were to be execs. Jno. Laurence, Thos. Hobbs, and Geo. Clark wit. the will.{AAWB EV#1 (#33):82}

On 2 Nov 1786, for 1 s., Hannah Barnes conv. to her son James Barnes of Adam 196 a. part of *Dorsey's Grove.*{AALR NH#2:544}

Hannah d. by 11 Sep 1792 when her estate was appraised at £127.11.5. The final accounting of her estate was rendered 6 March 1798 by the admin. James Barnes.{AAAD JG#3, 1797-1802:34}

Adam and Hannah (Dorsey) Barnes were the parents of: HENRY; JOHN; SOPHIA. m. 1st, William Petticoate, and 2nd, Thomas Greenwood; RUTH, m. Dawson Stephens;[1] SUSANNA, m. (N) Linthicum; JAMES; PATIENCE, m. John Norwood; HANNAH, m. John Hood; and MICHAEL.

5.   JAMES BARNES, son of James (1) and Ketura (Shipley) Barnes, d. in AA Co. in 1740.

---

[1] In April 1773, Dawson Stephens, and Ruth his wife, sold their 105 acres of *Invasion* to Edward Dorsey of John.{AALR IB#4:525}

On 10 March 1729, James Barnes, of AA Co., signed his name to a mortgage for some livestock, made to Lance Todd for £11.2.5.{AALR TI#1:196}

On 6 Oct 1730, he patented 80 a. called *Barnes Luck* in AA (now HO) Co. In 1737, he patented 235 a. called *Day's Discovery*.{MPL PL#7:608, MPL EI#6:7}

In his will dated 4 June 1740 and proved 18 April 1740 [sic], he named his bros. Peter and Adam Barnes as execs., and named children {MWB 22:214}: RICHARD; JAMES; and JOHN.

6.   PETER BARNES, son of James (1) and Ketura (Shipley) Barnes, d. in AA Co. in 1759, having m. Rachel (N).

On 31 Aug 1730, his mother deeded some property to him on the understanding that he pay debts owing to Philip Hammond. On 13 March 1733, Peter Barnes assigned 146 a. to Robert Shipley and patented the land known as *Shipley's Search*. In return, Shipley sold 145 a. of the new tract back to Peter Barnes. On 24 Oct 1733, Peter Barnes assigned all his right, title, and interest in 64 a. warranted land to his bro. Joshua Barnes. On 7 July 1740, Richard Barnes conv. to Peter 103 a. called *Eve's Dower*, part of a larger tract called *Adam the First*. In return, Peter Barnes, with his wife Rachel consenting, made over 146 a. of *Shipley's Search* to Richard Barnes.{MPL EI#3:98; AALR IH&TI#1:2, RD#2:69, RB#1:17}

Peter and Robert Barnes patented 154 a. known as *Brother's Level* on 13 June 1734, and the same day Peter Barnes patented 116 a. known as *Ovenwood Thicket*.{MPL EI#3:107, EI#4:21}

Peter Barnes patented a number of other tracts: 105 a. called *Boiling Spring* on 14 May 1745; 95 a. *Fine Soil Forest* on 15 May 1745; 250 a. *Barnes' Friendship* on 18 March 1746; and on 29 Sep 1749, with Robert Barnes, 420 a. *Addition to Brother's Level*.{MPL PT#1:338, LG#C:496, TI#3:56, and BY&GS#2:508}

On 28 Jan 1745, Joshua Barnes and wife Ruth conv. him part of *Joshua's Refuge*, part of *Shipley's Search*.{AALR RD#2:277}

By 1750, Peter Barnes had acquired much land; he was listed in the 1750 AA Co. Debt Book as owning 116 a. part *Ovenwood Thicket*, 103 a. *Eve's Dowry* (part *Adam the First*), 106 a. *Joshua's Refuge* (part of *Shipley's Search*), 105 a. part *Boiling Springs*, and 144 a. part *Barnes' Friendship*.{AADB 1750}

Other patents and deeds involving Peter Barnes included a patent for 585 a. *Henry and Peter* on 1 April 1751, sale of 197 a. of the latter tract to Henry Howard on 12 May 1753, purchase of 32 a. *Curry Galls* from Michael and Sarah Wallis on 4 April 1755, purchase from Levin Lawrence of part of *Benjamin's Addition*, purchase from Robert Barnes of *Addition to Brother's Level*, sale by Peter and Rachel on 9 Aug 1756

8

of 103 a. *Eve's Dower* to John Hawkins.{MPL BY&GS#4:371; AALR RB#3:33, AALR BB#1:35, 165, and 212}

In Nov 1741, he was appointed Constable of Patuxent Hundred, and in Nov 1752 held the same position in Bare Ground Hundred.{AAJU Nov 1741:323 and Nov 1751:431}

He d. leaving a will signed 5 Oct 1747 and proved 19 Feb 1759. In his will, he named his wife Rachel and the children listed below.{MWB 30:631}

The estate of Peter Barnes was appraised on 26 April 1759 by Michael and Ph. Dorsey, who set the value at £314.6.11. The creditors were John Dorsey of Edward and John Stewart for himself and for Dun. Campbell. Adam Barnes and Robert Barnes signed as next of kin and James Barnes was exec.{MINV 67:533}

Peter Barnes and wife Rachel were the parents of (bequests listed): CHARLES (to have 105 a. *Boiling Springs*); PETER (to have 95 a. *Fine Soil Forest*); JAMES (to have 250 a. *Brother's Friendship*); NICHOLAS (to have *Eve's Dowry*); HAMMUTAL; PATIENCE; and VACHEL (to have the dwelling place *Ovenwood Thicket*).

7.   JOSHUA BARNES, son of James (1) and Ketura (Shipley) Barnes, was living as late as 1745. He m. Ruth (N).

On 13 June 1734, he patented 64 a. called *Barnes' Hunt,* on vacant land he had been granted by his bro. Peter. Robert and Elizabeth Shipley, on 15 Oct 1744, sold to Joshua Barnes *Joshua's Refuge,* being part of *Shipley's Search.* On 28 Jan 1745, Joshua, and his wife Ruth, conv. this latter tract, 106 a. to Peter Barnes.{MPL EI#2:75; AALR RB#2:177}

On 20 Aug 1748, Joshua Barnes of AA Co. conv. 64 a. *Barnes' Hunt* to John Hood of AA Co. Joshua's wife Ruth consented.{PCLR EI#8:488}

He served on the Grand Jury of AA Co. in Nov 1743 and was summoned to court in Nov 1756.{AAJU Nov 1743:283 and June 1756:566}

No will or inventory was filed in the Prerogative Court of MD prior to 1777. To date it is not known if Joshua Barnes left MD, or d. without any estate.

Joshua and Ruth seem to have been the parents of: 40. PHILEMON; and 41. JOSHUA, living in 1771.

8.   KETURA BARNES, dau. of James (1) and Ketura (Shipley) Barnes, m. Richard Shipley on 22 Oct 1728, in St. Anne's Parish, Annapolis.{Barnes, *MD Marriages, 1634-1777*:163} Ketura's husband was a son of Richard and Lois Shipley.

The couple were the parents of: JOHN SHIPLEY; ADAM SHIPLEY; EZEKIEL SHIPLEY; RICHARD SHIPLEY; JAMES SHIPLEY; SUSAN SHIPLEY; and BENJAMIN SHIPLEY.

9.   SUSANNA BARNES, dau. of James and Ketura (Shipley) Barnes, may have m. Charles Porter.

10.   NATHAN BARNES, son of James and Ketura (Shipley) Barnes, was b. 18 June 1717, and d. in AA Co. in 1760, having m. Ellis (N).{St. Anne's Parish Register}

On 20 July 1742, Nathan Barnes purchased 140 a. *Shipley's Discovery,* from Robert Shipley of Adam. On 11 Nov 1746, Nathan Barnes mortgaged to Philip Hammond 140 a., part of *Shipley's Discovery.*{AALR RB#1:166, RB#2:250}

He d. leaving a will dated 6 Sep 1759 and proved 12 March 1760. In his will he named his wife Ellis, and left to his children, unnamed, the land where he was living.{MWB 31:88}

His estate was inventoried on 1 April 1760 by Robert Davis and Vachel Dorsey, and the personal estate was valued at £85.6.10. John Dorsey and John Wood signed as creditors, and Adam and Robert Barnes signed as next of kin. Ellis Barnes, the extx., filed the inventory on 13 June 1760.{MINV 71:27}

Nathan and Ellis Barnes were the parents of{AALR IB#5:114, 116, 118, 120, 217, NH#6:221}: NATHAN, m. Milcah (N); SARAH, m. Thomas Barnes; JOHN; RACHEL, m. Samuel Musgrove; ELIJAH; ELLIS, m. Ely Dorsey; and ELIZABETH BARNES, m. Samuel Glover.

Third Generation

11.   BENJAMIN BARNES, son of Richard (2) and Sarah (Stevens) Barnes, was b. on 3 Oct 1716, and bapt. on 29 July 1717, and was still alive in Aug 1764. By 27 June 1763, he was m. to Martha (N).{St. Anne's Parish Register}

In 1745, he patented 50 a. *Barnes' Level,* in what is now CR Co. The following year he conv. this tract to William Gosnell.{MPL PT#1:346; BALR TB#E:328}

Benjamin also owned a tract called *Mount Pleasant* (60 a. of which he sold to Robert Gilchrist), *Absolom's Chance,* and *Absolom's Chance Resurveyed,* part of *Buckingham's Good Will,* and part of *Cargaferghus,* all in BA Co. By 1766, he had sold all of these tracts. {Index to BALR, MSA}

Proof of his mother's descent is found in a deed dated 27 June 1763 in which he described himself as a planter of BA Co., "the son of a certain Sarah Stevens Barnes, who was the sister of a certain William Stevens, who devised to his sister part of a tract called *Timber Neck,* originally surv. for Charles Stevens, father of the sd. William and Sarah. Now Benjamin, and his wife Martha, sold to Charles Hammond and others that part of *Timber Neck.*{AALR BB#3:29}

On 1 Aug 1764, Benjamin Barnes paid to the estate of Philip Hammond, dec., the unpaid sum on a mortgage made by Richard Barnes on 5 May 1730, to the sd. Philip Hammond.{AALR IB#5:106}

In the *Maryland Gazette* for 23 March 1769, John Campbell offered for sale a tract of land adjoining where Benjamin Barnes "formerly lived."{William B. Marye, "The Great Maryland Barrens," MHM 50:134}

No record of Benjamin's estate or heirs has been found.

12.   RICHARD BARNES, son of Richard (2), was living in March 1745/6 when "Richard Barnes, Jr.," was indicted for a breach of the peace.{AAJU IB#6:3}

It may be this Richard Barnes, or Richard (30) Barnes, son of James, who is described in the following records. In 1759, Richard Barnes of BA Co., patented 20 a. called *Barnes' Choice.* The tract was surv. on 15 July 1759, and was located in what is now CR Co., on a branch of Morgan's Run, adjacent a tract taken up by Edward Fell, and also adjacent *Shipley's Choice.*{MPL, BC&GS#13:387; Dr. Arthur Tracey, Notes on Carroll County Tracts, at the Carroll County Historical Society in Westminster}

The BA Co. Debt Books show that Richard Barnes owned this tract from 1759 until 31 Aug 1765 when Richard Barnes, and wife Sophia, sold 20 a. of the land to George Shipley.{Index to BA Co. Debt Books, 1759-1765, MSA; BALR B#0:571}

No record of Richard's estate or heirs has been found.

13.   JOSHUA BARNES, son of Robert (3) and Lois (Porter) Barnes, was living as late as 1779 and may have been alive in 1790.

From 1759 to 1763, he was listed as a bachelor in Bare Ground Hundred, Queen Caroline Parish, and as such had to pay a special tax. {Christ Church, Queen Caroline Parish, AA [now HO] Co., Vestry Proceedings, MSA}

On 5 April 1769, his father deeded him part of *Barnes' Purchase* and part of *Addition to Brother's Level.*{AALR IB#1:336}

In Aug 1770, he "undertook" for Peter Barnes [this probably means that he gave assurances that Peter would appear in court] and on 4 Sep 1770 he was chosen [Tob.?] Inspector for Queen Caroline Parish. {AAJU Court for Aug 1770:148-149}

On 24 Dec 1770, he surv. 16 a. of land in (then FR Co.) called *Pleasant Meadows,* adjacent *Hay Stack Meadow Glade.* On 19 March 1774, he assigned his interest in this tract to John Dorsey of AA Co.{MPL BC&GS#(?):489}

Sometime in 1778, Joshua Barnes took the Oath of Fidelity and Support to the State of MD, before Richard Davis, in WA Co. [which had been created in 1776 from FR Co.]. {Gaius M. Brumbaugh, *Revolutionary Records of Maryland*:13}

A lawsuit between John Dorsey and Joshua Barnes "of Robert" was recorded 1 April 1779. {WA Co. Circuit Court Record RR BG:27} The addition of the identification may be an indication that there was another Joshua Barnes who was a contemporary residing in the same county.

In Aug 1779, Joshua Barnes, Sylvanus Barnes, and Ezekiel Barnes of WA Co. conv. to James Brown of AA Co. 100 a. of *Barnes' Purchase* and *Addition to Brother's Level*, for which Brown had paid their father Robert Barnes on 19 Aug 1773. The three grantors sold the land as execs. and heirs-at-law of their father's estate. {AALR NH#13:45}

On 6 March 1783, Joshua sold to Henry Barnes of WA Co., MD, for £12, two black mares with Switchtails. John Stull was a witness. {WALR C:265-266; abstracted in *Western Maryland Genealogy* 3 (4) Oct 1987:185}

Joshua Barnes is listed in the 1790 Census of WA Co. with one white male over 16 [probably himself], one white male under 16 [a son], and two white females [a wife and dau.?]. He is not listed in the 1800 Census of WA Co.

Joshua Barnes may be tentatively identified as the father of at least three children: JOSHUA, Jr., b. by 1790; HENRY "of Joshua;"[2] and (N), (dau.), b. by 1790.

14.	NATHAN BARNES, son of Robert (3) and Lois (Porter) Barnes, was living as late as 1778.

On 26 Feb 1768, Nathan Barnes, of Robert, mortgaged to Richard Talbott, of AA Co., all his tob. houses. By 1770, Nathan Barnes had moved to FR Co., where he leased from Samuel and Bennett Chew lots 26 and 33 of *Chew's Farm,* each lot being 100 a. Later he assigned his lease of lot 33 to Thomas Gassaway of AA Co. {AALR IB&JB#1:12, FCLR N:363, and FCLR V:24}

Nathan Barnes took the Oath of Fidelity to the State of MD along with his bro. Joshua. {Brumbaugh, *op. cit.*:13}

Nathan Barnes may have been the father of at least one son: JOHN, of Nathan, who on 18 Aug 1770 leased lots 6 and 28 of *Chew's Farm.* {FCLR N:352, 354}

---

[2] Henry purchased horses from Joshua Barnes on 14 March 1783. {WALR C:265} A Henry Barnes later appeared in Fayette Co., PA, with Sylvanus and Ezekial, and one later appeared in Fleming Co., KY.

15. RACHEL BARNES, dau. of Robert (3) and Lois, was possibly b. after 1726, and may have been the mother of three children mentioned in her father's will:{See *Western Maryland Genealogy* 5 (1) (Jan 1989):20} JOSHUA (surname not determined); ROBERT (surname not determined); and NATHAN (surname not determined).

16. ROBERT BARNES, son of Robert (3) and Lois (Porter) Barnes, was still living in 1790.

In June 1756, Robert Barnes, of Robert, along with Nathan Linthicum and Joshua Barnes, was summoned to testify for Dawson Stephens at the suit of His Lordship.{AAJU ISB#3:566}

Like his bro. Joshua, he was listed and taxed as a bachelor in Bare Ground Hundred, Christ Church Queen Caroline Parish, from 1759 through 1763.{Christ Church, Queen Caroline Parish, AA [now HO] Co., Vestry Proceedings, MSA}

On 19 Aug 1773, Robert Barnes, Sr., of AA Co., gave a bond of conveyance to his son Robert Barnes, Jr., for 100 a. of *Barnes' Purchase,* and *Addition to Brother's Level.*{AALR NH#13:345}

In 1790, Robert Barnes was a resident of WA Co., with one white male over 16, four white males under 16, three white females, and four slaves.{*Heads of Families at the First Census of the United States Taken in the Year 1790: Maryland.* Reprinted Baltimore: Genealogical Society Publishing Co., Inc., 1972 (hereafter cited as 1790 Census of MD):118}

Robert Barnes would seem to have m. and had the following children: ROBERT Barnes, of Robert, listed in the 1790 Census of WA Co., with one white male over 16, one white male under 16, five white females, and two slaves{1790 Census of MD:118}: (N) (son), b. after 1774; (N) (son), b. after 1774; (N) (son), b. after 1774; (N) (son), b. after 1774; (N) (dau.), b. by 1790; and (N) (dau.), b. by 1790.

17. KAT(E?) BARNES, dau. of Robert (3) and Lois, possibly b. after 1726, may have been the mother of one son, named in her father's will: PETER (surnamed not determined).

18. SYLVANUS BARNES, son of Robert (3) and Lois (Porter) Barnes, was alive as late as 1790. On 21 June 1779, Sylvanus Barnes and Sarah Phelps were m. in WA Co.{Leisenring, "Maryland Marriages, 1777-1804," MS, MHS}

In 1776, he was named in his father's will, and in 1779 he joined his bros. in conveying land to James Brown.

On 24 March 1778, Sylvanus Barnes, of WA Co., farmer, rented to Shadrach Williams 50 a. of *Chew's Farm.* Williams was not to cut timber, cultivate, or sell the timber. Richard Davis wit. the deed. {WALR B:91-95}

He may be the "Lillranius" Barnes who took the Oath of Fidelity before Richard Davis in 1778, WA Co.{Brumbaugh, *op. cit.*:14}

Sylvanus Barnes must have moved to PA soon after taking the Oath, because during the Revolutionary War, Sylvanus Barnes was named in the Westmoreland County Pennsylvania Associators and Militia Men's list.{*Pennsylvania Archives*, Ser. II, 6:400}

In 1785, Sylvanus Barnes was living in Springhill Township, Fayette Co., PA, where he paid taxes in 1785 and 1786.{*PA Archives*, Ser. III, Vol. 22}

Sylvanus Barnes was listed in the 1790 Census for Fayette Co., PA, with one white male over 16 [himself], two white males under 16, and three white females.

A court record written sometime between 1788 and 1842 for Wood Co., VA, contains a petition to show the necessity of the road from Sam's Creek to where it intersects the old road above Mr. Woodyard's, because of the back water of Mr. Enoch's mill run and long lengths of Amity Bottom. Among those signing the petition were: Rezin, John, Sylvanus, and Rob and Joshua Barnes. Other signers included William Dyar, Hugh Craig, Richard Deputy, John Robison, Francis Langfill, Simon Simpson, Jedediah Darby, D. Baurshamp, Selomon Deputy, Charles Rockhold, Jacob Trumbo, Thomas Pribble, Wm. Powell, Manyard Rockhold, James White, James Woodyard, Benjamin Rigg, Tonly Rigg, Richard Bee, Henry Stewart, Jesse See, Del. Lowther, Henry Deputy, and Elizah Rockhold.{Wood Co., WV, Court Records, unclassified En 1-25, 1785-1842; microfilm in custody of Archives of WV at College Library, Morgantown, WV}

On 15 April 1800, Hugh Phelps (bro.-in-law to Sylvanus Barnes), and his wife Hannah, sold to Sylvanus and Reason Barnes 100 a. on the w. side of Little Kanewha.{Wood Co., WV, Deed Book DB#1:20, 80; Deed Book DB#3:27. A Plat Map showing April 1800 land of Sylvanus and Reason Barnes, 100 a. *Wood Co. Deed Books I, II, III*, by DAR}

Sylvanus Barnes and his family were living in Wood Co., VA, in 1810 and 1820, but could not be found in the 1830 Census Index. He may have emigrated to OH.{1810 Census of Wood Co., VA; 1820 Census of Wood Co., VA}

Sylvanus and Sarah were the parents of: REASON, m. Mary Langfitt in 1808 in Wood Co., (now West) VA; ROBERT, m. Jane Langfitt in 1808 in Wood Co.; (N) (dau.), b. by 1790; PRISCILLA, b. 24 Jan 1786, m. Alexander Westfall; JOHN, m. Fanny Davis in 1816, Wood Co.; JOSHUA; GATHERS, m. Mary Gerlick in 1818 in Wood Co.; SYLVANUS, Jr., m. Christina Drenned on 20 June 1825 in Wood Co.{Wood Co., WV, Court Records; microfilm in custody of Archives of WV College Library, Morgantown, WV}

19.   EZEKIEL BARNES, son of Robert (3) and Lois (Porter) Barnes, was living in Fayette Co., PA, in 1790.

His movements closely follow those of his bro., Sylvanus Barnes. He took the Oath of Fidelity before Richard Davis, and by 1785 was a taxable in Springhill Township, Fayette Co., PA. By 1790, his household was in Georges Township, Fayette Co., with himself, two males under 16, and three females.

He d. in Wood Co., (now West) VA, in 1811. He m. Nelly (N).

He was the father of{Donald F. Black, *History of Wood Co., VA,* in custody of Archives of WV College Library, Morgantown, WV}: ELIAS; EZEKIEL; ELIJAH; NOAH; GATES; SIMPSON; LUTHER; LASSY; SALLEY; ELEANOR; and HANNAH, m. Alfred Mattox in 1814.

2O.   HENRY BARNES, son of Adam (4) and Hannah (Dorsey) Barnes, was mentioned in his father's will, and may have moved to AL Co.

The card index to Anne Arundel Judgments at the MD State Archives give some indications of his activities in court. In June 1753, he was a defendant against Thomas Colvill (folio 607); in Nov 1754 he was Constable of Elk Ridge Hundred (folio 44); in June 1755 he received instructions for taking a census (folio 164); in June 1758 he was sued by Basil Dorsey (folio 278), and in 1770 he was sued by Obed Pierpoint (folio 262).

He appears to have been the father of: HENRY, who may be the Henry Barnes, "Jr.," who was a witness for R. Barnes, Jr., in Aug 1772, and who was in AL Co. in 1790 when he sold 50 a. of *The Invasion.* {AAJU Court for Aug 1772:90; AALR NH#8:51}

21.   JOHN BARNES, son of Adam (4) and Hannah (Dorsey) Barnes, was b. c1735 in AA Co., and d. in BA Co. in 1800, having m. Hammutal (N).

For many years family historians have accepted Hammutal, wife of John Barnes, as a dau. of Robert Tivis, but this theory has been dissolved by the discovery that Hammutal Tivis m. 1st, Adam Shipley, and 2nd, John Lindsay.{Correspondence from Nancy Lesure of McLean, VA, to the compiler. See also Nancy Pearre Lesure, "Hammutal Tivis and Robert Shipley: A Cautionary Tale," *BMGS* 31 (3) 161-164}

Having demonstrated that John Barnes' wife Hammutal was not a Tivis, Mrs. Lesure has thoughtfully compiled a list of other possible Hammutals, taken from the parish registers of AA Co., and made it available to this compiler.

In Nov 1761, John Barnes, of Adam, was appointed overseer at Upton, and then, on 27 July 1765, Adam Barnes deeded to son his John 126-3/4 a., part of *Invasion,* and 46 a., part of *Conclusion.* His grandfather, John Dorsey, of Col. Edward, in his will proved 13 Nov

1764, left John Barnes, of Adam, a negro boy.{AAJU Court for Nov 1754:48; AALR BB#3:416; MWB 33:44}

On 2 March 1778, John Barnes, of Adam, took the Oath of Fidelity to the State of MD.{CMSP, The Red Books, No. 4, Part 3, item 150}

On 5 March 1795, John Barnes sold his AA Co. land, consisting of 126-3/4 a. *The Invasion,* 46 a. *Conclusion* and 94 a. *What Is Left,* to Edward Dorsey, of Caleb. His wife Hammutal did not sign a deed relinquishing her right of dower until 2 March 1797.{AALR NH#7:465 and AALR NH#8:486}

On the same day he sold his land in AA Co., John Barnes purchased land in BA (now CR) Co., 195-1/2 a. from David McMechen, known as *Stevenson's Deer Park, Trouting Streams,* and *Robert's Lot* On his death this property was divided among his children: John Barnes, Jr., Dorsey Barnes, and Rachel Petticoat. [In 1801 the latter two sold their interest in this tract to their bro. John].{BALR WG#QQ:533 and BALR WG#69:306}

John Barnes and his wife Hammutal (N) were the parents of: ADAM, d. 1809, m. Ruth Shipley; DORSEY; JOHN, d. 1822; and RACHEL, m. (N) Peddicoat.

22.   SOPHIA BARNES, dau. of Adam (4) and Hannah (Dorsey) Barnes, m. 1st, by 1764, William Peddicord (son of William and Sarah), and 2nd, on 3 Sep 1782, Thomas Greenwood.

On 22 Oct 1764, Adam Barnes conv. property to his five daus., including Sophia "Petticoate," to each a negro and a parcel of land.{AALR BB#3:282, 340, 342}

William Peddicord d. leaving a will dated 25 Sep 1777 and proved 10 March 1779. In his will he named his wife Sophia and the children listed below. The estate was to be divided when son Benedict was 14 years of age. Benoni Belt and Adam Peddicord were named as execs., but Belt refused to serve.{BAWB 3:374}

No record has been found to date showing any children that Sophia may have had by her second husband. By her first husband, William Petticoat, Sophia was the mother of: ADAM PEDDICORD, m. 25 Sep 1783, Eliza Zimmerman; JASPER PEDDICORD, m. BAML of 8 Oct 1785, Amelia Hobbs[3]{Dawn Beitler Smith, *BA Co. Marriage Licenses, 1777-1798,* Westminster: Family Line Publications, 1989:147}; WILLIAM PEDDICORD, m. by BAML of 5 Nov 1788, Elizabeth Hobbs {Smith, *op. cit.*:147}; BENEDICT PEDDICORD, not yet 14 in 25 Sep 1777; d., probably unm., leaving a

---

[3] She was a dau. of Thomas Hobbs, and sister of Cordelia Hobbs, who married Adam Barnes.

will dated July 1791 and proved 8 June 1793 {BAWB 5:110}; PLEASANT
PEDDICORD, m. 2 Jan 1794 Michael Elder.
{Barnes, *MD Marriages, 1778-1800*:67}

23.   JAMES BARNES, son of Adam (4) and Hannah (Dorsey) Barnes,
m. Elizabeth Shipley, dau. of George and Catherine (Ogg) Shipley.
On or about 5 July 1776, James Barnes, of Adam, was one of
several inhabitants of AA Co. who sent a petition to the Convention of
MD, stating that militia companies are "indifferently provided with
arms," and asking to be allowed to form an independent militia rife
company, limited to eighty, and with the right to choose their own
officers, except under fire. The petitioners felt this would save the state
1,000 pounds.{CMSP, The Red Books, No. 4, Part 3, item 15}
On 31 July 1786, James Barnes of Adam advertised for sale 305 a.
of land in AA Co., on the upper part of Elk Ridge, near Poplar Spring
Chapel. In Sep 1792, he was appointed Constable of Upper Fork
Hundred.{*Maryland Journal and Baltimore Advertiser*, 21 July 1786; AAJU Court for September
1792:226}
In the chancery case, "Ellicott vs. George and Adam Barnes,"
George Shipley dep. that, after James Barnes gave land to his three sons,
he came to live with the sd. Shipley.{MD Chancery Book #107:125, MSA}
James and Elizabeth (Shipley) Barnes were the parents of{*The Shipleys
of Maryland 1968*, Baltimore: King Bros., Inc., c.r. 1971 by The Shipleys of Maryland: 384-385, 420-421}:
HANNAH, m. by license dated 23 Dec 1790, George Ogg Shipley{BAML};
CHARLES ALEXANDER, m. Harriet Hobbs on 19 Dec 1805;
CATHERINE, m. Zachariah Barnes; AMELIA, m. Elisha Barnes on 11
Nov 1801; GEORGE, m. Mary Wilson on 6 Aug 1811; ELIZABETH, m.
James Barnes; ADAM, m. Cordelia Hobbs on 17 April 1805;
PATIENCE, m. Nicholas Watkins on 25 Jan 1806; MIRANDA, m.
Henry Hobbs, 22 Aug 1805; and MARY.

24.   PATIENCE BARNES, dau. of Adam (4) and Hannah (Dorsey)
Barnes, m. John Norwood who d. in AA Co. leaving a will dated 16 Nov
1814 and proved 20 Feb 1815.{AAWB JG#3:86-87} Patience evidently d. by
1802, when John Norwood m. 2nd, Elizabeth Hobbs.
John Norwood was a 2nd Lieutenant in MD during the
Revolutionary War.{National Society, Daughters of the American Revolution. *Patriot Index*.
Washington: The Society, 1966:500; some material on this family was compiled by Miss Pauline Hobbs of
Severna Park, MD}
John and Patience (Barnes) Norwood were the parents of:
HENRY NORWOOD, d. 1817, unm.; EDWARD NORWOOD, possibly
m. Jemima Howard; SAMUEL NORWOOD, m. Patience Howard;
MARY NORWOOD, m. 1st, in 1791 Denton Hobbs, and 2nd, in 1813,

Greenbury Treakle; HANNAH NORWOOD, m. Caleb Hobbs in 1793;
and ELIZABETH NORWOOD, m. Larkin Hobbs on 22 March 1799.

25.   HANNAH BARNES, dau. of Adam (4) and Hannah (Dorsey)
Barnes, d. 23 Feb 1772, having m. on 6 Jan 1771, John Hood, b. c1742,
d. 15 Dec 1794, in his 52nd year. John and Hannah (Barnes) Hood were
the parents of{"Hood Bible," *Maryland Genealogical Bulletin*, (ed. by Robert Hayes), 2:10; J. D.
Warfield. *The Founders of Anne Arundel and Howard Counties, Maryland.* Baltimore: Kohn and Pollock,
1905:472, 494}: SARAH HOOD, b. 5 Nov 1771.

26.   MICHAEL BARNES, son of Adam (4) and Hannah (Dorsey)
Barnes, d. by 1799, having m. by 1794, Patience Shipley, dau. of
William Shipley.
    In July 1776, he joined his bro. James Barnes of Adam in
petitioning the Convention of MD for permission to form an independent
militia rifle company. In March 1778, he took the Oath of Fidelity to the
State of MD before Samuel Meriwether.{CMSP, The Red Books, Number 4, Part 3, item
150}
    In Aug 1776, Michael Barnes contributed £0.7.6 for the relief of
the poor at Boston.{AMG 29 Aug 1776}
    In Dec 1781, he placed a notice in the *Maryland Journal and
Baltimore Advertiser* that the report he propagated at Montgomery Court
House in regard to Capt. Leaven Lawrence was false and without any
foundation. He had other legal troubles as well. In Nov 1783 and March
1784, he was sued by Richard Potts and Baker Johnson, but he did not
appear in court. In April 1793, he was sued again by (N) West and (N)
Oden, and again he did not appear in court.{Card Index to Anne Arundel Judgments,
MSA}
    In 1790, his family was listed in the Census as consisting of three
white males over 16, five white females and five slaves.{1790 Census of MD:13}
    He may be the Michael Barnes who was appointed as an ensign in
the AA Co. Militia on 18 June 1794.{Militia Appointments No. 1:22 and No. 2:40, 134,
MSA}
    On 13 Aug 1795, Michael Barnes of AA Co., and wife Patience,
conv. to Achsah Howard lands devised to Michael by his father Adam
which he [Michael] had not previously sold.{AALR NH#7:665. For other deeds
involving Michael Barnes, see AALR NH#6:665, 714 and NH#7:278, MSA}
    Michael d. by 28 March 1799 when James Barnes of Adam dep.
that Michael Barnes was "now dec." {MD Chancery Book #43:92, MSA}
    Michael and Patience (Shipley) Barnes had at least one son:
WILLIAM, b. c1771; age 19 on 9 Sep 1790, when he was bound to
Samuel Hutton to be taught the trade of coach making until the age of

21, and to be taught reading, writing, and arithmetic to the rule of 3.
{AAJU Aug 1791 Courts:147-148, MSA}

27.   RICHARD BARNES, son of James (5), was living as late as
1759. He m. Sophia, whose maiden name has not been discovered.
     On 3 Dec 1748, Richard Barnes, of BA Co., and James Barnes,
carpenter of AA Co., sold *Day's Discovery* to Gideon Howard.{AALR
RB#3:89, MSA}

     On 15 July 1759, Richard had surv. 20 a. called *Barnes Choice,* in
what is now CR Co. It was located on Morgan's Run, adjacent to
Shipley's Choice and a tract taken up by Edward Fell.{MPL BC&GS#13:387,
MSA} Richard Barnes and wife Sophia later conv. the 20 a. to George
Shipley.{BALR B#G:571, MSA}
     No record of any children or any estate has been found. However,
he may be tentatively identified as the Richard Barnes who was listed in
the 1773 Tax List of Delaware Hundred, BA Co., with one son.{Henry Peden.
Inhabitants of Baltimore County, 1763-1774. FLP}

     Richard may be tentatively identified as the father of: AQUILA,
over 16 in 1773. On 20 July 1776, he was enlisted by Michael Burgess
and passed by Col. Hyde in AA Co.{AARP}

28.   JAMES BARNES, son of James (5), was living as late as 1769.
No record of any wife has been found.
     With his bros. Richard and John, he inherited *Day's Discovery* and
Barnes Luck from their father.
     On 3 Dec 1748, Richard Barnes, of BA Co., and James Barnes,
carpenter of AA Co., sold *Day's Discovery* to Gideon Howard. On the
19th of the same month, James patented 150 a. in AA Co. called *Dung
Hill Ground Thicket.*{AALR RB#3:89, and MPL TI#4:269, MSA}
     The Debt Books show that, in 1750, James owned 80 a. *Barnes'
Luck* and 150 a. of *Dung Hill Ground Thicket,* and in 1769 he had
increased the size of the latter tract (perhaps by resurvey) to 384 a.{AA Co.
Debt Books for 1750 and 1769, MSA}
     No record of any marriage, children, or estate has been found.
However, he may be tentatively placed as the James Barnes who was
listed in the 1773 Tax list of Delaware Hundred, with three sons over 16
years.{Peden; Inhabitant of Baltimore County, 1763-1774}
     James Barnes, of BA Co., took the Oath of Allegiance before the
Hon. Reuben Meriwether on 2 March 1778, the same day his cousin
James Barnes, of Adam, and his own son, James Barnes, of James, as
well as other Barneses, took the Oath.{AARP}
     If he is the James of the 1773 Tax List, then his children may be
tentatively identified as: JAMES, of James, who took the Oath in 1778;
CALEB, over 16 in 1773 (did not take the Oath of Allegiance in AA or
BA Cos.); SAMUEL, over 16 in 1773; and DAVID, over 16 in 1773.

29.   JOHN BARNES, son of James (5), was living as late as 1771. On 24 Sep 1751, as [John?] James Barnes, of AA Co., planter, he sold 80 a. *Barnes Luck* to James Creagh of London who was then in MD.{AALR RB#3:422, MSA}

On 1 July 1762, he purchased part of *Boiling Springs* from Charles Barnes, of Peter, and shortly thereafter he sold the tract to Henry Ridgely. On 20 May 1765, he sold to Benjamin Fowler, of AA Co., all that tract called *Day's Discovery* over and above 210 a. On 14 March 1771, he sold to Henry Ridgely another 50 a. of *Boiling Springs* at the head of a small branch leading into Snowden's River.{AALR BB#2:667, 735, IB#2:347 and IB#3:139, MSA}

As "John Barnes, of James" he was named in a bastardy case in June 1753. In 1754, he was named overseer of Upper Severn Hundred. {Card Index to Anne Arundel Judgments, MSA}

No record of any estate or children has been found.

30.   CHARLES BARNES, son of Peter (6) and Rachel was not yet 21 in 1747 when he was named in his father's will. In 1759, he inherited 105 a. of *Boiling Springs* from his father.

Between 1759 and 1763, he was taxed as a bachelor, living in Bare Ground Hundred, Queen Caroline Parish. In Aug 1763, he was a defendant against Joshua Warfield, but the case was entered "agreed," and in June 1767, as Charles Barnes, of Peter, Gent., he undertook for J. Barnes.{Index to Anne Arundel Judgments, MSA; Queen Caroline Parish, AA Co., Vestry Proceedings, MSA} He was evidently unable to sign his name, as on deeds between 1762 and 1770 he made his mark. As late as 1770, no wife joined him in any deeds.

On 1 July 1762, he sold a number of parcels of land: to Peter Barnes part of *Benjamin's Addition, Ovenwood Thicket* and *Addition to Brother's Level;* to John Barnes [of James?] part of *Boiling Springs;* and to Jacob Cramblich part of *Henry and Peter.*{AALR BB#2:666, 667, 668, 670, MSA}

A short time later he sold parts of *Henry and Peter, Boiling Springs* and *Curry Galls* to Henry Ridgely, and he sold *Barnes Hunt* and *Barnes Fellowship* to James Barnes.{AALR BB#3:29, 624, 630, MSA}

He patented 150 a. called *Boiling Springs* on 2 Dec 1767.{MPL BC&GS#10:580, MSA}

On 12 Nov 1770, he sold 150 a. *Pleasant Meadows* to John Barnes, of Adam. On 17 Nov 1770, he deeded to Henry Ridgely, planter, the following tracts: *Fine Soil Forest* (90 a. granted to Peter Barnes, Sr., and increased by 490 a. vacant land to 580 a.); *Boiling Springs* (105 a. granted to Peter Barnes), and 32 a. *Curry Galls* (formerly conv. to the afsd. Peter Barnes by Michael Wallace).{AALR IB#3:49, 51, MSA}

No record of any estate or any family has been found.

31.   PETER BARNES, son of Peter (6) and Rachel, m. before 3 June 1775, Eleanor (N), who joined him signing a deed on that date.

In 1747, he was described in his father's will as not yet being 21, and as the recipient of *Fine Soil Forest*. AA Co. Deeds show that he purchased from his bro. Charles part of *Benjamin's Addition, Ovenwood Thicket* and part *Addition to Brother's Level*. {AALR BB#2:666, 668, MSA}

The AA Co. Debt Book for 1769 show that he owned 116 a. of *Ovenwood Thicket*, 151 a. of *Barnes Friendship*, 105 a. of *Boiling Springs*, 60 a. of *Brother's Level* and 140 a. of *Benjamin's Addition*. The following year he is shown as owning only the 1st, 4th and 5th of those tracts. {AA Co. Debt Books for 1769 and 1770, MSA}

On 3 June 1775, with the consent of his wife Eleanor, he sold 60 a. of *Ovenwood Thicket* to James Barnes, of Adam. On 5 March 1779, he purchased *Invasion* and *Woodford* from Edward Dorsey of Col. John, and between 1787 and 1788 he sold parts of *Invasion* and *Anything* to his son Vachel. {AALR IB#5:258, IB&JB#1:322 and NH#3:124, 128}

The 1790 Census of AA Co. shows Peter Barnes living in AA Co. with three white males over 16, three white males under 16, and three females. {1790 Census of MD:13}

Peter Barnes had mortgaged some property to Charles Warfield. On 13 Sep 1794, Warfield received payments of £40.7.4 from Eleanor, widow of Peter Barnes, for the original loan made in 1787. Warfield released the mortgage. {AALR NH#7:275, MSA}

The children of Peter and Eleanor included: VACHEL, probably b. by 1766; PETER, over 16 in 1790; (N), probably a son, under 16 in 1790; (N), probably a son, under 16 in 1790; (N), probably a son, under 16 in 1790; (N), probably a dau.; and (N), probably a dau.

32.   JAMES BARNES, son of Peter (6) and Rachel, was b. after 1726, and was living as late as 1777. He m. Catherine (N) by 1768.

In his father's will he was not yet 21, and he was to have 250 a. *Brother's Partnership* after his father's death.

On 7 April 1768, James Barnes, of Peter, conv. to John Hood 92 a. of *Barnes' Friendship*. James' wife Catherine consented. {AALR IB&JB#1:43, MSA}

The AA Debt Book for 1769 shows that he owned 52 a. part *Conclusion* and 17 a. part *Barnes' Pleasant Meadows*, both purchased from John Hood, and in 1770 he had acquired 154 a. *Barnes' Friendship*. {AA Co. Debt Books for 1769:7, 1770:5, and 1771:7, MSA}

On 27 Oct 1771, he sold to John Hood 17 a. *Barnes' Pleasant Meadow*, 158 a. *Barnes' Friendship*, and 51 a. part *Conclusion*. {AALR IB#5:488, MSA}

The card index to AA Judgments at the MD State Archives shows that James Barnes, of Peter, was on the jury in June 1761 (June 1761

Court:171), and in Nov 1770 he was a defendant against John Stewart and Duncan Campbell.{November 1770 Court:428}

On or about 5 July 1776, he joined James Barnes, of Adam, and others in petitioning the Convention of MD for permission to form an independent militia rifle company.{CMSP, The Red Books, Part 3, item 150}

No record of any children has been found.

33.   NICHOLAS BARNES, son of Peter (6) and Rachel, was b. after 1726, since he was not yet 21 when his father made his will. By that will, he was to receive *Eve's Dowry,* but his father sold that tract in 1756, so Nicholas may have d.

34.   VACHEL BARNES, son of Peter (6) and Rachel, was b. after 1726 since he was not yet 21 in his father's will, by which he was to inherit the plantation *Ovenwood.*

He is probably the Vachel Barnes who joined his bro. James Barnes, of Peter, and other inhabitants of AA Co. in petitioning the Convention of MD for permission to form an independent militia rifle company.{CMSP The Red Books, Part 3, item 150}

No other record seems to have been found.

35.   PHILEMON BARNES is placed as a son of Joshua and Ruth, because on 18 Sep 1771, as "Philemon Barnes, of Joshua" he was listed as a debtor in the inventory of William Hall of AA Co.{MINV 107:339-355} He was b. c1723, and d. 12 Dec 1813, aged about 90.{Diary of John Evans (hereafter cited as Evans Diary), deposited at Lovely Lane Museum, Baltimore, MD.}

Philemon Barnes m. 1st, by 1756, Mary, b. 10 Oct 1730, dau. of George and Mary (Potee) Ogg. He m. 2nd, Rachel, who, as wife of Philemon Barnes, d. 27 Nov 1801.{Evans Diary}

On 22 Sep 1752, Philemon Barnes patented 1,200 a. of land called *Horse Pasture,* at the head of Sam's Creek. This land was later resurv. by John Hood.{MPL Y&S #6:309, MSA}

In Nov 1756, George Ogg conv. property to his granddau. Mary, dau. of Philemon Barnes.{BA Co. Chattel Records TR#E:228, MSA} The only dau. of George Ogg not accounted for is his dau. Mary, b. 10 Oct 1730, so she was probably the first wife of Philemon Barnes.

Philemon Barnes was listed as a debtor in the inventory of James Dixon of FR Co., filed 15 June 1767.{MINV 94:217-252, MSA}

His plantations included 100 a. *Horse Pasture* (1752), *What You Please* (1762), and 259 a. *Dodson's Tent* (1785).

On 2 March 1778, he took the Oath of Fidelity in AA Co.{CMSP, The Red Books, Part 3, item 150}

In 1790, he was in Two Delaware Hundreds, BA Co., with two white males over 16, four white males under 16, and five white females.

On 17 Feb 1802, Philemon Barnes, of FR Co., sold to Archibald Barnes 152-1/2 a. of *Dodson's Tent,* and 21 a. *What You Please.* On the same day, he sold Thomas Barnes 121 a. part *Dodson's Tent,* and 5 a. part *Resurvey on Horse Pasture.*{FRLR WR#23:220, 222, MSA}

Philemon Barnes was the father the following children, many of whose dates of birth are given in the Evans Diary: MARY, living in 1756; LEVIN, b. 9 April 1759, d. 17 April 1831, aged 72 years and 8 days{Evans Diary};[4] ZADOC, b. 23 or 25 May 1764; ZACHARIAH, b. 14 Oct 1765; AIREY, was b. c1767, named as a sister in the 1836 will of her bro. Archibald Barnes[5]; ARCHIBALD, b. 25 Jan 1769, d. 19 Dec 1837, aged 69; THOMAS, living 1802; (possibly) PHILEMON, Jr. (he may be the Philemon Barnes who m. Ruth Penn by BAML dated 24 Feb 1782); and ELISHA, d. 5 Jan 1856 in his 73rd year.{Evans Diary}

36.   JOSHUA BARNES, son of Joshua and Ruth, was living on 18 Sep 1771 when he was listed as a debtor in the estate of William Hall of AA Co.{MINV 107:339-355}

37.   NATHAN BARNES, son of Nathan and Ellis, m. Milcah (N), and was living as late as 1796.

Samuel Musgrove and Rachel Musgrove, in 1774, conv. to Nathan Barnes, of Nathan, 15-2/9 a. *Shipley's Discovery.*{AALR IB#5:120}

On or about 5 July 1776, he joined several of his Barnes cousins and other inhabitants of AA Co. in petitioning the Convention of MD for permission to form an independent militia rifle company.

On 2 March 1778, Nathan Barnes, of Nathan, took the Oath of Fidelity to the State of MD.{CMSP, The Red Books, No. 4, Part 3, item 148}

He advertised as a tavern keeper in Nov 1779. In Nov 1788, he was a defendant against William French.{AAJU Nov 1788:181, MSA; *Maryland Journal and Baltimore Advertiser,* 16 Nov 1779}

In March 1792, he bought and sold several parcels of land. On 14 March, he bought 16-2/9 a. of *Shipley's Discovery* from his bro. Elijah Barnes; Elijah had inherited the land from their father Nathan. On the same date, Nathan also purchased from his sister Elizabeth, now wife of

---

[4] He is evidently not the Levin Barnes who m. Hannah Slack by license dated 4 Sep 1783 in BA Co. That Levin has been identified as a son of Richard and Elizabeth Barnes.

[5] Miss Airey Barnes d. 10 Aug 1838, age 71 years, 5 mos., 20 days.{Evans Diary}

Samuel Glover, her share of the same tract. The following day, with the consent of his wife Milcah, he sold to Walter Worthington 128 a. of *Shipley's Discovery.* {AALR NH#6:217, 221, 223, MSA}

Nathan Barnes was granted a warrant from the land office to lay out 50 a. of vacant land adjacent tracts called *Polecat* and *Eppington Forest.* This was surv. for him on 8 Feb 1794, and called *Nathan's Morsel.* On 14 Dec 1796, he had surv. an adjacent 19-3/4 a. which he called *Addition to Nathan's Morsel.* These tracts were in BA Co. {BA Co. Unpatented Certificates #56 and #1093, MSA}

38.   SARAH BARNES, dau. of Nathan (10) and Ellis, m. Thomas Barnes, with whom she sold the share of *Shipley's Discovery* she had inherited from her father. {AALR IB#5:116}

Thomas Barnes, husband of Sarah, may be the Thomas to whom William Bellison, on 20 April 1791, conv. two tracts of land, *Charles Delight* and *Baker's Desire,* which Bellison had purchased from Elias Dorsey. Thomas assigned his right to these tracts to Dennis Barnes sometime prior to 1814. {Maryland Chancery Paper #757, MSA}

Thomas and Sarah may have had at least one son (although definite proof still has to be found that Thomas, the husband of Sarah, and Thomas, the father of Dennis, are the same person): DENNIS.

39.   JOHN BARNES, son of Nathan (10) and Ellis, sold his share of *Shipley's Discovery* to his bro. Nathan c1774-1778. {AALR IB#5:118, MSA}

In Nov 1767, he was a defendant against Nathan Dorsey, and in Nov 1770 he "undertook" for James Barnes, of Peter. {AAJU November 1767 Court:202 and November 1770 Court:428, MSA}

As John Barnes of Nathaniel, living in BA Co., he took the Oath of Fidelity to the State of MD. {CMSP, The Red Books, No. 4, Part 3, item 150}

40.   ELIJAH BARNES, of Nathan (10) and Ellis, was b. c1755, and d. 13 Aug 1840. He m. Catherine Shipley on 17 Aug 1784 in St. Paul's Parish, BA Co. {Leisenring, "MD Marriages, 1777-1804," MS, MHS:166}

Absolom Shipley, of BA Co., d. leaving a will dated 20 Jan 1804 and proved 6 Feb 1809, naming his wife Usley (Ursula?), son Absolom, and dau. Catey Barnes. {BAWB 8:359, MSA}

Elijah Barnes fought in the Revolutionary War in Capt. Daniel Dorsey's Company, Col. Hall's Regiment, according to his application for a pension. He enlisted in AA Co. in 1776, and served in the PA Continental Line for months. He was taken prisoner on 16 Nov 1776 and held until Jan 1777. {*Soldiers of the Revolution Who Lived in Ohio, Vol. 3,* 1959} He stated that he had removed from MD to OH, and then to Decatur Co., IN, where he appeared before Justice of the Peace to make his declaration. He stated that he intended to live with his son. It appears that his widow did receive

a pension.{Revolutionary War Pension Application of Elijah Barnes, W-9717, National Archives}
On 14 March 1792, Elijah Barnes, of BA Co., sold to his bro.
Nathan, 16-2/9 a., his share of his father's land, *Shipley's Discovery.*
{AALR NH#6:217 MSA}

In 1840, at age 85, he was living with Absolom Barnes in Decatur
Co., IN, where he d. on 13 Aug of that year.{*Census of Pensioners, 1840;* and Indiana
DAR, *Roster of Soldiers and Patriots of the American Revolution Buried in Indiana.* 1938}

Elijah and Catherine were the parents of: ABSOLOM; (possibly)
ZACCHEUS, m. Rachel Stilwell on 31 Jan 1819 in Hamilton Co., OH.
{Letter to the compiler from Lea Sharp of Hesperia, CA, dated 27 Feb 1983}

41.   ELLIS BARNES, dau. of Nathan (10) and Ellis, m. Ely Dorsey.
Two dates have been found for the marriage. Leisenring states the couple
were m. in 1785 by Rev. William Ringgold, but a BAML states they
were m. on 21 Feb 1778 by Rev. Chase.{Leisenring, "MD Marriages, 1777-1804,"
MHS:145; Smith, *BA. Co. Marriage Licences*:8}

42.   ELIZABETH BARNES, dau. of Nathan (10) and Ellis, m. Samuel
Glover in AA Co. on 24 Feb 1778, by Rev. Macgill.{Robert Barnes. *Maryland
Marriages, 1778-1804.* Baltimore: Genealogical Publishing Co., Inc., 1978:83} Samuel Glover was
b. c1756 in AA Co., MD, and d. c1813. His wife, Elizabeth, probably d.
c1813.{Data on the Glover descendants was generously supplied by Mrs. Marion Riggs, of Fort Thomas,
KY} On 24 March 1792, Samuel and Elizabeth Glover, then of BA Co.,
sold Elizabeth's share of *Shipley's Discovery* to her bro. Nathan Barneş.
{AALR NH#6:221}

Samuel and Elizabeth (Barnes) Glover were the parents of{Data
supplied by Mrs. Marion Riggs}: JOHN, m. Prudence Lamb in Mason Co., KY;
EZEKIEL, b. 23 July 1780, MD, d. 6 July 1831, Louisville, KY; ELIJAH
BARNES, b. 6 May 1782, MD; JOHNSA, b. c1784; NATHAN, b. 24
March 1786; JOSHUA; SARAH, m. John M. Thornton; SAMUEL;
ASA, m. Sarah White; ANNA, b. 27 June 1796; MARGARET, b. 1789
in Mason Co., KY; AZEL, b. 27 Sep 1800; and ELIZABETH BARNES,
b. c1802, d. c1818.

Fourth Generation

43.   JOSHUA BARNES,[6] son of Joshua Barnes, of WA Co., was probably b. sometime prior to 1750 since he had a son b. c1772.[7]

Joshua Barnes' name appeared on the tax lists of Bourbon Co., KY, in 1787, which then included Mason and Fleming Counties. In the spring of 1787, "the Barnes and Williams families" accompanied George Stockton and wife, Rachel Dorsey Stockton (dau. of Edward Dorsey of AA Co., MD), and Stockton's cousin, Isaiah Keith, from s.w. PA, down the Monongahela and Ohio Rivers to Fleming, KY, where they built a stockaded settlement known as Stockton's Station.{R. S. Cottrell, *History of Fleming County*:24} The "Williams family" included Basil, John, Jarred, Thomas, Laurence, and Zadock (who was killed by the Indians in 1788) Williams - all from WA Co., MD. The "Barnes family" included Joshua Barnes, whose wife was Delila Williams, and possibly others.

His will was written 31 May 1806 and probated at July Term, 1806, Fleming Co., KY.

Joshua Barnes had a dau. named Lois (probably named after his grandmother, Lois Porter) and a grandson named Joshua Porter Barnes. The name of the eldest son, Basil/Bazle, may be for Basil Williams; it is interesting, however, to note the following: Bazil Barnes sued Frances Castiol in a case of ejectment in WA Co., MD, Prothonotary Court, April Term 1782. The deposition of Thomas Pollock "of Kentucky" was taken and the case was dismissed in 1784 [Appearance Docket 1782-1792, p.41, case 106].

Joshua m. Delila Williams, and they were the parents of (not necessarily listed in the order of birth): BASIL, b. c1770/1780; JOSHUA; LOIS; HENRIETTA; ANARY/ANN/ARAH, m. 5 Oct 1813 John Calerman or Colterman, Jr.; CYNTHIA, b. c1786/1787, PA, d. 3 May 1857, Fleming Co., KY, m. 17 Feb 1807 William Dudley, Jr.; RACHEL, b. March 1795; d. 26 March 1835, m. 28 April 1818 Thomas Salathiel Fitch; and DELILAH, b. 20 Nov 1796, d. 15 Feb 1834, m. 21 Dec 1830 Elisha Fitch.

---

[6] The two basic sources of information for this branch of the Barnes Family are: 1) the article by Carol Ruth Gehrs Mitchell in the *BMGS*, Vol. 32, No. 1; and 2) Larry D. Bowling and Pat Donaldson's article "The Barnes Family of Fleming Co., Kentucky," in *BMGS* ... . The Barnes Family arrived in Fleming Co. in 1787, along with several other Marylanders to establish the first white settlement in that county.

[7] Larry D. Bowling, "The Barnes Family of Fleming Co., Kentucky," typescript in the possession of the compiler.

44.   JOHN BARNES, son of Nathan, was in FR Co. on 18 Aug 1770 when he leased lots 6 and 28 of *Chew's Farm.* {FCLR N: 352, 354}

45.   ROBERT BARNES, son of Robert, is listed in the 1790 census of WA Co., with one white male over 16, one under 16, five white females and two slaves. If his wife were still living, his family could have consisted of one son and four daus. {1790 Census of MD:118}

He is probably the Robert Barnes described in Henry Peden's *Marylanders to Kentucky.* {Westminster: Family Line Publications, 1991:6} He moved to Clark County, KY, c1806, and d. c1830. He m. Jane Peddicord who d. c1825.

The Robert Barnes who is believed to be the ancestor of Larry D. Bowling, joined Joshua Barnes at Stockton's Station by 1 Nov 1793, which is the date Robert's name first appeared on the Mason Co. (parent county of Fleming), KY, tax list. Listed as a white male over age 21, sharing his household was a male over 16 but under 21. This would put his birth prior to 1756 if the male is his child (probably his son, Robert, Jr.) In the 1800 tax list of Fleming Co., Robert Barnes, Sr., had two additional white males over age 21 in his household, and one white male between 16 and 21. Adding Robert Barnes, Jr., who is now listed separately, the number and approximate age brackets of these males now closely match the Robert Barnes of the 1790 census of WA Co., MD.

In 1798, the year Fleming Co. was formed, Robert purchased 200 a. of land there from Michael Cassidy, who was also from MD. Robert Barnes, Sr., was still alive in Sep 1809 when "he conv. the plant. whereon I now live cont. 100 a. and Robert is to live there and use as much of the cleared land as he chooses rent free for and during his natural life" to Samuel Barnes. On 11 March 1812, the Sheriff of Fleming Co. "as a result of a judgment in favor of Alexander Dougherty against Robert Barnes, Jr., Robert Barnes, Sr., and Samuel Barnes, the deputy seized, advertised and sold lots #75, 77, 79 in Flemingsburg to William P. Roper, the high bidder, for $12." This is the last time Robert Barnes, Sr., is mentioned in the court records or other documents. Additionally, no will was found. Based entirely upon circumstantial evidence, the following is presented as that possible family unit.

Research by Larry Bowling of Pittsburgh (see his article in the *BMGS*) indicates that this Robert was the father of: ROBERT, Jr., b. c1772/1774, m. 1st, before 1798, Maryan (N), m. 2nd, Ann (Hineman/Hindman/Hyneman Nichols), dau. of John Hineman and widow of John Nichols; JOSEPH, b. by 1779 (date and place of death are unknown since no will has been found), m. 20 Feb 1800, Phebe Stockton (b. 22 Sep 1782, d. 7 April 1830, bur. Stockton Station Cemetery), dau. of George Stockton; ALFRED, b. 1 June 1790, MD, m.

Helen Lackland, dau. of Aaron Lackland, in 1816;[8] EPHRAIM, b. between 1765 and 1775 according to census data (from his appearance on the tax lists it would appear that his birth was c1774), d. by March 1836; SAMUEL, b. c1781, d. by 29 Aug 1820 (the date when his inventory was filed in Fleming Co., KY. [Will Book B]), m. 27 Feb 1806 in Mason Co., KY, to Anna Waller, dau. of Thomas Waller; HARRIET, b. by 1787, (if m. at age 18; Robert Barnes was the bondsman for her marriage) m. Samuel McDonald on 3 Oct 1805 in Fleming Co.; RACHEL, b. c1780-1790, (Robert Barnes was the bondsman for her marriage), m. William Davis 25 June 1808 in Fleming Co.

46.   REASON BARNES, son of Sylvanus and Sarah, m. Mary Langfitt in 1808, in Wood Co., (now West) VA.

47.   ROBERT BARNES, son of Sylvanus and Sarah, m. Jane Langfitt in 1808, in Wood Co., (now West) VA.

48.   PRISCILLA BARNES, dau. of Sylvanus and Sarah (Phelps) Barnes, was b. 24 Jan 1786 in Fayette Co., PA, and d. 8 March 1874 in Weldon, Clark Co., IA, aged 88 years, 1 mo., 22 days. She was bur. in Smyrna Friends Cemetery, Clark Co. She is listed as a dau. of Sylvanus Barnes in the Wood Co., VA, History, and named one of her sons Sylvanus Barnes Westfall.
    She m., by 1805, Alexander Westfall, son of George Westfall. He was b. 27 Aug 1784 in VA, and d. 27 Dec 1862 in Knox Co., IL, aged 68 years. He was bur. in the Westfall Cemetery, Knox Co., IL.
    In 1805, Alexander Westfall, and his wife Priscilla, of Wood Co., VA, sold to James Davis, for $150, 45 a. in Wood Co., s. of the Little Kanawha River. The deed was wit. by James Neale, Jr., Thomas Tavenner, and James Laidley.
    On 7 Oct 1807, Alexander Westfall and Francis Langfitt gave bond to Robert Triplett for the sum of $9.58. Triplett sued Westfall, and the sheriff took Westfall into custody. The dispute was over a black and white cow, which Westfall wished to keep in his possession.
    In 1810 and 1820, Alexander Westfall was enumerated as the head of a family in Wood Co., (now West) VA.{1810 Census of Wood Co., VA; 1820 Census of Wood Co., VA}

In 1830, 1840, and 1850, he and Priscilla were living in Scipio Township, Meigs Co., OH. In 1850, Alexander was age [60?], and Priscilla was age 65.{1830 Census Meigs Co., OH, Scipio Township, p. 266; 1840 Census Meigs Co., OH, Scipio Township, p. 35; 1850 Census Meigs Co., OH, Scipio Township, p. 24}

---

[8] Helen d. in 1849, and Alfred moved to Callaway Co., MO, in 1853.{Peden, *Kentucky Ancestor,* 12 (4) 213, and *BMGS* 27 (3) 382}

On 6 Sep 1842, while living in Meigs Co., Alexander and Priscilla sold 120 a. to David Daugherty for $800. On 6 Oct 1845, Westfall paid $31 for a tax sale of land, 40 a., in Meigs Co., sold to George Westfall. There was a penalty of 1,613 cents and 6 mills. In April 1847, David M. Daugherty and Fanny, of Athens Co., OH, sold land to Westfall, still a resident of Meigs Co.{Meigs Co., OH, Deeds}

In 1860, Alexander, age 76, and Priscilla, age 75, were listed in the Census as living in Knox Co., IL. Living with them was their son Sylvanus, his wife Samantha, and their children{1860 Census Knox Co., IL, p. 11}

Priscilla Barnes Westfall was about 85 in Oct 1871, when she made the long trip by covered wagon from Knox Co., IL, across the Mississippi and halfway across the State of Iowa to the vicinity of Weldon, IA, with her son Sylvanus and family.{Collene Adair Taylor, *Our Family History of the Westfalls and Related Families, 1964-1966*:28-30}

Alexander and Priscilla (Barnes) Westfall were the parents of eight children {Taylor, *op. cit.*, 1982 edition}: (possibly) SARAH, b. c1808, m. (N) Hapenstall; SYLVANUS BARNES WESTFALL, b. 31 Aug 1809, VA, d. 31 Aug 1885 in Clark Co., IL, bur. in Smyrna Cemetery, and removed to Hebron Cemetery, Clark Co., m. on 14 Sep 1837, in Meigs Co., OH, Samantha Jane Bailey, dau. of Robert and Elizabeth 'Betty' (Hysell) Bailey; GEORGE, b. 17 Nov 1811 in Elizabethtown, Wood Co., WV, d. 9 Aug 1894 in Knox Co., IL; HIRAM P., b. 1814 in VA, d. 3 May 1849 in OH, bur. in Woodyard Cemetery, Pageville, OH, m. on 1 Oct 1839 Elizabeth Tewkesbury in Athens, OH; MARY, b. c1815 in Elizabethtown, d. age 24, m. William Cornell on 26 Sep 1833; FANNY, b. 1818 in Elizabethtown, d. 12 March 1882 in Athens Co., OH, bur. 1882 in Henning Cemetery, Scipio Township, Athens Co., OH, m. on 19 March 1835, David Daugherty; REBECCA, b. 26 Nov 1822 in Elizabethtown, d. 11 April 1874 in Knox Co., IL, bur. 1874 in the Westfall Cemetery, Knox Co., m. on 7 May 1840, Jabez W. Crouch; ELIZABETH REEVES, b. 19 March 1826 in Athens Co., d. 29 Nov 1900 in E. Gal., IL, bur. 1900 in the Westfall Cemetery, Knox Co., IL, m. 3 Nov 1842, Lewis Mitchell.

49.   JOHN BARNES, son of Sylvanus and Sarah, m. Fanny Davis in 1816, Wood Co., (now West) VA.

50.   GATHERS BARNES, son of Sylvanus and Sarah, m. Mary Gerlick in 1818 in Wood Co., (now West) VA.

51.   SYLVANUS BARNES, Jr., son of Sylvanus and Sarah, m. Christina Drenned on 20 June 1825 in Wood Co.{Wood Co., WV, Court

52.   HANNAH BARNES, dau. of Ezekiel and Nelly, m. Alfred
Mattox in 1814.

53.   HENRY BARNES, son of Henry, on 6 Nov 1790 sold 50 a. *The
Invasion* to James Barnes, of Adam. The deed stated that his father was a
son of Adam Barnes, of AA Co. Henry's wife Mary consented.
{AALR NH#5:400}
    He may be the Henry Barnes, "Jr.," who was a witness for R.
Barnes, Jr., in Aug 1772, and who was in AL Co. in 1790 when he sold
50 a. of *The Invasion*.{AAJU Court for Aug 1772:90; AALR NH#8:51}
    On 22 Nov 1795, Henry Barnes, planter, of AL Co., and wife
Mary, sold 3 or 4 a. of *The Invasion* to James Barnes of Adam.{AALR
NH#8:51}

54.   ADAM BARNES, son of John Barnes and Hammutal (N) Barnes,
was b. c1761, and d. in BA Co. in 1809, having m. Ruth Shipley on 2 (or
5) Aug 1784. He may have been previously m. to an unidentifed first
wife. Ruth Shipley Barnes is said to have m. 2nd (N) Miller. For more
information on Ruth Shipley's parents, see Nancy Pearre Lesure's article,
"Hammutal Tivis and Robert Shipley, A Cautionary Tale."{*BMGS* 31 (3) 161-
164}
    On 30 May 1775, Adam Barnes leased from Joseph Beasman 85
a. of *Beasman's Discovery*.{BALR AL#M:535} On 8 Dec 1790, he purchased
from John Beasman an adjacent tract called *Hopewell,* cont. 144 a.{BALR
B#F:253} *Hopewell* was near the village of Gamber, CR Co., on Nicodemus
Road.
    Adam took the Oath of Fidelity in BA Co. in 1778.{Oaths of Fidelity, Box
3, folder 21, p. 8, MSA; Hodges, "Unpublished Revolutionary Records of Maryland," 6:105; typescript at MHS}
    The 1783 Tax List of Delaware Upper Hundred, BA Co., shows
Adam Barnes owning 144 a. *Beasman's Discovery*, with a household
consisting of one free male, and six white inhabitants.
    Although Adam Barnes was an Anglican in his younger days, he
became a Methodist, and on 28 Nov 1808 he and a group of citizens of
this vicinity were Methodist Vestrymen and purchased a tract of land for
the erection of a church and public school.{BALR WG#101:214}
    The will of Adam Barnes, dated 2 May 1809 and proved 17 June
1809, names the children listed below.{BAWB 8:416} Adam's estate was
inventoried on 4 or 11 July 1809, and filed by Robert Barnes on 30 Sep
1809. The inventory came to $401.88, and was signed by Edmund
Howard, Joshua Barnes, and William Baseman.{BA Co. Inventories 26:113}

Robert Barnes admin. his father's estate on 6 April 1811, and again on 26 April 1815. After the second account, there was a balance due of $300.06.{BAAD 18:361 and 20:74}

Adam Barnes was the father of: ROBERT; RACHEL; ADAM; NAOMI, m. Lloyd Pool (see The Poole Family); JOSHUA; ZACHARIAH; HAMUTAL; MARY (POLLY), m. Benjamin Haines; HENRY; JOSIAH; MARGARET; RUTH; SARAH ANN; SUSANNA; ANN; SAMUEL; and CASSEENER.

55.   DORSEY BARNES, son of John and Hammutal (N) Barnes, m. Lydia Musgrove, dau. of John Musgrove.{See Chancery Paper #3178, MSA}

In 1790, he was living in Two Delaware Hundreds, with one white male over 16, four white males under 16, and three females.

On 28 Oct 1801, he and his sister, Rachel Petticoat, deeded to their bro., John Barnes, *Stevenson's Deer Park.* Dorsey's wife, Lydia, consented.{BALR WG#69:306} On 24 Nov 1826, Dorsey deeded 3 a. of *Stevenson's Deer Park* to Moses Barnes.{BALR WG#185:413}

In 1809, Dorsey Barnes, Sr., and Dorsey, Jr., were sureties for the administration of the estate of Adam Barnes.{BAAD}

Dorsey and his wife were the parents of: MOSES, m. 6 Feb 1808, Airey Poole; ADAM; DORSEY; and JOHN.

56.   JOHN BARNES, son of John and Hammutal, d. 1822. He m. Elizabeth (N), who d. c1826 in AA Co.

In 1803, John Barnes, of John, and wife Elizabeth, deeded to Matthias Pool 187-3/4 a. of *Robert's Lot, Stevenson's Deer Park,* and *Trouting Streams.*{BALR WG#77:337. See also WG#69:306, 308, for information on how John Barnes of John acquired this land}

On 6 Jan 1804, James Porter sold to John Barnes, of John, parts of *Shipley's Discovery,* cont. 30 a., 35 a., and 25 a.{AALR NH#12:355} James Porter's wife, then residing in Ross County, OH, confirmed the sale on 6 Sep 1804.{AALR NH#12:526} On 27 July 1817, John Barnes, of AA Co., sold Andrew Mercer 2 a. of *Shipley's Discovery.*{AALR WSG#5:396}

John Barnes d. by 16 April 1822 when his estate was admin. It was admin. again on 15 July 1822.{AAAD TTH#2:204, 208}

Elizabeth Barnes d. by 19 April 1826 when the first and final account of her estate was made.{AAAD TTS#4:384} In 1827, Peregrine Elder gave an account of his guardianship of the orphans, Rhoda C., Thomas, James A., John D., Benjamin, and Rufus D. Barnes.{AAAD TTS#3:385, 386}

John and Elizabeth were the parents of: HANNAH, b. c1700, m. Joshua Young by BAML dated 17 Dec 1808; MARCELLA, m. 1 Nov 1822 (BAML 1 Nov 1822) Perry G. Elder; THOMAS, b. 10 Nov 1805, m. Louisa Ann Pool; JOHN DORSEY, b. c1806, m. Eliza Pool; BEN-JAMIN, b. c1810; JAMES A., b. c1812/6, m. 1st, on 3 Sep 1844, Sarah

A. Fountain, and 2nd, on 3 Nov 1847, Catherine Shipley; RHODA C.; RUFUS; and HENRY.

57.　ADAM PEDDICORD, son of William and Sophia (Barnes) Peddicord, m. Eliza Zimmerman on 26 Sep 1782. They had at least one son: JOHN PEDDICORD, m. Catherine Huish.

58.　JASPER PEDDICORD, son of William and Sophia (Barnes), m. by BAML dated 8 Oct 1785, Amelia Hobbs. She was a dau. of Thomas Hobbs, and sister of Cordelia Hobbs, who m. Adam Barnes.

On 30 May 1840, Jasper Peddicord, of Belmont Co., OH, and wife Amelia, and Wilson L. Peddicord, and wife Keturah B., of the same place, conv. to Asbury Peddicord, of HO Co., land which Jasper and Amelia had already conv. to Wilson L., and which Wilson had conv. to Asbury. The purpose of this deed was to quiet the title. {HOLR JLM#1:320}

Jasper and Amelia were the parents of: WILLIAM ASBURY PEDDICORD, b. c1794; THOMAS, b. c1800, m. Mary Landon; JOSEPH H., b. c1801, m. Ann E. Barnes; WILSON B., m. Keturah B. (N); and BENJAMIN.

59.　WILLIAM PEDDICORD, son of William and Sophia (Barnes), m. by BAML dated 5 Nov 1788, Elizabeth Hobbs.

William and Elizabeth (Hobbs) were the parents of: SOPHIA, m. Stephen Musgrove; MARY, m. Richard Warfield; ELEANOR, m. Jacob Thompson; GERARD; and JERUSHA ELIZABETH.

60.　BENEDICT PEDDICORD, son of William and Sophia (Barnes), was not yet 14 on 25 Sep 1777, he d. probably unm., leaving a will dated July 1791 and proved 8 June 1793. {BAWB 5:110}

61.　PLEASANT PEDDICORD, dau. of William and Sophia (Barnes), m. 2 Jan 1794 Michael Elder. {Barnes, *MD Marriages, 1778-1800*:67}

62.　HANNAH BARNES, dau. of James and Elizabeth (Shipley) Barnes, m. by BAML dated 30 Dec 1790, George Ogg Shipley. They were the parents of: TALBOT SHIPLEY; PATIENCE SHIPLEY, m. Eli Shipley; and AMANDA SHIPLEY.

63.　CHARLES ALEXANDER BARNES, son of James and Elizabeth (Shipley) Barnes, m. Harriet Hobbs on 19 Dec 1805. They were the parents of: ANN ELIZABETH, b. c1808, m. by BAML 25 Nov 1825, Joseph H. Peddicord, son of Jasper and Amelia (Hobbs) Peddicord;

CATHERINE MARGARET; MARCELLA SHIPLEY; CAROLINE; and THOMAS HOBBS, b. c1814.

64.   CATHERINE BARNES, dau. of James and Elizabeth (Shipley) Barnes, m. by AAML dated 14 Feb 1794, Zachariah Barnes (see #77 below).

65.   AMELIA BARNES, dau. of James and Elizabeth (Shipley) Barnes, m. Elisha Barnes on 11 Nov 1801.
    On 21 May 1810, James Barnes, of Adam, for $4,200, sold Amelia Barnes part of *Dorsey's Grove.* {AALR NH#16:240}
    Amelia and Elisha were the parents of: LEWIS; WASHINGTON, b. 10 July 1804, d. 25 Oct 1873, m. 11 March 1829, Mary Bartholow; LOUISA; ALFRED, b. c1809; GEORGE; ANN; and CHARLES ALEXANDER.[9]

66.   GEORGE BARNES, son of James and Elizabeth (Shipley) Barnes, m. Mary Wilson on 6 Aug 1811.

67.   ELIZABETH BARNES, dau. of James and Elizabeth (Shipley) Barnes, m. James Barnes.

68.   ADAM BARNES, son of James and Elizabeth (Shipley) Barnes, was b. 1778 and d. 1861. He is bur. in the Old Northern Cemetery, Jackson Township, Belmont Co., OH. He m. Cordelia Hobbs on 17 April 1805. She was b. c1783, a dau. of Capt. Thomas Hobbs, d. 1852, age 69, and is bur. in the same cemetery.
    In 1818, Cordelia Barnes dep. giving her age as 35. {MD Chancery Book 107:124, MSA}

    Adam and Cordelia were the parents of: MARTHA, b. 1806, d. 1859, m. John Koontz, d. 1857, age 51; RACHEL W., b. 1809, d. 1880, m. Camm Thomas, Jr.; RUFUS, m. Ruth (N); JAMES, b. 1812, d. 1835, age 23, bur. in the same cemetery as his parents; EDWARD S., b. 21 May 1815, d. 1878, m. Mary (N), b. 21 April 1818, d. 1903; and CHARLES T., b. c1815; m. Euphemia (N).

69.   PATIENCE BARNES, dau. of James and Elizabeth (Shipley) Barnes, m. Nicholas Watkins on 25 Jan 1806.
    Nicholas and Patience (Barnes) Watkins were the parents of {letter to the compiler from David Charles Becker}: JAMES BARNES WATKINS, b. 14 Aug 1814, went to KY c1840/5; THOMAS WORTHINGTON WATKINS,

---

[9] On 17 July 1826, Charles Alexander Barnes was apprenticed for six years to learn the trade of shoemaker. {AALR WG#12:87}

came to KY; SARAH ELIZABETH WATKINS; ELVIRA ANN
WATKINS; PATIENCE RACHEL WATKINS; and WILLIAM
WATKINS.

70.   SARAH HOOD, dau. of John and Hannah (Barnes), was b. 5 Nov
1771 and d. 17 June 1833. She is bur. at Shawan. On 12 Sep 1786, in BA
Co., she m. Walter Worthington, b. 15 Feb 1765, son of Samuel and
Mary (Tolley) Worthington.
        Walter and Sarah (Hood) Worthington were the parents of{Newman,
Anne Arundel Gentry}: MARY TOLLEY WORTHINGTON, m. Charles
Worthington Dorsey; MARTHA WORTHINGTON, m. John Raedel;
SAMUEL WORTHINGTON; CHARLES WORTHINGTON; JOHN
TOLLEY HOOD WORTHINGTON; HANNAH WORTHINGTON, m.
Charles Wayman Hood; ELIZABETH WORTHINGTON, m. James Tolley
Worthington; and COMFORT WORTHINGTON, m. Jacob Wilderson.

71.   WILLIAM BARNES, son of Michael and Patience (Shipley), was b.
c1771. He was age 19 on 9 Sep 1790, when he was bound to Samuel Hutton, to
be taught the trade of coach making until the age of 21, and to be taught reading,
writing, and arithmetic to the rule of 3. {AAJU Aug 1791 Court:147-148}
        He was the father of at least two sons: SAMUEL, b. c1803, m.
Elizabeth Sampson; MICHAEL, living on 18 Sep 1843 when he
executed a deed as an insolvent debtor to Wesley Whalen.{HOLR 4:471}

72.   CALEB BARNES, tentatively placed as a son of James Barnes
(son of James who d. in 1740), was over 16 when he was listed with
James, Samuel, and David as a taxable in Delaware Hundred, BA Co.[10]
        He may be the Caleb Barnes who was listed as a taxable in Elk
Ridge Hundred, AA Co.{1782 Assessment List for AA Co.}
        Research by Ethel Albin indicates that he m. Honor Stevens, and
sometime in the 1770s settled in Bedford Co., PA. His bro. James may
have settled on land adj. him.
        Caleb first appears in Bedford Co. Tax Lists in 1787. He d. in
Bedford Co. before the 1820 Census was taken.
        Caleb and Honor (Stevens) Barnes were the parents of {Research by
Ethel Albin}: DAWSON, d. after 1850 in Southampton Township, Bedford
Co., PA; MARY, b. c1780; OSCAR (or OZIAS), b. c1784;
ELIZABETH, b. c1793, d. after 1850 in AL Co., MD, may have

---

[10] Sources used in compiling this chapter include A) research by Ethel Albin; B) *The
Barnes Bulletin*, Vols. 1-13; and C) *The Barnes Bulletin 2.0*, Vol. 1.

m. c1817 Denton Poole; CALEB, Jr., b. 1 Nov 1795, Bedford Co., PA;
PHILEMON, b. c1801, Bedford Co., PA.

73. VACHEL BARNES, son of Peter and Eleanor (N) Barnes, was
living in FR Co. on 15 May 1788 when he m. Charity McDougal.
    The 1790 census shows Vachel Barnes living in FR Co. with one
free white male over 16, one free white male under 16, and one free
white female.
    On 15 Sep 1794, Vachel Barnes, of FR Co., mortgaged to Henry
Ridgely Warfield, two tracts, *Invasion* (149 a. conv. him by his father
Peter Barnes), and 56 a. called *Anything*.{AALR NH#7:277}
    On 28 March 1796, Vachel Barnes sold to Hoopes Chamberlain of
AA Co. 28-1/2 a. of *Anything*, and 119 a. *The Invasions*. Vachel's wife,
Charity, consented, and his mother, Eleanor, renounced her dower right.
{AALR NH#8:127}
    Vachel and Charity may have been the parents of at least one
child: (N), son, b. by 1790.

74. PETER BARNES, probably son of Peter and Eleanor, was b. 3
June 1770, and d. 20 March 1848 in Belmont Co., OH. He m. 1st Ann
(N), b. 27 Aug 1797, d. by 1820. He m. 2nd, on 5 June 1821, in Belmont
Co., Nancy Phillips, b. 1787, d. in the 1860s, in Belmont Co. She was the
widow of David Barton, and the dau. of Evan and Jane Phillips.
    Peter was the father of five children by his first wife and four by
his second wife: SAMUEL, b. 1797; RUTH, b. 1803; PETER, b. 1805;
VACHEL, b. c1807; ELIJAH, b. 1809, d. 4 March 1852; ELI, b. 28 May
1821, d. 18 Nov 1885, m. 28 Aug 1844, Christina Ball; ELENORA, b.
1825, d. 1899, m. Robert Gillespie on 30 Oct 1845; MATILDA, b. 1826,
d. 22 Dec 1900, m. John Huntsman on 1 Feb 1853; and BENJAMIN, b.
1829, m. 13 June 1852, Caroline Anderson.

75. ZADOCK BARNES,[11] son of Philemon, was b. either 23 or 25
May 1764 or on 15 April 1768'{Evans Diary, or C. Ray Barnes, "Genealogy of C. R. Barnes," typescript, Jan 1,
1937, in possession of the compiler} and d. 18 April 1849, age 81 years{Tombstone} He m.
Ann Elizabeth Paulson by FRML dated 28 Jan 1794. Ann Elizabeth was
b. 15 March 1773, d. either 16 June 1854, age 82 years, or 2 March 1855,
age 82. {C. Ray Barnes, op. cit; Jacob M. Holdcraft. *Names in Stone*. Baltimore: Genealogical Publishing Co., Inc.,
1985} Both are bur. at Taylorsville Methodist Church.[12]

---

[11] The compiler is indebted to Wanda Barnes Hall of Joppa, MD, for generously sharing
her research on the descendants of Zadock Barnes.
    [12] The tombstone of Zadock Barnes states that he d. 18 April 1849, age 81 years. A
History of Vigo County, IN, gives his birth date as 23 May 1767. Ann Elizabeth's
tombstone states she d. 2 March 1855, age 82 years. The History of Vigo County says she
was b. 24 Aug 1772.{Wanda Barnes Hall}

Zadock was a teamster in the New Windsor area of CR Co. He drove a team of horses, and was a poor man, although he did own several tracts of land.{Statements by C. Ray Barnes}

Ann Elizabeth Paulson's uncle was John Evans, who started Methodism in CR Co., after being converted by Robert Strawbridge. All the Barnes children were Methodists. Many gave land to start a church, as did Zadock's grandson, William H. Barnes, who gave land to build Taylorsville Methodist Church. Zadock also deeded part of his land to build Ebenezer Methodist Church in Winfield.

Zadock and Elizabeth were orignally bur. on their farm in Taylorsville. After Taylorsville Church was built, their tombstones, and that of son Andrew, were moved to the church. The bodies were left on the farm, in a grove of trees. I have viewed this area. Nothing marks the original burying ground.{Statement by Wanda Barnes Hall}

Zadock and Elizabeth were the parents of{T. J. C. Williams and Folger McKinsey. *History of Frederick County, Maryland.* 2 vols. Reprinted Baltimore: Regional Publishing Co., 1967}

: ANDREW P., b. 1 May 1796, d. 16 June 1854, age 58, m. by FRML of 12 April 1820 Mary Ann Arnold, b. c1797, d. 15 May 1854. Both are bur. at Taylorsvill{Dielman-Hayward File, MHS} JAMES PETER, b. 28 May 1800, d. 3 Jan 1874, age 73 years, 7 mos., 6 days, m. Mary A., d. 3 Jan 1895, age 77 years, 10 mos., 16 days. Both are bur. at Unionville Methodist Church {Holdcraft, *op. cit.*}; LEVI ZADOC, b. 22 April 1802, age 58 in 1860, m. by FRML of 19 Oct 1823 Susan Lindsay, b. c1807, she was age 53 in 1860; RACHEL, b. 3 March 1804, d. 6 Aug 1892, m. David Buckingham (his second wife). Both are bur. at Taylorsville Methodist Church{Holdcraft, *op. cit.*}; SLINGSBERRY LETHANY, b. 1 April 1806, d. 15 May 1891; PRUDENCE, b. c1807; THOMAS E. F., b. 13 Feb 1811, d. 1 April 1896; ELVIRA, b. 19 Feb 1813, m. Thomas Condon; ELIZABETH, d. 11 Feb 1829, having m. John Lindsay 10 April 1828{Evans Diary} AMELIA, d. 3 Sep 1835, having m. John Conoway on 2 Oct 1832{Evans Diary}; NANCIFER, named in father's will; and ASBURY, m. Ann, dau. of Charles Franklin, on 17 April 1828.{Evans Diary}

76.   ZACHARIAH BARNES, son of Philemon, was b. 14 Oct 1765. He m. Catherine (N), who d. 18 Sep 1803.{Evans Diary} Zachariah Barnes m.

by AAML dated 14 Feb 1794 in AA Co., Catherine, dau. of James and Elizabeth (Shipley) Barnes.

According to *The Shipleys of Maryland*, Zachariah and Catherine were the parents of: ELIZABETH, d. 28 July 1823, m. Samuel Baker (had a dau. Marcella){Evans Diary}; JAMES FRANCIS ASBURY; and MATILDA.

77.   ARCHIBALD BARNES, son of Philemon, was b. 25 Jan 1769, and d. 19 Dec 1837, aged 69.{Evans Diary}

In 1818, he was listed in the 6th District of BA Co., assessed at $615, including 282-1/2 a. *Abington Forest* and other tracts assessed at $565, and improvements assessed at $50.{Tax List of BA Co., 6th District, 1818:4, typescript at MHS}

Archibald Barnes d. in CR Co. leaving a will dated 8 March 1836 and proved 22 Jan 1838. He named his bro. Thomas (exec.), and sister Airey, nephew Alfred (to have all his land on the s. side of the New Liberty Road, and part of the land purchased from Jacob Tener). He also named niece Louisa Buckingham and nephew Archibald Barnes. Joshua Gist, Joshua Franklin, and Benjamin Bennett were execs.{CRWB 1:38}

78.   THOMAS BARNES, son of Philemon, was living in 1802. In 1836, he was named as a bro. in the will of Archibald Barnes. He m. by 20 March 1839 Violette (N). On that day, Thomas Barnes, and wife Violette, of CR Co., for $600, conv. to James C. Attlee 20 a. of *Eppington's Forest, John's Industry,* and *Lawrence's Pleasant Valleys.* On the same date, for $200, Thomas and Violette sold Henry Cover 20 a., part of *Lawrence's Pleasant Valleys*.{CRLR WW #3:301, 316}

Thomas Barnes d. leaving a will dated 1843 in CR Co.{CRWB 1:272}

Thomas and Violette were the parents of: ARCHIBALD; and SALLY.

79.   ELISHA BARNES, son of Philemon Barnes, d. 5 Jan 1856 in his 73rd year. His wife Ann d. 13 March 1826.{Evans Diary}

80.   DENNIS BARNES, possibly son of Thomas and Sarah (Barnes), d. 1831 in BA Co. He m. 1st, on 14 Oct 1793, Sarah Cord, and 2nd, on 18 Aug 1803, Leah, dau. of James Hood.

On 29 Aug 1808, Dennis Barnes was named a Captain in the Militia.{Militia Appointments, Liber 2, folios 22, 44, 138, MSA}

In 1812, he was listed with Nathan Barnes as owing a debt to the estate of Joshua Porter on a note bearing interest from 14 Aug 1801.{MD Chancery Book 148:51}

On 9 Sep 1813, he was deeded part of *Bachelor's Refuge* by Araminta Shipley, Hamlet Gillis, Pantus Gillis, and Elizabeth Leatherwood.{BALR WG #124:624}

In 1814, he appeared on the BA Co. Tax List for Lower Delaware Hundred. He was listed as owning 50 a. *Charles Delight,* and 29 a. *Resurvey on Charles Delight.* In 1818, he was listed in the 6th District of BA Co. as owning 540 a. *Baker's Desire,* 29 a. part of *Charles' Delight,* and 25 a. part *Bachelor's Refuge.*

On 5 July 1819, Dennis Barnes and wife Leah, Henry H. Warfield and wife Rachel, all of BA Co., and George Wolfe and his wife Letitia, of FR Co., for $680 sold John Hood, of James, certain tracts of land, their share of the estate of James Hood, Sr.{AALR WSG#6:445}

Dennis Barnes was listed in the 6th District of BA Co. with one male 45+, one female 26-45, one male 16-26, two females 10-16, two females under 10, and three males under 10.

The estate of Dennis Barnes was admin. by execs. Leah Barnes and Joseph Elsom Barnes, on 23 Feb 1832, 19 Nov 1832, and 22 June 1833.{BAAD 30:20, 315 and 31:28}

Dennis Barnes was the father of: MARGARET, b. 24 Dec 1794{St. Paul's Parish Register 1:275}; JOSHUA; THOMAS; LETITIA, m. by BAML dated 26 Oct 1825, Joseph Elsom; ANN; and ELIZA.

81.   ZACCHEUS BARNES, possibly son of Elijah and Catherine (Shipley) Barnes, m. Rachel Stillwell, 31 Jan 1819 in Hamilton Co., OH.

Fifth Generation

82.   BASIL BARNES, son of Joshua (43), was b. c1770/1780 (probably the male 16-21 who first appears with Joshua in 1792); dec. by Oct 1833 when his son, Joshua Porter Barnes, was named admin. of the estate. Basil m. 11 May 1809 in Fleming Co., KY, Priscilla Williams.

83.   ROBERT BARNES, Jr., son of Robert (45), was b. c1772/1774, m. 1st, before 1798, Maryan (N), and 2nd, Ann Hineman/Hindman/Hyneman Nichols, dau. of John Hineman and widow of John Nichols, of Mason Co., KY, by bond dated 25 Feb 1808.

Robert Barnes, Jr., purchased some town lots from the trustees of Flemingsburg on 14 May 1798. He and his wife, Maryan, sold part of these on 11 Sep 1798. From 1798 through 1820, these are the only two men named Robert Barnes found in Fleming Co. Consistently designated as Jr. and Sr., they are believed to be father and son and will be treated as such from this point forward. Robert, Jr., was listed in the 1820 Census of Fleming Co., KY, as a male 45+. In his household was one female 45+, one female 26-45, two females 16-26, one female 10-16, one male 10-16, and one male 0-10. His name appeared on the tax lists of Fleming Co. for the year 1824. In 1826, Robert Barnes, Jr., of Nicholas Co., KY, sold lot 39 in Fleming Co. to James Graham. {Fleming Co. Deeds 0:130} He was taxed in Nicholas Co. in 1826 and 1827, but was gone from the lists in 1830 and 1831. From 1835 through 1837, he was taxed in Mason Co., but again disappeared in 1838. An unidentified Daniel Barnes appeared on the tax lists of Mason Co. for the first and only time in 1838.

Robert Barnes was probably the father of: MARGARET, b. c1800, m. 6 Feb 1821 Simeon Lloyd (She listed MD as the birthplace of both of their parents when the 1880 Census of Fleming Co. was taken.); ALVIN, b. c1803, d. after 1880 (He also listed MD as the birthplace of both of his parents when the 1880 Census of Fleming Co. was taken.); NATHAN, m. Amelia Roper 13 Sep 1825; THOMAS m. Melvina Jackson 18 July 1825; and SALLY ANN m. Robert Stockwell 27 Jan 1825.

84. JOSEPH BARNES, son of Robert (45), was b. before 1779, the date and place of his death are unknown since no will has been found. However, much can be determined about his family by court documents in Fleming Co. He m. 20 Feb 1800, Phebe Stockton, b. 22 Sep 1782, d. 7 April 1830, bur. in Stockton Station Cemetery, dau. of George Stockton.

Joseph last appeared on the 1834 Fleming tax list. He is undoubtedly the male 50-60 living with his son, George F., in the 1830 U. S. Census; thus, Joseph would have been b. between 1770-1780. On 5 July 1830, Joseph gave guardianship of his minor children, Leakem and Ruan Barnes, to Leaken D. Stockton. G. F. Barnes was security.

Joseph and Phoebe had issue: JOHN S.; GEORGE F., d. 12 May 1864, Fleming Co.; JOSHUA, moved to Mason Co., KY; RACHEL; PHEBE; RUAH; LEAKUM/LAKIN D., resided in Bourbon Co., KY, in 1850.

85. EPHRAIM BARNES, son of Robert (45), was b. between 1765 and 1775 according to census data, and from his appearance on the tax lists it would appear that his birth was about 1774. He d. by March 1836, when Andrew Yeates filed his mortgage foreclosure and listed Ephraim's heirs.

In Fleming Co. May Court 1831, "Sally Ann Barnes came into court and by and with the consent thereof chose Abram Hillis as her guardian."{Fleming Co. Order Book E:292} Ephraim Barnes last appeared on the 1825 tax list, and in 1826, James, his oldest son, appeared for the first time with the same amount of personal property. Moreover, on the 1829 tax list, Andrew Yeates is listed with the 100 a. on Triplett Creek which is the subject of the 1836 mortgage foreclosure. Thus, it would appear that Ephraim may have d. in 1826. Ephraim Barnes was undoubtedly m. in

---

Fleming Co., as a bond was filed there 2 Feb 1801 for the pending marriage of Ephraim Barnes to Elizabeth McIntyre, with James McIntyre as the bondsman.

Ephraim Barnes and Elizabeth McIntire of Fleming Co., KY, were the parents of: JAMES G., b. c1803, d. between 1870 and 1880, Fleming Co., KY, m. 21 March 1825, Lucinda M. Choate, b. July 1810, d. after 1900 Montgomery Co., KS, dau. of Richard Choate, had 13 children; SAMUEL, b. 1800/1810, m. 1st, on 24 Feb 1825, Cynthia Choat, dau. of Edward Choat, 2nd, on 17 Oct 1829, Sarah Oxley;[13] ALFRED or ALVIN, b. 16 March 1808, KY, d. 16 April 1884, Des Moines, IA, m. 12 March 1835 in Brown Co., OH, Margaret Shick, b. 1815, d. 11 Feb 1888, KS, had 11 children; SARAH ANN, b. 16 Sep 1812, d. 3 July 1888, Burt Co., NE, m. 3 May 1831, Fleming Co., KY, Stephen Hester, had 7 children; JOSEPH, b. c1812, d. after 1883, m. 1st, on 18 Oct 1834, Asenath Peddicord, b. 1811, d. 29 Sep 1860, by whom he had 8 children, m. 2nd, on 19 Jan 1862, Sarah Case, m. 3rd, Rebecca (Hall) Wright, had 2 children;[14] JOSHUA URIAH, b. 15 June 1814/1815, d. 15 April 1898, Cherokee Co., KS, m. 26 April 1837, Montgomery Co., IN, Paulina/Pearlina Barnhill, b. 3 Jan 1818, d. 3 Nov 1896, had 9 children; GARLAND BRADFORD, b. c1819, d. after 1887, probably in Burt Co., NE, m. 1st, on 20 July 1837, Montgomery Co., IN, Elizabeth Ann Westfall, had four children, m. 2nd, Mary A. (N); SUSAN, b. c1820/1825, d. 20 Aug 1855, m. 13 April 1842, Des Moines Co., IA, Franklin Loper, had 5 children.

86.   SAMUEL BARNES, son of Robert (45), was b. c1781, d. by 29 Aug 1820, the date of his estate inventory in Fleming Co., KY.{Fleming Co. Will Book B}, m. 27 Feb 1806 in Mason Co., KY, to Anna Waller, dau. of Thomas Waller.

A lawsuit was filed in Fleming Co. Circuit Court 4 Feb 1815 by Samuel Barnes in which he accused Robert Barnes, Jr., of taking numerous household items "which he (Robert) knew were rightfully his (Samuel's)." Earlier, on 3 Sep 1809, Samuel had sued Robert Barnes, Sr., in a case of "covenant broken." Perhaps the elder Robert had transferred his home and land to Samuel, with the stipulation, no longer satisfactory, that he be allowed to remain and live there. The raid on the household goods could have been Robert, Jr.'s, attempt to take some of the personal effects which would have remained in Robert, Sr.'s, home after his death,

---

[13] Samuel was in Pendleton Co., KY, in 1860. His son, Harrison, moved to Modale, IA, and to Douglas Co., NE, by 1900.

[14] In 1880, Joseph was with his son, Nicholas, in Smith Co., KS.

items which, not being specifically listed in the contract, might be considered part of his estate to be shared among the other children.

Anna appears as the head of the household in the 1820 census and later court documents identify the children of Samuel and Anna as: FREDERICK MORTIMER; SOPHIA ANN, m. Elias Wheatley; ELIZABETH ELEANOR, m. Thomas M. Small; ARY S.; and THOMAS WALLER.

87.   HARRIET BARNES, dau. of Robert (45), was b. by 1787 (if m. at age 18). Robert Barnes was the bondsman for her marriage to Samuel McDonald on 3 Oct 1805 in Fleming Co., KY.

88.   RACHEL BARNES, dau. of Robert (45), was b. c1780-1790. Robert Barnes was the bondsman for her marriage to William Davis on 25 June 1808 in Fleming Co., KY.

89.   SARAH WESTFALL, (possibly) dau. of Alexander and Priscilla (48) (Barnes) Westfall, was b. c1808, and m. (N) Hapenstall. {Data compiled by Carol Gehrs Mitchell, hereafter cited as CGM}

90.   SYLVANUS BARNES WESTFALL, son of Alexander and Priscilla (48) (Barnes) Westfall, was b. 31 Aug 1809 in VA, and d. 31 Aug 1885 in Clark Co., IL. He was bur. in Smyrna Cemetery, and removed to Hebron Cemetery, Clark Co. He m. on 14 Sep 1837 in Meigs Co., OH, Samantha Jane Bailey, dau. of Robert and Elizabeth 'Betty' (Hysell) Bailey. {CGM}

91.   GEORGE WESTFALL, son of Alexander and Priscilla (Barnes) (48) Westfall, was b. 17 Nov 1811 in Elizabethtown, Wood Co., WV, and d. 9 Aug 1894 in Knox Co., IL. He m. Susan Bailey. {CGM}

92.   HIRAM P. WESTFALL, son of Alexander and Priscilla (Barnes) (48) Westfall, was b. 1814 in VA, and d. 3 May 1849 in OH. He was bur. at Woodyard Cemetery, Pageville, OH. On 1 Oct 1839, he m. Elizabeth Tewkesbury in Athens, OH. {CGM}

93.   MARY WESTFALL, dau. of Alexander and Priscilla (Barnes) (48) Westfall, was b. c1815 in Elizabethtown, and d. age 24. She m. William Cornell on 26 Sep 1833. {CGM}

94.   FANNY WESTFALL, dau. of Alexander and Priscilla (Barnes) (48) Westfall, was b. 1818 in Elizabethtown, and d. 12 March 1882 in Athens Co., OH. She was bur. in 1882 in Henning Cemetery, Scipio

Township, Athens Co., OH, having m. on 19 March 1835, David Daugherty. {CGM}

95.   REBECCA WESTFALL, dau. of Alexander and Priscilla (Barnes) Westfall, was b. 26 Nov 1822 in Elizabethtown, and d. 11 April 1874 in Knox Co., IL. She was bur. in 1874 in the Westfall Cemetery, Knox Co. She m. on 7 May 1840, Jabez W. Crouch. {CGM}

96.   ELIZABETH REEVES WESTFALL, dau. of Alexander and Priscilla (Barnes) (48) Westfall, was b. 19 March 1826 in Athens Co., and d. 29 Nov 1900 in E. Gal., IL. She was bur. in 1900 in the Westfall Cemetery, Knox Co., IL, and she m. 3 Nov 1842, Lewis Mitchell. {CGM}

97.   ROBERT BARNES, son of Adam (54) and Ruth (Shipley) Barnes, was b. c1788, and d. in CR Co. in 1855. On 18 Dec 1845, he m. Sarah, dau. of John and Sarah (Arnold) Smith. She d. in 1866 in CR Co.
    On the death of his father, Adam Barnes, Robert was made exec. of the estate, and the property was to remain in his hands until his youngest sister reached the age of 16. According to the Chancery Case that ensued, Robert continued to live on the homestead after his marriage until the property was sold in 1820.
    Robert Barnes d. leaving a will dated 16 April 1852 and proved 21 May 1855. In his will, he left a portion of the tract *Hopewell* to his son Adam, describing it as "the old home place." His wife Sarah was to have a tract called *Kinfauns,* which Robert had bought from John Smith, Sr., on 3 July 1837.
    Sarah Smith Barnes also d. testate, leaving a will dated 30 April 1863 and proved 15 Jan 1866. {CRWB 3:380}
    The children of Robert and Sarah (Smith) Barnes were: ROBERT S. Barnes, b. c1818, m. Sarah Smith by CRML dated 6 Dec 1845; RACHEL; SARAH, m. by CRML dated 2 Jan 1846, Richard Frizzell; LEVI TIVIS, b. 19 Nov 1827; NIMROD HENRY, b. 18 Sep 1829; BURGESS NELSON, m. by CRML dated 1 April 1853, Susan Lescaleet; ADAM S., m. by CRML dated 14 Oct 1858, Elizabeth A. Barnes; ELIZA A., b. c1833, m. William H. Hughes.

98.   RACHEL BARNES, dau. of Adam (54) and Ruth (Shipley) Poole, m. by BAML dated 12 Jan 1811, Vachel Pool.

99.   ADAM BARNES, son of Adam (54) and Ruth (Shipley) Barnes, d. in CR Co. in 1840, having m. by BAML dated 11 April 1801, Mary Parish. They were the parents of: LUCINDA EMILY; and LEWIS HANSON.

100. NAOMI BARNES, dau. of Adam (54) and Ruth (Shipley) Barnes, was b. 10 June 1785, and d. 12 May 1873, age 87 years, 11 mos., and 2 days. She m. by BAML dated 17 March 1807, Lloyd Pool, b. c1782, d. 22 Feb 1863, age 81 years, 8 mos., 11 days. Both are bur. at Mt. Pleasant M. E. Church, Gamber, MD.

On 23 March 1805, George Whips, of AA Co., and wife Susanna, conv. to John Whips Pool and Lloyd Pool portions of *First Choice,* 21 a., *Hood's Friendship,* 6 a., and part of *Whips Hill Resurveyed.*{AALR NH#14:25}

On 23 March 1807, John Whips Pool and Lloyd Pool stated they were indebted to George Whips, who was intending to move shortly to KY.{AALR NH#13:655}

Lloyd Pool d. leaving a will made 23 Jan 1864 and proved 10 Feb 1864. In his will, he left 1/3 of his farm, 1/3 of his money, and 1/3 of his property to his wife Naomi. He also named his children Henry Pool, Joseph Pool, Reuben Pool, Asenath Shipley, Ketura Shipley, Sarah Ann Grimes, Hammutal Wilson, Mary Ann Creswell, and Martha Ann Pool. {CRWB 3:117}

According to interviews with family members conducted many years ago by the late Dr. Caleb Dorsey, Naomi Barnes Pool was an excellent horsewoman, and was trained in the art of healing, quite an advantage in a day and time when doctors were practically non-existent. She once rode a horse after dark into that part of CR Co. known as "Wolf Bottom," to rescue a little girl who had wandered into the wolf-infested forest.

Lloyd and Naomi (Barnes) Pool were the parents of: JOSEPH POOL, b. 14 April 1809; REUBEN POOL, b. 21 Feb 1812; ASENATH POOL, m. (N) Shipley; KETURA POOL, m. Frederick Shipley; SARAH ANN POOL, m. Dennis Grimes, by CRML dated 22 Nov 1838; HAMMUTAL POOL, b. c1826, d. 21 March 1850, age 23 years, 7 mos., 26 days, m. (N) Wilson; MARTHA ANN POOL, b. 23 Sep 1829, d. 18 Nov 1893, m. 11 March 1847, Elisha Griffee; HENRY POOL, b. c1821; and MARY ANN POOL, m. (N) Criswell.

101. JOSHUA BARNES, son of Adam (54) and Ruth (Shipley) Barnes, was b. c1786, and d. in 1853. He m. Elizabeth, dau. of William Parrish, by BAML dated 17 April 1807. His grandson, George Barnes, told Dr. Caleb Dorsey that Joshua Barnes had been killed by a falling rock when he and his son were sawing off a piece of soapstone to be used in the construction of a top for a still (for the distillation of wormseed, an important industry in CR Co. at the time).

Joshua Barnes d. leaving a will proved 5 Sep 1853.{CRWB 2:88} In his will he named children: JOSHUA TEVIS; SOLOMON; MARY, m. Benjamin Williams; ELIZABETH; NAOMI, m. George Williams; and EURITH, m. (N) Demoss.

102.   ZACHARIAH BARNES, son of Adam (54) and Ruth (Shipley) Barnes, was b. c1787 in AA (now HO) Co., MD, and d. in 1863 in Barnesville, Belmont Co., OH, where he m. 1st, on 12 July 1812, Elizabeth Clifton. He m. 2nd, on April 1824 (N) (N), and 3rd, on 20 March 1833, Jemima Barnes. {Data compiled by Erma Brown, 609 N. Gleanoaks Boulevard, Burbank, CA 91502}

In 1850, Zachariah Barnes, age "60" was living with Thomas N. Hayes in Warren Township, Belmont Co., OH. {1850 Census Belmont Co., dwelling 289, fam. 295} In 1860, Zachariah was listed as age 72, and was still living with Thomas N. Hayes.

Zachariah Barnes was the father of (by his second wife): RUTH JANE, b. 1826 at Barnesville, Belmont Co., and d. 1874, m. 22 Aug 1843, Thomas N. Hays. {Data from Erma Brown}

103.   MARY BARNES, dau. of Adam (54) and Ruth (Shipley) Barnes, m. by BAML dated 8 Jan 1817, Benjamin Haines, probably son of Daniel Haines, who was b. c1794, and d. 20 Dec 1885, "age 98," at Gamber, CR Co. His obituary gives his age as 98 and states that he fought in the War of 1812. {Obituary in the Westminster *Democratic Advocate*, 2 Jan 1886}

In 1850, the ages of Benjamin Haines and his wife were given as 56.

Benjamin Haines, age 85, applied for a pension on 22 May 1878, claiming he was a private in Capt. Burgett's [Burgess'] Co. of MD Militia during the War of 1812. He stated he volunteered on 1 Aug 1814 and was discharged in Oct 1814. After his discharge, he resided in AA Co., MD, until about 1828, when he returned to CR Co. where he bought his residence in Mechanicsville. He was described as having black hair and light colored eyes, and as being 5'10" in height. William H. Lamotte and Edwin Shipley were witnesses. His application was rejected on 23 Sep 1878 because his name was not shown on the rolls of either Capt. Roderick Burgess or Capt. Thomas Burgess. {Pension Application SO-33084}

Benjamin and Mary (Polly) (Barnes) Haines were the parents of at least four children: WILLIAM HAINES, b. c1823, m. Emmaline Barnes; MARY A. HAINES, b. c1831; LEWIS FRANCIS HAINES, b. 17 Dec 1834, d. 1924, m. Agnes Jane Shipley; and ABRAHAM HAINES, b. c1837; m. by CRML dated 11 June 1857, Margaret Ann Eckman.

104.   HENRY BARNES, son of Adam (54) and Ruth (Shipley) Barnes, was b. c1795, and d. 28 April 1851 in CR Co., having m. Mary Smith by BAML dated 11 Sep 1817.

He fought in the War of 1812, in Captain I. T. Randall's Company, MD Militia, from 27 July 1814 to 13 Oct 1814, and it is claimed that he was at both the Battle of Bladensburg and the Battle of North Point, and that he was a substitute for Robert Barnes. {Pension Applications W.O.14821 and W.C.8561} His widow, Mary Smith, d. c1881.

Henry and Mary (Smith) Barnes were the parents of: GEORGE, b. c1820, m. Ann B. M. Craft; RICHARD ADAM, b. 24 July 1822, m. Ursula Carr; WILLIAM H., b. c1823; and THOMAS, b. c1832.

105.   JOSIAH BARNES, son of Adam (54) and Ruth (Shipley) Barnes, was b. c1798, and m. Rebecca (N), b. c1797. They were the parents of: JOHN, b. c1821; JOSHUA, b. c1826; ANN, b. c1833; RUTH H., b. c1835; and MARY I., b. c1839.

106.   RUTH BARNES, dau. of Adam (54) and Ruth (Shipley) Barnes, was b. c1800 and d. 4 Feb 1859 in Erie Co., OH. She m. Wesley Driver, son of James and Lucy (Hobbs) Driver, b. c1794, d. 20 Nov 1851 at Erie Co. Ruth and Wesley are bur. at Cranberry Creek Cemetery.

Wesley and Ruth (Barnes) Driver were the parents of: ADAM DRIVER, b. May 1817 in MD, d. 1903 probably at Fort Wayne, IN, having m. Abigail (N); JAMES A. DRIVER, b. c1823; WILLIAM DRIVER, b. c1824, m. Abby (N), and d. probably at Fort Wayne, IN; NANCY DRIVER, b. 1 Jan 1830, d. 7 Jan 1904 at Joppa, Erie Co., OH, m. Alvin Minkler, bur. at Peaks Cemetery; SARAH DRIVER, b. 26 Feb 1832, d. 6 June 1920, m. George Shoop; JOHN WESLEY DRIVER, b. c1836, OH, m. Abgeline Bradley; WILSON DRIVER, b. 4 Nov 1839, OH, d. 18 March 1906, bur. at Cranberry Creek Cemetery, m. Eliza Minkler; and MARY DRIVER, m. Wales Higgins, d. at Fort Wayne, IN.

107.   CASSANDRA BARNES, dau. of Adam (54) and Ruth (Shipley) Barnes, m. Isaac Driver by BAML dated 22 Aug 1821.

108.   MOSES BARNES, believed to be the son of Dorsey (55) and Lydia (Musgrove) Barnes, was b. c1777, m. Airey Poole, b. c1785, by BAML dated 6 Feb 1808. Both Moses and Airey were living in 1850.

On 30 Dec 1846, Aquila Garrison Barnes, and wife Urith, conv. to Moses Barnes part of *Flag Meadow Resurveyed,* consisting of 2-1/2 a. {CRLR JS#8:284} On 4 Aug 1847, Moses Barnes, of CR Co., leased to John Williams, Ephraim Triplett and Thomas Mitchell, of BA Co., the rights to *Sewell's Folly,* which Moses Barnes had purchased from James M. Shellman. {CRLR JS#7:255} On 8 March 1851, Moses Barnes, and wife Airy, deeded to Moses Barnes, Jr., part of *Stevenson's Deer Park, Trouting Streams and Roberts' Lot,* comprising 100 a. of land. {CRLR JBB#12:116}

Moses and Airey were the parents of: AQUILA GARRETTSON, m. Urith (N); BENJAMIN FRANKLIN, d. unm.; MOSES, Jr.; SUSAN, m. Isaac Kellar, moved to IN (had nine children in five births); JABEZ;

EMALINE, m. by CRML dated 16 March 1846, William Haines; CARILLA, m. by CRML dated 14 April 1838, Lewis Jewett Grove; TABITHA, m. by CRML dated 17 July 1846, William G. Holmes; and EURITH.

109.   ADAM BARNES, son of Dorsey (55) and Lydia (Musgrove) Barnes, was b. c1779 in MD, and in 1850 was living with his m. dau. and her husband.{1850 Census of CR Co.}

On 27 Aug 1803, Adam Barnes, son of Dorsey, appeared before the Court of Chancery and testified that he had delivered a court order to Stephen Cramblich.{MD Chancery Book, 48:130, MSA}

On 3 Sep 1838, James Orr, and his wife Hetta, of Belmont Co., OH, sold to Adam Barnes, of CR Co., MD, lot #30 of *Colross,* cont. 160 a., for $1,100. On 8 March 1841, Adam Barnes sold the same lot to Robert M. Barnes for only $10. On 1 April 1842, Adam Barnes, of CR Co., sold to John Smith, of Richard, the tract *Caledonia,* or *Edinburgh,* 161 a., for $800.{CRLR WW#2:410; WW#6:43, and JS#1:190}

Adam Barnes was the father of: ELIZABETH, m. by BAML dated 27 Aug 1833, John Smith of R.; and ROBERT M., b. c1816, m. by CRML dated 20 July 1840, Elizabeth Ann Smith.

110.   JOHN BARNES, son of Dorsey (55), joined the BA Co. Militia in 1794. No other data has been found.{Militia Registration Card File at MSA}

111.   MARCELLA BARNES, dau. of John (56) and Elizabeth, m. by BAML dated 1 Nov 1822, Perry G. Elder. On 29 Feb 1832, Perry G. Elder, and wife Marcella, sold to Thomas and John D. Barnes, for $200, Marcella's 1/9th of the estate of John Barnes, dec., *Pool's Chance,* and *Shipley's Discovery.*{AALR WSG#17:167}

112.   THOMAS BARNES, son of John (56) and Elizabeth, was b. 10 Nov 1805 in AA Co., MD, and d. 26 May 1893 in Aurora, NE. Sometime before 1829, he m. Louisa Ann Pool, who d. 18 Dec 1886 in Newton, IA.

On 18 June 1844, Thomas Barnes, and wife Louisa, of Howard District, for $1,280, conv. to Margaret Wayman 78 a. of *Shipley's Discovery* and *Pool's Chance.*{HOLR 5:439} On 23 Aug 1847, Thomas and Louisa Barnes, and John and Louisa Hood, all of Howard District, for $4,433, sold 41 a. of *Shipley's Discovery* to Mary Forsyth.{HOLR}

Thomas Barnes' obituary in the Aurora newspaper stated that 12 children were b., and eight were still living; two sons and one dau. were in Hamilton Co., NE.

Thomas and Louisa Ann (Pool) were the parents of (the first 10 were definitely b. in MD): SARAH E., b. c1829; MARTHA L., b. c1833;

WILLIAM L., b. c1835; ELIZA E., b. c1837; RICHARD B., b. c1839; JAMES H., b. c1842; EMMA E., b. c1844; FRANCIS M., b. 3 July 1845; JOHN D., b. c1848; and EMORY, b. c1850.

113.   JOHN DORSEY BARNES, son of John (56) and Elizabeth, was b. c1806, and m. 15 Jan 1833, Eliza Pool, b. c1813.

By 1889, he was living in Genssee, IL. {The obituary of his bro. Benjamin Barnes.}

John and Eliza were the parents of {1850 and 1860 Censuses of HO Co., MD}: ELLEN I., b. c1836; MARIA L., b. c1837/8; JOHN A., b. c1838/40; SARAH, b. c1840; TABITHA, b. c1842; LEONORE, b. c1845; AMANDA, b. c1844/8; MATILDA, b. c1846; MARCELLA, b. c1848; and FLORENCE, b. c1858.

114.   BENJAMIN BARNES, son of John (56) and Elizabeth, was b. 5 Sep 1810 in AA Co., MD, and d. 1 April 1889 in HO Co., MD. He was bur. 4 April 1889 in McKendree Cemetery, HO Co. On 17 Dec 1853, he m. 1st, in BC, Ann Elizabeth Brenneison, b. 6 July 1812 in FR Co., dau. of John and Margaret Brenneison. She d. 27 Dec 1851. Benjamin m. 2nd, on 18 Oct 1853, Elizabeth Henry, b. 3 Sep 1809, d. 29 Dec 1885, age 76 years, 3 mos., and 26 days. She is bur. at Liberty Baptist Church.

Benjamin Barnes was a wheelwright and a member of the Lisbon Methodist Church. At the time of his death, he was the oldest member of the Church. {Typed copy of his obituary in possession of the compiler}

According to the Barnes Bible, owned by Sarah Hughes of Leonardtown, MD, Benjamin had no children by his second wife. By his first wife he was the father of: WILLIAM THOMAS, b. 25 June 1835, d. 22 July 1835; (N), son, b. and d. 21 April 1836; JOHN EMERY, b. 11 March 1837, d. 30 Dec 1907; MARGARET ELIZABETH, b. 6 Oct 1838, d. 1 Dec 1913, m. John Wesley Barnes, of Baltimore; ALMIRA LOUISA, b. 29 Jan 1842, d. 11 Jan 1860; MARY ANDELUE, b. 18 June 1844, d. July 1905, m. Charles Knock, of near Lisbon; BENJAMIN FRANKLIN, b. 19 Sep 1845, d. 13 Sep 1915, bur. McKendree Church, m. 26 June 1873, Mary Elizabeth Smith; DAVID THOMAS, b. 17 Jan 1847, d. 13 Sep 1915, m. 28 May 1883, Hannah C. Bunn; SARAH AMELIA, b. 6 Oct 1848, d. 6 Oct 1918 at Westminster, CR Co., MD, m. 27 Oct, 1875, in Baltimore, Rev. Reuben Kolb, a minister of the ME Church; JAMES ALBERT, b. 29 April, d. 3 July 1850; and EMILY LAIN, b. 6 Dec 1851, d. 7 March 1852.

115.   JAMES A. BARNES, son of John (56) and Elizabeth, was b. c1812/6, and was living as late as 1872. He m. 1st, by HOML dated 3 Sep 1844, as "Joshua Barnes," Sarah Ann Fountain, and 2nd, by BAML dated 3 Nov 1847, Catherine Shipley.

He lived near the intersection of Route 97 and old Route 40 in HO Co., in an old stone house. He was a blacksmith. His son George was b. in Cooksville, HO Co. {Data from Julia Wagner, of Westminster, and Leslie A. Barnes, of Winfield} He d. in 1927 leaving a will. {CRWB 13:318}

His family can be reconstructed from a) the 1850 Census, and b) the 1860 Census of Franklin District, CR Co. James A. Barnes was the father of (by Sarah Ann Fountain): SARAH or SUSANNAH, b. c1836/8, m. (N) Easton; MARGARET, b. c1844/5, m. (N) Shipley; MARCELLA, b. c1848/9; MARY S. or I, b. c1849; GEORGE W., b. c1851, d. 11 Feb 1935; DORA, b. c1853, m. (N) Robertson; LENORA (or MIRANDA or MEDORA), b. c1855, m. George Aldridge; WILLIAM H., b. c1858, twin; REZIN H., b. c1858, twin, d. 8 April 1948, m. Annie Horton Ebenezer; LAURA, b. c1863, m. (N) Franklin; OLIVIA, b. c1866, d. 23 Sep 1939, m. Nathan C. Franklin; LEWIS, b. 25 Feb 1872, d. 28 Nov 1938, bur. at Ebenezer Church of God; and CHARLES C.

116.   WILLIAM ASBURY PEDDICORD, b. c1794, is probably the Asbury Peddicord, son of Jasper (58) and Amelia (Hobbs) Peddicord, b. c1794, d. Jan 1851, who m. by BAML dated 17 Jan 1823 Eliza Rowles, dau. of Eli Rowles.

The children of William Asbury and Eliza (Rowles) Peddicord were{HOLR 19:234 and 27:236; also HO Co. Equity Record Book 3:539}: ELI T.; LEANA(?), m. by HOML 6 Dec 1847, Charles A. Hobbs; VIOLETTE, m. by HOML dated 9 May 1846, Mahlon A. Etchison; SOPHIA A., m. Edward Green; GEORGE S.; FRANKLIN A.; SARAH C.; and BASCOM E.

117.   THOMAS PEDDICORD, son of Jasper (58) and Amelia (Hobbs) Peddicord, was b. c1800, and m. Mary Landon. According to Scharf's *History of Western Maryland,* they were the parents of: WASHINGTON A. PEDDICORD, m. by 1839, Rebecca Crawford.

118.   JOSEPH H. PEDDICORD, son of Jasper (58) and Amelia (Hobbs) Peddicord, was b. c1801, and m. by BAML 25 Nov 1825, Ann Elizabeth Barnes, b. c1808, dau. of Charles Alexander and Harriet (Hobbs) Barnes (see above).

In 1850, they were living in Somerset Township, Belmont Co., OH, with the following children{1850 Census}: CAROLINE, b. c1822 in MD; THOMAS, b. c1831 in MD; LYCURGUS, b. c1833 in MD; THEOPHILUS, b. c1837 in OH; EVALINE, b. c1840 in OH; MARIETTA, b. c1844 in OH; ELIZABETH, b. c1843 in OH; HARRIETT, b. c1846 in OH; and ZACHARY TAYLOR, b. c1849 in OH.

48

119.   THOMAS HOBBS BARNES, son of Charles Alexander (63) and
Harriet (Hobbs) Barnes, was b. c1814, and was probably the Thomas H.
Barnes living as late as 1850 when he was listed in the census of Franklin
Township, Monroe Co., OH, as age 36. Listed with him was his wife
Ruth (N), b. c1818 in MD, and the following children, all b. in OH{1850
Census, Franklin Township, Monroe Co., fam. 154}: OVILLA, b. c1837; OLIVER, b.
c1840; CATHERINE, b. c1842; MARTHA, b. c1845; THOMAS, b.
c1847; and WESLEY, b. c1849.

120.   WASHINGTON BARNES, son of Elisha and Amelia (Barnes)
(65) Barnes, was b. 10 July 1804, and d. 25 Oct 1873. On 11 March
1829, he m. Mary Bartholow, b. 24 Oct 1810, d. 21 July 1898. He and his
wife were bur. at Stone Chapel Methodist Church, New Windsor, where
his tombstone gives his parents' names.
        In 1850, he lived in the 7th District of CR Co. {See 1850 Census of CR Co.;
The Shipleys of Maryland; and Scharf's *History of Western Maryland,* 2:904}
        Washington and Mary (Bartholow) Barnes were the parents of:
ELIVIRA, b. c1830; ALFRED H., b. 20 Jan 1834, d. 15 Oct 1897;
FRANCINA, b. c1839; SARAH E., b. c1843 (as Betty Barnes, she d. 14
Feb 1889, age 45 years, 4 mos., 27 days); MARTHA W., b. c1848; and
MARY H., d. 16 May 1869, age 21 years, 4 mos., 4 days.

121.   ALFRED BARNES, son of Elisha and Amelia (Barnes) (65)
Barnes, m. by CRML dated 31 March 1848, Elizabeth Condon, b. c1819,
d. 10 Nov 1858. She was bur. in the Presbyterian Cemetery, New
Windsor, CR County.
        Alfred and Elizabeth were the parents of{1850 Census of CR Co.}:
THOMAS W., b. c1838; JESSE H., b. c1840; ELVIRA A., b. c1843; and
JOHN W., b. c1848.

122.   CHARLES T. BARNES, son of Adam (68) and Cordelia (Hobbs)
Barnes, was b. c1815 in MD, and by 1850 was living in Malaga
Township, Monroe Co., OH. Joseph Howiler, 18, laborer, b. in OH, was
living in his household in 1850.
        By his wife, Euphemia (N), b. c1820 in Germany, Charles T.
Barnes was the father of (all b. in OH):{1850 Census, Malaga Township, Monroe Co., OH,
fam. 72}: MARTHA C., b. c1832; FRANCIS A., b. c1834; CHARLES W.,
b. c1836; SUSANNA, b. c1838; and THEODORE B., b. c1839.

123.   MARY TOLLEY WORTHINGTON, dau. of Walter and Sarah
(Hood) (70) Worthington, m. by BAML dated 26 May 1812, Capt.
Charles Worthington Dorsey. He was known as "Twisted Mouth

Charles," and served as a Captain of the 32nd MD Regiment during the War of 1812. Captain Dorsey d. 24 May 1864.

Charles and Mary (Worthington) Dorsey were the parents of {Newman, *Anne Arundel Gentry*}: ELIZABETH DORSEY, d. in infancy; THOMAS BEALE DORSEY, d. in infancy; SARAH ANNE DORSEY, d. Aug 1847, m. Thomas Watkins Ligon, Governor of MD (his first wife); CALEB DORSEY; ELIZABETH WORTHINGTON DORSEY; MARY TOLLEY DORSEY, m. Thomas Watkins Ligon, Governor of MD (his second wife); PRISCILLA DORSEY, d. unm.; and COMFORT AUGUSTA DORSEY.

124.   MARTHA WORTHINGTON, dau. of Walter and Sarah (Hood) (70) Worthington, m. in Nov 1822, Dr. John Didier Readel of Baltimore. He d. in 1854.{His obituary appeared in the Towson *Baltimore Co. Advocate* of 30 Sep 1854} John and Martha (Worthington) Readel were the parents of: (N), son, d. 1846; (N), son; (N), son, d. 1851; (N), son; and (N), dau.

125.   SAMUEL BARNES, son of William Barnes (71), was b. c1803, and d. 19 Aug 1879. On 26 July 1833, he m. (possibly as his second wife, according to the Records of the First M. E. Church, Baltimore) Elizabeth Sampson, b. c1810, d. 29 Aug 1885, age 75, in HO Co. Samuel and Elizabeth are bur. in Trinity Chapel Cemetery, HO Co., 6th District, across from St. John's Evangelical Lutheran Church.

According to a notebook in the possession of S. Norman Gardner of Baltimore, Samuel Barnes was m. (before his marriage to Elizabeth Sampson). Children of this marriage included Rufus Barnes and others.

On 27 June 1843, Samuel Barnes applied for relief as an insolvent debtor. The court appointed Nimrod Burchett a trustee. Samuel Barnes turned all of his property over to Burchett.{HOLR 4:213, 458}

In 1850, Samuel Barnes, 45, shoemaker, was listed in the Census for Howard District, AA Co., with his wife Elizabeth, 40, Sarah Ellen, age 14, Samuel T., age 10, Fanceanna, age 8, Michael Denton, age 6, Anne E., age 5, and George W., age 2.

In 1880, Elizabeth Barnes, 70, was living with her son Michael Barnes in Mt. Vernon, BA Co.{1880 Census of BA Co., 9th District, enum. district 243, dwelling 294, fam. 294}

Samuel Barnes had one son by his first wife, and six children by Elizabeth Sampson. His children were: JAMES W.; (by ELizabeth): SARAH ELLEN, b. 29 May 1835, d. 1 May 1909, m. Samuel Thompson; SAMUEL T., b. 1840; FRANCEANNA, b. c1841/2; MICHAEL DENTON, b. 23 Dec 1842 or 1843; ANN E., b. c1845; and GEORGE WASHINGTON, b. c1848.

126.   DAWSON BARNES, son of Caleb (72) and Honor, d. after 1850 in Southampton Township, Bedford Co., OH. He m. Mary Poole on 29 Sep 1794 in FR Co. Mary was probably the dau. of Samuel Poole who moved to Bedford Co., PA, c1807. She also d. after 1850. Dawson and Mary are probably bur. in the cemetery located on the farm of Caleb Barnes.

Dawson and Mary were the parents of{Data from Ethel Albin}: HONOR, b. 16 July 1795, d. 27 Oct 1873 in Bedford Co., m. c1814/5, Levin Shipley, son of Elijah Shipley, d. 19 Aug 1882 in Mann Township, Bedford Co., PA; SAMUEL, b. c1797, d. c1849 in AL Co., MD, m. 1st, c1820, Susan Weimer, and 2nd, Sarah (N).

127.   CALEB BARNES, son of Caleb (72) and Honor (Stevens) Barnes, was b. 1 Nov 1795 in Bedford Co., PA, and d. 6 Aug 1878 in Perry Co., OH. He m. 1st, c1818 in Bedford Co., Mary Cavinee, dau. of Edward and Rebecca (Gordon) Cavinee. He m. 2nd, in Perry Co., OH, Nancy Wilson.

Caleb was the father of (by Mary Cavinee): HONORA,[15] b. 23 July 1819, Bedford Co., PA, d. 24 Oct 1905, m. 27 May 1838, Perry Co., OH, Moses Powell; JOHN, b. 9 June 1820, Bedford Co., PA; OZIAS, b. 1 Dec 1824, Bedford Co., PA; REBECCA, b. c1825/30, Bedford Co., d. by 14 Oct 1869, m. (Nicholas?) Breen; MARY ANN, b. 13 April 1831, Perry Co., OH, d. there on 26 June 1915, m. on 13 April 1854, in Perry Co., Michael Diller, son of John and Julia (Whiteline) Diller; and DAWSON, b. c1835, Perry Co., OH, d. by 14 Sep 1878, Perry Co., where he m. on 13 March 1859, Mary Catherine Palmer.

128.   ANDREW P. BARNES, son of Zadock (75) and Ann Elizabeth, was b. 1 May 1796, in FR Co., MD, and d. 16 June 1854, age 58. He m. on 12 April 1820, Mary Ann or Sarah Ann Arnold, b. March 1796 and d. 15 May 1854. Both are bur. at Taylorsville.{Data compiled by Wanda Barnes Hall}

The following information was written 2 Sep 1977 by Georgia R. F. Gosnell, as it was told to her by her grandmother, Mary Catherine Barnes Fleming, dau. of Andrew and Sarah:

"Andrew P. and his wife were bur. in the family lot on the farm, which was later owned by Augustus C. Barnes. About 1910, their stones were taken away and placed in Taylorsville Church Cemetery, Taylorsville, MD.

Andrew P. Barnes was my great-grandfather, and his wife, Sarah Ann Arnold, was my great-grandmother. Her parents lived in PA and were very wealthy in those days. Andrew was of a poor family and lived

---

[15] She was the great-great-grandmother of Ethel Albin.

in MD. Andrew Barnes was a great horseman, and like the gallant, Sir Lancelot, attracted Miss Arnold very much; so they eloped on horseback and were married.

After her marriage to Andrew P. Barnes, Sarah Ann Arnold was disinherited by her family. Before her marriage, she never so much as washed a pocket handkerchief. When she was confronted with a sheet, she just cried.

Uncle George Arnold was a merchant of some renown. He was the only one of the Arnolds that would visit her. He drove a stage coach and wore knee breaches with silver buckles at the knee. When he came, he would bring bolts of calico to make dresses for Sarah Ann's girls, and other provisions for them, too."

The will of Andrew P. Barnes was presented to Orphans Court of CR Co. on 26 June 1854. The witnesses to the will were David Buckingham, Thos. Hood, and Zacheride W. Hedridge. The will had been held by his sister, Clementine Franklin.

Andrew and Sarah Ann Arnold were the parents of: WILLIAM; LOUISA, m. David Buckingham; RACHEL, m. (as second wife?) David Buckingham; MARY CATHERINE, m. Charles Thomas; ELIZABETH, m. James Steele of Westminster, MD; CLEMENTINE, m. (N) Franklin, lived at Taylorsville; and JANE, m. (N) Frizzell.

129.   JAMES PETER BARNES, son of Zadock (75) and Ann Elizabeth, was b. 28 May 1800, and d. 3 Jan 1874. He m. on 10 May 1842, Mary A. Buckingham, b. 1817, d. 3 Jan 1895. Both are bur. at Unionville Methodist Church Cemetery, FR Co., MD. He was a farmer.

130.   LEVI ZADOC BARNES, son of Zadock (75) and Ann Elizabeth, was b. 22 April 1802, and d. 20 Oct 1862. He m. 19 Oct 1825, in FR Co., Susannah Lindsay, b. 18 Aug 1806, d. 2 Sep 1881, dau. of John and Sarah (Baile) Lindsay.

According to Williams' *History of Frederick County*, page 966, Levi Zadock Barnes was a poor boy and received no education but what he acquired in the old log school house, yet he was an expert mathematician. He learned shoemaking and worked at the trade for many years. After his marriage, he settled on land near Oak Orchard, on which now stands the residence of Isaac Nusbaum. At this time he had but fifty cents with which to buy food. He invested in a sack of flour and middlings. This was soon consumed and no work came in. As he had no cash, he went to the mill and asked for flour on credit, which, after some hesitation was given him.

Levi Zadock Barnes persevered and worked and saved until finally he was able to buy five or six a. of land near Oak Orchard. He now abandoned his trade at which he had worked successfully for many years, and on his land sold general merchandise and began business as a huckster.

He was a successful merchant and continued the business until his death. During this time, he was postmaster of Oak Orchard for fifteen or twenty years. He was a member of the Whig party. He and his wife are bur. in the graveyard adj. Linganore Methodist Chapel.

Levi Zadock and Susan (Lindsay) Barnes were the parents of {Williams, *op. cit.*:966}: SARAH A.; F. WASHINGTON, d. Feb 1908, having m. Ellen Reese; ELIZABETH, m. William R. Curry; CATHERINE, m. John Waltz; JOHN THOMAS; AMELIA, d. 1904, m. Hamilton Lindsay; AUGUSTA, m. William Ecker; RACHEL E.; and LUCRETIA, m. (N) Dudderar.

131. RACHEL BARNES, dau. of Zadock (75) and Ann Elizabeth, was b. 3 March 1804, and d. 6 Aug 1892. On 29 Sep 1851, she m., as his second wife, David Buckingham, b. 11 Jan 1811, d. 9 Feb 1902. Both are bur. at Taylorsville Methodist Church Cemetery, Taylorsville, MD.

132. SLINGSBERRY LETHANY BARNES, son of Zadock (75) and Ann Elizabeth, was b. 1 April 1806, and d. 15 May 1891 in Largo, Wabash Co., IN. On 18 Feb 1835, in Montgomery Co., OH, he m. Sarah Niswonger, b. 19 Jan 1817, d. 1 July 1895, dau. of Samuel and Ellen (Dillon) Niswonger. Slingsby and Sarah are bur. in the Largo, IN, I.O.O.F. Cemetery. Slingsby and Sarah were parents of seven children.

Slingsby moved to OH as a young man and founded the town of Arlington, OH, near Dayton, in Nov 1838. Slingsby and Sarah moved to Wabash Co., IN, in Feb 1865, to avoid the ill feelings of the Niswongers, who fought in the Confederacy during the Civil War. {Data from James W. Haupert, in 1979, was living in Wabash, IN, who used an 1882 History of Montgomery County, OH, and 1884 and 1901 Histories of Wabash County, IN}

133. THOMAS E. F. BARNES, son of Zadock (75) and Ann Elizabeth, was b. 13 Feb 1811, and d. 1 Apr. 1896.

A biography of his appears in *The History of Vigo County, Indiana,* by H. C. Bradsby, c1891, page 670.

Thomas E. F. Barnes was raised in MD, where he lived until he was 23 years of age. He, like many of the pioneer children, when but little more than a toddler, trudged his way 2-1/2 miles to school, and then received only a limited education. About 1835, he left his native state, and went to Montgomery Co., OH, near Dayton, where he was engaged in farming for three years, and from there he moved to Miami Co., where he worked on a farm for one year. In 1840, he went to Clay Co., IN, entered 320 a. of land, and began to improve a farm. In 1842, he returned to Montgomery Co., OH, and m. Miss Sarah Hosier, a native of that place, and a dau. of Abram and Lucy (Key) Hosier.

Mr. Barnes resided in Clay Co. for 18 years when he disposed of his farm and came to Vigo Co., IN. He purchased 40 a. of land, which he farmed until 1878, and thereafter resided in Terre Haute. He owned two lots in the city, and 53 a. of valuable land. He cast his first presidential vote for Adams, and was always affiliated with the old Whig party during this time.

His obituary adds that he and his wife were m. 54 years. They were constant companions and enjoyed life together. He was of a genial and jovial disposition and was always welcome in the company of any social gathering. He was a very honest and upright man. He was very fond of little children and took delight in entertaining them. He was bur. in Woodstock Cemetery, Terre Haute, IN. He left two daus., two granddaus., and three great-grandchildren.

134.   ELVIRA BARNES, dau. of Zadock (75) and Ann Elizabeth, was b. 19 Feb 1813, and m. Thomas Condon. She was named in her father's will.

135.   AMELIA BARNES, dau. of Zadock (75) and Ann Elizabeth, d. before 1849. She m. (N) Conaway. Her father's will mentioned a granddau., Elizabeth, who was to inherit her share at age 18.

136.   ELIZABETH BARNES, dau. of Zachariah (76) and Catherine (Barnes) Barnes, m. Samuel Baker, and had at least one dau. {*The Shipleys of Maryland*}: MARCELLA.

137.   JAMES F. ASBURY BARNES, son of Zachariah (76) and Catherine (Barnes) Barnes, m. by FCML dated 15 April 1828, Susan Ann Franklin, dau. of Charles Franklin.

James F. A. Barnes was a blacksmith, and lived at New London, FR Co. He was a member of the Methodist Church.

They were the parents of{Williams, *op. cit.*:1462}: FRANCES, m. Westminster Singler; CLEMENTINE, d. young; JOHN RANDOLPH; WILLIAM, m. Sarah Hobbs and moved to VA; SUSAN, m. her cousin Alfred Barnes; JOSEPHINE, m. George Zepp; and TOMSEY AMELIA, d. age 20.

THE BASIL FAMILY

1.   RALPH BASSELL, the progenitor, claimed land for service in 1658.{MPL Q:70} Ralph Bazzell, of AA Co., claimed land for service again in 1662.{MPL 5:531}

He d. leaving a will dated 20 Feb 1665 and proved 24 June 1672. He named his wife Mary as extx., and stated that his son Ralph was to have 50 a. of land at age 17 years.{MWB 1:406}

Ralph and Mary were the parents of: RALPH, Jr., b. after 1648.

2.   RALPH BASIL, son of Ralph and Mary, was under 17 years of age in 1665. He m. Rose Hopper on 23 Sep 1697 in All Hallows Parish, AA Co. He may be the Ralph Bassil who was bapt. there on 22 Jan 1698. {AACR:7, 8}

Like many colonial planters, Ralph Basil was involved in a number of land transactions. On 9 Nov 1685, Ralph Bazill, of AA Co., conv. to Jno. Norris 50 a. called *St. Thomas' Neck.* {AALR IH#3:106} On 24 July 1685, John Gray had surv. 184 a. called *Gray's Adventure.* It was assigned to Ralph Bazil, and by 1707 was owned by Jno. Cooly's Orphans. {MRR:259}

Ralph "Basill" patented 316 a. in PG Co. called *Ralph's,* on 10 Oct 1708. {MPL DD#5:390, PL#3:1} On 26 March 1709, he paid 4000 lbs. tob. to Benjamin Williams and wife Margaret for 83 a. known as *The Old Plantation.* {AALR PK:58}

On 22 Feb 1717, Ralph Basil, carpenter, of AA Co., with consent of his wife, conv. to John Turner a tract called *Raepho* in PG Co., 402 a. {PGLR F:Old Series 6:86/634}

"Raphael" Bazil and Richard Shald appraised the inventory of John Keys of AA Co. on 6 Nov 1718. {MINV 1:458}

Ralph Basil must have been prosperous enough to loan money to his neighbors. On 25 May 1697, he received a payment from the estate of John Cooley of AA Co. {INAC 14:130} On 18 April 1698, he was paid from the estate of John Rowell of AA Co. {INAC 16:69} On 17 June 1709, Ralph Bazill was listed as one of the creditors of Richard Cheney of AA Co. {INAC 29:256}

Ralph Bazzell, cooper, of AA Co., d. leaving a will dated 27 March 1728 and proved 27 June 1728. He left 10 s. each to his sons Robert and John, left his real estate to his wife Rose (extx.), and at her death to his sons James and Joseph, and named Ruth, wife of Walter Phelps, Sr., and Mary, wife of Walter Phelps, Jr. Walter Phelps, Rich. Phelps, and William Fish were witnesses. {MWB 19:527}

The inventory of Ralph Bazell of AA Co. was taken on 2 Sep 1728 by Anthony Bedingfield and Thomas Richardson. William Chapman and John Welsh signed as creditors, and Walter Phelps, Sr., and Walter Phelps, Jr., signed as kin. Rose Bazell, extx., filed the inventory on 24 Sep 1728. {MINV 13:313}

Ralph Bazill's estate was admin. on 27 Nov 1729. There were two inventories totalling £101.2.4 and £33.14.8. Payments were made to a number of people, including Mr. William Black, merchant in London. {MDAD 10:82}

Mrs. Rose Bazill was mentioned in the 1761 deposition of John Phelps, Sr. {AALC 2:553-557}

Ralph and Rose (N) Basil were the parents of (b. in All Hallows Parish, AA Co.){AACR:4, 5, 11, 12, 13, 14, 19, 22, 24, 30, 33, 44, 195, 200}: RUTH, b. 16 May 1698, bapt. 12 June 1698; ROBERT, b. 25 June 1699, bapt. 23 July 1699; JOHN, b. 13 Feb 1700, bapt. 6 April 1701; RALPH, b. 2 April 1702, bapt. 21 June 1702 (he is probably the (N), child, bur. 23 Aug 1702); RALPH, bapt. 17 April 1704; MARY, b. 10 April 1706, bapt. 30 June 1706, probably d. young; MARY, b. 13 Sep 1707, bapt. 26 Oct 1707, m. Walter Phelps on 9 Jan 1727; ELIZABETH, b. 27 Dec 1709, bapt. 27 April 1712, m. John Smith on 15 Sep 1730 in All Hallows Parish; SARAH, b. 11 Jan 1711, bapt. 27 April 1712, m. John Phelps on 9 Aug 1730 in All Hallows Parish; JAMES, b. 20 May 1714, bapt. 20 June 1714, may have d. young; SUSANNA, bapt. 21 Sep 1716; JAMES, bapt. 11 Oct 1719; and JOSEPH, bapt. 15 May 1722.

3.   ROBERT BASIL, son of Ralph and Rose, was b. 25 June 1699 and was bapt. 23 July 1699. He may be the Robert Basil living in DO Co., who wit. the will of Robert Thornwell on 15 Jan 1716.{MWB 14:173}
        Robert Basil m. Ruth Morrice. They were the parents of: JAMES, b. 15 Nov 1722, bapt. 11 Dec 1722 in All Hallows Parish. {AACR:35}

4.   JOHN BASIL, son of Ralph and Rose, was b. 13 Feb 1700 and bapt. 6 April 1701. He gave his age as 59 in 1761 and 65 in 1766.{AALC 2:554-557, 674}

5.   JOSEPH BASIL, son of Ralph and Rose, was bapt. 15 May 1722. He gave his age as 36 in 1757.{AALC 2:475}
        On 3 Oct 1760, he wit. the will of Walter Phelps of AA Co.{MWB 32:60}

Unplaced

BASIL, JOHN, m. by 9 May 1753, Elizabeth, dau. of John Perry of PG Co.{MWB 28:500}

THE BATEMAN FAMILY

1.   WILLIAM BATEMAN was bur. in All Hallows Parish on 3 Feb 1706.{AACR:21} He m. Sarah Wells in All Hallows Parish, AA Co., on 27 Jan 1696.{AACR:7}
        William was in AA Co. by 1 Jan 1682 when he wit. the will of John Taylor.{MWB 2:200}

In 1698, Leonard Wayman conv. him 150 a. *Poplar Ridge.*{AALR IH#1:184}

By Mary (N), he had an illegitimate son: WILLIAM, bur. in All Hallows Parish on 27 Nov 1701.{AACR:10}

William Bateman d. in AA Co. leaving a will dated 23 Jan 1706 and proved 10 March 1706/7. He left his entire estate to his wife Sarah, whom he named extx. After his wife's death, his real estate was to pass to Agnes Chambers, dau. of Samuel and Ann Chambers.{MWB 12:84}

William Bateman was the father of: WILLIAM; and HENRY, b. c1686.

2.   HENRY BATEMAN, son of William, was b. c1686. Henry Bateman, aged 27, dep. 10 Sep 1713 that his father, William Bateman (now dec.), stated about 16 years earlier ... .{AAEJ: Hill, Henry} On 7 Feb 1723, Henry Bateman, one of the people called Quakers, dep., giving his age as c36, and naming his father, William Bateman.{MCHP 4:138} As Henry Bateman, Quaker, he dep. again, giving his age as 44 in 1731, and 72 in 1760.{AALC 2:65, 522-523}

Unplaced

BATEMAN, HENRY, m. Sarah Powell on 22 Dec 1707 in St. Anne's Parish.{AACR:65} Henry and Sarah had one child{AACR:66}: RUTH, bapt. --- 1708.

BATEMAN, HENRY, m. Mehitabel Holland on 31 July 1722 in St. Anne's Parish.{AACR:90} Sometime between 1724 and 1728, Henry Bateman and wife Mehitabel sold 102 a. *Welsh's Adventure* to Samuel Peele.{AALR SY#1:168}

BATEMAN, HENRY, Jr., wit. the will of Snowden Taylor of AA Co. on 10 Feb 1742/3.{MWB 23:35}

BATEMAN, HENRY, Jr., m. Anne (N). They were the parents of {AACR:53}: BENJAMIN, b. 19 Feb 1752.

BATEMAN, HENRY, Jr., m. by 1759, Elizabeth, who joined him in selling to John Wilmot, Jr., land that had formerly been owned by William Wintersell, dec.{AALR BB#2:248}

BATEMAN, JOHN, d. by 1708, when he was mentioned in a deed as formerly owning part of *Timber Neck.*{AALR PK:483}

BATEMAN, SARAH, m. James Mouat on 20 Feb 1706 in All Hallows Parish.{AACR:22}

BATEMAN, WILLIAM, of AA Co., d. by 18 April 1686, when his estate was appraised at £4.15.9 by Lawrence Draper and Jacob Harnis.{INAC 9:1}

BATEMAN, WILLIAM, m. Anne (N), by whom he had a dau.{AACR:66}: CATHERINE, bapt. --- 1708 in St. Anne's Parish.

THE BATTEE FAMILY

1.	FERDINANDO BATTEE was in AA Co. by the 1660s, and d. by April 1706. He m. 1st, Millicent (N), and 2nd, Elizabeth (N), who m. Thomas Hood on 30 July 1707.{AACR:24}
	On 18 July 1663, he and Andrew Skinner surv. 300 a. called *Hopewell* near Herring Creek Beaver Dams. This land was later held by the Widow Battee for herself and her orphans.{MRR:125} On 8 July 1663, he surv. 300 a. called *Essex*. This also was later held by the Widow Battee.{MRR:144} On 14 Aug 1672, he surv. 48 a. called *Kent*. By about 1707, this was held by Samuel Battee.{MRR:148}
	On 24 Sep 1684, Ferdinando Battee, with the consent of his wife Millicent, conv. to his only son, Seaborn, who was "about to enter the state of matrimony," 127 a. of *Kent* and *Essex*, and 52 a. *Suffolk*.{AALR WH#4:199}
	Ferdinando d. leaving a will dated 21 Dec 1705 and proved 2 April 1706, naming his wife Elizabeth and sons Benjamin and Ferdinando, not yet 18, daus. Dinah Brewer and Mary and Elizabeth Battee, and grandchildren Samuel Battee, Thomas Knighton, Samuel Smith, Mary Harwood, and Elizabeth Simmons.{MWB 3:744}
	The first inventory of Ferdinando Battee's estate was taken by Thomas Larkin and Samuel Chambers on 22 June 1706. Mary and Elizabeth Battee and John Brewer were mentioned. The extx., Elizabeth Battee, was dec.{INAC 25:275}
	A second inventory of Ferdinando Battee's estate was taken by Thomas Larkin and Thomas Chambers, and valued at £56.7.4. The extx., Elizabeth, now wife of Thomas Hood, filed the inventory on 18 April 1709.{INAC 29:120}
	Battee's estate was admin. on 18 April 1709. Inventories totalling £420.16.4 were mentioned. Dinah Brewer was a legatee.{INAC 29:226}
	Ferdinando and Millicent were the parents of: SEABORN.
	Ferdinando and Elizabeth were the parents of (births are recorded in All Hallows Parish Register){AACR:1, 4, 10, 18, 22}: JOHN, b. c1698; BENJAMIN, b. 24 May ---, bapt. 23 July 1700; DINAH, b. 31 Dec 1690,

m. 1st, Thomas Knighton, and 2nd, John Brewer on 14 Feb 1704;
FERDINANDO, b. 22 April 1697, bapt. 23 July 1700; MARY, b. 5
March 1698, bur. 13 Oct 1707; and ELIZABETH, b. 30 June 1701, bapt.
13 April 1703.

2.   SEABORN BATTEE, son of Ferdinando (1), d. leaving a will
dated 2 Jan 1687 and proved 3 March 1687/8. About 24 Sep 1684 (when
his father conv. him several parcels of land), he m. Elizabeth (probably
dau. of Henry and Eliza Hanslap), who later m. (N) Chew.
     In his will of Jan 1687, Ferdinando named his wife Elizabeth, only
son Samuel, and sister Dinah, wife of Thomas Knighton.{MWB 4:286}
     Eliza Hanslap, widow, of AA Co., drew up a will on 7 Jan 1702.
She named her grandson Samuel Battee, and her son and dau. Joseph and
Eliza Chew.{MWB 3:8}
     The estate of Seaborn Battee was appraised by John Gresham and
James Sanders on 24 March 1687, and valued at £178.16.1.{INAC 9:491} The
undated administration account of his estate mentioned an inventory and
other assets of £244.10.10. Dinah Knighton, wife of Thomas Knighton,
was named as a legatee, and the widow Elizabeth, now wife of Joseph
Chew, filed the account.{INAC 10:313}
     On 31 Aug 1711, Eliza Chew, widow of Seaborn Battee, and now
wife of (N) Chew, and her son Samuel Battee, conv. 50 a. of *Kent* to
William Barton of AA Co., cooper.{AALR PK:57}
     Seaborn and Elizabeth were the parents of one son: SAMUEL,
bapt. 12 June 1698 in All Hallows.{AACR:8}

3.   JOHN BATTEE, son of Ferdinando (1) and Elizabeth, was b.
c1698. In 1745, he dep. giving his age as c47.{AALC IB#1:208}

4.   BENJAMIN BATTEE, eldest son of Ferdinando (1) and Elizabeth
(Hood), was bapt. 23 July 1700. He m. in Aug 1717 in St. James Parish,
Ann Evans, dau. of Lewis and Lois (Gongo) Evans, b. c1680/90.{AACR:163}
     On 25 March 1716, Benjamin and Ferdinand "Batte" were named
as legatees in the administration account of Anthony Smith of AA Co.
{INAC 38A:86}
     On 15 Oct 1718, he and his bro. Ferdinando divided the lands.
Ann Battee, wife of Benjamin, consented.{AALR IB#2:517}
     Benjamin Battee, of AA Co., d. leaving a will dated 2 Jan 1741
and proved 25 May 1741. He named his wife Anne, extx., and left her a
life interest in the dwell. plant. and 1/3 of *Hopewell*. To his daus.,
Elizabeth Sherbutt and Ann Battee, he left *Coles Point* and *Coles
Quarter,* which belonged to the testator as heir-at-law of Mary Keely,
widow of John. He left personalty to his grandchildren Ann and Mary
Sherbutt. He also named his bro., Ferdinando, and his father, Ferdinando.

The will was wit. by John Franklin, Abraham Simmons, and Isaac Simmons.{MWB 22:395}

Benjamin and Ann (Evans) Battee were the parents of{Jourdan; *Early Families of Southern Maryland,* 2:214}: ELIZABETH, m. Thomas Sherbutt; and ANN.

6.   FERDINANDO BATTEE, son of Ferdinando (1) and Elizabeth, m. Elizabeth Wooden on 11 Dec 1718. A Quaker, she was b. c1698, and gave her age as c47 in 1745.{AALC IB#1:207}

Ferdinando Battee, of AA Co., d. leaving an undated will that was proved 29 April 1745. He named his wife Elizabeth, and sons Fardo, Samuel, and John, and daus. Elizabeth and Dinah. Wife Elizabeth and son Samuel were execs. The will was wit. by Thos. Spring, Thomas Sparrow, and John Talbott.{MWB 24:109-110}

Ferdinando and Elizabeth were the parents of{IGI}: ELIZABETH, b. April 1724; DINAH; FERDINANDO; and SAMUEL.

7.   SAMUEL BATTEE, son of Seaborn (2) and Elizabeth, d. by Dec 1717.

On 3 Sep 1717, he conv. to Nicholas Watkins, 125 a. *Essex,* which he inherited by the will of his father Seaborn, except for land sold earlier to William Barton, Negro.{AALR IB#2:389}

Samuel Battee, of AA Co., d. leaving a will dated 4 Sep 1767 and proved 7 Dec 1767. He named his wife Anne, and children Ferdinando, Samuel, Ann, and Elizabeth. He mentioned tracts *Rich Neck,* formerly owned by Robert Welsh, and *Smith Fields,* adj. land of Samuel Smith. Wife Anne was extx. The will was wit. by Samuel Smith, Keely Lewis, and Kinsey Sparrow.{MWB 36:114}

Samuel and Ann were the parents of: FERDINANDO; SAMUEL; ANN; and ELIZABETH.

Unplaced

BATTEE, JOHN, m. by 17 Nov 1770, Henrietta, sister of Charles Connant of AA Co.{MWB 38:271}

THE BEARD FAMILY

1.   RICHARD BEARD, the earliest known ancestor, d. in 1680. He came to MD as a free adult with his wife and two children.{BDML} Skordas states that Richard Beard, Rachel Beard, and Richard Beard the son, immigrated to MD c1650.{MPL 5:585} Beard had probably been in VA from 1646. He m. c1646 Rachel, dau. of Edward Robins, b. 1602, d. by 1646,

of Accomack Co., VA. Rachel's sister Elizabeth m. William Burgess, b. c1622, d. 1686/7.{BDML}

Richard represented AA Co. in the Lower House of the Assembly in 1662, 1663-4, and 1666.{BDML}

He was summoned for jury service in 1660, but he refused to swear the required oath. In 1674, he and some others presented a petition requesting a law that would exempt Quakers from having to take an Oath. No doubt it was his religious convictions as a Quaker that prevented him from holding public office.

On 18 Sep 1666, he was granted 30 a. called *Johns Cabin Ridge;* on 1 Aug 1668 he conv. this to James Sanders. In the deed, he described himself as a boatwright.{AALR IH#2:170}

On 13 Nov 1666, Richard Beard, with the consent of his wife Rachel, sold to John Maccubbin 100 a. called *Brampton*.{AALR WH#4:285}

On 6 Oct 1674, Richard Beard was listed as a debtor of George Puddington, of AA Co.{INAC 1:92} About 1675-7, he was listed as one of the creditors of Neale Clarke of AA Co.{INAC 4:249} On 9 March 1677, he was listed as a creditor of John Medley of SM Co.{INAC 4:624}

Beard d. leaving a will dated 24 July 1675 and proved 10 Aug 1671. He named his wife Rachel extx., and left her the home plant. for life. Sons Richard and John were to have the home plant. after his wife's death. Dau. Ruth was to have part of *Timber Neck*. Dau. Rebecca and her sons were to have part of *Indian Range*. Dau. Rachel Clarke was to have all of the lands mentioned above if his other children s.p. Bro.-in-law William Burgess and his own sons were named overseers. The will was wit. by Geo. Green, Jno. Raster, Eliza Cornton, and Thomas Pinethwickie.{MWB 2:143}

At his death, his estate was valued at 19,067 lbs. of tob. by Thomas Beason and John Gray.{INAC 7C:6} He also owned over 14,385 a. of land.{BDML}

Rachel Beard was living on 23 Feb 1683 when she and her son Richard Beard, Jr., were listed as debtors of Dr. William Fisher, of AA Co.{INAC 8:136}

Sometime after the death of Richard Beard the Elder, a question arose as to what had happened to his will. On 4 July 1710, depositions were taken to determine if his son Richard Beard had cut the will out of the books after the death of Col. Burgess. Walter Phelps dep. that he knew Elizabeth Carrington, Elizabeth Mash, who m. a Jones, George Green, and John Rutter and his wife Alice. Anne Bradley dep. that she had been a servant to Richard Beard, and that her husband John Stopkins had been a witness. Mrs. Mehitable Peirpoint dep. that when Beard's will was made, Henry Bonner, the clerk of the court was absent and so records were committed to the care of Otho Holland, her then husband. Holland told her that Beard the Younger had spent much time with the books one day, and that the page with his father's will was missing.{MCHR PC:668}

Richard and Rachel (Robins) Beard were the parents of{BDML}: RICHARD, b. c1648, d. 1703; JOHN, d. by 1678; RACHEL, d. after 1724, m. 1st, Neal Clarke, d. c1676, 2nd, John Stimpson, d. by 1692, 3rd, Robert Proctor, d. by 1695, 4th, Richard Kilburne, d. by 1698, and 5th, Thomas Freeborne{BDML}; REBECCA, m. Col. John Nicholson; and RUTH, m. John Gaither.

2.   RICHARD BEARD, son of Richard (1) and Rachel, was b. 1648 and d. 1703. He was a Justice of AA Co. and made the first map of Annapolis. He m. Susanna (N), who, as Mrs. Susanna Beard, was bur. in St. Anne's Parish on 14 Oct 1708.{AACR:67}

Richard Beard, age 40, dep. in 1696, mentioning John Coode and Mrs. Nicholas Sporne.{ARMD 20:493-493, 23:480}

Susannah Beard, of AA Co., d. leaving a will dated 4 Oct 1708 and proved 15 Oct 1708. She left her estate to her son John and dau. Rachel, as son Matthew had already been provided for. Thomas Bordley was the exec. The will was wit. by John Beale, Edmond Benson, and Ann Barnett.{MWB 12:299}

Richard and Susanna were the parents of{AACR:67}: MATTHEW; JOHN; and RACHEL, m. Thomas Bordley on 26 Dec 1708 in St. Anne's.

3.   JOHN BEARD, son of Richard (1) and Rachel, d. in AA Co. by 2 May 1679, when his estate was inventoried by William Ramsey and James Sanders. Richard Beard, Sr., and John Stimpson were among the debtors.{INAC 6:95}

4.   MATTHEW BEARD, son of Richard (2) and Susannah, was described in his mother's will as already having been taken care of. He d. by 11 July 1721, having m. Mary (N), who also d. by 11 July 1711.
{AACR:88}

Matthew and Mary were the parents of (b. in St. Anne's Parish) {AACR:65, 68, 88}: MARY, bapt. 19 Aug 1708, d. 11 July 1721; SUSANNA, bapt. 30 March 1710; and RICHARD.

5.   JOHN BEARD, Esq., son of Richard (2) and Susannah, was b. c1694, and d. in AA Co. on 15 Dec 1719.{AACR:85} He gave his age as 23 in 1717.{AALC 1:15}

On 4 March 1719, his estate was inv. by Cesar Ghiselin and Thomas Jobson and appraised at £89.17.6. Rachel Freeborn and Hester Warman signed as next of kin.{MINV 3:316}

On 18 Oct 1722, his estate was admin. by Rachel, wife of Thomas Bordley.{MDAD 5:74}

On 12 Jan 1725, his estate was admin. by his sister, Rachel, late wife of Thomas Bordley. After debts were paid, the estate was dist. to [Thomas Bordley] in right of his wife Rachel, sister of the dec., to Mary Beard, and to Susannah and Richard Beard, children of Matthew Beard. {MDAD 7:226}

Unplaced

BEARD, ANDREW, m. Hannah (N). Andrew d. by 16 June 1730, when his estate was appraised by John Jacobs and Richard Williams, and appraised at £29.3.8. Mary Cheney and John Cheney, Jr., signed as next of kin. Hannah Beard, admx., filed the inventory on 16 June 1730. {MINV 16:26}

On 13 Sep 1718, John Cheney, of AA Co., Gent., with consent of wife Mary, conv. to Andrew Beard, planter, 100 a., part of *Waterford*. {AALR IB#2:506}

Andrew and Hannah were the parents of (b. in All Hallows Parish) {AACR:27, 35, 38, 39, 42, 68, 199}: ELIZABETH, bapt. 25 April 1709; SUSANNA, bapt. 30 March 1710 (she may be the Susanna Beard who m. Aaron Rawlings in All Hallows Parish on 14 Dec 1725); RICHARD, b. 10 March 1716; ANDREW, b. 12 Jan 1718, bapt. 1 March 1718; JOHN, b. 10 May 17--; ELIZABETH, b. 1724, bapt. 23 Aug 1724; and RACHEL, bapt. 26 Nov 1727.

BEARD, JOHN, son of Andrew, was b. 10 May 17--. He m. by 16 April 1772, Elizabeth, dau. of Thomas Watkins.

On 16 April 1772, Thomas Watkins made his will, naming his dau. Elizabeth Beard, and naming her sons Stephen and Joseph, and mentioning his dau.'s four children. {MWB 38:837}

BEARD, Richard, son of Andrew, was b. 10 March 1716. As Richard Beard of Annapolis, age 68, he dep. 22 April 1784 that he was the bro. of John Beard, father of the libellant [Stephen Beard?], and that Thomas Watkins had informed the deponent that he had left ... to his [the deponent's] bro.'s son, Stephen Beard. Stephen Beard had a bro. Joseph Beard. {AAEJ: Beard, Stephen, Lydia's Rest}

THE BEDINGFIELD FAMILY

ANTHONY BEDINGFIELD d. in AA Co. by May 1740. He m. 1st, Mary (N), and 2nd, by May 1717, Eliza (N). He m. 3rd, Mary Jones (dau. of William and Mary Jones), who survived him.

Anthony Beddenfield, of AA Co., d. leaving an undated will probated 15 May 1740. He left 1 s. to his daus. Elizabeth, Mary Ann, and Easter, and son Anthony. He named his wife Mary extx. The will was wit.

by William Phelps, Jonathan Taylor, and Thomas Cheney.{MWB 22:171}

Mary Beddingfield, age over 60, dep. 17 April 1744, mentioned her parents William and Mary Jones, and her dec. husband, Anthony Beddingfield.{AAEJ: Jennings, Thomas and wife Rebecca}

Anthony and Mary were the parents of (bapt. in All Hallows Parish unless otherwise noted){AACR:17, 20, 39, 199, 201}: JOHN, bapt. 20 Sep 1703; ELIZABETH, bapt. 1 May 1705, m. John Rickeots on 4 Feb 1724; GEORGE, bapt. 13 March 1717; (by Eliza): ANNE, bapt. 5 May 1717; SARAH, bapt. 26 June 1720; and EASTOR.

Unplaced

BEDINGFIELD, LAWRENCE, was in SM Co. by 18 Jan 1684 when he wit. the will of Samuel Maddox.{MWB 4:93}

THE BELT FAMILY[16]

First Generation

Refs.: A: "Belt Genealogy," by Christopher Johnston, in *MD Genealogy,* 1:28-35. B: Shirk. *Descendants of Richard and Elizabeth (Ewen) Talbott.*

1.   HUMPHREY BELT, age 20, was transported from London to VA in the *America*, by William Barker, by certificate from the Minister of Gravesend, 23 June 1635.{Coldham; *Complete Book of Emigrants, 1607-1660:* 152}

Humphrey Belt is stated by some to have been a son of Sir Robert and Grace (Foxcroft) Belt, but Marilyn Roth suggests he was of a Scottish branch of the family because the arms used by the family were different from those used by the branch from Bossal Hall, Yorkshire, and because Joseph Belt patented a tract called *Chevy Chase*.{AL}

Zellow Belt and others state that Humphrey m. Ann (N), b. c1621, but Marilyn Roth states he was m. by Oct 1649 to Margery Craggs, for whose transportation he was granted land in Lower Norfolk Co.{Va. Patents, 3:268}

---

[16] See also Elise Greenup Jourdan, *Early Families of Southern Maryland* (Westminster: Family Line Publications, 1993) 1:286-306.

He seems to have still been in VA by 1652 when Thomas Cartwright was granted land in Lower Norfolk Co. adjacent Humph. Belt's.{Nugent; *Cavaliers and Pioneers*, Vol. I:174}

On 8 June 1654, he was granted 220 a. in Linhaven Parish, Lower Norfolk Co., for the transportation of five persons.{Nugent; *Cavaliers and Pioneers*, Vol. I:289}

Humphrey, Ann, John, and Sarah Belt were transported to MD c1663.{MPL 5:373}

Shirk states that "Humphrey, the Maryland Settler," was a son of the Humphrey who was transported to MD c1663.{B:30} Boyd feels that there were two separate Humphreys, father and son, and they both came to MD c1650.{Boyd; *The Parrish Family*:329}

Humphrey d. in AA Co. in 1698, aged 83.{Hardy, *Colonial Families of the United States*}

Humphrey Belt was probably the father of: JOHN; ANN; and SARAH.

Second Generation

2.   JOHN BELT, possibly son of Humphrey, d. testate leaving a will dated 13 May 1697 and proved 11 Nov 1698. He m. Elizabeth (N), who later m. John Lamb. It should be noted that Boyd identifies the 2nd generation immigrant to MD, father of John, Jeremiah, Richard, Leonard, and Joseph Belt, as Humphrey, but provides no documentation for this. {*The Parrish Family*:329}

John Belt lived in AA Co., but on 29 April 1678 purchased 300 a. called *Belt's Prosperity* in BA Co. from Thomas and Rebecca Lightfoot. {BALR RM#HS:123} (This land was bequeathed to his sons Joseph and Benjamin.)

A John Belt is named as a legatee in the will, made 9 April 1675, of John Roberts of SM Co.{MWB 2:53} John Belt is also mentioned as a legatee of the estate of John Wheeler of AA Co. in the latter's account filed 1 Oct 1688.{INAC 10:87}

John m. Elizabeth Tydings, dau. of Richard Tydings. On 25 July 1701, in All Hallows Parish, Elizabeth m., as her 2nd husband, John Lamb.{AACR:13} On 2 Feb 1687, John Belt wit. the will of Richard Tydings, of AA Co. Tydings had a son John, and daus. Charity, Elizabeth, Pretiosa, and Mary.{MWB 6:40} Now Michael Pasquinet m. Charity, dau. of Richard Tydings, sometime before 27 Dec 1726, when they executed a power of attorney to their "loving cousin John Belt [Jr.]" of BA Co.{BALR IS#I: 36, 71}

John Belt d. leaving a will dated 13 May 1697 and proved 11 Nov 1698, naming his wife Elizabeth and sons John, Joseph, and Benjamin, and daus. Elizabeth, Charity, and Sarah. There was a son Jeremiah, b.

after the will was made. His will also named a nephew Thomas Ramsey.
{MWB 6:175}

Elizabeth Lamb, of AA Co., d. leaving a will dated 1 Aug 1737
and proved 14 Dec 1737, naming sons John, Joseph, Benjamin, and
Jeremiah Belt (each to have 20 s.), daus. Charity Mulliken, Sarah
Harwood, and Margaret Watkins, son-in-law Nicholas Watkins, and
grandchildren Mary Norwood, and Nicholas, Elizabeth, and Anne
Watkins.{MWB 21:815}

The inventory of Elizabeth Lamb was filed 5 Aug 1738 by
Nicholas Watkins, exec. Thomas Stockett and Ferdinand Battee
appraised the estate at £282.19.4. Jeremiah Belt and Samuel Chew signed
as creditors, and Joseph Belt and Jeremiah Belt signed as kin.{MINV 23:213}

John and Elizabeth (Tydings) Belt were the parents of{AACR:18}:
JEREMIAH, b. c1672, AA Co., probably d. young; RICHARD, b.
c1674, AA Co.; LEONARD, b. c1677, AA Co.; JOHN, b. 1678, d. 1761
in PG Co.; Col. JOSEPH, b. 1680, d. 26 June 1761; BENJAMIN, b.
1682, d. 1773; JEREMIAH, b. 1698, bapt. 14 Dec 1703, m. 1st, 1714,
Sarah Lamb, and 2nd, 1725, Mary, dau. of John Wight; ELIZABETH,
bapt. 14 Dec 1703, m. Basil Waring; CHARITY, bapt. 14 Dec 1703, d.
1740, m. in 1737, James Mullikin; and SARAH, bapt. 14 Dec 1703, m.
11 Sep 1718, Thomas Harwood.

Third Generation

3.   JOHN BELT, son of John (2) and Elizabeth, is said to have been
b. 1678 and to have d. 1761 in PG Co.

He inherited 200 a. *Velmead* in AA Co. After selling the property
to Gilbert Higginson of London, England, in 1724, John and his wife
moved to BA Co.{A:29} No record of a will or estate has been found, but
he was living as late as 1727.{A:29}

John Belt was a member of the Society of Friends, and m. at
William Richardson's, West River Meeting, on 10 Feb 1701/2, Lucy,
dau. of Benjamin Lawrence.

On 22 April 1720, the Assembly passed an Act to "supply certain
defects" in the conveying lands from Henry Gibbs, son and heir of
Edward Gibbs of SO Co. ... to Benjamin Lawrence and John Belt and
Lucy his wife ... .{B:30}

In 1720, John Belt, of AA Co., Gent., and wife Lucy sold 400 a.,
being 1/2 of *Belt's Hills*, in BA Co., on the s. side of the Patapsco Falls,
to Benjamin Stevens of BA Co.{BALR RM#HS:685}

On 20 Oct 1724, John Belt, of AA Co., merchant, and wife Lucy,
sold to John Taylor the plantation which he had inherited from his father,
and which he had mortgaged in 1710 to Gilbert Higginson of London.
{AALR SY#1:79}

On 12 Feb 1727, John Belt, of BA Co., Gent., attorney for his cousin Mrs. Charity Tydings Pasquinet, of Bath Co., NC, conv. to John Belt, Jr., 375 a. *Nanjemoy* on the Gunpowder River.{BALR IS#1:61}

John and Lucy were the parents of{A:30}: JOHN, b. 1703, d. 1788; MARY, m. c1726, Greenbury Dorsey (not in Shirk); MARGARET, b. 10 June 1719, d. c1770, m. 1 Dec 1743, Basil Lucas (not in Shirk); LEONARD, d. by Sep 1793; HIGGINSON; JOSEPH; SARAH; LUCY, m. William Beckwith; and ELIZABETH, m. Lameth Beckwith.

4.   Col. JOSEPH BELT, son of John (2) and Elizabeth, was b. 1680, and d. 26 June 1761. He m. 1st, Esther, dau. of Col. Ninian Beall, and 2nd, Margery, widow of Thomas Sprigg, and dau. of John Wight. {B:30-31}

Joseph owned land in BA Co., was a Presiding Justice of the PG Co. Court, and represented the county in the Assembly from 1725 to 1737.

On 8 Sep 1719, he was the exec. of, and admin. the estate of, John Lashley.{MDAD 2:233} On 19 July 1723, he admin. the estate of Thomas Burton.{MDAD 5:188}

Mrs. Margery Belt, wife of Joseph Belt, was extx. of the estate of Thomas Sprigg, Gent., and admin. his estate on 30 June 1737.{MDAD 15:341}

The estate of Col. Joseph Belt was appraised on 13 Nov 1761 by Richard Duckett and Thomas Williams and valued at £2209.6.7. Jeremiah Belt, Jr., and John Belt, Jr., signed as kin, and Humphrey Belt, exec., filed the inventory on 18 Dec 1761.{MINV 75:193}

Joseph Belt was the father of 10 children{A:31}

By his first wife he was the father of: JOHN, b. 13 March 1707, m. 4 March 1727/8, Margaret Queen; ANNE, b. 1708/9, d. 1762, m. 1st, 1724, Thomas Clagett, and 2nd, Ignatius Perry; RACHEL, b. 13 Dec 1711, m. 11 July 1727, Osborn Sprigg; JOSEPH, b. 19 Dec 1717, d. 6 May 1761; TOBIAS, b. 20 Aug 1720, d. 1785; MARY, b. 24 Dec 1722, m. 1st, Edward Sprigg, and 2nd, Thomas Pindle; JEREMIAH, b. 4 March 1724, d. 1784; and JAMES, b. 23 July 1726.

By his second wife, Joseph was the father of: HUMPHREY; and MARGERY, m. 1st (N) Lyle, and 2nd, (N) Perry.

5.   BENJAMIN BELT, son of John (2) and Elizabeth, was b. in 1682, and was age 66 in 1748 and 73 in 1755. He made various depositions in PG and AA Co., giving his age as 56 in 1738, 66 in 1748, 73 in 1755, and 83 in 1765.

He m. Elizabeth (probably Middleton, since they had a son named Middleton Belt), probably d. by 1745.{A:32}

He inherited 200 a. part of *Belt's Prosperity* in BA Co., but in 1745 he sold his share to Stephen Onion.{A:31; BALR TB#E:334}

In Nov 1714, Benjamin Belt was Overseer of Highways for Patuxent Hundred.{PGCP G:694} In Nov 1715, Benjamin Belt was allowed 1,000 lbs. tob. for keeping Eliza Norman's child.{PGCP H:16}

On 26 March 1759, Benjamin Belt and Zachariah Harris signed the inventory of Rachel Harris as the next of kin.{MINV 65:217}

Benjamin Belt d. leaving a will dated 19 June 1772, and proved 28 May 1773 in PG Co. and in Annapolis. He named children Benjamin Belt, Joseph Belt, Sophia Beall, Anne Brashers, Eliza Waring, and Hester Watkins, and grandsons Benjamin and Stephen. The will was wit. by James Drane, Daniel Clark, and Thomas Williams.{MWB 39:142}

His estate was appraised on 4 Sep 1775 by William Deakins and James Pearre, who appraised his personal property at a total of £357.3.4. {MINV 123:238}

Benjamin and Elizabeth were the parents of{A:32}: Col. JOSEPH, b. 1716, d. 16 June 1793; MIDDLETON, d. unm. in 1745; BENJAMIN, d. 1775; SOPHIA, m. (N) Beall; ESTHER, m. John Watkins; ANNE, m. Basil Brashears; and ELIZABETH, m. Basil Waring.

6.   JEREMIAH BELT, son of John (2) and Elizabeth, was b. 1698, and bapt. 14 Dec 1703. He m. 1st, 1714, Sarah Lamb, and 2nd, 1725, Mary, dau. of John Wight.{A:29}

On 2 June 1727, as exec. of Ann White [sic], he admin. her estate. {MDAD 8:240}

Fourth Generation

7.   JOHN BELT, son of John (3) and Lucy (Lawrence) Belt, was b. c1703 and d. 1 Dec 1788, age 85 years, an Elder of Gunpowder Meeting. He m. Lucy (N).{A:32}

On 12 Feb 1727, his father, John Belt, "the Elder," conv. him 375 a. called *Nanjemy*.{BALR IS#1:61} On 16 Sep 1783, John Belt conv. the whole *Nanjemy* plant. to Leonard Belt.{BALR WG#R:218}

He d. leaving a will dated 24 Sep 1788, leaving 222 a. to his son John. To his sons Nathan and Joseph, he left all of *Aquila's Reserve*; he also owned 64 a. on a fork of Piney Run, with reversion to his daus. Sarah Randall, Lucy Malone, and Mary Belt.{BAWB 4:350}

John and Lucy Belt were the parents of{A:32; B:41; Boyd; *The Parrish Family*:330}: JOHN; RICHARD, m. 1760 Keturah Price; SARAH, m. Thomas Randall;[17] NATHAN; JEREMIAH;[18] LEONARD, not in his

---

[17] He d. in BA Co., leaving a will dated 23 Feb 1812 and proved 21 March 1812, naming wife Sarah, and children: CHARLES, CHRISTOPHER, WILLIAM, NICHOLAS Beale, CATHERINE Poe, ELLEN Randall, REBECCA Cullison, LUCY Randall, and HANNAH Randall.{BAWB 9:225}

[18] Stated in Boyd, probably erroneously, to have m. Mary Sprigg, dau. of Dr. John Sprigg, but Johnston states that the Jeremiah who m. Mary Sprigg was a son of Joseph of

father's will, he may have been disowned for marrying contrary to discipline{B:275}; LUCY, b. 25 Nov 1744, m. 6 Dec 1779, Thomas Watkins; MARY, b. 30 June 1747; and JOSEPH, b. 10 June 1750.

8.   LEONARD BELT, son of John (3) and Lucy (Lawrence) Belt, d. probably unm. in MO Co., where he left a will dated 14 Sep 1793 and proved 20 Sep 1793, naming nephew John (exec.), son of bro. Higginson, Lucy, widow of William Beckwith, sister Sarah Peddicord (her dau. Althea, who m. William Sellman), Rebecca, wife of Jasper Peddicord, Elizabeth, wife of Samuel Beckwith, bro. Joseph Belt, Henry Watson, Jr., John Watson, son of Henry, and Mary Belt, dau. of John. The will [was wit. by] William Glaze, Edward Harding, and Kinsey Gittings of Benjamin.{MOWB C:117}

9.   HIGGINSON BELT, son of John (3) and Lucy (Lawrence), is stated in a Family record of Julia Belt, dau. of John Lloyd Belt of Rock Hall, Dickerson, MD, to have m. 1st, Sarah Lawrence, b. c1714 in PG Co., MD, by whom he had Higginson and Carlton, and to have m. 2nd, Sarah Marshall. On the other hand, Zellow C. Belt states that Higginson Belt, Sr., m. Dorothy (nee Williams?), widow of John Rogers, and she was the mother of his children.

Higginson Belt was granted a tract named *Spring Garden,* near Laytonsville, in what is now MO Co., in 1738.{Scharf's *Western MD,* p. 652}

The 1755/6 Debt Book of FR Co. states that he owned 250 a. *Spring Garden,* and 200 a. *Rogers Chance.*{*Western MD Genealogy,* 7:132}

Higginson Belt took the Oath of Fidelity to the State of MD on 2 March 1778, in MO Co., before Elisha Williams.{Brumbaugh; *Revolutionary Records of Maryland:*10}

On 23 Feb 1781, through principles of conscience, he freed 14 slaves.{B:41, cites MOLR A:401}

He d. leaving a will dated 15 July 1786, leaving household furniture to his wife Sarah, and the residue of his personal estate to his sons John, Carlton, and Higginson, and dau. Becky Peddicord; also named dec. son Greenberry (who left two sons Westley and Higginson). {MOWB B:361}

Higginson and Sarah were the parents of{B}: JOHN, possibly b. c1764; CARLTON; HIGGINSON, d. 1795 in FR Co.; REBECCA, m. Jasper Peddicord; and GREENBERRY, d. in his father's lifetime.

John.

10.　JOHN BELT, son of Joseph (4) and Esther, was b. 13 March 1707, and m. 4 March 1727/8, Margaret Queen{A} She is placed as a dau. of Samuel and Katherine (Marsham) Queen.

　　Samuel Queen d. in SM Co., leaving a will dated 10 Jan 1711 and proved 18 March 1711/2, naming wife Katherine, father-in-law Richard Marsham, and children Samuel, Marsham, William, Katherine and Margaret Queen, and son-in-law Richard Brooke.{MWB 13:389}

　　John Belt gave his age as 56 in 1765, when he stated he was a nephew of John Belt, dec.{Peden, *More Maryland Deponents*}

　　There are no probate records for anyone named John Belt prior to 1823.

　　John and Margaret (Queen) Belt are known to have had at least two children, and probably at least one other{B}: KATHERINE, b. 18 March 1729; SARAH HADDOCK, b. 18 March 17--; MARSHAM; (W. E. Belt, Jr., writes that John and Margaret may have also had): Col. JEREMIAH; ESTHER; JOSEPH; and OSBORN.

11.　JOSEPH BELT, son of Joseph (4) and Esther, was b. 19 Dec 1717, and d. 6 May 1761. His estate was inv. on 24 Sep 1761 by William Bowie and William Lock Weems, who valued it at £539.2.0. Tobias Belt and John Belt, Jr., signed as next of kin. Edward Sprigg, the admin., filed the inventory on 13 Jan 1762.{MINV 75:203}

　　Joseph m. Anne, dau. of Thomas Sprigg and Margery (Wight), and had issue{A:32}: THOMAS; JOSEPH; CHARLES; WILLIAM; ELIZABETH; ANNE; and MARY.

12.　TOBIAS BELT, son of Joseph (4) and Esther, was b. 20 Aug 1720, and d. 1785. He m. 1st, Mary Duvall, and 2nd, Mary Gordon, widow of George Hamilton, who was b. c1724 in PG Co., MD, and d. c1795 in PG Co., MD. Mary Gordon was a dau. of George Gordon by his wife Christian Hannah Forbes, dau. of George Forbes.{Data from Mary Belt Taylor}

　　He was listed in the 1755/56 Debt Book of FR Co. as owning 129 a. *Lost Hatchett,* 290 a. *Oronobia,* and 120 a. *Belt's Delight.*{WMG 7:133}

　　On 10 May 1764, George Gordon, of PG Co., made his will naming, among others, his dau. Mary, wife of Capt. Tobias Belt, and grandchildren Horatio, Joshua, Lucy, and Dryden Belt.{MWB 34:313}

　　On 10 Oct 1763, Tobias and Humphrey Belt appraised the estate of Thomas Mullican, planter, of PG Co.{MINV 83:155}

　　Data compiled by Mary Belt Taylor indicates that he may have been the father of (by 1st wife): HORATIO, b. c1746; JOSHUA, b. c1748; LEVIN, b. c1750; (by 2nd wife): LLOYD CARLTON, b. c1752,

PG Co., MD;[19] FORBES, b. c1754; LUCY, b. c1766, m. John Addison; DRYDEN GEORGE, b. c1758, d. 1 May 1825, m. by MOML dated 17 March 1783, Robert Brad Tyler; RACHEL, b. c1762, m. by MOML dated 12 Feb 1803, John Wilkes Pratt; and ELIZABETH, b. c1763, d. 15 July 1834, m. by MOML dated 13 Nov 1786, John Magill.

13.   JEREMIAH BELT, son of Joseph (4) and Esther, was b. 4 March 1724, and d. 1784. He d. leaving an undated will which was proved 18 Jan 1785.{PGWB T#1:202} He m. on 21 June 1746, Mary, b. 15 Dec 1723, dau. of Thomas and Margery (Wight) Sprigg.

Jeremiah and Mary were the parents of{A:33; Doliante, *Maryland and Virginia Colonials:*903}: RICHARD, b. 26 Dec 1747; EDWARD, b. 15 March 1749; JOHN SPRIGG, b. 10 Sep 1752, m. Rachel Griffith, dau. of Joshua;[20] GEORGE, b. 1 March 1755; THOMAS SPRIGG, b. 19 July 1756; MARY, b. 18 Aug 1758; FIELDING, b. 29 March 1761; MARGERY, b. 18 Jan 1764, m. 28 April 1800, in PG Co., Beale Duvall, son of Samuel and Mary (Higgins) Duvall; and TOBIAS, b. 1766, m. 31 Jan 1789, Rebecca Beall, dau. of Capt. Richard Beall.

14.   Col. JOSEPH BELT, son of Benjamin (5) and Elizabeth, was b. 1716, and d. 16 June 1793 in MO Co., MD. In 1734, Joseph Belt, son of Benjamin, gave his age as 18.{PGLR T:364}

On 25 April 1780, John Murdock, of MO Co., conv. to Joseph Belt and wife Esther, for the term of both their lives, 200 a. part of *Friendship*.{MOLR A:538}

Col. Joseph Belt m., in or before 1739, Esther, dau. of William and Jane (Edmonston) Smith, of PG Co. Esther was b. c1722, and d. 12 July 1796, age 74. William Smith, in his will, named his son-in-law Joseph Belt, son of Benjamin.

The inventory of Joseph Belt, late of MO Co., dec., was filed 12 Aug 1793, and valued at £309.12.3. Middleton Belt was the admin.

Joseph and Esther (Smith) Belt were the parents of{A:34}: Capt. MIDDLETON, b. 1747, d. 1807; ESTHER, b. 1744, d. 1814; m. Dr. Walter Smith; ANN, b. 1751, may have m. Col. John Murdock of Montgomery Co., PA.

15.   MIDDLETON BELT, son of Benjamin (5) and Elizabeth, d. unm. leaving a will dated 25 Feb 1745 and proved 21 May 1746, naming

---

[19] Although Mary Belt Taylor placed him as a son of the first marriage, he is not named as a grandson in the will of George Gordon.

[20] He was Captain of the 4th Co., 1st Regiment, MD Line, and was a Member of the Society of the Cincinnati.

Middleton Brashear, son of Basil Brashear, and his father Benjamin Belt, who was named as exec. [The will was wit. by] George Wells and John Brashears.{MWB 24:403} No inventory of his estate has been found.

16.   BENJAMIN BELT, son of Benjamin (5) and Elizabeth, d. 1775. He m. Ruth (N).

Benjamin Belt d. leaving a will dated 11 April 1775 and proved 28 June 1775. In his will, he named his sons Benjamin, Thomas, and Middleton, and daus. Elizabeth (Nixon), Esther, and Rachel. He appointed his wife Ruth extx. The will was wit. by Andrew Beall, John Pearre, Archy Lanham, and George Hoskinson.{MWB 40:418}

Benjamin and Ruth (N) Belt were the parents of{A:34}: BENJAMIN; THOMAS; MIDDLETON; ELIZABETH, m. (N) Nixon; ESTHER and RACHEL.

Fifth Generation

17.   JOHN BELT, son of John (7) and Lucy (N), was b. 27 April 1729, and d. age 10 mo., 1 day, 1788, in BA Co. He m. Dinah (N), who was b. 19 Sep 1739, and d. 12 Nov 1799.

He was received in membership by the Gunpowder Meeting on 28 da., 5 mo., 1755.{B}

Boyd states that John m. Lucy (N) and moved to Bedford Co., PA. {Boyd, *The Parrish Family*:330 cites BALR WG#AA:76}

John and Dinah were the parents of{B:274}: JOHN, b. 16 Oct 1759, d. 23 Dec 1814;[21] LUCY, b. 15 Nov 1767, may have m. Thomas Sprigg; JEREMIAH, b. 17 March 1772; GREENBURY, b. 11 Aug 1774; MARY, b. 2 July 1777, may have d. c1796/7, probably m. on 13 Jan 1795, Bennett Gwynn (his first wife).

18.   RICHARD BELT, son of John (7) and Lucy (N) Belt, d. in BA Co. leaving a will dated 18 March 1788. He m. Keturah, dau. of John Price, of BA Co., at Gunpowder Meeting on 24 Feb 1760.{B:61}

Richard Belt leased 50 a. *Richard's Chance* from the Lord Proprietor on 1 April 1758, and assigned it to Isaac Hammond on 16 Nov 1771.{BALR AL#D:184}

In his will, cited above, he left a life interest in his plant. to his wife Keturah, and named his sons John, Carlton, Aquila, and Benedict Belt. John Price, of John, and Joseph Belt, of John, were named as execs. {BAWB 4:350}

---

[21] He is the only child recognized by Shirk. He is listed in the DAR Patriot Index as having rendered Patriotic Service in MD during the Rev. War.

Richard and Keturah (Price) Belt were the parents of{B:61}: JOHN; CHARLTON, moved away, and m. by Sep 1804; MILCAH, b. 12 Jan 1765, m. James Matthews c25 Jan 1794; AQUILA, m. by 29 Sep 1804; BENEDICT; and (N), dau., who m. contrary to the good order of the Friends.

19.   JEREMIAH BELT, son of John (7) and Lucy (N) Belt, may be the Jeremiah Belt who was b. c1750, and d. 31 Dec 1819, having m. 1st, Eliza Skinner, 2nd, Susan Magruder, 3rd by MOML dated 4 March 1778, Priscilla Gantt, and 4th, Ann West. He rendered Patriotic Service in MD during the Revolutionary War.{DAR Patriot Index, Vol. I}

Records of St. Peter's P. E. Church, Poolesville, MO Co., show that Jeremiah and Ann (West) Belt had at least two children{WMG 2:56}: SARAH, b. 19 Nov 1797, bapt. 3 Nov 1799; and HARRIET WEST, b. 3 Sep 1799, bapt. 3 Nov 1799.

20.   LEONARD BELT, son of John (7) and Lucy, was not in his father's will. He may have been disowned for marrying contrary to discipline.{B:275} He m. on 27 da., 1 mo., 1762, Hannah Parrish, b. 16 da., 5 mo., 1748, of BA Co. Although she was a member of Gunpowder Meeting, the marriage was not accomplished in good order.{B} Hannah was a dau. of Mary Parrish.{BALR WG#55:190}

Leonard d. leaving a will dated 25 Jan 1808 and proved 2 March 1808, naming wife Hannah and children Leonard, Mordecai, and others. {BAWB 8:297-298}

Leonard and Hannah were the parents of{B; also Boyd, *The Parrish Family*:331}: ANNE, m. (N) Tanner and settled in OH; SARAH; RICHARD; ELEANOR, d. by May 1846, unm.{See BAWB 21:168}; LEONARD; MILCAH; MORDECAI; REBECCA; HARRIET; and possibly others.

21.   LUCY BELT, dau. of John (7) and Lucy (N) Belt, was b. 25 Nov 1744, and m. by MOML dated 6 Dec 1779, Thomas Watkins.

22.   JOSEPH BELT, son of John and Lucy, was b. 10 June 1750, and m. by BAML of 8 Oct 1793, Elnora (Ellen) Randall. He is bur. near Dover, BA Co. After his death, his widow and three children moved to Fairfield Co., OH. She disposed of parts of tracts called *Huggy Muggy* and *Aquila's Reserve,* 104-1/4 a.{BALR WG#157:176, 291}

Joseph and Ellen had four children{B; also Boyd, *The Parrish Family*:330-331}: JOHN, d. as a young man; REBECCA, b. 17 Jan 1796,

BA Co., d. 27 Dec 1830, age 34 years, m. 11 Aug 1879, John Parrish; BENJAMIN R., b. 10 Feb 1798; and NICHOLAS, b. 25 April 1800.

23.   JOHN BELT, son of Higginson (9) and Sarah, d. after Aug 1811. His wife has not been identified.

He inherited all of his father's real estate, and from his uncle Leonard Belt, he inherited 140 a., part of *Dann*.

He d. leaving a will dated 26 Aug 1811, naming his sons Evan and William, dau.-in-law Margaret, widow of his son Greenbury (and grandchildren Rebecca and Rufus Belt), dau. Mary Gatril, son Otho, son John Smith, and daus. Ann and Dolly. {MOWB H:321-324}

John Belt was the father of{B}: EVAN; WILLIAM; GREENBURY; MARY, m. (N) Gatril; OTHO; JOHN SMITH; ANN; and DOLLY.

24.   CARLTON BELT, son of Higginson (9) Belt, is stated by Shirk to have d. in MO Co., MD. A handwritten family record of Alfred Belt, son of Carlton Belt, and collected by Ann F. Jewell of Grand Junction, CO., states that he m. 1st, Mary Watson, and 2nd, on 26 Dec 1784 in Loudoun Co., VA, Anne, dau. of Col. Aeneas Campbell. Anne Campbell was b. 1768, and d. 13 March 1808 in MO Co., MD, having m. 2nd, on 30 March 1807, William Trail.

Williams' *History of Frederick Co.* states that he was the first sheriff of Loudon Co., VA, and was a Captain in the Flying Camp, and d. 21 Feb 1812. Shirk, however, states that he d. c1802 in MO Co., MD. {Brumbaugh; *Revolutionary Records of Maryland:*9}

On 2 March 1778, Carlton Belt took the Oath of Fidelity to the State of MD in MO Co., MD, before Aeneas Campbell. On 15 April 1780, Carlton Belt conv. to Basil Windsor 87-1/2 a. *Water's Forest.* His wife Mary consented, and Aeneas Campbell was a witness. {MOLR A:495}

Belt Family records compiled by Zellow C. Belt, and the DAR Application of Julia Catherine Killiam Henry {National No. 248566}, identify the children of Carlton Belt by his first wife. The Alfred Belt Family Record states that Carlton and Anne were the parents of (all b. in MO Co., MD): WATSON, b. 6 March 1769; HIGGINSON, b. 15 Nov 1778; CARLTON, Jr., b. 18 July 1772, d. 25 Dec 1798, m. Elizabeth Jones; LUCY, b. 12 May 1774; MARY, b. 19 June 1776, m. 1796 Joseph Magruder, by whom she had a son Lloyd Belt Magruder; WASHINGTON, b. 12 Dec 1779; and LEE, b. 11 June 1781.

By his 2nd wife, Carlton Belt was the father of: ESTHER, b. 24 April 1786, d. 24 Oct 1831, m. 18 Nov 1802, Daniel Trundle; AENEAS, b. 24 April 1786, d. 1828, m. 7 Dec 1816, Jane Clagett; ALFRED, b. 14 Feb 1788, d. 1872, m. 22 Dec 1809, Charlotte Trundle; TILGHMAN, b.

3 Sep 1789, m. 5 Feb 1811, Eleanor Slagle;[22] ANNE, b. 26 May 1791, d. in infancy; LLOYD, b. 25 May 1795, m. Julia Maria McPherson Berrien; ANNE or HANNAH, b. 17 Nov 1797, d. 5 Oct 1843, m. 18 Dec 1819, Daniel Duvall; ELIZABETH, b. 16 Dec 1799, d. 27 Jan 1846, m. on 16 March 1833, William Smith; and HENNE ANNE CAMPBELL, b. 1 Jan 1802, d. 11 April 1809.

25.   HIGGINSON BELT, son of Higginson (9) Belt, was b. c1745, moved to FR Co., where he d. in 1795. The 1776 Census of Sugar Land Hundred, FR Co., lists Higginson Belt, 31, Alley, 20, and one child {Shirk:42}: ELIZABETH, b. c1775 (age 1 in 1776).

26.   GREENBURY BELT, son of Higginson (9) Belt, d. by 12 June 1783, when his estate was appraised at £122.2.2. Sarah Belt, his admx., signed the inventory. Greenbury had at least two children{B:63}; HIGGINSON; and WESLEY.

27.   MARSHAM BELT is placed as a son of John (10) and Margaret (Queen) Belt. Direct evidence of the connection is lacking, but Richard Marsham d. leaving a will dated 14 April 1713 and proved 22 April 1713, naming granddaus. Catherine and Margaret Queen, and dau. Sarah Haddock.{R:560-561} Marsham would have been named for his great-grandfather, Marsham Belt.
        Marsham Belt m. Elizabeth (N) [said by some genealogists to be Elizabeth, dau. of Thomas and Sophia Cross, but definite proof is lacking]. In 1778, he took the Oath of Fidelity to the State of MD in PG Co.{V:2:274} In 1783, Marsham Belt appeared in the 1783 Assessment List, WA Co., for Marsh Hundred.{*Western Maryland Genealogy* 8:65} By 1800, Marsham Belt, Sr., and Marsham Belt, Jr., were in Fleming Co., KY.{Clift, Second Census of KY}
        Marsham Belt does not appear in the MO, PG, or WA Co. Land Records.{Indexes to the land records of those counties}
        Marsham Belt d. 8 Oct 1801 in Fleming Co., KY.
        Marsham Belt was the father of{Register of Queen Anne Parish, PG Co.; *WA Co., MD, Church Records of the 18th Century* (Family Line Publications); see also Fleming Co., KY, Land Records, A#2:454}: WILLIAM M., b. c1755; (N), dau., b. 6 Jan 1764; THOMAS, b. 15 June 1765; MARSHAM, b. July 1767, m. Margaret Norman; ELEANOR, b. 1772, m. John Faris; ALICE, m. James Chappell; MARY, m. Thomas Hutton; JOSEPH CROSS, m. Nancy (N); DENNIS; FIELDING; ELIZABETH; and MARGARET, m. Christian Fry.

---

[22] A deed dated 2 Jan 1822 mentions Tilghman Belt and his sister Anne C. Belt, now wife of Daniel Duvall, and their dec. sister Henney Anne Campbell Belt.{MOLR W:86}

28.   THOMAS BELT, son of Joseph (11) and Anne (Sprigg) Belt, inherited slaves and 1/2 of *Chevy Chase* from the 1761 will of his grandfather Belt. He is probably the Thomas Belt who m. Priscilla (N), and had at least two children, bapt. in King George Parish, PG Co.{B:278}: ESTHER, bapt. 19 Dec 1762; and RUTH, bapt. 19 Dec 1762.

29.   JOSEPH BELT, son of Joseph (11) and Anne (Sprigg) Belt, inherited the tract *Friendship* in FR Co. by the 1761 will of his grandfather Belt. He was the father of{B:278}: THOMAS, b. c1740, d. 1823 in Hagerstown.

30.   WILLIAM BELT, son of Joseph (11) and Anne (Sprigg) Belt, m. Elizabeth Smith Waters, b. 15 May 1786, dau. of Dr. Richard Waters and Margaret Smith.
       He inherited 1/2 of *Chevy Chase* from his father's will.{B:279}

31.   LLOYD CARLTON BELT, is stated by Shirk to have been a son of Tobias Belt (12) by his second wife, Mary Gordon. Lloyd Carlton was b. c1752 in PG Co., MD, and d. Sep 1854 in PG Co., MD.
       He may be the Lloyd Carlton Belt who m. Elizabeth Coslette Metcalfe Thomas, b. c1765, on 16 Dec 1790, at the German Reformed Church in Frederick. There is a possibility that the Lloyd who m. Elizabeth was a son of Higginson Belt.
       Lloyd Carlton and E. C. M. (Thomas) Belt were the parents of at least one son{Research by Mary Taylor of Burson, CA}: ENOS, b. c1819, d. c1859.

32.   EDWARD BELT, son of Jeremiah (13), was b. 15 March 1749. He may have been the father of two children{Belt Notes made available by W. E. Belt, Jr., of Flatonia, TX}: ELIZABETH; and RICHARD WATKINS, b. 1780, d. 1868, m. Eleanor Aldridge and had issue.

33.   JOHN SPRIGG BELT, son of Jeremiah (13) and Mary Belt, was b. 10 Sep 1752. He m. Rachel Griffith, dau. of Joshua.
       He was Captain of the 4th Co., 1st Regiment, MD Line, and was a member of the Society of the Cincinnati.

34.   TOBIAS BELT, son of Jeremiah (13) and Mary Belt, was b. 1766. He m. 31 Jan 1789, Rebecca Beall, dau. of Capt. Richard Beall.

35.   Capt. MIDDLETON BELT, son of Joseph (14) and Esther (Smith) Belt, was b. 1747 in PG Co., and d. 1807 in MO Co. On 25 March 1763, he m. Mary Ann Dyer, in St. John's Church, Surrey, England.

During the Revolution, he was a captain, and in 1789 served on the Grand Jury of PG Co.{Register of MD DAR, 1966}

Middleton and Mary Ann were the parents of{Ibid.}: ANNA MARIA, b. 24 Nov 1771, m. (N) McCormick in 1796; MIDDLETON (dau.), b. 24 April 1777, m. William Smith; MARY ANN, b. 29 March 1779; CLARISSA, b. 10 Nov 1781, m. Joshua Stewart, 1806; MIDDLETON (son), b. 13 Sep 1785; WILLIAM DYER, b. 26 Feb 1788; and JAMES HANRICK, b. 13 Jan 1792.

Sixth Generation

36.   SARAH BELT, dau. of Leonard (20) and Hannah, d. leaving a will dated 8 March 1848 and proved 24 April 1848.{BAWB 22:346} She m. Richard B. Chenoweth of Baltimore. He d. cDec 1845, leaving a will dated 31 Dec 1845 and proved 24 April 1846.

Richard B. and Sarah (Belt) Chenoweth were the parents of{B:93}: BENJAMIN THOMAS; RICHARD B.; and JULIANNA.

37.   LEONARD BELT, son of Leonard (20) and Hannah, was b. 6 April 1773, and d. 22 Nov 1829. He m. 17 Sep 1807, Catherine, dau. of William Almack of Baltimore. Catherine Almmack Belt was b. 27 April 1790 and d. 18 June 1828.

Leonard and Catherine (Almack) Belt were the parents of{B:93 cites Belt Family Bible}: CAROLINE, b. 10 Oct 1808; EPHRAIM, b. 15 Sep 1810; LEONARD, b. 24 April 1812; WILLIAM, b. 24 Jan 1814; JACKSON, b. 10 Feb 1816; THOMAS, b. 28 Oct 1817; DARBY, b. 10 March 1819; CHARLES, b. 9 Sep 1820; AMOS, b. 20 Dec 1822; ELIJAH, b. 22 Dec 1824; and JOHN DORSEY, b. 18 Oct 1828.

38.   MORDECAI BELT, son of Leonard (20) and Hannah, was b. 1776, and d. 12 April 1829. He m. on 24 or 25 April 1799 in BA Co., Priscilla Parrish, b. 10 May 1771, d. 30 Aug 1851 or 1861.

Mordecai Belt served in the War of 1812, and he and his wife lived near Dover, BA Co.

Mordecai and Priscilla were the parents of{Boyd; The Parrish Family:332, cites records of Hickman Belt}: HUMPHREY, b. 26 Dec 1799; JOSHUA, b. 11 April 1801, m. Keturah, dau. of Charles Ambrose;[23] RICHARD, b. 11 April 1803; MOSES, b. 5 Jan 1805, m. Mary Canoles; RACHEL ANN, b. 8 Oct 1807; SARAH ANNE, b. 19 Oct 1809; MARY ANN, b. 25 Feb 1812, m. Dorsey Osborn;[24] NATHAN, b. 6 Sep 1814,

---

[23] They had one dau.: ELIZABETH, m. John Dorsey Belt.
[24] They had at least one child: MIRIAM, who m. John Dorsey Belt.

m. Rachel Childs; HICKMAN, b. 6 Feb 1817, m. Ann Eliza Sindell; ELISHA, b. 5 April 1819, m. Barbara Emich; and JOHN GEORGE, b. 26 Aug 1822, m. Fanny Hunter.

39.   BENJAMIN R. BELT, son of Joseph (22) and Ellen (Randall), was b. 10 Feb 1798 in BA Co., MD, and d. 8 Nov 1863, probably in OH. He m. in Sep 1829, in OH, Angelica Parrish, dau. of Aquila and Rebecca (Tipton) Parrish. They had four children{B:94; See also Boyd, *The Parrish Family*:88-89} : GEORGE W.; REBECCA; SUSANNA; and ELLEN.

40.   NICHOLAS BELT, son of Joseph (22) and Ellen (Randall), was b. 25 April 1800, in BA Co., MD, and d. 8 June 1857, in Fairfield Co., OH., He is bur. in the Parrish Cemetery in Millersport, OH. He m. 1st, Rebecca Ann Parish, dau. of Nicholas and Mary (Ensor) Parrish, and 2nd, Tabitha Parrish, sister of Rebecca Ann. He had six children by his first wife, and five children by his second wife.{B:94; See also Boyd, *The Parrish Family*:143-148, 332}

Nicholas Belt was the father of{B:93}: JOHN; LEWIS; KINSEY; SARAH; MARY; REBECCA; BENJAMIN T., lived in Millersport, OH; HARRIET C.; RACHEL; JOSEPH, d. 1870; and JULIA.

41.   CARLTON BELT, son of Carlton (24), was b. 18 July 1772, in MO Co., MD, where he m. on 25 Feb 1799, Elizabeth Jones. They were the parents of{B:94}: SARAH ANN, b. 3 June 1801.

42.   AENEAS BELT, son of Carlton (24), was b. 24 April 1786, and d. 1828. He m. on 7 Dec 1816, Jane Clagett. No doubt he is the "Enos" Belt, orphan, age 16, who, on 24 April 1802, was bound to Matthias Buckey, tanner, to age 21. Anne Belt, his mother, consented.{*WMG* 5:161 cites FR Co. Indentures:369-370}

43.   ALFRED BELT, son of Carlton (24), was b. 14 Feb 1788, in MO Co., and d. 1 July 1872. He m. Charlotte Trundle, who was b. 6 Feb 1787, and d. 13 April 1824. After the birth of their second child, they moved to Loudon Co., VA, where Alfred Belt d. Alfred and his wife were bur. on the Trundle Plantation in MO Co., MD.{B:95 cites Ridgely's *Historic Graves*}

Alfred and Charlotte (Trundle) Belt were the parents of: ALFRED CAMPBELL, m. Mary Malls; RUTH, m. Samuel Sinclair; MARY, m. Cephas Hempstone; JOHN LLOYD, m. Sarah Eleanor MacGill; JAMES, m. Elizabeth Snouffer; and ANN ELIZABETH, m. J. M. M. Sellman.

44.   LLOYD BELT, son of Carlton (24), was b. 25 May 1795, in MO Co., MD, and d. 1824, in Burk Co., GA. He moved to GA in 1815 where he m. Julia, dau. of Senator Berrien. He was a member of the Medical and Chirurgical Faculty of Maryland.{B:95 cites Cordell, *Medical Annals of Maryland*}
    Lloyd and Julia (Berrien) Belt were the parents of:
WILHELMINA, m. 1st, (N) Connelly, and 2nd, Gen. Henningson; RICHARD R., M.D.; and LLOYD CARLTON.

45.   WILLIAM M. BELT, son of Marsham (27), is said to have been b. c1755, in PG Co., MD, and d. by 1826, in Jessamine Co., KY. He m. Deborah Waters, who was b. Feb 1776, PG Co., and d. by 1823 in Jessamine Co., KY. They were the parents of{DAR Application of Ethel Belt Harper}: TILGHMAN W.

46.   JOSEPH CROSS BELT, son of Marsham (27), m. Mary Armstrong, c1824, in Fleming Co., KY. They had a son: GEORGE W., b. 23 July 1825, moved to Platte Co., MO, by 1839.{Sprague, *Kentuckians in Missouri*:60}

47.   ENOS W. BELT, son of Lloyd Carlton (31) and Elizabeth C. M. (Thomas) Belt, was b. c1819, and d. c1859. On 11 Dec 1840, in the German Reformed Church, Frederick, he m. Mary Elizabeth Butcher, b. c1820, d. 1844. They were the parents of{Research by Mary T. Taylor of Burson, CA}: LLOYD CARLTON, b. c1841; and WILLIAM HENRY, b. c1844.

Seventh Generation

48.   TILGHMAN W. BELT, son of William M. (45) and Deborah (Waters) Belt, was b. c1800, at Jessamine Co., KY, and d. Jan 1861, at Millville, MO. He m. on April 1826, Aurelia T. Lampkin, b. 1809, in KY, d. c1860, at Millville, MO. They were the parents of{DAR Application of Ethel Belt Harper}: MARIA DEBORAH, b. c1829; GEORGE W., b. c1834; THOMAS G., b. c1836; ADONIJAH, b. c1839; CHARLES M., b. c1840; MARY E., b. c1845; and RICHARD ARTRIDGE, b. 12 March 1853.

THE BESSON FAMILY

Refs.: A: *Register of Baptisms, Marriages and Burials of the Parish of St. Andrew's, Plymouth, County Devon, A. D. 1581-1618, with Baptisms 1619-1633.* Ed. by M. C. S. Cruwys. Exeter: The Society, 1954. B: Coldham. *Complete Book of Emigrants, 1607-1660.* C: Foley.

Early VA Families: Vols. 2: Charles City Co., PG Co.; Vol. III: James City, Surry Counties. D: "Jones Bible Records," in *Maryland Genealogies,* 2:106-109.

I. The Family in England

The following entries may pertain to the family of Thomas Besson who came to VA and then to MD, but definite proof is lacking. More work needs to be done.

THOMAS BESSON of St. Andrew's, Plymouth, Devon, was the father of{A:58, 110, 199, 497, 511}: ELIZA, bapt. 26 Jan 1594/5; MARTHA, bapt. 20 June 1603; THOMAS, bapt. 11 Jan 1617/8 (may have d. young); PHILLIP_, (dau.), bapt. 17 June 1619; THOMAS, bapt. 26 July 1621; and JOAN, bapt. 31 Aug 1623.

II. The Family in Virginia

THOMAS BESSON, age 24, was transported to VA from London on the *Assurance,* by Mr. Isaac Bromwell in 1635.{B:157}
He had been transported to VA c1638 by Robert Freeman.{BDML: 1:132}
On 11 Sep 1638, Robert Freeman, merchant, was granted 700 a. in James City Co. for transporting a number of people, including Thomas Besson.{C:3:22} On 18 (?) 1640, Thomas Stegg was granted 1,000 a. in Charles City Co. for transporting a number of persons, including "Thomas Bessen."{C:2:13}
On 19 May 1649, Toby Smith gave bond in Lancaster Co. he would pay 295 lbs. tob. to Thos. Besson.{Fleet, *Virginia Colonial Abstracts,* 1:121}

III. The Family in Maryland

1.   THOMAS BESSON, was b. c1617 in England, and d. 1679 in AA Co. In 1649, he and his family immigrated to MD (his wife Hester is listed as having been transported c1650).{MPL Q:69 and 4:66}
He m. Hester, widow of Henry Caplin. After Thomas Besson's death, she m., by 1680, Thomas Sutton as her third husband.{BDML 1:132}
Besson was probably one of the Puritans who came from VA in 1649. He represented Providence, later AA Co., in the Assemblies of 1657 and 1666. He was a Justice of the AA Co. Court, 1658-1668, and was a captain [of the militia] in 1661.{BDML 1:132}
On 9 Dec 1658, he had surv. 450 a. called *Bessenden,* in South River Hundred. By 1707, most of the tract had passed out of the family, but 160 a. were held by Thomas and John Gassaway.{D:158} On 3 Nov

80

1650, he had 350 a. called *Bessenton* surv., also in South River Hundred. {MRR:159} On the same day, he had surv. 50 a. called *Younger Besson.* {MRR:160}

On 12 Oct 1664, he wit. the will of Philip Allenby of AA Co.{MWB 1:263}

When Thomas Besson was first elected to the Assembly, he owned 800 a. of land; at his death he owned three tracts of unspecified acreage.{BDML 1:132}

In 1674/5, Capt. Thomas Besson gave his age as 58. He mentioned James Stringer and John Collier in his deposition.{ARMD 51:79}

Thomas Besson, Sr., of South River, d. leaving a will dated 15 Oct 1677 and proved 29 April 1679, naming son John (to have land adjoining that of son[-in-law] Nicholas Gassaway), son William, son Thomas the Younger, dau. Martha, and wife Hester. The overseer was to be son Thomas the Elder. Edward Burgess, Robert Ward, and Jno. Greene were witnesses.{MWB 10:42}

On 29 April 1679, his estate was appraised by Richard Tydings and James Sanders, who valued the property at 16,296 lbs. tob. The list of debtors included Edward Piles, Edward Rawlings, Anne Cove--, John Gressam, Edmond Purdy, and Nicholas Aldridge.{INAC 6:105}

On 31 May 1680, the administration account of his estate was filed. His total inventory came to 16,286 lbs. tob., payments came to 10,498 lbs. of tob., leaving about 500 lbs. of tob. to be dist. to his heirs. The account named Martha Aldridge, and was filed by the extx. Hester, "very aged," wife of Thomas Sutton.{INAC 7-A:125}

The inventory of his estate totalled £80.18.0, and the final balance of his estate was £43.8.0.{BDML 1:132}

Thomas and Hester were the parents of: THOMAS, m. Margaret Saughier on 5 March ---{B:107}; THOMAS "The Younger;" WILLIAM; JOHN; ANNE, m. Nicholas Gassaway; and MARTHA.

2.	THOMAS BESSON, son of Nicholas and Hester, m. [probably in VA] on 5 March ---, Margaret Saughier, b. 1636, dau. of George Saughier, who was b. c1600 in Newport, England, and came to VA in 1620.{B:107} Thomas was living in AA Co. as late as c1704.

On 20 Oct 1711, Thomas and Margaret conv. to Henry Maynard 110 a. *Sturton's Rest.*{AALR PK:428}

Thomas and Margaret had issue{B}: THOMAS, b. Dec 1677; ANN, b. 26 Dec 1670, m. Richard Cromwell on 26 Oct 1697; MARGARET, b. 31 Jan 1673/4, m. John Rattenbury on 30 Dec 1701; NICHOLAS, b. 28 Dec 1677; and ELIZABETH, b. 1683.

3.   WILLIAM BESSON, son of Thomas and Hester, inherited 100 a. of *Bessenden* from his father. On 7 Oct 1687, he sold this land to Thomas Hutton.{AALR WT#1:136}

4.   JOHN BESSON, son of Thomas Besson, the Elder, was living in AA Co. as a carpenter on 16 Aug 1688 when he sold to Nicholas Gassaway 80 a. part of *Bessenden,* adj. the dividend of land which the sd. Thomas had devised to his sons John and William.{AALR WH#4:287}

5.   NICHOLAS BESSON, son of Thomas (who had been living in AA Co. c1704), was b. c1679, and d. in BA Co. by April 1761. In 1734, he gave his age as 55, and mentioned his father Thomas, who had been living in AA Co. c1704.{AALC IB#1:79} He m. Diana Haile on 3 Sep 1722 in St. Margaret's.{AACR:131} Diana was the admx. of Matthew Haile. {MDAD 6:118}

        On 11 July 1709, John and James Jackson, with consent of James' wife Sarah, conv. 150 a. *Jackson's Chance* to Nicholas Besson. {BALR TR#A:10}

        Nicholas may be the Nicholas "Beston" who wit. the will of William Slade of BA Co. on 2 April 1726.{MWB 20:276}

        Nicholas Beston, of AA Co., d. leaving a will dated 20 April 1759 and proved 6 Dec 1759. The heirs named were dau. Ann Bond, grandson William Bond, and son-in-law Jonathan McGlocklin, the exec. Beston mentioned tracts *Jackson's Chance, Fortune,* and *Long Bridge Run.* The will was wit. by Nathaniel Ramsey, John Walker, and George Morden (a Dutch Baptist or Dunker).{MWB 30:770}

        On 9 April 1761, the balance of Nicholas Beston's estate, totalling £450.14.12, was dist. by Jonathan McLockland, exec., with Thomas Jones and Daniel Chamier, sureties. Ann Bond was a legatee, and the balance went equally to the accountant and the grandchildren.{BFD 3:76}

        Nicholas and Diana were the parents of{AACR:114}: ANN, b. 30 Sep 1723, m. (N) Bond; DIANA, b. 8 Feb 1725; and ELIZABETH, b. 14 April 1727.

THE BICKERDIKE FAMILY

1.   RICHARD BICKERDIKE, Clerk of St. Anne's Parish, was bur. 31 Aug 1719.{AACR:85} He m. Anne Smith in St. Anne's Parish on 16 Oct 1704.{AACR:73} Anne m. 2nd, on 7 Jan 1719/20, John Talbott, of Annapolis.{AACR:86}

        The administration account of Elias Poleman, filed 19 Aug 1715, contains a payment to Dr. Monroe for Richard "Bickardick," a man with a wife and two small children."{INAC 36B:350}

Bickerdike's will, dated 30 Aug 1719 and proved 30 Sep 1719, left his estate to his wife, the extx., for her lifetime. Then it was to pass to the children. Thomas Williams was the only witness. {MWB 15:185}

Richard Bickerdike's estate was admin. on 8 Sep 1721 by Ann, wife of John Talbott. An inventory of £28.10.5 was mentioned. {MINV 3:152, MDAD 3:526}

John Talbott, scrivener of Annapolis, drew up his will on 3 Feb 1721. He left personalty to Richard (eldest son of Richard Bickerdike, dec.) and to William Bickerdike. Talbott named his own wife Anne. The will was proved 21 April 1723, and Thomas and Catherine Williams were the witnesses. {MWB 17:257}

Anne Talbot, of Annapolis, d. leaving a will dated 5 April 1722 and proved 4 March 1722. She named her children Mary, John, Amos, and William Bickerdike, and her dau. Jane [Talbott?]. Ann also mentioned Thomas and Katherine Williams. John Lawson, Charles Worthington, Robert Mackilwain, and Nicholas Hammond wit. the will. {MWB 18:160}

Richard and Anne were the parents of (births or baptism were recorded in St. Anne's Parish){AACR:65, 66, 69, 74, 75, 77, 81, 89, 90}: RICHARD, b. 29 Jan 1707; WILLIAM, bapt. 9 --- 1708, d. 12 April 1722; MARY, bapt. 3 Feb 1708 [sic],[25] m. William Hutton on 1 Dec 1722; JOHN, b. 24 June 1711; AMOS, b. --- 1713, bapt. 7 Nov ---; and ELIZABETH, b. 30 July 1716, bur. 5 Nov 1717.

2.   RICHARD BICKERDIKE, son of Richard (1) and Anne, was b. 29 Jan 1707. He m. [1st], Anne (N) in All Hallows Parish on 6 June 1728.{AACR:42} He seems to have m. 2nd, Rebecca (N).

Richard Bickerdike, carpenter, of Annapolis, in c1728/9, conv. to the Hon. Charles Calvert Lot #82 (formerly numbered Lot #103) in Annapolis. His wife Rebecca relinquished her dower. {AALR RD#1:84}

3.   JOHN BICKERDIKE, son of Richard (1) and Anne, was b. 24 June 1711.{AACR:69, 90} He may be the John Bickerdike of AA Co. who patented 100 a. called *Terrapin Bite* on 7 Sep 1754.{MPL GS#2:291, BC#1:326}

4.   AMOS BICKERDIKE, son of Richard (1) and Anne, was b. 1713. He was still living on 15 Nov 1731 when he wit. the will of Thomas Facer, shoemaker, of AA Co.{MWB 20:470}

---

[25] Her godparents were Thomas Reading and Elizabeth and Jane Tompson.

83

Unplaced

BICKERDIKE, MAJOR, tailor, in 1757 conv. a Lot #102 in Annapolis to Nicholas Minskie.{AALR BB#2, No. 1:72}

THE BIRD FAMILY

Refs.: A: Scisco. *Baltimore County Land Records, 1665-1687.* Baltimore: Genealogical Publishing Co.

JOHN BIRD d. by April 1691. He m. by 1680, Elizabeth, admx. of Henry Lewis. He may be the John Bird for whose transportation John Abington of CV Co. claimed land in Aug 1680.{MPL 28:34} He m., by Nov 1684, the widow of John Armstrong.

John Bird admin. the estate of Joseph Pearce of BA Co. on 8 Oct 1677.{INAC 4:337}

He was in AA Co. on 13 Jan 1679, when he wit. a deed between Robert Proctor and John Gater, and Marien Duvall.{AALR IH#2:1}

About 1680, Elizabeth, wife of John Bird, admin. the estate of Henry Lewis, Gent., of AA Co. She was extx. of the estate.{INAC 7B:8}

John Bird was back in BA Co. by 2 Aug 1681, when he was conv. 50 a. *Tuttle Fields* by Michael Judd and his wife Jane. It was part of a 200 a. warrant issued the previous 16 Feb.{BALR IR#AM:137} On 27 April 1683, Bird and his wife Elizabeth conv. this same 50 a. to Benjamin Bennett.{BALR RM#HS:44} On 1 June 1686, Thomas Richardson conv. him 100 a. of *Richardson's Prospect.*{BALR RM#HS:178}

As John Bird, of Broad Neck, AA Co., on 18 Aug 1679 he purchased 200 a. *Turner's Ridge* from Thomas Bucknall, of AA Co.{TALR 3:308} In 1681, Bucknall and his wife Mary conv. the tract to Bird.{TALR 4:105} On 6 Feb 1688, Bird, now living in TA Co., conv. the tract to John Howell of Stockton, England, merchant.{TALR 5:218}

Bird d. by 7 April 1691, when his estate was inv. by William Ebden and Lawrence Richardson, and valued at £20.12.8. His estate was admin. on 1 May 1694 by James Phillips, who reported the above inventory and additional assets of £24.16.9. Payments were made to Mr. Hedge, Madam Long, Joseph Sanders, and Timothy Dawson.{A; INAC 12:134}

THE BOYD FAMILY

Refs.: A: "Boyds of Maryland and Virginia," by Leroy Stafford Boyd, published in the *Boyd Family Journal,* No. 1, March 1925, pp. 10-17. B: "Notes on the Thomas Boyd Family," by Edward Kinsey Voorhees. 1930; at MHS.

1.   JOHN BOYD, emigrant, settled in AA Co., MD. On 30 June 1684, he patented 60 a. known as *Boyd's Chance.*{MPL 25:94, 33:108} He d. in 1704. John m. Mary (N), who d. in PG Co. by Dec 1722.

    The inventory of personal property of John Boyd, of PG Co., was taken on 19 July 1705 by Thomas Wells and Hugh Abrahams and appraised at £112.5.2.{INAC 26:75} His estate was admin. by the extx., Mary Boyd, on 30 Nov 1706.{INAC 26:109}

    Mary Boyd, of PG Co., d. leaving a will dated 16 Sep 1721 and proved 4 Dec 1722. She named her children Charles, John, Abraham, Martha wife of Thomas Wells, Isaac, and Mary Batterman (and the latter's son John). She mentioned property left by her husband, John Boyd, dec. Son John was named exec. The will was wit. by Richard Duckett, Mary Boyd, and John Perkins.{MWB 18:20}

    The personal estate of Mary Boyd was appraised by Robert Tyler and Ralph Crabb on 20 Dec 1722 and valued at £37.7.7. The inventory was filed 5 Feb 1722.{MINV 8:98}

    John and Mary were the parents of{A:10, 22}: CHARLES, m. Elizabeth Ray; JOHN, m. Eleanor Fitzredmonds on 28 March 1706; ABRAHAM, m. 16 Oct 1705, Mary Grey; ISAAC, m. 18 March 1727, Susannah Noble; MARY, m. Ishmael Bateman (Batterman in her mother's will); and MARTHA, m. Thomas Wells.

2.   CHARLES BOYD, son of John and (1) Mary, m. Elizabeth Ray. {A:10}

    They were the parents of{PGQA}: MARY, b. 17 Aug 1707; FRANCES, b. 16 Feb 1714; and MARTHA, b. 29 Feb 1716.

3.   JOHN BOYD, Jr., son of John (1) and Mary, d. c1756.{A:1}

    He lived on the 1,000 a. his father bought in 1694. He m. 1st, on 28 March 1706, Eleanor Fitzredmonds, said to be a niece of Charles Carroll of BA Co. He m. 2nd (N) (N) and mentioned his second wife and their children in a deed of 1748, but he did not name them.{A:10}

    On 5 March 1715, John Boyd and wife Elinor conv. to Abraham Boyd part of *Sway.*{PGLR F:612}

    On 27 June 1738, John Boyd conv. to his son John Boyd, Jr., a 233 a. tract *Boyd's Delay.*{PGLR T:595}

John Boyd and Eleanor were the parents of{A:11}: BENJAMIN, b. 13 Jan 1707; JOHN, III, b. 25 Sep 1709; ABRAHAM; WILLIAM; ELEANOR; MARY; MARGARET; MARCELLA; ANN; and SARAH.

4.   ABRAHAM BOYD, son of John (1) and Mary, is stated to have m. 16 Oct 1705, Mary Grey. He probably m. 2nd, Deborah Walley, on 8 Nov 1728.{PGQA}

He d. by 20 Sep 1737, when his estate was inv. by Thomas Harwood and John Lamar and appraised at £513.2.2. John Boyd and Benjamin Boyd signed as creditors. Mrs. Deborough Boyd, admx., filed the inventory on 29 March 1738.{MINV 23:172}

Abraham and Deborah were the parents of{PGQA}: MARGARET, b. 23 Sep 1730.

5.   BENJAMIN BOYD, son of John (3) and Eleanor, was b. 13 Jan 1707, and d. 10 July 1762, leaving a will. On 30 Oct 1733, he m. Elizabeth Harwood, dau. of Major Thomas Harwood.{A:11}

Benjamin Boyd, of PG Co., d. leaving a will dated 12 April 1762 and proved 22 April 1762. The heirs named were eldest son Thomas, son Abraham, eldest dau. Eleanor Watkins, 2nd dau. Sarah Boyd, and 3rd dau. Peggy Boyd. The execs. were sons Thomas and Abraham. The will was wit. by John Bateman, Abraham Woodward, and Benjamin Hall, son of Benjamin.{MWB 31:583}

The estate of Benjamin Boyd, of PG Co., was inv. on 6 May 1762 by Robert Tyler and Jeremiah Magruder, who appraised his personal property at £622.14.2. Eleanor Watkins and Sarah Harris signed as next of kin, and Thomas Boyd, the exec., filed the inventory on 29 Jan 1768. {MINV 95:220}

Benjamin and Eleanor were the parents of{A:11; PGQA}: THOMAS, b. 14 Sep 1734; ABRAHAM, b. May 1736, a colonel in the Revolutionary War; ELEANOR, m. Stephen Watkins; SARAH, m. (N) Harris; and PEGGY, m. Nicholas Watkins.

6.   JOHN BOYD, III, son of John (3) and Eleanor, was b. 25 Sep 1709. He m. Margaret Baldwin, and became head of the MO Co. branch of the family, which scattered all over n.w. MD, principally at Frederick and Hagerstown.{A} It is more likely that he m. Susan Baldwin on 8 May 1734.{PGQA}

He d. in FR Co., leaving a will dated 17 April 1760 and proved 18 May 1772. He named a wife Susanna, a son-in-law Aaron Prather, and children Benjamin, John, Abraham, William, Mary, Margaret, Marulla,

Elinor, Ann, and Sarah. The will was wit. by William Dent and Nicholas Baker.{MWB 38:629}

David Lynn and Samuel West appraised John Boyd's personal property on 26 May 1772, and valued it at £105.14.9. Mary Prather and Masiller Boyd signed as next of kin. Susannah Boyd, extx., filed the inventory on 22 Oct 1772.{MINV 109:373}

John Boyd's estate was dist. on 25 Oct 1775. Mrs. Susanna was extx., and William Dent and Samuel Swearingen were sureties. The balance of £22.15.11 was divided among his daus. Mary, Margaret, Marsula, Eleanor, Ann, and Sarah.{BFD 7:46}

John Boyd was the father of: BENJAMIN; JOHN; ABRAHAM; WILLIAM; MARY; MARGARET; MARULLA; ELINOR; ANN; and SARAH.

7.   THOMAS BOYD, son of Benjamin (5) and Eleanor, was b. 14 Sep 1734, and was a First Lieutenant in the 5th MD Regiment during the Revolutionary War, and an Original Member of the Society of the Cincinnati. He m. twice and had issue.{A}

Thomas Boyd m. Charity Duckett on 24 March 1757. They were the parents of{PGQA}: RICHARD DUCKETT, b. 28 Dec 1757; and others.

8.   BENJAMIN BOYD, son of John (6) and Susan (Baldwin), may be the Benjamin Boyd who m. Elenor Williams on 27 Feb 1758.{PGQA}

The DAR Patriot Index lists a Benjamin Boyd, b. 1734, d. 1784, m. Eleanor Taylor, who was a Private in MD during the Revolutionary War.

Eleanor Williams or Taylor is probably the Mrs. Eleanor Boyd, [b. c1737], d. 13 May 1830, aged 93 years, in Hagerstown, at the residence of her son, Mr. Joseph Boyd.[26]

Benjamin and Eleanor (Williams) may be tentatively placed as the parents of: JOSEPH, b. c1764.

9.   WILLIAM BOYD, son of John (6) and Susan Baldwin, may be the William Boyd who was listed in Voorhees as living at Herring Bay, MD, b. c1730/40, and m. Charity Talbot, said [without any documentation] to have been "a descendant of George Talbot a cousin of Lord Baltimore."{B}

William and Charity are stated by Voorhees to be the parents of: WILLIAM, Lieutenant in Gen. Arthur St. Clair's Army, killed at St.

---

[26] "Marriages and Deaths 1830-1837, Washington County, Maryland, Recorded in *The Republican Banner*," by Helen W. Brown, typescript, MHS, 1962, p. 5.

Clair's defeat; BENJAMIN, d. in childhood; and WALTER, m. Amanda
Alverson.

THE BURLE FAMILY

<u>Refs.</u>: A: Burle Family Chart, by Christopher Johnston, Johnston Genealogy
Collection, MHS.

1.   ROBERT BURLE, of AA Co., d. c1676. He m. Mary (N), who d.
by 1672.{A}
      Robert Burle immigrated in 1649.{MPL 5:12} Mary Burle, wife of
Robert, Robert Burle, Jr., and Stephen Burle were transported in 1649.
{MPL 2:608, ABH:39}

      Burle was a Justice from 1658-1676, and a Burgess in 1662 and 1666.
{A}

      On 28 Dec 1663, Abraham Holdman, of BA Co., made his will
naming Robert Burle as his bro.-in-law, and leaving him *Hunting Worth.*
{MWB 1:213}

      Robert Burle's will, dated 25 April 1672 and proved 27 June 1676,
left *Burle's Hill* (or *Burle's Bank)* to son Stephen, the exec. Dau. Rebecca
was to have *Burle's Town Land* and the personalty given her by
Gwelthian Hollman, widow of William Hollman. Dau. Susanna was to
have the personalty formerly owned by the dec.'s son John, dec. Dau.
Mary was to have the property given her by son Robert, dec. The testator
said his daus. were to be of age at 16, and directed that he be bur. with
his dec. wife Mary. The will was wit. by Jno. Norwood, Thomas Marsh,
Jacob Neale, and Josias Hall.{MWB 5:150}
      Robert and Mary were the parents of{A}: ROBERT, b. c1610,[27]
came to MD in 1649, but returned to England and d. by 1672;
STEPHEN, b. 1610; JOHN, d. by 1672; REBECCA; SUSANNA;
MARY; and ELIZABETH.

2.   STEPHEN BURLE, son of Robert (1) and Mary, was b. c1610,
and d. April 1683. He m. Blanche (N) who m. 2nd, Thomas Rider, and d.
28 Feb 1708/9. Stephen came to MD with his parents in 1649.{A}
      Stephen Burle, of AA Co., d. leaving a will dated 1 Jan 1683, and
proved 31 March 1684. He named his wife Blanche as extx., and named
as heirs son Stephen, son John, dau. Sarah, dau. Mary, and dau. Blanche.
Sons were to be of age at 18, and daus. at 17. The will was wit. by Jno.

---

[27] Robert Burle gave his age as c51 in 1661.{KE Co. Court Proc. B:99} In his
deposition, he named John Browne, Sr., and William Pither (or Piper).{ARMD 54:220-
221}

Andrew, Geo. Stourton, Edmund Duncalfe, and Wm. Martin.{MWB 4:30}

Thomas Ryder, of AA Co., made his will on 27 Dec 1703. He named his wife Blanche, John Burle, Sarah wife of Henry Brown, Blanch Wratten, and Eliza Stanton, all the children of his wife Blanch. {MWB 11:403}

Blanch Ryder, of AA Co., d. leaving a will dated 29 March 1707 and proved 14 April 1709. She named her eldest son Stephen Burle (to have 1 s.), daus. Blanch Wharton and Eliza Stanton, and son John (joint exec. with dau. Eliza.). The will was wit. by Robert Jubb, Robert Boon, and George Hodge.{MWB Part 2-12:13}

Stephen and Blanche were the parents of{A}: STEPHEN; SARAH, m. Henry Brown; MARY; BLANCHE, m. (N) Wratten or Wharton; possibly ELIZA, m. (N) Stanton; and JOHN, d. 1742.

3.   STEPHEN BURLE, son of Stephen (2) and Blanche, m. Sarah Gosling in St. Margaret's Parish on 14 Feb 1707.{A; AACR:130} Sarah Burle m. Hugh Merriken in St. Anne's Parish on 20 Nov 1716.{AACR:78}

Stephen Burle, of AA Co., d. leaving a will dated 8 Aug 1716 and proved 27 Aug 1716. He named his son John (to have *Pettibone's Rest*), son Stephen (to have dwell. plant. of *Burle's Hills*), daus. Mary and Rachel, not yet 16, and bro. John. Wife Sarah was named exec. The will was wit. by Robert Jubb, Nathan'll Stinchcomb, and Jno. Bucknell. {MWB 14:115}

The estate of Stephen Burle was admin. on 11 Nov 1718. An inventory of £326.4.9 was taken. Legatees included John Burle, bro. of the dec. Mr. Philip Sunter [or Smith], merchant in England, was mentioned. The account was filed by Hugh Merriken, admin. de bonis non.{MDAD 1:246} Another account was filed by 14 April 1719 by Hugh Merriken, who admin. that part of the estate unadmin. by Sarah Burle. {MDAD 1:391} A third account was filed 12 May 1719.{MDAD 1:421} A fourth account was filed 11 March 1727.{MDAD 8:535}

Stephen and Sarah were the parents of (b. in St. Margaret's Parish, AA Co.){A; AACR:110, 131}: SARAH, b. 12 Sep 1708; JOHN, b. 14 Oct 1710; and MARY, b. 27 Jan 1711, m. Joshua Gray on 25 Feb 1727.

4.   JOHN BURLE, son of Stephen (2) and Blanche, was b. c1683, and d. 1742 in AA Co. He gave his age as c45 in 1728.{AALR RD#2:137} He m. 1st, Elizabeth (N), who d. 16 April 1722.{A; AACR:138} John Burle m. 2nd, Ann Hawkins, in St. Margaret's Parish on 2 Dec 1731. {AACR:131}

Ann Hawkins Burle m. 2nd, Nathaniel Stinchcomb, in St. Margaret's Parish, on 20 May 1735. She m. 3rd, on 8 Sep 1743, also in St. Margaret's Parish, Philip Pettibone.{AACR:131, 132}

John Burle d. leaving a will dated 2 June 1742 and proved 23 Oct 1742. He named his children John and Stephen, execs., and Mary Boon, and grandchildren Charles, Margaret, and Ann Todd. The will was wit. by Alex. Cummings, Sterling Adair, and Whitman Marshe. {MWB 22:516}

John and Elizabeth were the parents of (b. in St. Margaret's Parish, AA Co.){A; AACR:110, 115}: ANNA, b. 20 July 1712, m. Lancelot Todd on 10 Oct 1727; MARY, b. 5 Oct 1714, m. (N) Boon; JOHN, b. 6 Dec 1716; STEPHEN, b. 26 Jan 1718[28]; and RACHEL, b. 18 Sep 1721.

John and Ann were the parents of one dau., b. in St. Anne's Parish {AACR:115, 119, 139}: MARY, b. 22 (or 23) March 1731, d. 22 Jan 1747.

5.   STEPHEN BURLE, son of John (4) and Elizabeth, was b. 26 Jan 1718, in St. Margaret's Parish, and d. in AA Co. by July 1743. He m. Anne (N).

Stephen left a will dated 4 July 1742 and proved 6 July 1743. He left his entire estate to his wife Anne, and after she d. the estate was to be divided between his bro. John and his sister Mary Boone. His will was wit. by Robert Boone, Samuel Wright, and William Davison. {MWB 23:161}

6.   MARY BURLE, dau. of John (4) and Ann, was b. 22 (or 23) March 1731, and d. 22 Jan 1747. {AACR:115, 119, 139}   She left a will dated 19 Nov 1747 and proved 15 Feb 1747, leaving her estate to her bro.-in-law Nathaniel Stinchcomb, then to sister Hammutal Stinchcomb, and then to bro. Thomas Stinchcomb. The will was wit. by John Merriken, Sr., Philip Pettybone, and Samuel Fowler. {MWB 25:319}

Philip Pettibone dep. on 15 Feb 1747 that the testatrix would have been 16 years old if she had lived until next March. Pettibone had m. the testatrix' mother{MWB 25:319}

Unplaced

BURLEY, ANNA, m. Humphrey Boone in St. Margaret's Parish on 2 Feb 1743. {AACR:132}

BURLEY, JOHN, m. Margaret Mortimore in St. Margaret's Parish on 23 June 1743. {AACR:132}

---

[28] He may be the Stephen Burle who d. leaving a will in AA Co. dated 4 July 1742 and proved 6 July 1743, naming his wife Anne as extx., leaving his entire estate to her, and, after her death, to his bro. John and sister Mary Boon. {MWB 23:161}

BURLE, RACHEL, m. Matthew Hawkins in St. Margaret's Parish on 25 July 1730.{AACR:133}

BURLEY, RICHARD, m. Sarah Lindsay in St. Anne's Parish on 27 Jan 1737.{AACR:98} They were the parents of{AACR:99}: SARAH, bur. in St. Anne's Parish on 16 Feb 1741.

THE BURRAGE FAMILY

JOHN BURRAGE was transported to MD by 1649.{MPL ABH:40, 2:614, 4:625} His wife Margaret, and daus. Elizabeth and Margaret, were transported prior to 1658.{MPL 4:625}

    Burrage surv. a number of tracts of land: on 20 March 1662, 500 a. *Burrage* and 150 a. *Burrage Blossom,* and on 6 Nov 1665, 150 a. *Burrages End*{MRR:15}; on 20 Oct 1663, 300 a. *Quick Sale*{MRR:138}; and on 8 Nov 1665 he surv. 100 a. *Herring Creek Road.*{MRR:126}

    John Burrage d. by 14 June 1679 leaving an estate worth 65,850 lbs. tob., admin. by Samuel Lane and wife Margaret Lane.{INAC 6:136}

    Samuel Lane d. leaving a will dated 18 Jan 1681. In addition to his wife Margaret, sons Samuel and Dutton, dau. Sarah, and nephew Thomas Lane, he named sons-in-law Samuel Smith and Francis Hutchins, and a dau. Grace Burridge.{MWB 2:185}

    Nathan Smith, of AA Co., made a will on 15 April 1684, in which he named his wife Margaret, and mentioned land which his wife inherited as an heir of John Burridge.{MWB 4:50}

    John Burrage and wife Margaret were the parents of{AALR WT#2:276}: ELIZABETH, b. outside of MD, m. by 1708, Francis Hutchins of CV Co., who was dec. by that time{AALR IH#3:85}; MARGARET, b. outside of MD, m. 1st, by 15 April 1684, Nathan Smith, and 2nd, by 25 March 1684, Thomas Tench;[29] and GRACE, b. in MD, m. by 5 March 1688, Benjamin Scrivener.{AALR IH#3:76-78}

Unplaced

BURRAGE, JOHN, on 3 Oct 1696 was paid out of the estate of Samuel Raniger of AA Co.{INAC 14:61} He may be the John Burridge who was bur. in All Hallows Parish on 20 May 1697.{AACR:7}

BURRIDGE, JOHN, of Lynn Regis, County of Dorset, on 11 Feb 1713, conv. to Richard Bennett 1,000 a. *Lyford* in TA Co., formerly in tenure of

---

[29] On the latter date, she made a will leaving *Burridge Blossom* to her son Nathan Smith.{MWB 7:16} Margaret and Nathan Smith had one dau.: Elizabeth, m. James Rigby.

Joseph Gundrey, who purchased it from George Yate. The tract had been granted to Yate on 10 April 1666.{QALR ETA:210}

THE CARPENTER FAMILY

1.   (N) CARPENTER was the father of at least three children{PCLR EI#9B:122}: JOHN; THOMAS; and DOROTHY.

2.   JOHN CARPENTER, son of (N), and bro. of Thomas and Dorothy, d. intestate in Annapolis by Feb 1749.
    On 3 July 1717, John Carpenter, of Annapolis, merchant, with consent of wife Elizabeth, sold to Jane Burnell, part of a lot where Carpenter was now living.{AALR IB#2:272}
    In Feb 1749, limited administration was granted to William Hunt, attorney for the relict, Elizabeth Carpenter.{AWAP:52}
    The inventory of Capt. John Carpenter, of AA Co., was taken 9 Sep 1749 by Michael Macnemara and Jonas Green, and valued at £860.19.10. George Johnson and Robert Swan signed as creditors. The admx., Elizabeth Plater, the late widow, filed the inventory on 12 Oct 1749.{MINV 41:152}
    John Carpenter left a widow Elizabeth, but no children.

3.   THOMAS CARPENTER, of Alphington, County Devon, son of (N) and bro. of John and Dorothy, d. before 3 May 1749, leaving two daus., Mary and Dorothy, who, with their spouses, on the above mentioned date, gave power of attorney to Brian Philpot.{PCLR EI#9B:120}
    He is probably the Thomas Carpenter, of County Devon, mariner, who, in 1697, was granted power of attorney by Henry Arthur and Daniel Ivy, English merchants, to be their agent in VA and MD.{AALR WT#2:119-121}
    In 1703, Thomas Carpenter surv. 400 a. *George's Park.* As Thomas Carpenter, of AA Co., merchant, he sold the land to George Miller, of AA Co., on 10 Feb 1703.{BALR TR#A:309} He returned to Alphington by 9 Jan 1735 when, as "Thomas Carpenter of Alphington, near Exeter, formerly of MD," he sold 300 a. *Hellmore* and 170 a. *Hellmore's Addition* to John Cockey.{BALR HWS#M:420}
    Thomas m. Dorothy Bulford on 6 Sep 1675 at Alphington, County Devon.{IGI} He was the father of the following children, all bapt. at Alphington{IGI}: ANN, bapt. 13 Nov 1685; MARY, m. on 7 April 1741, at Kenn, Devon, Joseph Elliott, of Exeter, Devon, leather dresser; FRANCIS, bapt. 17 Oct 1688; DOROTHY, bapt. 17 Oct 1688, m. on 9 Nov 1742 at Alphington, John Burnett, of Alphington, serge maker; and RICHARD, bapt. 6 Sep 1691.

92

4.   DOROTHY CARPENTER, dau. of (N), and sister of John and Thomas, m. on 7 Feb 1708 at Heavitree, Devon, Tristram Radcliffe, of Devon.{IGI} She had at least one dau.: ANN.{PCLR EI#9B:122}

THE CHIFFIN FAMILY

1.   WILLIAM CHIFFIN m. Rachel Mariarte (widow) on 21 May 1719 in All Hallows Parish, AA Co.{AACR:199}
       On 25 April 1741, Rachel Chiffin and John Mariarte signed the inventory of Edward Mariarte, shipwright, as next of kin.{MINV 26:37} On 17 March 1741, Rachel and Eleanor Chiffin signed the inventory of John Mariarte, of AA Co., as next of kin.{MINV 26:481}
       William and Rachel were the parents of{AACR:34}: WILLIAM; and ELEANOR, b. 2 May 1720 in All Hallows Parish, AA Co. She seems to have m. 1st, after 1741, Samuel Lockwood, and 2nd, William Reed.

2.   WILLIAM CHIFFIN, of AA Co., son of William and Rachel, d. by Feb 1768.
       On 24 Feb 1768, his estate was inv. by Lewis Lee and John Ijams, and valued at £109.17.8. James Dick and Ann Caton signed as creditors, and Eleanor Reed and William Lockwood signed as kin. John Reed was the admin.{MINV 96:33}
       The balance of William Chiffin's estate, totalling £41.11.3, was dist. on 27 July 1769 by John Reed, admin., with Robert Welsh and Edward Lee as sureties. The distribution was made equally to the dec.'s half-sisters, Margaret Stockett and Rachel Covington, and to his whole sister, Eleanor Reed.{BFD 5:203}

THE NEAL CLARKE FAMILY

1.   NEALE CLARKE, progenitor, was transported to MD c1649, and d. by July 1678.{MPL 2:608} He m. Rachel, d. after 1724, dau. of Richard and Rachel (Robins) Beard. She m. 2nd, John Stimpson, d. by 1692; 3rd, Robert Proctor, d. by 1695; 4th Richard Kilburne, d. by 1698; and 5th Thomas Freeborne.{BDML}
       In 1674, George Puddington mentioned the children of his "grandson" Neale Clarke.{MWB 2:6}
       Neal Clarke d. leaving a will dated 26 Sep 1675 and proved 3 July 1678. In it he named his wife Rachel, and sons Samuel and Richard (who were to be of age at 18). He mentioned his three daus. who were to have his lands if his sons s.p. His will was wit. by Richard Sidebottom and George Ardes.{MWB 5:71}

Sometime in late 1675 or early 1676, the administration account of Neale Clarke of AA Co. was filed. An inventory worth 30,309 lbs. of tob. was listed. John Stimson, admin., filed the account. {INAC 4:249} Another account was filed on 6 Dec 1677 by the extx. Rachel Stimson, widow of the dec., now wife of John Stimson. {INAC 5:58}

Rachel Beard Clarke m. 2nd, John Stimson or Stinson, of AA Co. On 11 Aug 1685, Rachel Stimson released her dower to 250 a. being sold by John Stimson to Richard Rawlins of AA Co. {AALR IH#2:125}

John Stimson d. leaving a will dated 22 Oct 1688 and proved 23 Jan 1688/9. He left his lands to his son John, Rachel, and Comfort. John was to be of age at 18, and daus. at age 17. If his children s.p., lands were to pass to Rachel Robinson and Ruth Clarke (daus. of his wife by her first husband). Jos. Smith, Ellinor Vaux, and Jno. Gartrell were wits. {MWB 6:49}

On 10 Sep 1694, Robert Proctor, of AA Co., innholder, and Rachel, his wife, conv. land to Andrew Norwood. Both Proctors made their marks as "RP." {AALR IH#1:266}

On 20 Feb 1694/5, Mrs. Rachel Proctor signed her name to a deed originally made on 9 Aug 1687 when Jno. Moriton sold land to her then husband John Stimpson. Col. Charles Greenberry, who m. Rachel, one of the daus. and coheirs of Thomas Stimson, requested that the deed be recorded. {AALR IH#3:2}

On 4 March 1700/1, Rachel Killburn, of the Town and Port of Annapolis, made deeds of gift in which she named her daus. Rachel Greenbury, Comfort Simpson, and Ruth Williams, grandchildren Joseph Williams and Rachel Clark, son-in-law William Kilburne, and dau.-in-law Elizabeth Kilburne. {AALR WT#1: 118} Elsewhere, these gifts are recorded in the form of a will dated 4 March 1700/1 and proved 13 Sep 1701. She disposed of a great deal of personal property. {AALR WT#1:197}

About 1727 (or 1707?), Rachel Freeborn, of AA Co., age 80 years or thereabouts, stated that about 56 years earlier there came into this province Alice Skinner, of the County of Devon, and a near relation, Mary Skinner. They came to her at the insistence and request of the deponent's grandmother, a certain Jane Puddington who, before her marriage to sd. Puddington, was the widow and relict of a certain Edward Roberts [sic]. {H}

On 6 Jan 1715, she conv. to her dau. Rachel Edney, formerly Rachel Robinson, for natural affection and motherly love, a negro man. {AALR IB#2:262}

Rachel Freeborn was still alive on 3 March 1716, when she conv. property to Charles Carroll of Annapolis. {AALR IB#2:364} No will, inventory, or administration account of the estate of Rachel Freeborn has been found.

Neal and Rachel (Beard) Clarke were the parents of: SAMUEL; RICHARD; RACHEL, m. 1st, by 1688, Thomas Robinson, and 2nd, by 6

Jan 1715, (Robert?) Edney; RUTH, unm. in 1688; and (N), dau., may have d. by 1688.

2.   RICHARD CLARKE, son of Neale (1) and Rachel, d. by 21 Aug 1705. At the time of his death, he owned *Clark's Inheritance*.{AALR WT#2:247}

On 2 Aug 1703, Richard Clarke mortgaged to Charles Carroll and Micajah Perry, 400 a. *Charles' Inheritance*.{AALR WT#2:118}

Richard m. Elizabeth (N). They were the parents of{AACR:3, 4, 6, 12, 14, 17, 22}: NEAL, b. 11 April 1695, bapt. 24 Feb 1701, and bur. 17 Jan 1707 in All Hallows Parish; RACHEL, b. 15 Aug 1697, bapt. 24 Feb 1701; ELIZABETH, b. 10 May 1700, bapt. 24 Feb 1701/2; RICHARD, b. 12 Feb, bur. 24 Feb 1701; and MARGARET, b. 7 Nov [1703].[30]

3.   NEAL CLARKE, was b. c1664/7. His father has not been identified, but he was probably a relative of Richard (2). He gave his age as c49, when he dep. on 11 Sep 1716 concerning the boundaries of *White Hall*.{MCHR CL:304} In 1720, he gave his age as c56, when he dep. in PG Co. concerning the tract *Ralpho*.{MCHR CL:612} In 1724, he gave his age as 60. {PGLR I:590}

He m. 1st, by Jan 1687, Ann (N). On 30 Jan 1687, Neale Clarke, with the consent of his wife Ann, conv. 60 a. *Clark's Luck* to William Griffith.{AALR IH#1:72}

Neal Clark m. 2nd, Jane Jones, on 17 Oct 1699, in All Hallows Parish.{AACR:9} William Jones, of AA Co., made his will on 31 May 1705, naming several children, including Jane, wife of Neal Clarke.{MWB 3:489}

Neal Clark patented three tracts of land: 165 a. *Clarke's Enlargement* on 20 June 1686; 60 a. *Clarke's Luck,* on 14 Oct 1684; and 333 a. *Turkey Island,* on 26 March 1696.{MPL 25:116, 274, 32:415, 33:438, 34:131, and 30:350}

On 21 Aug 1705, Neal Clark, of PG Co., and Thomas Robinson, of AA Co., with consent of Clark's wife Jane and Robinson's wife Rachel, conv. 400 a. *Clark's Inheritance,* formerly in occupation of Richard Clark, to John Brice.{AALR WT#2:247} On 7 Nov 1705, Neal Clark of AA Co., with consent of his wife Jane, conv. to John Mobberly, Sr., 200 a. part of *Neal's Delight,* now called *Mobberly's Purchase*.{AALR IB#2:250}

Neal was the father of{AACR:199}: THOMAS, b. c1688/9; NEAL, b. c1715; and ANN, bapt. in All Hallows Parish, 16 Feb 1718.

---

[30] On 12 May 1705, Aaron Rawlings, of AA Co., merchant, conv. a considerable amount of household furnishings to Margaret Clark, dau. of Richard and Elizabeth Clarke.{AALR WT#2:204}

4. THOMAS CLARK, son of Neal (3), was b. c1688/9. He gave his age as 36 in 1724.{PGLR I:88} He gave his age as 37 in 1726. In one deposition he named his father Neal Clark, and in another he mentioned Richard Clark, bro. of Neal, who bounded some land.{AALC IB#1:7, 20, 12}

5. NEAL CLARK, possibly son of Neal (3), was b. c1715. In 1753 he gave his age as 38.{AALC IB#1:387} As Neal Clark, age 63 or 64 in 1773, he mentioned his bro. Thomas Clark.{AALC 3:292-293}

THE CONANT FAMILY

1. ROBERT CONANT d. by May 1687. He m. probably 1st, Abigail (N), who was brought to MD by him, and 2nd, Lydia (N), who survived him.

Robert Conant was transported to MD by 1664.{MPL 7:469} Earlier, Robert Conant, of AA Co., immigrated c1663 and brought his wife Abigail, daus. Ann, Margaret, and Martha, and nine other persons. {MPL WC#2:50, 57, 89, 98}

He was in AA Co. by 23 July 1674 when George, John, and Robert Wells, Gentlemen, deeded part of *West Wells* to him.{AALR PK:25} On 13 Jan 1680, he sold 100 a. of *Herring Creek* to Leonard Coates.{AALR WT#1:254} On 26 Sep 1681, Coates sold 60 a. of *Broughton Ashley* to Robert Conant.{AALR WT#2:667}

On 17 July 1680, he patented 25 a. *Conant's Chance.*{MPL 28:19} On 9 Nov 1687, Lidia Conant wit. the will of Francis Holland of Herring Creek.{MWB 4:293}

On 7 Feb 1675, he wit. the will of James Ogdon.{MWB 5:104} He may be the "Roger Conants" who appraised the estate of Jery Sudenant on 22 April 1676.{INAC 2:218}

The estate of Robert Conant, planter, was appraised on 3 May 1687 by John Sollers and Robert Gover, and valued his personal property at £293.8.3. Some property at the house of Lydia Conant, the widow, was mentioned.{INAC 9:282} Another inventory was taken on 13 Sep 1688; no value was given.{INAC 10:92} Lydia Conant, admx., filed an administration account on 5 Oct 1688.{INAC 10:164}

Robert Conant d. leaving at least one son and probably three daus.: ROBERT; and (probably) ANN; (probably) MARGARET; and (probably) MARTHA.

2. ROBERT CONANT, son of Robert, d. by June 1715. On 9 May 1705, he m. Sophia Herrington in St. James Parish.{AACR:155}

On 12 April 1708, Robert Conant, planter, conv. 50 a. of *West Wells* to John Chew. Sophia Conant consented.{AALR PK:25} On 15 Oct

96

1708, he conv. 60 a. *Broughton Ashley* to William Holland. {AALR WT#2:667}
On 25 Nov 1712, he conv. 60 a. of *West Wells* to George Anderson.
Again Sophia consented. {AALR IB#2:31}
    On 11 June 1715, Richard Tucker and John Walter appraised
Conant's personal estate at £58.0.0. John Chew and Jean Macclaning
signed that they approved the inventory. {INAC 36B:171}
    Sophia Conant, admx., filed an administration account of her
husband's estate on 18 Oct 1717. {INAC 37B:82}
    Sophia probably m. 2nd, John Mackdannan, of AA Co., whose
will dated 2 June 1746 named his wife Sophia, son-in-law Charles
Conant, and Charles' three daus. {MWB 24:438}
    Robert and Sophia (Herrington) Conant were the parents of the
following children, all bapt. in St. James Parish {AACR:158, 160, 163}: LYDIA,
b. 5 Feb 1705 [1705/6?], bapt. 17 Nov 1709; ROBERT, b. 7 Jan 1712,
bapt. 5 April 1713; and CHARLES, b. 11 July 1715, bapt. 3 June 1716.

3.   CHARLES CONANT, son of Robert and Sophia, was b. 11 July
1715 (a month after his father's death). He d. by 30 July 1756. He m.
Sarah, dau. of Solomon and Sarah Wooden. {MCHR 10:25}
    By 2 June 1746, he had m. and was the father of three daus.,
named in the will of his step-father, John Mackdannan.
    On 10 Jan 1751, he was named as son-in-law and exec. in the will
of Sarah Wooden, of AA Co. {MWB 28:253}
    The will of Charles Conant was written on 13 July 1756, by
Thomas Caney, schoolmaster, and proved 30 July 1756. Charles named
his son Charles and left money for his education. He also mentioned
money in the hands of Silvanus Graves, John Buchanan, and William
Perkins, merchants in London. Benjamin Carr wit. the will. {MWB 30:292}
    Charles was the father of {MWB 24:438}: HENRIETTA, not yet 16 in
1746; ELIZABETH, not yet 16 in 1746; SARAH, not yet 16 in 1746; and
CHARLES, probably b. after 1746.

THE CRANDALL FAMILY

1.   FRANCIS CRANDALL d. in AA Co. by 30 Nov 1744. He m.
Esther Hill on 25 Sep 1707 in All Hallows Parish. {AACR:24}
    Francis Crandell appeared as a servant in the May 1699 inventory
of Henry Hawkins of CH Co. {INAC 19:127}
    Francis and Esther Crandall wit. the will of William Smith on 21
March 1718/9. {MWB 15:129}
    Francis Crandall d. leaving an undated will and proved 30 Nov
1744. Son Joseph was named as exec., and all the rest of the children
were to receive personalty. {MWB 23:639-640}

Francis and Esther were the parents of the following children, b. in St. James Parish, AA Co.{AACR:164, 183}: (probably) FRANCIS; WILLIAM, bapt. 14 May 1713; JOSEPH, possibly the Joseph (N), b. 3 Sep 1713; ABEL, b. 24 Aug 1715; THOMAS, b. 11 March 1718; ESTHER, named in will as Esther Gott, m. John Gott in 1727;[31] and ANN, named in will as Ann Gott, m. (N) Gott.

2.   FRANCIS CRANDALL is placed as a son of Francis (1) and Esther (Hill), because in St. James Parish Register he is referred to as Francis, Jr.

He m. Jane Atwood on 27 Dec 1733 in St. James Parish.{AACR:168} Jane, dau. of Henry and Ann (Jane) (nee Pratt) Atwood, was b. 19 March 1720 at St. James Parish.{AACR:164} Jane, wife of Francis Crandall, was bur. 2 June 1746.{AACR:169}

Francis, son of Francis and Esther, was probably the Francis Crandall who, sometime before 22 March 1745/6, was one of the Freeholders of MD who signed a petition to Gov. Thomas Bladen asking for an increase in allowances to jurors, as the rate was much lower than the actual expenditure on such occasions.{CMSP Black Books, item 511}

Francis Crandall, of AA Co., d. by 8 Jan 1765 when his estate was inv. by Jacob Franklin and Joseph Hill. H. (N.?) Norman and Thomas Crandell signed as kin, and Samuel Harris was the admin.{MINV 97:18}

Francis and Jane were the parents of the following children, b. in St. James Parish{AACR:168, 169}: HENRY, b. 4 Aug 1735; ESTHER, b. 1 Dec 1737; ANN, b. 27 Nov 1739; THOMAS, b. 16 April 1744; and JANE PRATT, b. 18 March 1746.

3.   WILLIAM CRANDALL, son of Francis (1) and Esther (Hill), of AA Co., was bapt. 14 May 1713, and d. leaving a will dated 24 April 1774 and proved 5 Nov 1776.

William Crandall is one of the co-execs. of the estate of Edward Thusby, of AA Co., whose estate was inv. on 20 March 1751.{MINV 47:39}

In his will, cited above, he named son Adam (to have part *Grammar's Parrott* and *The Lot*); if Adam s.p., the lands were to go to his grandsons William and Thomas, son William (age 11), and dau. Elizabeth Crandall.{MWB 41:153}

The estate of William Crandall was inv. on 12 Feb 1777, and valued at £249.18.6. Sarah Smith and Abel Hill signed as kin.{MINV -- }

---

[31] John and Esther had three children, two of whom moved to Bladen Co., NC.

The estate of William Crandall was admin. 14 Aug 1778 by exec. Adam Crandall, with John Holliday and John Dove as sureties. The accounts named sons Adam and William, daus. Elizabeth, Sarah and Mary, grandson William, and grandsons William and Thomas of Thomas.{AAAD ED (1777-1799):68}

William was the father of: ADAM; WILLIAM; THOMAS; SARAH, m. Nathan Smith; ELIZABETH; and MARY.

4.   ABEL CRANDALL, son of Francis, was b. 24 Aug 1715 in St. James Parish.

Abel Crandall, of AA Co., d. by 18 Jan 1755 when his estate was inv. by James Deale and Jacob Franklin and valued at £86.10.7. Kinsey Johns signed as creditor, and Samuel Ford and Francis Crandall signed as next of kin. Joseph Crandall was the exec. or admin.{MINV 60:693}

Abel Crandall's estate was dist. on 15 June 1767 by Walter Gott, admin. de bonis non. The widow, unnamed, was to have her thirds, and the balance was to be divided among his children.{BFD 4:15}

Abel Crandall was the father of: MARGARET; ESTHER; JOSEPH; JOHN; and FRANCIS.

5.   HENRY CRANDALL, son of Francis and Jane, was b. 4 Aug 1735 in St. James Parish,{AACR:168} and d. by 27 April 1759, when the inventory of his estate (valued at £102.13.1) was filed. Jacob Franklin and Thomas Norris were appraisers. Walter Gott and Henry Darnall were creditors. Joseph Gott and Nicholas Norman signed as kin, and Sibell Crandall was the admx.{MINV 67:542}

Henry Crandall's estate was dist. on 15 Oct 1761 by Sybil Crandall, admx., with Anthony Gott and Francis Crandall as sureties. The widow received her thirds, and the balance went to Henry Attwood Crandall.{BFD 3:93}

Sibell Crandall d. by 16 June 1767, when her inventory was filed by admin. Anthony Gott. Henry Crandall was mentioned.{MINV 93:34}

Henry and Sybil Crandall were the parents of: HENRY ATTWOOD.

Unplaced

CRANDALL, JOSEPH, was b. c1720, and dep. giving his age as 69 in 1789 and as 71 in 1791.{AALC 3:409, 420}

CRANDALL, THOMAS, was b. c1744, and dep. in 1791 giving his age as 47.{AALC 3:420}

THE CROSBY FAMILY

1.   BURDEN [or BURTON] CROSBY is the first known ancestor. He was in AA Co. and d. by 25 Jan 1734/5. He m. Elizabeth, dau. of Josias Towgood.

Burden Crosby wit. several deeds in 1732. In one deed, he was described as "commander of *The George,* transporting tob. to London." {AALR IH&TI#1:401,448, 471}

On 14 Aug 1734, a citation was issued by the Prerogative Court to Elizabeth Crosby, relict of Burden Crosby, ordering her to show cause why she did not administer the estate of her husband. In Sep 1734, Elizabeth Crosby appeared before the court, bringing a letter from her father Josias Towgood, stating that Burden Crosby had d. in England, but had left a will in which he named one Mason as exec. of Crosby's effects in England, and naming Elizabeth as sole extx. of his effects in MD. Both Elizabeth and her father had written to Mason, but he had not replied, so she could not proceed with the administration of her husband's estate. {MDTP 29:438, 447}

On 19 July 1736, Lewis Welsh posted bond as admin. of Burden Crosby's estate, with Robert and James Welsh as sureties. An inventory totalling £158.12.0 was appraised on 14 Aug 1736 by Henry Austin and Samuel Griffith. Lewis Welsh filed the inventory on 25 Oct 1736. {MDTP 30:184, 230; MINV 22:33}

Welsh filed an administration account on 28 May 1744. After the debts were paid, there was a balance of £146.83. Welsh asked for time to file an additional account, but none has been found. {MDAD 20:224}

Burden and Elizabeth (Towgood) Crosby were the parents of: JOSIAS; and RICHARD, who d. in CV Co. by 1 July 1772 when Mary and Joseph Crosby signed his inventory as next of kin. {MINV 112:90}

2.   JOSIAS CROSBY, almost certainly a son of Burden [Burton] and Elizabeth (Towgood) Crosby, was alive as late as 1789.

Josias owned three tracts of land in CV Co.: *Archer Hays, Gough's Purchase,* and *Turner's Pasture.*

In 1789, he and his son Josias, Jr., admin. the estate of his son John.

Josias Crosby was the father of: JOHN, d. c1789; BURTON; and JOSIAS, Jr.

3.   JOHN CROSBY, son of Josias, d. in AA Co. by 1789. He m. Rachel, dau. of Richard Brown, by AAML dated 4 Jan 1786.

On 5 Sep 1799, his estate was dist. He d. leaving a will naming Josias Crosby, Sr., and Josias Crosby, Jr., as execs. The widow Rachel received her thirds, and the balance of the estate went to Richard Crosby. {AADI JG#1:12}

John and Rachel (Brown) Crosby had one son, named in the will of Richard Brown as a grandson: RICHARD CROSBY.

4.   BURTON CROSBY, son of Josias, served in the CV Co. Militia during the Revolutionary War, and m. Ann Childs, by AAML dated 1 Jan 1785.

5.   JOSIAS CROSBY, son of Josias, d. in CV Co. intestate in 1796. {MCHP 8086} He m. Mary Carr in St. James Parish on 17 Feb 1784.{AACR:181}

He left one dau.: ELIZABETH, d. by 1822, having m. Nathan Ward, who was also dead by 1822.

6.   RICHARD CROSBY, son of John and Rachel (Brown) Crosby, was b. by 1789, and m. 1st, by AAML dated 16 Feb 1807, Elizabeth Norman, and 2nd, by AAML 25 July 1818, Juliet Trott. He was the father of: RICHARD, b. c1833; SARAH A., b. c1834; ANNE M., b. c1836; and RACHEL, b. c1841.

Unplaced

CROSBY, ELIZABETH, m. William Allen on 15 Dec 1776 in St. James Parish.{AACR:177}

CROSBY, ELIZABETH, m. Josias Hinton on 23 Dec 1779 in St. James Parish.{AACR:178}

CROSBY, RACHEL, m. Nathaniel Deal on 10 July 1794 in St. James Parish.{AACR:182}

THE CROSS FAMILY

The name Cross has sometimes been read as Crans, and there was a Robert Crane who was living in SM Co. very early.

1.   ROBERT CROSS, of AA Co., may be related to the Robert "Crans" who was transported to MD before 1676 when he claimed land for service, but a definite connection has not been established.{MPL 15:369} Robert Cross lived in St. Margaret's, Westminster Parish, AA Co., and d. by May 1720. He m. 1st, on 20 July 1710, Ann Board (Bourd) in All Hallows Parish.{AACR:25} She was almost certainly the widow of Francis Board and a dau. of Abraham and Anna (N) Dawson, and step-dau. of Francis Mead. Ann "Craws" d. 28 July 1712, and Robert m. 2nd, Hannah Gosnell, on 28 Nov 1712.{AACR:130} She m. as her 2nd husband, by 31 Oct 1721, John Buckingham.{MDAD 4:31}

On 30 Jan 1713, John Conoway, and his wife Ann Conoway, conv. to Robert Cross 80 a., being 1/2 of *Friendship*.{AALR IB#2:179}

Francis Mead named John and James Board [not Beard] in his will. He also named his granddau., Hannah Crans. Anna (?) Mead named her grandsons John and James Board.

On 10 March 1712/3, the account of William Gosnell, of AA Co., mentioned a legatee Hannah Gosnell, wife of Robert Cross.{INAC 33B:169}

Robert Crans/Craws may be the Robert Cross, planter, who d. by 29 May 1720 when his estate was appraised by Robert Edney and (N) Robesson. John Ronel and Peter Gosnell approved the inventory. {MINV 5:91}

The estate of Robert Cross was admin. on 31 Oct 1721 by the admx. Hannah, now wife of John Buckingham. An inventory of £134.12.10 was mentioned.{MDAD 4:31} A second administration account was filed on 12 Feb 1722.{MDAD 5:4}

Robert Cross (or Crans) was the father of{AACR:100, 111, 112} (by Ann Board): HANNAH, b. 28 April 1711; (by Hannah Gosnell): WILLIAM, b. 10 Dec 1713; and ROBERT (Craws), b. 3 Sep 1719.

2.   WILLIAM CROSS, son of Robert and Hannah (Gosnell) Cross, was b. 10 Dec 1713. He m. Dorcus Croscomb on 24 Dec 1738. She may be the Dorcas Cross who m. Hancelip Nelson on 10 Aug 1746.{AACR:131, 132}

William and Dorcus were the parents of the following children, b. in St. Margaret's Parish{AACR:117, 120}: OBADIAH BUCKINGHAM, b. 22 March 1738; and CHARLES, b. 15 Aug 1743.

3.   ROBERT CROSS, son of Robert and Hannah (Gosnell) Cross, was b. 3 Sep 1719, and was living as late as 1750. He m. Jemima Gosnell on 13 March 1744 in St. Thomas Parish, BA Co.{BCF:151}

On 12 May 1744, Joseph Cornelius conv. 100 a. *Curgafurgus* to Robert Cross. Robert and his wife Jemima conv. 50 a. of this land to William Mattox on 27 Oct 1749.{BALR TB#C:317, 674}

Robert and Jemima were the parents of{BCF:151}: ANN, b. 27 Nov 1748; HANNAH, b. 24 March 1754; NICODEMUS, b. 19 July 1759; BENJAMIN, b. 23 April 1760; and ANN, b. 13 Jan 1765.

THE CULLEN FAMILY

1.   JAMES CULLEN, of AA Co., d. by April 1710, leaving a widow Catherine, who m. 2nd, Thomas Brusse [or Bruff], and a son John.{AALR PK:139, IB#2:81}

It is likely he was the James Cullen, of SM Co., who was left personalty in the will, dated 5 Jan 1677, of Constantine Daniel, of SM Co.{MWB 5:325}

He was named as son-in-law and exec. in the will, made 27 March 1685, of Mark Cordea, of SM Co.{MWB 4:162} On 27 Feb 1686, Edmond Dennis, of CV Co., made his will, with James Cullen as wit.{MWB 7:41} On 5 Jan 1688, Nicholas White, of SM Co., made his will, naming James Cullen as exec.{MWB 6:48}

James Cullen, of SM Co., Gent., patented four tracts of land: 300 a. *Cullen's Lot* in BA Co., on 17 June 1683; 500 a. *Cullen's Addition* in BA Co., on 25 Sep 1683; and 381 a. *Hopewell*, also in BA Co., on 15 Jan 1687.{MPL 24:523, 25:49, 383; 32:578} The latter tract was later owned by William Bladen.{MRR:75} Cullen also patented 200 a. in AA Co. called *Beale's Gift* on 1 Nov 1701.{MPL DD#5:38, 34:354}

James and Catherine were the parents of: JOHN.

2.   JOHN CULLEN, son of James and Catherine, was living as late as April 1710.

On 17 April 1710, John Cullen, Gent., and Thomas Bruss, who m. the relict of James Cullen and mother of John Cullen, conv. a messuage of 144 square perches in Duke of Glo[uce]ster St., Annapolis, where Thomas Brusse [or Bruff] dwelt. Catherine Brusse [Bruff] released her right of dower.{AALR PK:139}

THE DAVIDSON FAMILY

Ref.: A: Margaret Wilmot Martin. *James Davidson of the 'Maryland Line,' and Some of His Descendants.* The Author: 1966. B: Margaret Wilmot Martin. *Supplement to James Davidson of the 'Maryland Line,' and Some of His Descendants.* The Author: 1970.

1.   JAMES DAVISON m. Ann, and they were the parents of the following children, whose births are recorded in All Hallows Parish, AA Co.{A; AACR:38, 41, 43}: JOHN, b. 24 Feb 1723/4, bapt. 12 --- 1724; THOMAS, bapt. 2 Feb 1726; and JAMES, b. 15 June 1729.

2.   JOHN DAVISON, son of James and Ann (1), was b. 24 Feb 1723/4. He is probably the John Davison who m. Eleanor Strachen on 14 Feb 1769 in All Hallows Parish.{AACR:58}

John and Eleanor had at least one dau.: ELEANOR, m. Thomas Harris, Jr. (son of Thomas and Ann), on 1 Nov 1795 in All Hallows Parish.{AACR:106}

3.   THOMAS DAVISON, son of James (1) and Ann, was bapt. 2 Feb 1726 in All Hallows Parish, AA Co. He m. Hannah (N) by whom he had the following children, whose births are recorded in All Hallows Parish {A; AACR:56, 57}: ANN, b. 7 Feb 1758; JAMES, b. 5 Nov 1760; MARY, b. 22 Nov 1763; and THOMAS, b. 12 Aug 1766.

4.   JAMES DAVISON, son of James (1) and Ann, was b. 15 June 1729. He m. Elizabeth (N). Elizabeth, wife of James, was bur. 4 Nov 1769.

James and Elizabeth were the parents of the following children, all b. in All Hallows Parish{AACR:55, 56, 57, 58}: RUTH, b. 27 Feb 1758; JOHN, b. 28 Feb 1762; SARAH, b. 15 April 1766, bapt. 25 May 1766; and JAMES, b. 30 April 1769, bapt. 16 May 1769.

5.   JAMES DAVIDSON, son of Thomas (2) and Hannah, was b. in All Hallows Parish on 5 Nov 1760. (A few sources say he was b. in Scotland, but these statements seem to have been made several generations after his life. However, it seems most unlikely that two men, with the same name and living in the same county would have been b. on the same day, or in the same county, one in Scotland.) James d. in AA Co. on 28 Nov 1841. He m. Amelia Reed, b. 27 Aug 1766, d. 9 Sep 1838, dau. of John and Eleanor (Chiffin) Reed.

James Davidson enlisted 20 April 1778 and served as a private in the 1st MD Regiment. He was captured 25 Jan 1780 at Elizabethtown, NJ, and spent 11 months in prison. He appears to have re-enlisted as a substitute and was wounded at the Siege of Yorktown, where he remained until he was able to return home. His service ended 15 Nov 1783 (his Revolutionary War Pension Application #S-8305).{A}

Martin, in 1966, discussed the confusion arising over the fact that there may have been several individuals of the same name living in AA and BA Cos. at the same time.

Davidson's tombstone reads: "Sacred to the memory of James Davidson, b. Nov 5, in the year of Our Lord 1760 and departed this life 28 Nov 1841, age 81 years and 25 days. He fought for his country in the Revolutionary War ..."

The children of James and Amelia (Reed) Davidson were{B:4}: ELEANOR, b. 22 Oct 1787, m. William Thumblert; PRISCILLA, b. 1790, d. 3 Oct 1834; JAMES, b. 1791, d. 15 Sep 1846, age 55; NELSON, b. 16 Feb 1794, d. 1856, m. Delia Raymond; JOHN, b. 1 Oct 1796, d. 1883, m. Mary Ann Upperman; THOMAS, b. 1800, d. 1868, m. Jane Welsh; MARGARET, b. 1804, d. 1853, m. Lewis J. Brooks; MATILDA (twin) b. 25 Nov 1807, d. 1877, m. John Wilson Iglehart; PERMELIA REED (twin) b. 25 Nov 1807, d. 1857, m. Rev. Samuel Kepler.

THE DAWSON FAMILY

1.   ABRAHAM DAWSON was transported into MD sometime between 1649 and 1662. He claimed land for service in 1663.{MPL 5:87, 487}

He was in AA Co. by 10 Jan 1674, when he and William Crouch appraised the estate of James Warner.{INAC 1:169}

He d. leaving a will dated 19 March 1675 and proved 27 March 1675. His wife was to be the extx., and he named the children listed below. Jno. Butter and Simon Herring were wits.{MWB 5:237}

The estate of Abraham Dawson was appraised by William Hopkins and Matthew Howard on 9 April 1677, and valued at 9,823 lbs. of tob.{INAC 4:138}

Abraham Dawson was the father of: THOMAS; ELIZA; HANNAH [Could she be the Ann who m. 1st, Francis Board, and 2nd, Robert Crans?]; SARAH; and (possibly) MARY,[32] m., by 1700, Henry Wright, and had a son, Dawson Wright.

2.   THOMAS DAWSON, of St. Margaret's, Westminster Parish, AA Co., possibly son of Abraham, m. Sarah Fuller on 2 Jan 1700 in St. Margaret's Parish.{AACR:129} Sarah was the widow of Edward Fuller, whose dau. Mary patented 80 a. *Fuller's Luck* on 10 Oct 1708.{MPL DD#5:517, PL#3:49}

On 25 May 1697, he was mentioned in the administration account of John Cooley of AA Co.{INAC 14:130} On 3 July 1707, Dawson and William Pennington appraised the estate of Joseph Conaway, of AA Co. {INAC 27:7}

On 18 April 1702, William Taylard sold to Thomas Dawson 100 a. *Swan Neck.* The deed mentioned 50 a. of the tract in possession of Francis Mead.{AALR WT#1:281}

Thomas Dawson and wife Sarah, of AA Co., on 28 July 1712, conv. to William Pennington 64 a. *Dawson's Chance.*{AALR PK:505}

On 4 Jan 1716, Francis Mead named him as a son-in-law in his will.{MWB 14:441}

Thomas and Sarah were the parents of the following children, b. in St. Margaret's Parish{AACR:107, 108}: ABRAHAM, b. 10 April 1702; THOMAS (twin) b. 31 Aug 1705; and ANN (twin) b. 31 Aug 1705.

---

[32] She would have been b. after her father's will was written. Abraham may not have even known his wife was pregnant or he would have provided for "the child my wife is carrying."

THE DISNEY FAMILY

This account was based on "The Disney Family," by the compiler, which was published in the *BMGS* 35 (3) 425-436. Since that time, additional material has come to light. The compiler is especially indebted to Alecia Tipton and Noreen Mack, both of Redding, CA, for generously sharing their research notes on The Disney family.

THE WILLIAM DISNEY FAMILY

1.   WILLIAM DISNEY, progenitor, d. in AA Co., MD, by June 1721. William m. 1st, Sarah (N), by whom he had two children, and 2nd, Mary (N), who m. 2nd, Francis Westley on 26 April 1722 in All Hallows Parish. She m. 3rd, Thomas Wells, in Oct 1723 in All Hallows.{AACR:37}[33]
Mary, wife of William Disney, was bapt. 21 Dec 1705.{AACR: 20}
     Alecia Tipton suggests that Sarah, first wife of William Disney, may have been Sarah, widow of Francis Watts. She also suggests that William's 2nd wife, Mary, may have been a dau. of Richard Snowden.
     William may be the William Disney who was transported into MD c1677.{MPL 15:430} He was in AA Co. by 10 Jan 1691, when he was listed as one of the debtors in the inventory of Capt. Nicholas Gassaway. {INAC 11A:36} On 6 Nov 1699, Disney and John Jacob appraised the estate of Simon Fine.{INAC 19 1/2 A:44}
     On 17 March 1711, William Disney, of All Hallows Parish, AA Co., conv. to Henry Leek, of the same parish, carpenter, part of 100 a. where Disney now lives, part of *Town Hill,* formerly conv. by Richard Snowden, Jr. William's wife Mary consented.{AALR PK:449}
     On 12 May 1718, William Disney and Stephen Warman signed the inventory of George Miller, of AA Co., as next of kin.{MINV 1:261}
     William Disney's will, dated 23 April 1721 and proved 20 June 1721, left his entire personal estate to his wife, who was also to have the use of the dwell. plant. for life. After her death, the dwell. plant. was to go to son James, who was also left 10 s. Sons Thomas, Snowden, and Richard, and dau. Eliza. were also left 10 s. each. No exec. was named. The will was wit. by Francis Westly and Thomas Lewis.{MWB 16:460}
     The inventory of William Disney's estate was appraised c1721 by James Lewur [Lewis?] and William Brewer and valued at £45.4.5. Francis Westley and Samuel Peele signed as creditors, and Thomas Disney and James Disney signed as kin.{MINV 7:270}

---

[33] Alecia Tipton states that the 1721 date for Thomas Wells' marriage to Mary Disney is in error.

Mary Disney, extx., admin. the estate of William Disney on 2 Oct 1722.{MDAD 4:158}

William had the following children, whose births were recorded at All Hallows Parish Register, AA Co.{AACR:1, 2, 5, 9, 10, 15, 16, 20, 23, 29, 30, 32, 33, 36} : (the two children by Sarah were not named in his will): MARGARET, b. 28 Dec 1686, m. John Stiffen, 24 April 1701; WILLIAM, b. 11 Aug 1693, d. Sep 1699; (by Mary): JAMES (named in will), b. 14 Feb 1695; THOMAS (in will), b. 4 May 1698, bapt. 5 June 1698, bur. 5 May 1722; SARAH, b. 10 July 1700, bapt. 4 Aug 1700 (probably the unnamed dau. who was bur. 10 Jan 1709); ELIZABETH, b. 12 Jan 1702 (in her father's will), probably the Elizabeth who m. John Watts, 5 June 1723; WILLIAM, bapt. 10 Dec 1704, bur. 16 Dec 1704; MARY, bapt. 1705 in All Hallows Parish; SNOWDEN, b. 3 March 1706, bapt. 9 April 1707, living in 1732; MARTHA, bapt. 11 Nov 1711; MARY, b. 17 May 1714, bapt. 5 Nov 1714; and RICHARD (in father's will), b. 8 March 1715, bapt. 20 March 1716 or 29 March 1717.

2.   JAMES DISNEY, son of William (1), was b. 14 Feb 1695, and d. in 1731. James Disney was bur. 14 Jan 1731. He m. Anne Ward, b. 5 Dec 1691,{AACR:1} dau. of Robert and Susanna Ward. Ann Ward Disney was bur. 26 March 1733.{AACR:45, 47}

The estate of James Disney was appraised on 21 April 1732 by William Brewer and Robert Welch and valued at £54.10.0. Richard Hill and Samuel Peele signed as creditors, and Snowden Disney and Richard Disney signed as kin. Anne Disney, the admx., filed the inventory on 10 June 1732.{MINV 16:643}

The estate of James Disney was admin. on 15 June 1737 by John Watkins, admin. of Ann Disney, the original admin.{MDAD 15:355}

Anne Disney d. by 10 April 1733 when her estate was appraised by William Sellman and Robert Welch, who valued her property at £44.17.5. Thomas Wells and Richard Hill signed as creditors, and Samuel Ward and Elizabeth Barton signed as kin. [These were Ann Ward's bro. and sister]. John Watkins, admin., filed the inventory on 13 June 1733.{MINV 18:148} In 1737, her estate was admin. by John Watkins.

James and Anne had the following children, b. in All Hallows Parish{AACR:32, 47, 195, 200}: WILLIAM, bapt. 28 Oct 1716; JAMES, bapt. 19 July 1719; THOMAS, b. 16 June 1721, bapt. 25 July 1721, and bur. 5 Nov 1733; and SARAH, b. 19 April 1724.

3.   THOMAS DISNEY, son of William (1), is probably the Thomas who m. 1st, by 1719, Jane Aldridge, and 2nd, Ann Leffels by banns on 29 June 1721. He was bur. 5 May 1722. Anne Leffels Disney may have m. 2nd, William Spicer on 28 Jan 1724.{AACR:33, 39}

Thomas Disney was the father of (by Jane): MARY, bapt. 7 May 1719, and bur. 4 Oct 1719{AACR:200}; and (by Anne): MARY, b. 2 Aug 1722, bapt. 23 Aug 1722.{AACR:34}

4.   RICHARD DISNEY, son of William (1) and Mary, was b. 8 March 1715/6 in AA Co., and d. 25 May 1798. He m. 1st, Sarah (possibly Burgess), and 2nd, on 11 Feb 1752, in All Hallows Parish, Elizabeth Gwinn.{AACR:53}

He gave his age as 33 in 1749. In 1749, he gave his age as 41 [sic] and mentioned his mother, Mary Disney, dec.{AALC 2:325, 326-7} Richard Disney, age c54, dep. again in 1770.{AAEJ: Anderson, James}

About 1774. Richard Disney purchased 100 a. *Duvall's Delight* from Charles Pickett, heir of William Pickett.{AALR IB#5:76}

Richard Disney d. leaving a will dated 1796 and proved 7 April 1798. He named his sons William and Richard as execs., left 100 a. *Duvall's Delight* to his son Richard, provided Richard would provide for the testator's dau. Ann{AAWB JG#2 (37):28}

The final administration account for Richard Disney was filed on 25 April 1800 by Richard Disney. The inventory, included in the account, totalled £47.1.4.{AAAD JG#3:252}

Richard was the father of six children by his first wife, and three by his second. His children were{AACR:49, 54}: (by Sarah): EDWARD, b. 22 June 1740, m. 1st, Susanna (N), and 2nd, Ann Phelps; MARY, b. 17 May 1742;[34] BENJAMIN, b. 13 March 1744; THOMAS, b. 5 Feb 1746; ELIZABETH, b. 25 Jan 1747/8; WILLIAM, b. 22 April 1750; (by Elizabeth): RICHARD, b. 17 March 1753, m. Ariana Porter; JAMES, b. 18 May 1755, m. Rachel Pickett, dau. of William and Rachel (Gaither) Pickett; and ANNE.

5.   SNOWDEN DISNEY, son of William (1) and Mary, was b. 3 March 1706 and bapt. 9 April 1707. He was living as late as 1732. {AACR:23}

Alecia Tipton suggests he may have been the father of: EZEKIEL, an adult in 1754; and AQUILA, who drowned.

6.   WILLIAM DISNEY, son of James (2), was bapt. 1716, and d. 1762. He m. Sarah Burgess, dau. of John and Jane (N) Burgess.

On 26 Sep 1738, William Disney wit. the will of widow Sarah Burgess, of AA Co.{MWB 22:268}

On 25 Nov 1755, Henry Leek, of FR Co., planter, conv. to William Disney, turner, part of *Town Hill* which William Disney,

---

[34] Mary may have m. John Watts on 19 Sep 1764 and had a son RICHARD Watts, b. 22 Aug 1756.{AACR:56}

grandfather of the grantee, sold to Henry Leeke, father of the grantor. {AALR RB#3, part 2:445}

William was one of the appraisers of the estate of Robert Welsh, of AA Co., on 11 May 1762. {MINV 78:139}

William Disney d. by 9 June 1762, when his estate was inv. by Robert Welsh and John James, Jr., and valued at £2320.6.1. Joseph Mayo and James Dick signed as creditors, and Richard Disney and Joseph Lecke signed as kin. The inventory was filed 23 April 1763 by Mr. James Disney and Sarah Disney, the execs. {MINV 80:341}

On 21 March 1765, Sarah and James Disney, execs., advertised they would sell 100 a. called *Town Hill*. {AMG 21 March 1765}

An additional inventory was filed on 6 April 1767 when his estate was inv. again by Robert Welsh and John Ijams, Jr., and valued at £82.2.6. James Dick and Joseph Mayo signed as creditors. Richard Disney and Edward Disney signed as next of kin. The inventory was filed 12 Aug 1767 by Sarah Disney and James Disney, the surviving execs. Sarah Disney filed a list of debts on the same day. {MINV 95:148, 149}

William and Sarah (Burgess) Disney were the parents of the following children, whose births were recorded in All Hallows Parish, AA Co. {AACR: 53, 54, 55}: JAMES, b. 7 March 1745/6, d. by 16 Feb 1837;[35] ANN, b. 28 Sep 1749; WILLIAM, b. 23 Jan 1750/1; JANE, b. 10 Jan 1753, d. Sep 1824; EZEKIEL, b. 23 Dec 1755; and SARAH, b. 23 May 1757.

7.   JAMES DISNEY, son of James (2), was b. 1719, and d. 1778. He m. Rachel, dau. of Samuel and Elizabeth (Durham) Burgess. Rachel d. 1789.

On 2 Nov 1748, James Disney, millwright, of AA Co., mortgaged to Samuel Preston Moore, and Mordecai, Richard, Thomas and Charles Moore, assorted personalty. {AALR RB#3:72}

He advertised in the *Maryland Gazette* in Sep 1760 that he would grind wheat "for toll or otherwise" at the windmill in Annapolis, which was in very good working order. {AMG 25 Sep 1760}

James Disney d. leaving a will dated 27 May 1778 and proved 25 July 1778, in which he appointed his wife Rachel extx., and named children: Rachel, Anne, James, and Samuel Burgess Disney. {AA Orig. Wills, Box d, folder 37, MSA; AAWB EV#1:70}

Rachel Disney admin. the estate in 1778, and stated that she had six children living with the accountant. Thomas Disney and James Disney were named. {AAAD ED:123}

Rachel Disney filed the final account on 5 Oct 1779, and William Faris and Richard Burgess were mentioned as securities. The estate was dist. to the widow and six children. Rachel Disney's legacy was mentioned, and a negro had by Thomas and James Disney. {AAAD ED:139}

---

[35] See his obituary in the Annapolis *Maryland Gazette,* 16 Feb 1837.

James and Rachel were the parents of the following children, whose births are recorded in All Hallows Parish Register{AACR:53, 55, 56; also Disney entries in the IGI}: ANN, b. 6 Nov 1748; JAMES, b. 4 Oct 1751, bapt. 9 Feb 1752, d. 1803, m. Mary (Ward), widow of Richard Weems,[36] 22 March 1783{AACR:170, 180}; RACHEL; ELIZABETH, b. 28 Feb 1756, m. Benjamin Nicholson c11 May 1784 in AA Co.; SARAH, b. 10 Aug 1760, m. Col. Nicholas Watkins, 1 Feb 1782 in AA Co., MD; and SAMUEL BURGESS, b. 23 Dec 1762, bapt. 10 July 1763.

8.   EDWARD DISNEY, son of Richard (4) and Sarah, was b. 22 June 1740, and d. by Dec 1784. He m. 1st, Susannah (N), and 2nd, on 4 Nov 1778, Ann Phelps.
    The inventory of Edward Disney's estate was taken 4 Dec 1784 by Richard Disney, admin.
    By Susanna, he was the father of{AACR:58}: RICHARD, b. 18 Aug 1760; JOHN, b. 14 Oct 1762; (probably) MORDECAI, b. 1760/5, m. Amelia Porter; EDWARD, b. c1770/4, d. 19 May 1807, m., by AAML 1 Dec 1795, Margaret Watkins.

9.   THOMAS DISNEY, son of Richard (4) and Sarah, was b. 5 Feb 1746, and d. c1813 in AA Co. He m. Ann (N). According to research by Alecia Tipton, Thomas and Ann were the parents of: WILLIAM, b. 1 Oct 1771; THOMAS M., b. 1773; RICHARD, b. 1779; (N), son, b. c1784-1800; and three daus.

10.   WILLIAM DISNEY, son of Richard (4) and Sarah, was b. 22 April 1750.
    He may be the William Disney of Richard mentioned in the 1811 list of debts of Edward Disney.{AA Co. Testamentary Papers, Box 100, folder 52, MSA} According to research by Alecia Tipton, he was alive in 1811 while the William who moved to BA Co. d. by 1810.
    According to Alecia Tipton, he was the father of: WILLIAM, b. 1782 in AA Co., MD, d. by July 1854, m. 1st, Caroline (N), and 2nd, Anna Maria Barry, and had several children.

---

[36] Richard Weems m. Mary Ward on 7 April 1768. They had a number of children.{AACR:172}

11.   RICHARD DISNEY, son of Richard (4) and Elizabeth (Gwinn), was b. 17 March 1753, and d. 1826. He m., by AAML dated 21 Aug 1784, Ariana Porter, dau. of John Porter.

John Porter d. leaving a will dated 1791 naming a grandson Mordecai Disney.{AAWB 37:72} When his estate was dist. on 16 July 1800 by exec. Richard Porter, half of the balance went to Arry [Ariana] Disney and half to Mordecai Disney.{AADI JG#2:45}

He also raised Mordecai Disney, who was either his nephew, or the nephew of his wife Ariana.

Richard Disney d. leaving a will dated 7 Sep 1822 and proved 17 Jan 1826, naming wife Airy, and children oldest son Richard, Mary Ann, Amelia Maria, Charlotte L., Benjamin, and Elizabeth Gaither.{AAWB JG (39):274}

Richard and Ariana were the parents of{Letter to the compiler from Doris Howard}: RICHARD, b. c1791; AMELIA MARIA, b. c1792;[37] ELIZABETH, m. Dennis Gaither on 14 Dec 1810 in AA Co.; BENJAMIN FRANKLIN, b. c1808, m. Sarah Ann Anderson, dau. of Samuel and Elizabeth; and CHARLOTTE LUCRETIA, b. c1805 (in 1850 she was living in HO Co. with her bro. Benjamin); and MARY ANN, bapt. 29 Aug 1802 in St. Paul's Parish, BA Co., m. on 8 May 1821, in AA Co., Lloyd Disney, son of William (15) and Ruth (Spurrier). {Disney entries in the IGI}

12.   JAMES DISNEY, son of Richard (4) and Elizabeth (Gwinn), b. 18 May 1755.{AACR:54} He d. by 1828. He m. Rachel Pickett, dau. of William and Rachel (Gaither) Pickett. He and his wife were the parents of: ELIZABETH, b. c1774, m. 8 Feb 1794 in AA Co., MD, Moses Deaver; WILLIAM I., b. 1778, d. 30 March 1842 in Knox Co., OH, m. Amelia Elliott; JAMES, b. c1780, d. between 1850 and 1860 in La Grange, IN, m. 1st, (N) (N), m. 2nd, Eliza Leisure; RICHARD, d. by 1840 in Knox Co., OH, m. Regina White on 19 April 1804 in BA Co., MD; MORDECAI, b. c1770/80, m. Achsah White, by BAML, 11 Oct 1811; and (possibly) (N).

13.   JAMES DISNEY, son of William (5), was b. 7 March 1745/6. {AACR:53} He d. by 16 Feb 1834.{See his obituary in the Maryland Gazette of that date.}

The 1776 Census of All Hallows Parish shows James Disney, of William, living with one white man (himself), one white woman, two

---

[37] Doris Howard says she was b. 14 June 1814, and d. 20 July 1872 in Rising Sun, IN. In 1850, she was living in HO Co. with her bro. Benjamin. She m. in 1825 at Rising Sun, IN, Henry James. {Letters to the compiler from Doris Howard and Mrs. Jan Bell Linn of Fresno, CA}

white children, and one black man; two taxables in all. {Gaius Brumbaugh, *Maryland Records*}

14.   MORDECAI DISNEY, probably son of Edward (8) and Susanna, was b. c1760/5, m. 1st, 8 Feb 1785, Amelia Porter.

On 16 July 1800, Richard Dorsey, exec. of John Porter, dist. the balance of Porter's estate. Half was paid to Mordecai Disney, and half to Arry (Ariana?) Disney. {AADI JG#2:45}

When John Porter wrote his will, he named his dau. Ariana Disney (who m. Richard Disney, above), and grandson Mordecai Disney. The grandson was made a ward of his uncle and aunt, Richard and Ariana Disney. {Research by Alecia Tipton}

Mordecai and Amelia were the parents of: MORDECAI, b. 1786, d. 1863 at La Claire, Scott Co., IA, m. Sarah Tudor by BAML dated 13 May 1813. Mordecai Jr.'s dau., Amelia Maria, was b. 14 June 1814, d. 20 July 1872 in Rising Sun (IN?), and m. Henry James, 12 April 1836, in Hamilton, OH. Henry James was b. 17 Oct 1797 in Frederick, MD.

15.   WILLIAM DISNEY, son of Thomas (9) and Ann, was b. 1 Oct 1771, and d. 18 Feb 1846 in AA Co. On 21 Feb 1794, he m. Ruth Spurrier, b. 1 July 1774. {Disney Bible Records, in NGSQ 20}

William and Ruth purchased *Truly Friend* and *Good Luck* in AA Co. from John Chew Thomas and his wife. {AALR WSG#2:159} The land was sold in the 1840s by William's heirs.

William and Ruth (Spurrier) Disney were the parents of: THOMAS SPURRIER, b. 28 Sep 1795; LLOYD, b. 15 Oct 1797, d. 8 June 1854; ELIZER, b. 2 Oct 1799; OWEN, b. 15 Dec 1801, d. 24 March 1877, m. Sarah Bryant on 4 Aug 1831; and JAMES, b. 29 Sep 1803.

16.   THOMAS M. DISNEY, son of Thomas (9) and Ann, was b. 1773, and d. 19 Feb 1830 in DO Co., MD. He m., by AAML dated 24 April 1802, Deborah Williams, b. 1774, and d. 1834 in DO Co. Both are bur. in Cambridge Cemetery. {Research by Alecia Tipton}

Thomas and Deborah were the parents of: ELENOR ELLEN, b. 11 Jan 1803, m. 1st, March 1821, William Douglas, and 2nd, 22 July 1827, Dawson Auld; EDWARD, b. 11 April ---; MARY ANN, b. 1808, d. 1811; REBECCA, b. 31 Aug 1813, m. 28 Feb 1828, (N) Jefferson; JOHN; and ELIZABETH, b. 10 May 1820.

17.   RICHARD DISNEY, son of Thomas (9) and Ann, was b. 1779, and d. after 1850, when he is shown in the AA Co. Census. Nicholas Disney lived next door. {Research by Alecia Tipton}

112

Richard Disney served in the War of 1812. He m. and had several children, among whom may have been{Tipton}: NICHOLAS; and JOSHUA.

18.   WILLIAM DISNEY, son of William (10), was b. 1782 in AA Co., MD, d. by July 1854. He m. 1st, Caroline (N), and 2nd, Anna Maria Barry. He left a will dated July 1854 and proved 4 Oct 1854.{AAWB BEG#1 (41):238}

Alecia Tipton places William as the father of (by Caroline): JOHN, d. before 1854, m. Julia Ann Harman; PHILIP, b. 13 Oct 1809, m. 1st, Ann M. Gardner, and 2nd, Louisa A. Harman; WILLIAM, b. 26 Jan 1814; MARY ANN, b. 5 Dec 1816; PRISCILLA, b. 16 Jan 1819, m. Enos Shipley; (by Anna Maria Barry): ELIZABETH, b. 16 --- 1822, m. Elias Harman; LEMUEL, b. 17 June 1823, m. Mary Harman; EMILY MAHAILY, b. 16 Jan 1825, m. John Gardner; GRAFTON, b. 22 Nov 1827, d. 1856; LOUISA A., b. 28 Oct 1832; VERLETTA, b. 7 Oct 1834, m. Dr. Alphonso White; RANDOLPH NELSON, b. Oct 1837, d. 1861; JAMES HENRY (twin), b. 23 March 1842, d. by 1850s; and JULIANN (twin), b. 23 March 1842.

19.   RICHARD DISNEY, son of Richard (11) and Ariana (Porter) Disney, was b. c1791, and m. Mary Ann Duvall on 27 Oct 1817.{BAML}
Richard and Mary Ann were the parents of: THEODORE, b. c1818, d. 1893, m. 1st, Mary Ann (Jones) Clagett, and 2nd, Sarah Ann Parker; ARIANA, b. c1821, m. Roderick Aldridge, and had a dau. Mary, b. 1849; GEORGE W., b. 1822, d. 1887, m. Elizabeth Jane Todd; JOHN, b. c1825, m. Elizabeth (N); JONATHAN, b. c1829, m. Mary Ann Pierce; CHARLES H., b. c1834; AMELIA, b. c1836; ELIZABETH, b. c1838; BENJAMIN, b. c1841, m. Martha A. Gibbons; and BEAL, b. c1846.

20.   BENJAMIN F. DISNEY, son of Richard (11) and Ariana (Porter) Disney, was b. c1808, and on 22 Jan 1847, he m. Sarah Ann Alban (Cora Delaney says she was Sarah Ann Anderson), b. c1817.
In 1850, he lived in the 4th District of AA Co., age 42, a farmer, owning real estate worth $1,000. Living with him were his wife Sarah, age 33, sister Amelia, age 58, sister Charlotte L., age 45, and two children, Elizabeth, age 2, and Eli, 8 months.{1850 Census of AA Co., 4th District}
Benjamin F. and Sarah Ann (Alban or Anderson) Disney were the parents of: ELIZABETH A., b. c1848; ELI, b. 19 Feb 1850, d. unm.; SAMUEL RICHARD, b. 7 May 1851, moved to KS in 1879; BENJAMIN FRANKLIN, b. 2 Feb 1854, moved to KS c1879, and d. 4 April 1929, unm.; MARY HANNAH, b. 7 July 1855; WILLIAM THOMAS, b. 30 Dec 1855, moved to KS, d. unm.; ARIANA ANN

PORTER, d. unm.; SARAH CHARLOTTE, b. 23 March 1860; and
JEFFERSON, b. 1862, d. in infancy.

21. JOSHUA DISNEY, b. c1802, is tentatively placed as a son of
Richard (11) and Ariana (Porter) Disney. However, Tipton suggests he
may have been a son of Richard (17), son of Thomas.

In the 1850 census, he lived near Benjamin F. Disney. The two
men may have m. sisters. He m. 1st, Edith Mallonee, by AAML 5 Dec
1827, and 2nd, by AAML of 1831, Catherine Anderson.

In 1850, he lived in the 4th District of AA Co. (he is listed as
"John," age 48) with Catherine, 38, and the following children{1850 Census of
AA Co., 4th District}: LEONARD, 22, b. c1822; JOSHUA B., b. c1825;[38]

JOHN W., 19, b. c1831; SARAH SUSAN, 17, b. c1833; HARRIET A.,
16, b. c1834; EDWARD A., 14, b. c1836; ELIZA, 13, b. c1837;
RICHARD T., 12, b. c1838; SELIMA, 11, b. c1839; ANDREW, 9, b.
c1841; MARY C., 7, b. c1843; LYDIA E., 6, b. c1844; JAMES D., 4, b.
c1846; HENRIETTA, 3, b. c1847; OWEN, b. 6 Jan 1851; MARGARET;
and RACHEL.

22. WILLIAM I. DISNEY, son of James (12), was b. 17 Dec 1778.
He m. Amelia Elliott, dau. of Jacob Elliott, on 25 Feb 1807 in BA Co.,
MD.

William and Amelia were the parents of{IGI}: FREDERICK J. J., b. 20
Jan 1808 in AA Co.; WILLIAM A., b. 11 Feb 1813 in AA Co.; GEORGE N.,
b. 24 Nov 1816 in AA Co.; LEROY S., b. 12 Nov 1819 in AA Co.; AMELIA,
b. 1823 in AA Co.; and MORDECAI, b. May 1824 in AA Co.

23. OWEN DISNEY, son of Joshua (21) and Catherine (Anderson)
Disney, was b. 6 Jan 1851, and m. on 17 April 1870, in Ashton [OH?],
Mary Elizabeth Johnson, b. 10 July 1852 at Ashton.{Unverified data in LDS
Ancestry File} Owen and Mary Elizabeth were the parents of the following
children, all b. at Simpsonville, HO Co., MD.: SARAH ELLEN, b. 10
Nov 1871; JOSHUA DALLAS, b. 7 Aug 1873, m. Amelia O. Johnson;
ANNIE ELIZABETH, b. 10 Nov 1874, m. John Pethebridge; CARRIE
SAVILLA, b. 10 Nov 1877, m. Harry Easton; JOHN LEONARD, b. 10
Aug 1880, m. Myrtle Corkran; ALICE MAY, b. 23 March 1882, m.
Charles Waters Brown; MARY CATHERINE, b. 9 June 1884, m. Cecil
F. Cole, b. c1884; and WILLIAM OWEN, b. 29 June 1885.

---

[38] He d. at Highland, HO Co., MD, on 25 May 1901, age 75 years, 3 months, 7 days.
Born in MD, he was a wheelwright. He m. Catherine V. and had 3 children living.{HO Co.
Register of Deaths, 1898-1903, MSA}

THE SNOWDEN DISNEY LINE

William and Mary Disney had a son Snowden, b. 3 March 1706. He was living in 1732, and then seems to have disappeared. There is a possibility that the following Snowden Disney family is connected somehow to the Disneys of AA Co.

1.   SNOWDEN DISNEY d. intestate in BA Co. in 1834. He m. Rachel Deaver, by AAML dated 2 Oct 1793.
      Snowden and his wife were the parents of{Chancery Book 171: 373, MSA}: ELIZABETH, d. 29 March 1869 in Pascogoula, MS, m. John Grant, by BAML of 5 May 1816; AARON, b. 1799, m. by BAML dated 27 Nov 1824, Nancy Boone; SNOWDEN, Jr., b. c1802; CHARITY, m. James Morgan, by BAML of 18 Dec 1828; ALEXANDER; and JARED, d. 1845, m. Mary Ann Carrick, by BAML of 8 July 1832.

2.   AARON DISNEY, son of Snowden (1) and Rachel, was b. 1799 and m. 27 Nov 1824, in BA Co., MD, Nancy Boone.
      The 1860 Census of BA Co. lists Aaron Disney, age 62, hotel keeper, Nancy, age 55, Rachel, age 21, Richard, age 16, and Mary Stevens, age 75.{1860 Census of BA Co., Pikesville District, dwelling 1923, family 1923}
      Aaron and Nancy were the parents of: ELIZABETH; CHARITY; RACHEL; WILLIAM; RICHARD; and ISABELLA.

3.   SNOWDEN DISNEY, Jr., son of Snowden (1) and Rachel, was b. c1800/2, and m. Elizabeth Rutter on 21 June 1825.
      The 1860 Census of BA Co. shows Snowden Disney, 58, carpenter, MD, Emily, age 23, Nelson, age 16 (farm hand), Isaac, age 10, Mary E., age 2, David, age 1, and Charity Morgan, age 55.{1860 Census of BA Co., Pikesville District, dwelling 1932, family 1932}
      Snowden seems to have been the father of: OLIVER H., b. c1829; JOSEPH, or JOSIAH, RUTTER, b. c1831, d. 7 Dec 1854, m. Elizabeth J. Owings on 7 Dec 1854 in BA Co., MD; SNOWDEN, b. c1833; ANN R., b. c1839; JOHN W., b. c1842; NELSON K., b. 27 Feb 1845, d. 30 Sep 1885; ISRAEL, b. c1849; and (possibly) MARY ELIZA, b. 10 March 1858, d. 4 July 1950, m. Charles Henry Penn.

4.   JARED DISNEY, son of Snowden (1) and Rachel, d. 25 Jan 1845, having m., 17 Aug 1820, Anne Jeffries. She d. 16 July 1882 at Woodbury, in her 80th year, widow of "Jarrett Disney."{Towson, *The Maryland Journal*, 22 July 1882}

      Anne Disney, 57, Mary, age 23, Caroline, age 22, and Richard Disney, age 16, were listed in the 1860 Census of BA Co. Charles

Fleischer, 46, was also listed in the family. {1860 Census of BA Co., Pikesville District, dwelling 1551, family 1549}

According to MD Chancery Records, Jared and Anne were the parents of{Chancery Record 171:373, MSA}: RACHEL; PROVIDENCE; SNOWDEN; MARY; CAROLINE; RICHARD JAMES; and JOSHUA.

5.   JOSEPH, or JOSIAH, RUTTER DISNEY, son of Snowden (3) and Elizabeth (Rutter) Disney, was b. c1831. He m. Elizabeth J. Owings on 7 Dec 1854 in BA Co., MD.
    The 1860 Census of BA Co. lists Josiah Disney, 28, factory hand, Elizabeth, 25, and the following persons: Maria, 4, Silas, 16, Henry, 14, Jacob, 12, George F. or T., 10, Albert, 8, and Robert, 2. {1860 Census of BA Co., Pikesville District, dwelling 1673, family 1674}

Unplaced

DISNEY, MARY, m. Thomas Wells on 17 Oct 1721 in All Hallows Parish. {AACR: 37}

DISNEY, WILLIAM, was b. 22 Nov 1781 in BA Co., and d. 1 July 1850 in Cincinnati, OH. He was not the son of William, of Richard, but may possibly have been a son of William (10) and Ann. {Research by Alecia Tipton} He m. on 20 Nov 1802, in BA Co., MD, Mary Moren, b. c1782, d. 1825 in Cincinnati, OH. {Unverified material found in The Ancestral Files of Church of Jesus Christ of LDS}
    William and Mary (Moren) seem to have been the parents of: DAVID TIERNAN, b. 25 Aug 1803, in Baltimore, d. 14 March 1857 in Washington, DC., bur. in Spring Grove Cemetery, Cincinatti, m. Sarah Carter. He was a member of the U.S. House of Representatives from OH, 1849-1855; declined appointment by President Buchanan as U.S. Minister to Spain{Who Was Who in America, 1607-1896}; MARY, b. 1805 in Baltimore, d. 1824; RICHARD, b. 1807 in Baltimore; WILLIAM, b. c1810, d. 1849, m. Ann Metcalfe; ANN, b. c1806/8, d. 14 April 1828 in Hamilton Co., OH; AMELIA MARIA, m. 1836 in Hamilton Co., OH, Edmond Townsend; and MARY FRANCES, b. c1815.

THE DRURY FAMILY

Refs.: Unless otherwise noted, the material in this account is based on a typescript history of the Drury Family by Harry Wright Newman, in the possession of the compiler.

1.   CHARLES DRURY was in PG Co. by 20 Oct 1711, when he was listed as having made a payment to the estate of John Johnson of PG Co. {INAC 33A:39}

On 7 Dec 1715, he and John Bradford wit. a deed.{PGLR F:547}

On 23 Nov 1725, William Scott recorded his apology for several times having called Charles Drury a "perjined [perjured?] rogue."{PGLR Liber F, Old Series 6:690}

Charles Drury and William King appraised the estate of Michael Daniell of PG Co. on 2 Feb 1725.{MINV 11:223}

On 26 March 1726, John Bradford made his will and named Drury as overseer of several tracts of land.{MWB 18:464}

Charles Drury's first wife may have been Mary (N), since Mary Drury wit. the document by which Walter Hoxton appointed Charles Drury his atty.{PGLR M:451}

James Bright, Sr., of DO Co., d. leaving a will dated Oct 1732, in which he named, among others, a dau. Elizabeth Drury.{MWB 20:713}

Moses Adney, of St. Anne's Parish, AA Co., d. leaving a will dated 11 Jan 1732/3 and proved 25 Jan 1732/3. The heir named was wife Alice, extx., she to have the entire estate. The will was wit. by Jacob Lusby, John Lusby, Jr., and William Ruley.{MWB 20:792}

Drury seems to have moved to PG Co., where he patented two tracts of land: 27 a. *Drury Lane,* on 27 Nov 1735{MPL EI#3:428, EI#4:365}, and 143 a. *Drury's Good Luck,* on 23 April 1736.{MPL EI#2:413, EI#5:290}

Charles Drury, of PG Co., d. leaving a will dated 27 Aug 1740 and proved 3 Aug 1740. He named wife Alice, who was to have *Essex Land,* except for a part sold to Francis King; after her death to pass to Edward, son of Charles and Sophia Butler; dau. Sarah was to have *Drury's Adventure*; son Charles, and daus. Esther Selby, Mary Dart, and Sophia Boteler, 10 s. each. The extx. was wife Alice. The will was wit. by Thomas Hodgskins, George Luxford, Gabriel Swain, and William Fallowell.{MWB 22:257}

Charles Drury was probably m. earlier, since his children seem to have been adults when he made his will. A study of the available land records has identified Charles' first wife.

Charles and Mary (N) Drury were the parents of: CHARLES; SARAH; ESTHER, m. Nathan Selby; MARY, m. (N) Dart; and SOPHIA, m. (N) Boteler.

2.   CHARLES DRURY, Jr., son of Charles (1), d. in 1766. He m. 1st, by 8 June 1738, Elizabeth, widow of Samuel Roberts, of AA Co. He m. 2nd, Mary (N).

Charles Drury, Jr., on 31 Jan 1735/6, wit. the will of Edmund Evans, of AA Co.{MWB 21:591} Thus, he was probably b. c1714, which would have made him at least 21 in 1735/6.

In his will, he disposed of several tracts. A study was undertaken to discover if Charles may have acquired them through his second wife, but an examination of AALR shows that he purchased them from others.

Newman states that the children of Charles Drury, Jr., were by his second wife. The distribution of Charles Drury's estate was made 15 July 1769. There was a balance of £2334.19.7 to be dist. Samuel Lane and Thomas Stockett were sureties, and Mrs. Mary Drury was the admx. The legatees were Sarah, Elizabeth, Margaret, Mary, Ann, and Easter. The balance was dist. with 1/3 to the widow, and the residue to three sons and six daus.: William, Samuel, Charles, Sarah, Elizabeth, Margaret, Mary, Ann, and Easter.{BFD 5:219}

Charles Drury was the father of (by Elizabeth): SARAH, m. (N) Hodge; (by Mary): WILLIAM, not yet 21 in 1766, m. Elizabeth Ijams; ELIZABETH, not yet 16; MARGARET, not yet 16, probably the one who m. John Pindell in 1770; MARY, not yet 16; ANNE, not yet 16; CHARLES, not yet 21; ESTHER, not yet 16; SAMUEL, not yet 21 in 1766, m. Ann Ijams; and JERNINGHAM.

3.   SAMUEL DRURY, son of Charles (2) and Mary, was b. in 1759, and d. leaving a will dated 28 Jan 1842 and proved 17 July 1850. On 29 May 1779, he obtained a marriage license in AA Co. to marry Ann Ijams, dau. of Plummer and Ruth Ijams. They were m. in St. James Parish.

Samuel Drury, Sr., was an ensign in Capt. William Simmons' Co. in the West River Battalion in 1778, and he took the Oath of Allegiance before the Hon. Samuel Lane on 1 March 1778.{AARP:57}

Samuel and Ann (Ijams) Drury were the parents of: ELIZABETH, m. (N) Lyles; ELIZABETH, m. Benjamin Welch; ANN, m. (N) Gardner; MARY, m. (N) Humphreys; PLUMMER IJAMS; SAMUEL; HENRY CHILDS; and Dr. JOHN IJAMS.

4.   HENRY CHILDS DRURY, son of Samuel (3) and Ann (Ijams) Drury, was stated by Newman to have been b. in 1795, and to have d. in 1873. He is certainly mentioned in his father's will of 1842.

Henry C. Drury, d. 17 Feb 1873, at 76 years of age. Mary A. Drury d. 6 July 1870, age 68. Both are bur. in the Drury Family Cemetery, Bristol, AA Co.

There were several Henry C. Drurys in AA Co. Henry C. Drury, of William, age 76, testified on 12 Dec 1850 that Henry C. Drury, of Charles, volunteered around 18 June 1813, was in Capt. Jacob Franklin's Co., and was discharged at Halls Crossroads. On 18 Dec 1850, Elizabeth Drury, age 73, widow of Henry C. Drury, of Charles, stated that her husband enlisted 1 July 1813, that she m. him on 27 Oct 1816 and her family name was Elizabeth Franklin. She said that her husband d. at home on 9 Aug 1840.

Newman states that Henry C. Drury (of Samuel) m., by license dated 22 Oct 1822, Mary Franklin Owens, sister of Nicholas, James, and William Owens.

AA Co. Marriage Licenses show that Henry C. Drury was m. four times, or there were several different individuals of that name: Henry C. Drury and Elizabeth Mills, license dated 16 May 1806; Henry C. Drury and Sarah Elson, license dated 25 Nov 1808; Henry C. Drury and Elizabeth Franklin, license dated 2 Dec 1816 (he is the son of William); and Henry C. Drury and Mary Owens, license dated 22 Oct 1822.

Henry Childs Drury was the father of: ANN FRANKLIN; PRISCILLA, m. Joseph Shepherd; SARAH JANE, m. Joseph Chaney; MARY FRANCES, m. Robert Montgomery Pindell; EMILY, m. 1st, (N) Hill, and 2nd, Benjamin Jones; and JAMES O., m. Mrs. Elliott.

Unplaced

DREWERY, JOHN, was in SM Co. by 25 March 1770, when he wit. the will of William Shercliffe.{MWB 12:157}

John Drury d. by 4 May 1726, when his estate was admin. by Mary Drury, the admx. An inventory of £56.19.1 was mentioned. Payment was made to a Robert Drury.{MDAD 7:333}

THE CADWALLADER EDWARDS FAMILY

Refs.: A: Matilda P. Badger. *Genealogy of the Linthicum and Allied Families.* B: Harry Wright Newman. *Anne Arundel Gentry, Revised and Augmented, Volume II.*

1. CADWALLADER EDWARDS, was b. c1685, and d. in 1744. He m. 12 April 1710, Catherine (N), widow of Henry Bourne, in All Hallows Parish.{AACR:68} He m. as his second wife, Anne (N), who survived him.

In 1705, he constructed the altar and font for St. Anne's Church, Annapolis.{A} Newman added that in 1710 an Act of the MD Assembly authorized him to be paid for work done on the State House after it had been destroyed by fire, and in 1711 he was commissioned to make window shutters for the same building. In 1713, he did some work for St. Anne's Church.{B}

On 2 June 1713, Cadwallader Edwards, of Annapolis, joiner, mortgaged his dwelling house with its lot, standing in Annapolis, near the

Gate House, next to the houses of John Slaughter and Thomas Docwra, to Charles Carroll, of Annapolis.{AALR IB#2:44}

Cadwallader Edwards d. intestate prior to 15 Jan 1744/5, when letters of administration were granted to his widow Anne. Jonas Green was her surety. His estate was inv. at £52.15.6 and Edward Edwards was named as son and heir. By 16 May 1746, the widow Anne had m. Thomas Howard.{B}

Cadwallader and Catherine were the parents of{AACR:70}: EDWARD; and CADWALLADER, b. 14 Aug 1713, bapt. 16 Aug 1713 in All Hallows Parish.

2.   EDWARD EDWARDS, son of Cadwallader (1) and Catherine, was b. 7 June 1711 and bapt. 8 July 1711 in All Hallows Parish. He m. 1st, in Jan 1734, in All Hallows Parish, Jemima Welsh.{AACR:29, 48, 69}

Newman adds that Jemima was bapt. 19 April 1717 in All Hallows Parish, dau. of Robert and Catherine (Lewis) Welsh. Jemima Welsh Edwards d. in 1741.{B}

When Robert Welsh made his will in 1756, he mentioned the heirs of his dau. Jemima Edwards.

Edward m. 2nd, Elizabeth (or Elinor) Chilton (or Clinton), on 18 Nov 1742, at St. Anne's Parish.{AACR:99} By this marriage, he acquired the tract *Bold Venture* which he sold to Richard Barnes on 8 May 1744, with wife Elinor waiving her right of dower.{AALR RB#1:383}

Edward Edwards evidently d. intestate and there was no formal administration of his estate by his son and heir.

Edward and Eleanor Edwards were mentioned in a deposition of Adderton Skinner.{AMG 5 May 1747}

Edward and Jemima (Welsh) Edwards were the parents of: EDWARD, Jr.

3.   EDWARD EDWARDS, Jr., son of Edward (2) and Jemima, d. in 1786, having m. Anne (N), b. c1738 in St. Anne's Parish; she may have been a relative of the Linthicum family.{A}

In 1752, Edward Edwards purchased the mortgage of *Linthicum Walk,* which Thomas Linthicum had mortgaged to Philip Hammond.

In 1778, Edward Edwards and his son Aquila took the Oath of Allegiance to the State of MD.{CMSP: The Red Books, No. 4, Part 3}

Edwards wrote his will on 17 April 1786, and it was filed on the following 18 May.{AAWB TG#1 (34):336} Letters of administration on the estate were granted on 19 June 1786.

Anne Edwards, Aquila Edwards, William Edwards, Cadwallader Edwards, and Jonathan Edwards, execs., advertised they would settle his estate.{AMG 6 July 1786}

When the final administration account of his estate was filed, there was a balance of £1475.14.8 to be dist. among the heirs.{B}

On 23 Sep 1793, his estate was dist. by his admin., William Edwards. Sureties were Thomas Bicknell and Jonathan Edwards. The balance of the estate was divided into tenths, and dist. to{AADI JG#1:45}: children of Jemima Evans; children of Catherine Lusby; William Anderson, husband of Elizabeth Edwards; Sarah Edwards; Cephas Waters, husband of Mary Edwards; John Linthicum, husband of Mary Edwards [sic]; John Fonerden, husband of Margaret Edwards; William Edwards; Cadwallader Edwards; and Jonathan Edwards.

Edward and Anne (N) Edwards were the parents of: CATHERINE, m. [Edward] Lusby; ELIZABETH, m. William, son of William and Susannah (Meek) Anderson; JEMIMA, m. (N) Evans; MARY, m. Cephas Waters, son of John and Mary (Ijams) Waters; SARAH, m., as his second wife, William Anderson, who had m. her sister Elizabeth; ANNE, m. John Linthicum; MARGARET, m. John Fonerden; AQUILA, s.p.; WILLIAM, m., by AAML dated 20 July 1789, Ann Chalmers; CADWALLADER, m., by AAML 1786, Sarah Chalmers; JONATHAN; and EDWARD, s.p.{Newman says it was his estate that was dist. on 23 Sep 1793}

THE FREEBORNE FAMILY

1.   RICHARD FREEBORNE, of Catherington, Hampshire, m. Jane (N). They were the parents of{IGI}: THOMAS, bapt. 9 Dec 1650; RICHARD, bapt. 6 July 1652; GILES, bapt. 23 Oct 1654; JOHN, bapt. 18 Feb 1655; and CLEMENT, bapt. 16 March 1657.

2.   THOMAS FREEBORNE, son of Richard (1) and Jane, was bapt. 8 Dec 1650 at Catherington, Hampshire. He may be the Thomas Freeborn who came to AA Co. by 1674 and d. 4 Jan 1713 in St. Anne's Parish.{AACR:68; BCF} A Mrs. Freeborn was mentioned in the inventory, made 16 May 1701, of Orlando Greenslade, of AA Co.{INAC 20:98}

Freeborne patented two tracts of land in AA Co.: 80 a. *Freeborne's Enlargement,* on 17 Oct 1684{MPL 27:328}. and 600 a. *Freeborne's Progress,* on 10 Dec 1695.{MPL 40:321} On 2 June 1684, Freeborne purchased 100 a. *Petticoat Rest* from William Petticoate.{AALR IH#3:16} On 18 Aug 1687, he purchased 103 a. *Norwood's Angles* from Andrew Norwood of AA Co.{AALR IH#3:25}

On 1 July 1686, Freeborne and William Formar appraised the estate of Walter Smith.{INAC 9:151} On 3 Dec 1696, Freeborne and Richard Kilburne, as execs., filed an administration account of Elizabeth Burnett, of AA Co.{INAC 14:46}

Thomas Freeborne d. by 21 Jan 1713/4, when his estate was appraised at £117.3.0 by Thomas Docwra and Richard Young.{INAC 35A:38} Nothing more was done until his estate was admin. on 19 July 1717 by

Richard Freeborne, exec. The same inventory of £117.3.0 was mentioned. Payments were made to legatees Sarah Sampson, Priscilla Freeborne, and Ann Freeborne.{INAC 38A:55}

Thomas Freeborne was the father of (order of birth uncertain): ANNE, m. by 1720, David Thomas; JANE, m. Robert Thomas on 18 Jan 1704 in St. Anne's Parish{AACR:73}; PRISCILLA, m. by 22 Aug 1723, Samuel Howell; RICHARD; and SARAH, m. (N) Sampson.

3.   JANE FREEBORNE, dau. of Thomas (2), m. Robert Thomas on 18 Jan 1704 in St. Anne's Parish.{AACR:73} On 13 June 1720, she gave power of attorney to Thomas Tolley to divide parcels of *Johnson's Bed* and *Johnson's Rest* (which her father Thomas Freeborne had purchased in Aug 1697 from John and Ann Johnson{BALR IS#IK:177}) where her bro. Richard Freeborne had lately lived, and which at his death descended to his four sisters, Eliz. Garrison, Mary Tolley, Priscilla Freeborne, and herself.{BALR RM#HS:661}

4.   RICHARD FREEBORNE, son of Thomas (2), was living in 9 Nov 1717, but d. in BA Co. c1720.

On 9 Nov 1717, Richard Freeborne conv. to Thomas Bordley three tracts lately occupied by Thomas Freeborne, dec.: 100 a. *Petticoats Rest,* 103 a. *Norwood's Angles,* and 80 a. *Freeborne's Enlargement.* Bordley agreed that Freeborn and his heirs could visit the grave of Thomas Freeborne whenever they wished.{AALR IB#2:407}

Richard Freeborne's undated administration account was filed by the admx., Priscilla Freeborn, c1720. An inventory of £75.11.8 was mentioned. A payment was made to David Thomas who m. Ann, sister of the dec.{MDAD 3:26}

Another administration account was filed 22 Aug 1723 by the extx., Priscilla, now wife of Samuel Howell.{MDAD 3:338}

THE FRENCH FAMILY

OTHO FRENCH, cordwainer, was b. c1708. He gave his age as 33 in 1741.{MDTP 31:181} He m. Emm Dowling in All Hallows Parish on 30 July 1727.{AACR:41}

Emm was a dau. of Emm Dowling, late servant of Thomas Rutland, who, in Jan 1702/3, petitioned the court that she had been deluded and overcome by William Reid, servant to Charles Carroll, and begot a child, who d. Emm Dowling asked that her corporal punishment be remitted.{AAJU G:10} Emm Dowling, the mother, was indicted again in 1709.{AAJU Nov 1709:91} She petitioned the court in June 1714 and was summoned to testify in court in March 1746.{AAJU June 1714:275, March 1745/6:5}

Emm Dowling, the mother, had at least one son, ROGERS, who, in Jan 1708, was bound to Thomas Rutland{AAJU Jan 1708:672}, and EMM, who m. Otho French on 30 July 1727 in All Hallows Parish.{AACR:41}

Otho and Emm were the parents of the following children, b. in All Hallows Parish{AACR:52, 53}: SAMUEL, b. 11 Dec 1729; OTHO, b. 24 Nov 1731; ANN, b. 21 Feb 1733; AGNES, b. 20 April 1736; BENJAMIN, b. 20 Nov 1738; WILLIAM, b. 24 May 1744; MARTHA, b. 3 May 174-; ISRAEL, b. 16 Sep 1746; EMM (twin), b. 11 Dec 1749; and JOANNA (twin), b. 11 Dec 1749, m. William Pearce in All Hallows Parish on 22 May 1768.{AACR:57}

OTHO FRENCH, son of Otho and Emm, was b. 24 Nov 1731. He was living as late as 1764 when he gave his age as 33.{AALC 2:615-616}

WILLIAM FRENCH, son of Otho and Emm, was b. 24 May 1744. He may have m. Susanna Morgan, whose son William was b. 16 Jan 1770. {AACR:60}

William and Susanna were the parents of{AACR:60, 62}: WILLIAM, b. 16 Jan 1770; NICHOLAS, b. 3 April 1781; and EMM, b. 26 Nov 1788.

THE GADSBY FAMILY

1.   JOHN GADSBY d. by June 1710. Sometime before 28 May 1701 he m. Johanna, admx. of George Norman.{INAC 20:109, 22:66} On 29 March 1708, Johannah joined him in selling several tracts.{AALR WT#2:631}

John Gadesby and Mr. Richard Sorrell appraised the estate of John Smith, Irishman, on 12 April 1698.{INAC 16:36}

On 16 Dec 1699, he wit. a deed.{AALR WT#1:5}

On 2 May 1700, he paid £100 for 1,000 a. *Brown's Adventure* from Thomas Brown, who patented it on 10 Nov 1695.{AALR WT#1:89} (For other transactions see AALR WT#2:50, 76, 451, 504)

By 1707 he owned 100 a. *Hopkins Fancy,* surv. in Oct 1662 for William Hopkins, 25 a. *Norman's Fancy,* surv. in June 1669 for Geo. Norman, 100 a. *Randall's Purchase,* surv. in April 1680 for Christopher Randall, 190 a. *Gray's Increase*, part of 300 a. surv. in June 1680 for John Gray, and other tracts.{MRR:235, 246, 251, 252}

On 23 June 1703, John Gadsby and Thomas Robson were listed as appraisers of the inventory of Hans Inghambrixon.{INAC 1:648}

Gadsby d. by 27 June 1710, when his estate was appraised by Abraham Child and Maurice Baker. Personal property was valued at £59.1.6. Johanna Gadsby and Hen. Rate signed as approvers.{INAC 31:331}

An additional appraisal was made 2 March 1710 and valued at £8.16.0.
{INAC 32B:50}

Christopher and Thomas Randall admin. the estate on 20 Aug
1711.{INAC 32C:116, INAC 39A:11)}

On 19 Nov 1722, Maurice Baker, age c47, dep. that he was with
John Gadsby, "grandfather-in-law" to the heirs of George Norman.{MCHR
CL:1015}

THE ANTHONY AND FAITH GONGO FAMILY

1.   ANTHONY GONGO was in AA Co. by c1676, when his account
was listed in the inventory of Thomas Stockett.{INAC 2:294} He is placed as
the father of the Gongo children by the administration account of the
estate of Lewis Evans, whose widow stated that Anthony Gongo was the
father-in-law of the dec.

On 20 Feb 1667, John Peart, of AA Co., made his will naming
Anthony "Congoe" as the sole legatee.{MWB 1:317}

Faith Gongo, evidently the widow of Anthony, d. in AA Co.,
leaving a will dated 23 Feb 1693/4 and proved 13 March 1694. Dau.
Lois, wife of Christopher Vernon, was to have personalty. Dau. Mary,
wife of Robert Trevett, and her heirs were to have 50 a., part of 150 a.
Kithenton, while daus. Ann and Faith were each to have 50 a. of the same
tract. The last two daus. were named execs. Samuel Chew and Samuel
Griffith were named overseers, and Thos. Hughs and Abraham Symons
were wits.{MWB 2:262}

The estate of Faith Gongo was inv. by William Powell and
Augustine Hawkins on 18 April 1694. The estate included 1,900 lbs. of
tob., and was valued at £50.5.6.{INAC 13A:139}

Anthony and Faith Gongo were the parents of: LOIS, m. 1st,
Lewis Evans, and 2nd, Christopher Vernon; MARY, m. 1st, Robert
Trevett; ANN, m. Samuel Guichard; and FAITH; m. Richard Hall.

Their Daughters

2.   LOIS GONGO, dau. of Anthony (1) and Faith, m. 1st, Lewis
Evans, and 2nd, Christopher Vernon. Lewis Gongo was a creditor of
George Symons, of AA Co., listed in the latter's inventory c1681.{INAC
7B:298}

Lewis Evans, of Herring Creek, d. leaving a will dated 10 Dec
1690 and proved 11 March 1690/1, naming his wife "Lues" as extx., and
naming four daus. who were to be of age at 16: Eliza, Sarah, Katherine
(to have 100 a. *Jerico)*, and Anne. Thomas Tench, Jno. Chappell, and
Edm. Evans were wits.{MWB 2:209}

On 22 April 1704, Lois Evans, now wife of Christopher Vernon, admin. the estate of Lewis Evans, of AA Co. Anthony Gongo "father-in-law" of the dec. was named in the account.{MWB 3:411}

Lois m., as her 2nd husband, Christopher Vernon.

Lois Gongo was the mother of the following children, whose births were recorded in St. James Parish (by Lewis Evans): ELIZA EVANS, b. c1674, d. c1762, m. 1st, Francis Anctill, and 2nd, Moses Faudrie{AACR:157; Jourdan, *Early Families of Southern Maryland*, 2:212}; SARAH A. EVANS, m. Samuel Griffith on 26 Nov 1702 in St. James Parish {AACR:153}; KATHERINE EVANS, who was to have 100 a. *Jerico*; ANNE EVANS, b. c1680/90, m. in Aug 1717, Benjamin Battee; (by Christopher Vernon): EPHRAIM VERNON, b. 18 Feb 1691, bapt. 11 June 1704, d. c1761 at Port Vernon Plantation, Brunswick Co., NC, having m. 2nd, c1723 at Richmond, VA, Ann Smith Lucas, and 3rd, c1751, at Brunswick, NC, Ann Nancy Gott{AACR:154; Jourdan, *Early Families*, 2:215}; WILLIAM VERNON, b. 23 Jan 1693, bapt. 11 June 1704{AACR:154}; LOIS VERNON, b. 1 Oct 1697, bapt. 11 Sep 1698, possibly the "Lucy," dau. of Christopher and Lois, who was bur. 27 Sep 1718{AACR:149, 163}; THOMAS VERNON, b. 27 Jan and bapt. 1 March 1701, and "sucked his mother until he was age 10," d. in Bladen Co., NC, after 1758{AACR:153; Jourdan, *Early Families*, 2:215}; and ANN VERNON, d. c1773 in Bertie Co., NC, m. 1st, c1722, Capt. George Martin, mariner, who d. c1734, and 2nd, Joseph Anderson.

3.   MARY GONGO, dau. of Anthony (1) and Faith, m., by 22 Feb 1693/4, Robert Trevitt. Robert Trevett d. by 7 Dec 1698 when his estate was appraised at 1,369 lbs. of tob. and an additional 1,325 lbs. of tob. Thomas Tench was the admin.{INAC 19½A:24} Mary was in AA Co. as Mary Gongo by 19 May 1707, when Samuel Greychard (Guichard) requested that her cattle marks be recorded.{AALR WT#2:564} She m., as her 2nd husband, Peter Tibbido. Peter and Jos."Topedo" signed the inventory of Samuel Guichard as next of kin.

Mary Tepedo, widow, of AA Co., d. leaving a will dated 17 April 1744 and proved 18 June 1748. She named her son Joseph Tepedo, exec., who was to have her 50 a. near Herring Creek, called *Knighton's Choice*. Her grandson Joseph Mumford was to enjoy the tract. The will was wit. by James Trott, Thomas Borer, and John Gardner.{MWB 25:326}

Mary Gongo was the mother of the following children, bapt. in St. James Parish (by Robert Trevett){AACR:151}: BRIDGET TREVET, b. April 1692, bapt. 11 June 1699; WILLIAM TREVET, b. June 1693, bapt. 11 June 1699; (by Thomas Ventam): GRACE TREVETT, b. 25 Oct 1699, bapt. 27 9br [Nov] 1699; (by Peter Tibbido){AACR:154, 156, 158}: MARY TIBBIDO, b. 14 March 1703, bapt. 14 May 1704; JOSEPH TIBBIDO, b. 15 Jan 1705, bapt. 25 March 1700; and FAITH TIBBIDO, b. 12 July 1708, bapt. 25 April 1709.

4.   ANN GONGO, dau. of Anthony (1) and Faith, m. Samuel
Guishard on 2 Nov 1704 in St. James Parish, AA Co.{AACR:162} Samuel
Guichard d. in AA Co., MD, in 1733, having come to MD in 1682 as an
indentured servant. On 19 June 1711, he dep. that he had been b. in
Geneva, had come to MD at age 16, and had been here 28 years. He had
served his time with Thomas Knighton the Elder.{(MCHR:19} On 12 May
1716, Guichard dep., giving his age as c51.{MCHR:35} Samuel Guichard
was bur. in St. James Parish on 26 Sep 1733.{AACR:165}

On 19 Jan 1682, Edward Calignon, Jean Louys Patrone,
Augustine Soux, and Samuel Gueshard were bound as apprentices to
James Goullay, of MD. They appeared before a Judge and declared
themselves willing to serve their master according to their indentures.
{Ghirelli; *List of Emigrants ..., 1682 to 1692*:15} A search of the *Publications and

Proceedings of the Huguenot Society of London* has failed to reveal any
information on Samuel Guichard's family or residence in England before
coming to MD.

Samuel Guishard, of AA Co., planter, was naturalized 15 Nov
1712.{ARMD 38:159} He was bur. in St. James Parish on 26 Sep 1733.
{AACR:165}

On 23 June 1714, Richard Hall, of CV Co., and wife Faith, sold to
Samuel Guishard, of AA Co., planter, 50 a., the residue of a 150 a. tract
called *Kickeytan,* which had been left to Faith Gongo, now wife of
Richard Hall, by the will of her mother Faith Gongo, made 28 Feb
1693/4. The deed states that 50 a. were also given to Mary Trevitt, then
wife of Robert Trevitt, and 50 a. to Ann Gongo.{AALR IB#2:158}

On 12 June 1716, Abraham Birckhead, of AA Co., conv. 300 a.
Quicksale to Jonathan Jones and Samuel Guishard, planters, of AA Co.
{AALR IB#2:284}

On 1 April 1717, Benjamin Holland sold 100 a. called *Holland
Range* to Guichard.{AALR IB#2:402}

Guichard d. in AA Co., leaving a will dated 12 Oct and proved 22
Oct 1733. To his son Anthony he left his dwell. plant. If Anthony d.
without legitimate heirs, the land was to go to the testator's son Mark, or
the nearest of kin. Son Mark was to have *Quicksale.* Dau. Hannah and
her heirs were to have 225 a. in BA Co. and personalty. If Hannah d.
without heirs, the land was to be divided between sons Anthony and
Mark. Wife Anne was to be the extx. William Worrell, Martin Fisher,
and William Simmons wit. the will.{MWB 20:816}

The estate of Samuel Guichard, of AA Co., was appraised by
Roger Crudgington and Abraham Simmonds on 9 Nov 1733. His
personal property was valued at £433.18.4. Ephraim Gover and Jo.
Camilton signed as creditors, and Peter Tepedo and Jos. Tepedo signed
as next of kin. Ann Guichard, the extx., filed the inventory on 12 March
1733/4.{MINV 18:186}

Samuel and Ann (Gongo) Guichard lived in St. James Parish, AA Co., where their children were b.

However, Samuel seems to have had a liason with Faith Gongoe, by whom he had a son: SAMUEL, b. 3 April 1700, bapt. as Samuel Gongoe in St. James Parish on 19 May 1700.{AACR:151}

Samuel and Ann (Gongo) Guichard were the parents of the following children, bapt. in St. James Parish{AACR:155, 156, 157, 159, 162, 183}: HANNAH, b. 30 Oct, bapt. 26 Dec 1704; ELIZABETH, b. 28 Feb 1705, bapt. 25 March 1706, bur. 2 Nov 1708; ANTHONY, b. 17 June, bapt. 24 Oct 1708; GEORGE, b. 19 July, bapt. 15 Oct 1710; ANN, b. 11 Dec 1713, bapt. 6 Jan 1713; MARK "GUIST," son of Samuel, bapt. 29 April 1716.

5.   FAITH GONGO, dau. of Anthony (1) and Faith, had a liaison with Samuel Guichard by whom she had a son, Samuel Gongoe, b. 3 April 1700, bapt. as Samuel Gongoe in St. James Parish on 19 May 1700. {AACR:151} By 23 June 1714, she was m. to Richard Hall. On that date, she and her husband conv. 50 a. of *Kickeytan* (left Faith Hall by her mother), to Samuel Guichard.{AALR IB#2:158}

Faith Gongo was the mother of the following children, b. in St. James Parish{AACR:129, 151, 158}: ELIZABETH GONGOE, b. 10 March 1698/9, bapt. 11 June 1699; (by Samuel Guichard): SAMUEL GONGOE, b. 3 April 1700, bapt. in St. James Parish on 19 May 1700; (by Richard Hall): FAITH, b. 12 Oct 1704 in All Saints Parish, CV Co., bapt. 25 April 1709 in St. James Parish; JOHN, b. 2 Aug 1705, bapt. 25 April 1709; and RICHARD, b. 1 Oct 1708, bapt. 25 April 1709.

The Grandchildren

6.   ELIZA EVANS, dau. of Lewis and Lois (2) (Gongo) Evans, was b. c1674 and d. c1762. She m. 1st, Francis Anctill, in St. James Parish, on 19 Aug 1708, and 2nd, Moses Faudrie, who d. c1729.{AACR:157; Jourdan, *Early Families of Southern Maryland,* 2:212}

Moses Faudrie, of Herring Creek, St. James Parish, d. leaving a will dated 31 Aug 1728 and proved 22 April 1729. He named his wife Elizabeth as extx. John Elliott Brown and William Vernon were wits. {MWB 19:809}

Elizabeth "Fodory," of CV Co., d. leaving a will dated 8 Sep 1755 and proved 17 Sep 1762. She named her sister Katherine Thornbury, Zachariah Maccubbin, Lewis Stephens, son of John and Rachel Stephens, the other children of John Stephens, Ann Vernon, Elizabeth Vernon, Sarah Jones, and Rachel Stephens. Execs. were her sister Catherine Thornbury and friend Zachariah Maccubbin.{MWB 31:769}

Elizabeth Evans was the mother of{Jourdan, *Early Families*, 2:212}: (by Francis Anctill): FRANCIS; GEORGE; BARNABY, who d. testate in SM Co., leaving a will dated 21 Feb 1732 and proved 12 April 1733. He named a wife Elizabeth, and cousin Jean Thompson.{MWB 19:809} When his estate was inv. on 6 June 1733, it was appraised at £141.19.6. Lewis Griffith and Hannah Griffith signed as next of kin.{MINV 17:320} His estate was admin. by Elizabeth Anctill on 20 Aug 1734.{MDAD 12:526}

7.   SARAH EVANS, dau. of Lewis and Lois (Gongo) Evans, may be the Sarah Evans who m. Samuel Griffith on 26 Nov 1702 in St. James Parish.{AACR:153} Samuel Griffith m. 1st, on 26 Nov 1702, at St. James Parish, Sarah Evans, dau. of Lewis and Lucy Evans, and 2nd, (date unknown) Anne Skinner, dau. of Clarke Skinner, of CV Co.{Jourdan; *Early Families of Southern Maryland*, I:196} For her descendants, see The Griffith Family.

8.   CATHERINE EVANS, dau. of Lewis and Lois (Gongo) Evans, was b. c1680/90, and d. by 1768. She m. 1st, John Clark, b. 13 June 1686, AA Co., son of Mathias and Elizabeth Clark, and 2nd, William Thornbury, who d. 1750.{Jourdan, *Early Families*, 2:213}
     William Thornbury d. leaving a will dated 22 Dec 1746 and proved 6 July 1750. The heirs named were wife Catherine, cousin William Vernon, sons-in-law William Scrivener and John Car, children of dau.-in-law Lewsey Car, dau.-in-law Elizabeth Scrivener, William and Elizabeth, children of John and Lewsey Carr. The will was wit. by Ephraim Gover and James Pickering.{MWB 27:277}
     The estate of William Thornbury, of AA Co., was appraised on 12 Oct 1750 by Richard Smith and John Brown and valued at £901.17.6. Henry Darnall and John Hamilton signed as creditors, and Katherine Thornbury, the extx., filed the inventory on 9 March 1750/1. {MINV 44:419}
     Catherine Thornbury d. leaving a will dated 24 Dec 1767 and proved 23 Nov 1768. The heirs named were grandson John Scrivener, son of William, who was to have *Kequotan's Choice,* grandchildren William, Elizabeth, Catherine, and Ann Carr, Susanna Weems, and John Scrivener, son of Elisha. The execs. were John Scrivener and William Carr. The will was wit. by William Child, William Parrett, and Thomas Parrett.{MWB 39:655}
     Catherine Evans was the mother of the following children: (by John Clark): ELIZABETH CLARK, m. William Scrivener; and LOIS (LEWSEY) CLARK, m. John Carr.

9.   ANNE EVANS, dau. of Lewis and Lois (Gongo) Evans, was b. c1680/90, and m. Benjamin Battee in Aug 1717. For her descendants, see The Battee Family.

10.   WILLIAM VERNON, son of Christopher and Lois (Evans) Vernon, was b. 23 Jan 1693 and bapt. 11 June 1704. He m. 1st, on 27 Nov 1733, in AA Co., Mary Brown, and 2nd, by 1735, Sophia (N). He d. by 24 Jan 1740, when his estate was inv. at a total of £66.15.0. Thomas Vernon and Ann Battee signed as next of kin. Sophia Vernon, admx., filed the inventory on 12 March 1740.{Jourdan, *Early Families*, 2:215; MINV 25:390}
   Sophia Vernon had two illegitimate children, b. in St. James Parish{AACR:170}: JOHN, b. 28 March 1748; and JOHN, b. 19 Jan 1748/49.
   William and Sophia had one child{AACR:166}: ANNE, b. 4 Oct 1735.

11.   MARK GUISHARD, son of Samuel and Anne, was bapt. 29 April 1716.{AACR:162} He m. 1st, by 8 June 1748, Dinah (N), who joined him in selling 100 a. *Green's Park* and 58 a. *Greer's Improvement* to Thomas Starkey. In June 1754, Mark and Dinah admin. the estate of Roger Crutchington.{BALR TR#C:2; BA Co. Court Proceedings BB#A: 185, 188} He m. 2nd, Sarah (N), who m. as her 2nd husband, James Wolfe.
   Mark d. by 14 Sep 1772, when Benkid Wilson and Abraham Britton appraised his personal property at £455.14.6. Sarah Guishard, admx., filed the inventory on 26 March 1773.{MINV 116:29}
   On 9 July 1768, Sarah Guishard and Prudence Sickkey signed the inventory of Richard Hendon, of BA Co., as next of kin.{MINV 98:259}
   Sarah Guishard admin. the estate on 23 March 1773. As Sarah Wolfe, she admin. his estate on 6 June 1778.{BAAD 7:233, 8:36}
   On 16 Sep 1778, the following children of Mark Guichard were made wards of James Wolfe, with Abraham Wright and Henry Hendon were sureties{BA Co. Orphans Court Proceedings, WB#1:23}: DAVID GUICHARD; HANNAH GUICHARD; HENRY GUICHARD; RICHARD GUICHARD; and SAMUEL GUICHARD.

THE GRIFFITH FAMILY

Refs.: A: Jourdan. *Early Families of Southern Maryland, Vol. I.*

1.   SAMUEL GRIFFITH, progenitor, was in MD by June 1651.{A} Samuel Griffith wit. the will of Edmund Joy in 1665.{MWB 1:260} Samuel may be the father of{A}: SAMUEL.

2.   SAMUEL GRIFFITH, possibly son of Samuel, who immigrated c1651, d. leaving a will proved 3 Sep 1717.{A:191 cites MD Original Wills, Box G, folder 78, MSA} He m. Elizabeth (N), who d. by July 1720.

He may be the Samuel Griffith who was left personalty in the will, dated 30 March 1685, of Philip Soones.{MWB 4:90} On 10 Dec 1690, Samuel Griffin was named as a trustee in the inventory of Lewis Evans.{INAC 11A:13½}

In his will proved 3 Sep 1717, Samuel Griffith named his children Martha Evans (and her dau. Elizabeth), Elizabeth Miles, Mary Bowers (and her dau. Mary), Sarah Duvall, Rebecca Moberly, and Rachel Giles (and her dau. Rachel), as well as son Samuel, Jr. (and his dau. Elizabeth). {A:195}

On 21 Nov 1717, John Giles entered a caveat stating that Samuel Griffith was not capable of making his will, and that it was worded by his wife, Elizabeth, in order to defraud the rest of his children.{A:195} The Commissary General ordered the will not to be recorded until further orders.{A:195}

On 17 Dec 1718, Elizabeth Griffith, of CV Co., made a deed of gift to her son Samuel, who was to pay the following gifts after her decease: to Elizabeth Miles, Mary Bowers, Sarah Duvall, Rebecca Mobley, and Rachel Giles.{MWB 15:170}

The estate of Samuel Griffith, Sr., of AA Co., was admin. 18 Feb 1718 by the execs., Elizabeth Griffith, the widow (one of the people called Quakers), and Samuel Griffith, Jr. An inventory of £249.3.1 was mentioned.{MDAD 1:365}

Elizabeth Griffith, widow, of CV Co., d. by 28 July 1720, when her son, Samuel Griffith, admin. the estate. An inventory of 3,500 lbs. of tob. was mentioned. Legatees were Elizabeth, wife of Thomas Miles, Mary Bowers, a widow, Rebecca, wife of Edward Mobberly, and Rachel, wife of John Giles.{MDAD 3:131}

Samuel and Elizabeth (N) Griffith were the parents of: SAMUEL, b. c1681, bapt. 15 Feb 1708 at St. James Parish; MARTHA, d. by 16 Dec 1718, m. (N) Evans; ELIZABETH, d. by 16 June 1751, m. 1st, c1688, Guy White II, and 2nd, on 23rd da., 10 mo., 1714, at West River Monthly Meeting, Thomas Miles (Samuel Griffith was a wit.){QRSM:23}; MARY, m. (N) Bowers, a widower; SARAH, b. c1685, d. after 12 June 1748, m. c1710, Mareen Duvall, the Younger, who was b. 1687 and d. after 3 Dec 1741; REBECCA, b. 13 May 1696, m. Edward Mobberly; RACHEL, b. c1689, bapt. 15 Feb 1708, age 19, m. 9 Dec 1710, John Giles; and ZIPPORAH, b. 11 Feb 1691, bapt. 8 July 1705, and may have d. young.

3.   SAMUEL GRIFFITH, son of Samuel (2), was b. c1681, and was bapt. 15 Feb 1708, age 27, at St. James Parish in AA Co. He d. in CV Co. leaving a will dated 2 Oct 1741 and proved 2 Nov 1741.

Samuel m. 1st, on 26 Nov 1702 at St. James Parish, Sarah Evans, dau. of Lewis and Lucy Evans, and 2nd, Anne Skinner, dau. of Clarke Skinner, of CV Co.{A:196}

The will of Samuel Griffith, written 2 Oct 1741, named son Samuel (to have land in BA Co.), son Lewis, son John, son Benjamin (to have land he inherited from his grandfather, Clarke Skinner), Richard Steele, and daus. Ann, Rebecca and Bathsheba. Sons Lewis and John were to be execs. The will was wit. by Henry Austin, Nathan Smith, and Elizabeth Brown.{MWB 22:398; MDAD 27:154}

Samuel Griffith was the father of{A:196-197}: ELIZABETH, b. 8 Nov 1703, m. by 11 Nov 1749, Samuel White; JOHN (birth date uncertain, but probably b. by 1706); SAMUEL, b. 25 May 1705; LEWIS, b. 19 June 1707; SARAH, b. 28 Feb 1708, m. by 11 Nov 1749, Lewis Jones; RACHEL, b. 26 Feb 1710, m. by 11 Nov 1749, John Stephens; LOIS or LUCY, b. 8 Oct 1713; MARTHA; BENJAMIN (definitely by second wife);[39] ANNE, m. by 11 Nov 1749, Benjamin Duvall; REBECCA, m. by 11 Nov 1749, Notley Thomas; BATHSHEBA, in 1749 she was a ward of John Griffith.

4.　　JOHN GRIFFITH, son of Samuel (3) and Sarah (Evans), d. in AA Co. by March 1765.[40] He is placed as a son of Samuel by his second wife Jourdan, but in this compiler's opinion, he must have been a son by the first wife if he was the father of John b. c1726. Moreover, he and his bro. Lewis were named as execs. by their father Samuel.{MWB 22:298} He was named as exec. of his bro. Benjamin.

Lewis Griffith and John Griffith appraised the inventory of Joseph Smith, Quaker, of CV Co., on 30 May 1763.{MINV 82:16}

John Griffith, of CV Co., d. by 7 March 1765, when his estate was appraised by William Lyles and William Smith, and valued at £173.17.0. Ralph Forster signed as creditor for James Gordon and Co. Lewis Griffith and Lewis Jones signed as next of kin, and Ann Griffith, admx., filed the inventory on 25 June 1765.{MINV 88:38} An additional inventory, totalling £65.2.8, was filed by Ann Griffith on 13 Oct 1766. Only Lewis Griffith signed as kin.{MINV 89:262}

---

[39] He d. in CV Co. leaving a will dated 10 Jan 1750/1 and proved 13 Nov 1751, naming his sister Bathsheba, sister Ann Duvall, bro. John, and the latter's daus. Sarah and Elizabeth. Bro. John was to be exec.{MWB 28:227}

[40] A John Griffith d. leaving a will dated 6 Jan 1750 and proved 28 Feb 1750, naming son-in-law Henry Hardesty as exec., and daus. Susanna, Sarah, Priscilla, Elizabeth Marshall.{MWB 27:511} He is almost certainly a different John, and not the father of John, b. c1726.

John Griffith was the father of: JOHN, Jr.; SARAH, named in the will of her uncle Benjamin; and ELIZABETH, named in the will of her uncle Benjamin.

5.   SAMUEL GRIFFITH, son of Samuel (3) and Sarah (Evans), was b. 25 May 1705 in AA Co., and d. c1744/5 in BA Co. He m. Mary (N).
{A:198}

On 25 Feb 1724/5, Ephraim Gover conv. 50 a. *Elburton* to Samuel Griffith, Jr. On 6 March 1733, Griffith conv. 50 a. of the tract to Samuel Gover, Sr., of AA Co.{BALR IS#H:91, HWS#M:89} On 17 Aug 1737, Samuel Griffith, with consent of his wife Mary, conv. 104 a. *Planter's Paradise* to James Lee.{BALR HWS#1-A:4}

Samuel Griffith d. leaving a will dated 14 March 1744 and proved 24 June 1745, leaving *Refuse, Abel's Forest* and *Williamson's Hope* to his eldest son Luke, his dwell. plant. to his son Samuel, and lands in CV and AA Co. to his wife Mary. He also named his daus. Mary, Elizabeth, and Sarah. His wife and friend Solomon Hillen were to be execs.{MWB 24:222}

The estate of Samuel Griffith was inv. on 1 Sep 1746 by John Mathews and James Osborn, and valued at £747.17..8. Jacob Giles and Isaac Webster signed as creditors, while Luke and Samuel Griffith signed as next of kin. Mary Griffith, the extx., filed the inventory on 4 Aug 1748.{MINV 37:7}

Samuel and Mary (N) Griffith were the parents of{A:198-199}: LUKE, b. c1729, m. 13 June 1759, Blanch Carvill; SARAH, b. 11 Sep 1734, possibly m. 2 Oct 1749, Thomas Deadman; SAMUEL, b. 7 April 1737, d. 8 Jan 1803, m. 1st, Frenetta Garrison; and 2nd, Mrs. Martha Presbury; MARY, b. 25 Sep 1739, m. 5 April 1761 at St. George's Parish, HA Co., Edward Ward, Jr.; ISAAC, b. 1743, and d. 1743/4; AVARILLA (twin), b. 23 Nov 1744, may have m. John Griffith; and PRISCILLA, (twin), b. 23 Nov 1744.

6.   JOHN GRIFFITH, b. c1726, is placed by Jourdan as a son of John Griffith, who d. 1750, but this compiler feels his father was the John who d. in 1765. John, Jr., d. in HA Co. leaving a will 14 Sep 1779 and proved 17 Jan 1780. He m. Averilla, b. c1742, dau. of James Pritchard, Sr. Avarilla Pritchard, dau. of James and Elizabeth, was b. 8 Jan 1738.{Reamy and Reamy, *St. George's Parish Register, 1689-1793*:57}

It should be noted that Jourdan identifies his wife as a cousin, Avarilla Griffith, b. c1744.{A}

In 1776, John Griffith, age 50, and Avarilla, age 34, lived in Susquehanna Hundred. Living with them were Hannah, age 14, Elizabeth, age 12, Fanney (Frances), age 9, Mary, age 8, James, age 4, and William, age 2.{Peden, *Early Harford Countians*:171}

In his will, John Griffith named his two eldest sons, James and William (who were left negroes). James was to have 60 a. *Gravelly Bottom* and *Woods Close*. Son John was to have a negro, and he and William were also to have 100 a. *Perriman's Revise*. John Griffith also left negroes to his daus. Hannah Crawford, and Elizabeth, Frances, and Mary Griffith. Execs. were to be his father-in-law James Pritchard, Sr., and the testator's wife Avarilla.{HAWB AJ#2:227}

John Griffith's estate file was dated 17 Jan 1780. Avarilla Griffith was the extx. No distribution was found in the file. James and Obadiah Pritchard were next of kin.{HA Co. Estate File No. 183, HA Co. Court House}

John and Avarilla were the parents of{Peden; *Early Harford Countians:* cites HA Co. Orphans Court Proceedings, 1778-1810}: HANNAH, 14 in 1776, m. (N) Crawford by 1779; ELIZABETH, 12 in 1776; FANNEY (FRANCES), age 9 in 1776, m. John Smith in 1787; MARY, age 8 in 1776; JAMES, age 4 in 1776; WILLIAM, age 2 in 1776; and JOHN, b. 25 Nov 1776.

THE GROCE FAMILY

1. ROGER GROCE, progenitor, is not listed in Skordas, but he was in MD by 21 Oct 1652 when he surv. 600 a. later called *Watkins' Purchase*. Gross sold the land to John Watkins.{MRR:141}

In 1657, Frances Smith testified she was his servant, and that Roger Scott was the father of her unborn child.{ARMD 10:525-526}

On 10 April 1663, he wit. a deed in AA Co.{AALR IH#1:153} On 25 Aug 1663, Anthony and Jane Griffin conv. to Roger Grosse, of AA Co., a patent for 700 a. called *Price's*.{TALR 1:2}

Roger Grose d. by 19 Feb 1675, when his widow and admx., Ann, now wife of John Welsh, filed an inventory valued at 190,480 lbs. of tob. She mentioned John Grose, who had d. in the interim.{INAC 1:541}

Roger Gross's estate was admin. prior to 13 Nov 1676 when a distribution was made to John Gross as guardian to the other orphans listed below.{INAC 5:143}

Roger and Anne seem to be the parents of: JOHN, d. by 18 April 1676{TALR 3:34}; ELIZABETH, living 1676, m. Richard Snowden; ROGER, living 1676; WILLIAM, living 1676; and FRANCES, under 16 on 4 Dec 1675. (By 10 June 1681 she had m. John Hawkins, Gent. On that day, they gave power of attorney to Vincent Lowe to sell 150 a. on Miles River called *Fausley*, left by John Grose to his sister, the sd. Frances.){TALR 4:46}

2.   JOHN GROSS, son of Roger, of AA Co., d. leaving a will dated 4 Dec 1675 and proved 18 April 1676, naming bros. Roger and William (the latter not yet 21), and sisters Eliza, wife of Richard Snowden, and Frances (not yet 16). He also mentioned lands on the Wye and Mills Rivers.{MWB 5:30}

On 14 March 1676, John Watkins, exec., of John Gross, Gent., who was the son and heir of Roger Gross, sold 200 a. on Wye River to John Davis.{TALR 3:34}

On 16 Sep 1677, his estate was admin. by John Watkins. Two inventories valued at £413.12.0 and £268.17.11 were recorded, and various disbursements were made, one being a payment made to Philemon Lloyd for Roger Grose, his part his father's estate [the wording is not clear].{INAC 4:300}

Roger Gross d. leaving a son John, who in turn d. leaving a surviving dau. and heir-at-law, Elizabeth, wife of John Carpenter. John and Elizabeth Carpenter sold 600 a. near Road River to John Watkins. {AALR SY#1:16}

John Gross, son and heir of Roger, d. by 14 March 1676, leaving his exec., John Watkins, to sell 200 a. on Myles River to John Davis. {TALR 3:34} John Grose, of AA Co., by his last will and testament dated 4 Dec 1675, conv. 250 a. on Miles River called *Fausley* to his dau. Frances, wife of John Hawkins, Gent.{TALR 4:46}

John Gross seems to have left two children: ELIZABETH, m. John Carpenter; and FRANCES, m. John Hawkins.

4.   ROGER GROSS, son of Roger and Ann, probably d. s.p. at *Ashby,* in TA Co., which was passed from Roger, Sr., who surv. it in 1663, to Roger, Jr., and then to William.

On 1 Aug 1676, Roger Grosse sold 100 a., part of *Ashby*, laid out for sd. Grosse, to Nathaniel Chance.{TALR 3:22}

Roger Gross sold part of 800 a. *Ashby* to Charles Bardon on 29 April 1678. The land was formerly owned by Roger Gross, Sr., of AA Co.{TALR 3:195}

5.   WILLIAM GROSS, son of Roger and Ann, m. by 10 Jan 1691, Hester, dau. of Nicholas Gassaway, and had a dau. Eliza Gross. Mother and dau. were mentioned in Gassaway's will.{MWB 2:228}

William Grosse patented 2 tracts of land in TA Co.: 24 a. *Gross's Addition* on 22 April 1684{MPL 25:113, 30:160}, and 200 a. *Ashby's Addition*, on 21 Jan 1689.{MPL 25:416, 34:33}

On (date illegible), William Grosse and wife Hester sold a tenement of 250 a. to Anthony Mayle. On 18 Nov 1684, William gave bond to Mayle for 40,000 lbs. of tob.{TALR 1:356, 357}

On 10 Sep 1683, William Gross and wife Hester conv. 200 a., a moiety of *Abington,* laid out for Roger Gross, Gent., to Richard Sweatnam, Gent.{TALR 4:227}

On 8 Oct 1700, Mrs. Hester Gross was mentioned as having received a payment from the estate of Capt. Nicholas Gassaway.{INAC 20:41}

William must have d. by 1704, for Esther Groce m. Stephen Warman on 2 July 1704 in All Hallows Parish.{AACR:18} However, on 28 Nov 1714, Hester Gross was listed as a debtor in the administration account of James Parnall.{INAC 35A:261}

On 18 Oct 1715, Hester Warman, lately called Hester Gross, was mentioned as having been a tenant in Col. Edward Dorsey's house. {AALR IB#2:252}

William and Hester were the parents of: ELIZA, b. by 1691; and possibly ANNE, who as Anne, dau. of William Gross, of BA Co., patented 200 a. *Ann's Dowry* on 22 Sep 1683.{MPL 25:99, 32:353}

Unplaced

GROCE, ANN, m. Thomas Davis on 7 April 1708.{AACR:24}

GROSSE, JACOB, d. by Feb 1732. He m. Sarah (N) who survived him.

He was in BA Co. by 3 Aug 1720 when Francis Dallahide conv. him 150 a. *Chestnut Neck.*{BALR TR#DS:227}

As Jacob Groce, of BA Co., he patented two tracts of land: 100 a. *Jacob's Privilege* on 8 May 1729{MPL PL#7:208, IL#B:41}, and 50 a. *Gross' Outlet,* on 9 May 1729.{MPL PL#7:147 and IL#B:42}

Jacob Groce d. by 14 Feb 1732, when his estate was admin. by Anthony Asher, admin. An inv. of £179.10.4 was mentioned, and payments were made to John Stone, who m. Susanna, dau. of the dec., Isaac Groce, son of the dec., and the widow Sarah Groce, as well as others.{MDAD 11:635}

Jacob Groce was the father of: ISAAC; and SUSANNA, m. John Stone.

GROSS, LAWRENCE, was in KE Co. by 22 June 1708 when he was listed as having been paid out of the estate of Ambrose Asiz of KE Co. {INAC 28:225}

GROCE, MARTHA, m. John Sellman on 4 Dec 1707 in All Hallows Parish.{AACR:24} On 22 Feb 1715/6, John Sellman, for the love he bore his wife Martha and children, John, Benjamin, Lawrence, and Martha Sellman, conv. to them livestock and furniture.{AALR IB#2:217}

GROCE, NICHOLAS, was transported to MD in 1651.{MPL 4:584} He was mentioned in 1671 in a deposition made by Nathan Bentley of CH Co. {ARMD 60:355}

Nicholas m. Rose (N) by 22 May 1690, when she released her dower on a 40 a. tract of land called *Eagle's Nest,* granted to Gross on 24 July 1679, being part of a warrant for 2,891 a. of land assigned to Thomas Daborne and which George Yate assigned to Gross. Gross sold the land to Mathias Hughs.{MPL 24:164, 28:177; AALR WH#4:49}

On 10 Oct 1683, Nicholas and Rose Groce wit. the will of Thomas Parsons of AA Co.{MWB 4:28}

He was bur. 5 Feb 1698/9 in All Hallows Parish.{AACR:8} Rose Groce, his wife, had been bur. 28 Dec 1695.{AACR:8}

The estate of Nicholas Grose was admin. on 12 Feb 1702 by James Lewis. An inventory worth £25.14.0 was mentioned.{INAC 23:83}

Nicholas and Rose were the parents of{AACR:15}: MARY, b. 1 July 1693, bapt. 26 July 1702; and ELIZABETH, b. 23 Dec 1689, bapt. (date not given).

THE HEARN(E) FAMILY

1.   DANIEL HEARN, possible first known ancestor of the family, d. sometime after Nov 1756. His wife's name has not been determined.

On 13 May 1717, Charles Carroll, of Annapolis, for £70, conv. to Daniel Carroll and Daniel Hearne, of AA Co., 203 a. called *Chance.* {AALR IB#2:383}

Daniel Hearn was listed in Dec 1728 as living at Mr. Carroll's plants. beyond Elk Ridge.{AMG 24 Dec 1728} He was still living there in July 1761 when he advertised he had a stray mare at his plant.{AMG 2 July 1761}

Daniel Herne was listed as one of the debtors owing the estate of Amos Garrett, of AA Co., in the latter's inventory filed 15 Aug 1729. {MINV 15:46-73}

On 29 June 1743, Daniel Hearn, Basil Dorsey, and James McCollum wit. the will of Eleanor Herbert of AA Co.{MWB 23:232}

Daniel Hearne, planter, appeared in Anne Arundel Judgments between June 1746 and Nov 1756. At the June 1752 Court, he was sued by John Hanbury and Co.{AAJU June 1752:360} In Nov 1752 and Nov 1755, two of his slaves were made levy free.{AAJU November 1752 Court:426 and November 1755 Court:335}

In Jan 1749, Daniel Hearn, Dr. Joshua Warfield, and Za. McDonnell wit. the will of Henry Rooker of AA Co.{MWB 27:268}

In Aug 1756, he was made levy free and in Nov 1756 the court made him an allowance and described his house as "being distressed." {AAJU August 1756 Court:711 and November 1756 Court:795}

Daniel Hearn was probably the father of: DANIEL, Jr., who in March 1749/50, was sued by Richard Snowden{AAJU March 1749/50 Court:501}; MICHAEL; and JOHN.

2.   MICHAEL HEARN, probably son of Daniel (1), was b. c1740/50 and d. 1813. He is the first definitely known progenitor of the Hearn family.

He was in AA Co. by Aug 1761 when he was a defendant against Richard Snowden.{AAJU August 1761 Court:228}

Michael Hearn and John Hearn are listed as debtors in the inventory, filed 18 Sep 1771, of the estate of William Hall of AA Co. {MINV 107:339-355}

On 2 March 1778, Michael Hearn took the Oath of Fidelity to the State of MD before Thomas Dorsey.{CMSP Red Books, Part 3, item 147}

On 26 May 1790, Henry Ridgely conv. to Michael "Heron" 75 a. part of *Grimmit's Chance.*{AALR NH#5:290} On 26 April 1800, Henry Ridgely, son of Henry Ridgely, conv. 30 more a. of *Grimmith's Chance* to Michael Hearn.{AALR NH#10:366}

Michael Hearn, planter, of AA Co., on 20 Dec 1805, gave bond he would convey to his sons Isaac, William, and John, part of *The Grove* and part *Second Addition to Snowden's Manor.*{AALR WSG#2:168}

A deed dated 21 Jan 1813 stated that, on 9 Aug 1803, Michael Hearn had obtained a conveyance from James Worthington for 300 a. of land, part *The Grove* and part *Second Addition to Snowden's Manor.* He also obtained two different conveyances for portions of *Grimmitt's Chance.* The deed also stated that Hearn had d. intestate without conveying the 300 a. to his three sons, and now disputes have arisen among his heirs. Now Edward Iglehart and wife Sophia, Isaac Hearn, John Hearn, Cornelius Iglehart and wife Anne, conv. all the land by deed of trust to Thomas Worthington.{AALR WSG#2:169} There is a possibility that Sophia was a widow and not a dau. of Michael Hearn.

Michael was the father of: ISAAC; ANNE, m. Cornelius Iglehart in 1802 (their son Tilghman m. his first cousin, Ann Hearne); JOHN; (possibly) CALEB; WILLIAM; and (possibly) SOPHIA, m. by 1813, Edward Iglehart.

3.   ISAAC HEARN, son of Michael, was b. c1771, and was living in 1853, m. Elizabeth (N), b. in the 1770, and d. by 1853, according to a deed dated 16 Aug 1853.{HOLR WHW#14:35}

On 23 Aug 1815, he executed a deed of partition with John Hearn (presumably his bro.), for part of *The Grove* and *Second Addition to Snowden's Manor.*{AALR WSG#4:40}

On 23 May 1849, Isaac Hearn, and wife Elizabeth, conv. to Tilghman Iglehart part *Second Discovery* and *Howard's Resolution,* 272

a. in all, except for 82 a. conv. by deed of same date to Rebecca, wife of Richard Hearn, and the sd. Isaac also reserved a life estate in the sd. tracts for himself and wife Elizabeth.{AALR EPH#9:114}

MD Chancery paper #10079 contains a petition of John Orem, of Howard District, stating that Isaac Hearn, of Howard District, executed two bills of obligation dated 13 May 1848, payable to the petitioner. Hearn then took advantage of the insolvent debtor laws and conv. all his property to his sons Artemus, Alfred, Richard (with wife Rebecca), and Benjamin Hearn, and to T[ilghman] Iglehart and wife Nancy.

The 1850 Census of Howard District shows Isaac Hearn, Sr., age 79, wife Elizabeth, age 7-(?), and Isaac, age 35 or 38, living with Trueman Iglehart, 40, and wife Anne, 35.{Census of Howard District, dwelling 1296, family 1313}

Isaac and Elizabeth were the parents of: ARTEMAS, b. c1805/7, d. 8 June 1885; ANN, b. c1809, d. 17 Feb 1895; ALFRED C., b. c1812; ISAAC, b. c1812/5, d. by May 1851; RICHARD, b c1815; and BENJAMIN, b. c1816, d. 1902.

4.   JOHN HEARN, son of Michael, was living on 23 Aug 1815 when he and Isaac Hearn executed a deed of partition for part of *The Grove* and *Second Addition to Snowden's Manor*.{AALR WSG#4:40-ff.} In 1813, John Hearn, living near Richard Owings' mills on Elk Ridge, registered a stray.{AALR WSG#2:175}

5.   CALEB HEARN, possibly son of Michael, d. cSep 1835. In Dec 1818, he m., in PG Co., Maria Green.

He was drafted in AA Co. in 1814 for service in the War of 1812.

Caleb d. in HO Co. (then AA Co.) in Sep 1835.{Wright; *Maryland Militia, War of 1812, Vol. 4: AA and CV Cos.*} His pension application stated that the name was sometimes pronounced Herring.

6.   WILLIAM HEARN, son of Michael, m., by 17 Oct 1813, Rachel (N), and moved to Washington Co., PA, when he and his wife conv. their share of his father's estate to Isaac Hear.{AALR WSG#2: 631}

7.   ARTEMAS HEARN, son of Isaac and Elizabeth (N) Hearn, was b. c1807, and d. 8 June 1885, age 78 years. He is bur. in the Tilghman Iglehart Graveyard.{HOCM 3:48}

He m. 1st, Elizabeth Close, b. c1812, d. 20 April 1858, age 46, by BAML dated 20 Nov 1830. He m. 2nd, Rebecca (N). Elizabeth is also bur. at the Tilghman-Iglehart Graveyard near Triadelphia Road and Rosemary Lane.{HOCM 3:47}

Artemas was the father of ten children by his first wife (their ages are taken from the 1850 and 1860 Censuses of HO Co.) and two children by his second wife.

138

By Elizabeth Close, he was the father of: ELIZABETH, b. c1832, age 18 in 1850; SAMUEL CHASE, b. c1836, d. 14 Oct 1914 in his 79th year, m. Rida Miller; SUSAN R., b. c1836/7, age 13 in 1850 and 24 in 1860; MARY JANE, b. c1839, age 11 in 1850;[41] CATHERINE, b. 22 Aug 1840, d. 23 Nov 1867, bur. at Wavertree{The Tilghman Iglehart Graveyard; HOCM:3:47}; SARAH T., b. 8 Jan 1843, age 7 in 1850, and 15 in 1860, m. William A. Iglehart and had six children living. She d. of Pulmonary tuberculosis on 30 Jan 1903, age 60{HO Reg. of Deaths} and was bur. in the Tilghman Iglehart Graveyard{HOCM 3:47}; ISAAC FLETCHER, b. c1846/7, age 4 in 1850 and 13 in 1860; BARBARA R., b. c1849, age 1 in 1850, 11 in 1860; CHRISTIAN, b. c1853, age 7 in 1860; and WILLIAM, b. c1856, age 4 in 1860.

By Rebecca, Artemas Hearn was the father of: NANNIE; and NAOMI.

8.   ANN HEARN, dau. of Isaac and Elizabeth, was b. c1809, and d. 17 Feb 1895 in her 87th year. She m. Tilghman H. Iglehart by, BAML dated 22 Jan 1833. She was bur. at Wavertree, Glenelg, HO Co.{HOCM 3:48} Ann (or Frances) and Tilghman Iglehart had at least one son: WILLIAM AUGUSTUS IGLEHART, d. 3 June 1902, age 66 years, 2 months, 27 days.[42]

9.   ALFRED C. HEARN, son of Isaac and Elizabeth, was b. c1812. He m. Matilda Carr by HOML dated 13 July 1849. On 29 Oct 1863, Alfred C. Hearn and his two children, Charles E. and Catherine E., mortgaged property to Enoch Selby.{HOLR 22 WWW:593}

10.   ISAAC HEARN, son of Isaac and Elizabeth, was b. c1812/5, d. leaving a will dated 30 Dec 1850 and proved 20 May 1851, naming the following relatives: bro.-in-law Tilghman H. Iglehart, niece Ann Eliza Iglehart, sister Ann Iglehart, bros. Artemus Hearn, Alfred C. Hearn, and Benjamin Hearn.{HOWB 1:261}

11.   RICHARD HEARN, son of Isaac and Elizabeth, was b. c1815, and m. Rebecca Ford by HOML dated 18 July 1846.

---

[41] Another source says she was b. 7 Dec 1833, and d. 29 April 1900. She m. Benjamin Franklin Nichols. They are buried at St. Mark's Episcopal Church, Highland, HO Co.

[42] A farmer, he m. Sarah T. Iglehart and had six children living.{HO Co. Register of Deaths} William A. Iglehart, b. 6 March 1836, d. 3 June 1902, bur. with wife [see above] on Tilghman Iglehart Graveyard.{HOCM 3:47}

12.   BENJAMIN HEARN, son of Isaac and Elizabeth, was b. c1816, d. 1902. He was bur. at Wavertree, Glenelg, HO Co.{HOCM 3:47} He seems to have had two death certificates registered in HO Co. The first states that he d. 14 June 1902 at Glenelg, age 83, son of Isaac Hearn. He was a widower and a laborer.{HO Register of Deaths} The second states that he d. 14 May 1902 at Glenelg, son of Isaac and Elizabeth Hearn, unm., age 82, paralysis listed as cause of death.{HO Register of Deaths}

Unplaced

HEARN, JOHN. On 20 Feb 1777, Thomas Dorsey and John Dorsey of Elk Ridge wrote to the Council of Safety recommending that the bearer, John Hearn, should be an officer in the troops being raised; he served with the Elk Ridge Battalion from the first of the disputes with Great Britain, and would have cheerfully marched to reinforce Gen. Washington, at the Council's request, had he been backed by a sufficient number.{CMSP Red Books, Part 2, item 933}

HARN, JOHN, III, on 12 March 1778, took the Oath of Fidelity to the State of MD before John Dorsey.{CMSP Red Books, Part 3, item 155}

HEARN, JOHN, is listed in the 1783 Assessment List of Elk Ridge Hundred, AA Co., but he did not own any land.

HARN, JOHN, is listed as dec. in November 1788 Court. Mary Harn appears for him.{AAJU November 1788 Court:149}

HEARN, MICHAEL, wit. a deed in 1736.{AALR RD#2:376}

HEARN, THOMAS, d. leaving a will dated 4 Nov 1814 and proved 24 Nov 1814, naming wife Priscilla (to have all his real estate), mother Sarah (to have farm on Stoney Creek called *Bachelor's Inheritance*); after death of his wife Priscilla all his property to be divided among his bros. and sisters and his wife's bros. and sisters.{AAWB 38:70}

THE HOLBROOK FAMILY

JOSEPH HOLBROOK m. 1st, Temperance Wade, in All Hallows Parish, on 4 Feb 1696/7.{AACR:7} Temperance was bur. on 16 Jan 1705. {AACR:21} Joseph m. 2nd, on 8 Aug 1711, Dorothy Callingood.{AACR:25}

Dorothy, wife of Joseph Holbrook, was bur. 18 July 1716.{AACR:195} Joseph m. 3rd, Mary (N).

Joseph and Dorothy Holbrook wit. the will of John Durden of AA Co. on 9 Oct 1715.{MWB 14:87}

Joseph and Temperance were the parents of{AACR:7, 19}: JOSEPH, b. 26 Sep 1697; and ANNE, b. 2 April 1704, bapt. 6 June 1704.

Joseph and Mary were the parents of{AACR:186}: RACHEL, bapt. 2 Oct 1717.

JOSEPH HOLBROOK m. Mary Culver in All Hallows Parish on 27 Dec 1730.{AACR:45}

JOHN HOLBROOK and Ann Jones were m. in All Hallows Parish on 8 Feb 1721/2.{AACR:33}

JOHN HOLBROOK m. Jane (N). They were the parents of: AMOS, b. 27 Feb 1722, bapt. 12 May 1723.{AACR:36}

AMOS HOLBROOK son of John and Jane, was b. 27 Feb 1722. {AACR:36}

By 12 March 1760, he was in BA Co., where he wit. the will of Mary Bowen.{MWB 31:748}

THE HOMEWOOD FAMILY

THOMAS HOMEWOOD was the father of two sons, named in the Aug 1681 will of his bro. John. His sons were: JAMES; and THOMAS.

JOHN HOMEWOOD d. in AA Co. by Aug 1681. He m., by 17 April 1675, Sarah, sister of John Meers of AA Co.{MWB 2:72}

John Homewood, of AA Co., d. leaving a will dated 21 Aug 1681 and proved 28 Sep 1682. He named his wife Sarah, and nephews James and Thomas, sons of his bro. Thomas Homewood.{MWB 4:70}

JAMES HOMEWOOD, possibly son of Thomas and nephew of John, m. Mary (N). He may be the James Homewood, "husband of Marah," who d. 11 Jan 1703.{AACR:136}

James and Mary were the parents of two children, b. in St. Margaret's Parish, AA Co.: SARAH, b. 20 Jan 1700; and THOMAS, b. 27 May 1704.{AACR:107, 108}

THOMAS HOMEWOOD d. 25 Oct 1709.{AACR:137}

JEAMES HOMEWOOD d. 15 March 1709/10.{AACR:137}

Capt. THOMAS HOMEWOOD, son of Thomas and Mary, was b. 27 May 1704, and d. 19 May 1739.{AACR:138} He dep. on 12 Jan 1735, giving his age as c31 years.{MDCHR:84} Thomas Homewood m. Rachel Merriken on 9 Jan 1727 in St. Margaret's.{AACR:131}

He m. Anne, dau. of Charles Hammond, on 16 Dec 1731, also in St. Margaret's.{AACR:131} After Thomas Homewood's death, she m. 2nd, William Govane.{MDCHR:100} In July 1752, Ann Govane petitoned the Court of Chancery, stating that she owned a great deal of property that came to her from her father and her former husband. She stated that her present husband (Govane) treats her in such a cruel manner that she wants to gain possession of her property.{MDCHR:98}

Thomas and Anne (Hammond) Homewood were the parents of three children who were infants under the age of 21 in May 1753, when their grandfather, Charles Hammond, petitioned the Court of Chancery. The children were b. in St. Margaret's Parish{AACR:117; MDCHR:100}: CHARLES, b. 22 April 1734; ANNE, b. 12 June 1736; and and REBECCA, b. 27 Oct 1738.

Unplaced

HOMEWOOD, MARY, m. John Ingram in St. Margaret's Parish on 3 Sep 1705.{AACR:129}

HOMEWOOD, SARAH, m. William Worthington in St. Margaret's Parish, on 5 Nov 1717.{AACR:133}

THE HOOKER FAMILY

After the publication of *Baltimore County Families, 1659-1759,* (Baltimore: Genealogical Publishing Co., 1989), subsequent research revealed that two generations were actually one. That research and the discovery of a reference to property in New York has led to a revision of the first two generations.

1.   THOMAS HOOKER, d. c1684. He m. Joane (N), who d. 12 da., 12 mo., 1675.{QRSM:1}

On 25 March 1658, Thomas Hooker was assigned 600 a. *Brownton* by John Brown and John Clark.{AALR IH#I:310}

On 14 June 1671, Thomas Hooker, of AA Co., was assigned 350 a. *Elberton's* on Great Choptank River by Thomas Thurston of BA Co. {DOLR 3 Old:2, 12} On 5 March 1673, Hooker, of AA Co., conv. the 350 a. of *Elberton's* to John Willson.{DOLR 3 Old:2, 12}

On 10 May 1673, John Edmondson, of TA Co., and wife Sarah, conv. to Thomas Hooker, of AA Co., 600 a. *Walnut Ridge.*{TALR 2:78}

About 1674, Thomas Hooker admin. the estate of John Deaving (?) of BA Co.{INAC 1:35}

A Yearly Meeting of Clifts/West River was held at the house of Thomas Hooker on 23rd da., 3rd mo., 1679.{QRSM:67}

Thomas Hooker patented 154 a. *Hooker's Chance* on 2 June 1683 and 31 a. *Corrant* on 25 June 1683, both in AA Co.{MPL 29:320, 31:93}

The will of Thomas Hooker, of West River, was dated on 8 Nov 1683 and proved on 9 May 1684. To his son Thomas he gave *Brownton,* except for 1-1/2 a. already given to the Quakers. Sons Jacob and Benjamin were to have jointly 600 a. *Black Walnut Ridge* in TA Co. Son Benjamin was to have 210 a. *Hooker's Addition* in AA Co. Daus. Damaris Hooker and Johanna Clarkson were left personalty. Execs. were to be his son Thomas and William Richardson and Benjamin Lawrence. Samuel Garland, Alis Bridgwater and Mary Woodlea wit. the will.{MWB 4:28}

On 17 Jan 1685, Hooker's estate was inv. at £152.12.6 and 8,600 lbs. of tob.{INAC 8:338}

The births of the children of Thomas and Joane were recorded in West River Monthly Meeting. Thomas and Joan were the parents of {QRSM:1, 12}: JOANNA, b. 15 da., 1 mo., 1660/1, m. 1st, John Hillen (d. 1682 in AA Co.), and 2nd, (N) Clarkson; THOMAS, b. 13 da., 5 mo., 1660/1; MARY ANN, b. 31 da., 6 mo., 16--, d. 2 da., 7 mo., 1678; JACOB, b. 12 da., 6 mo., 1665; DAMARIS, b. 29 da., 11 mo., 1667; and BENJAMIN, b. 15 da., 11 mo., 1670.[43]

2.   THOMAS HOOKER, son of Thomas and Joane, was b. 13 da., 6 mo., 1660 and d. by Nov 1744. He m. 1st, by 1689, Sarah (N), and 2nd, by 1720, Eleanor (N). He dep., giving his age as 66 or 67, in 1727. {AALC 2:20, 21, 22}

On 6 Oct 1683, Hooker, of West River, MD, gave a power of attorney concerning property in NY to John Edmondson, also of MD. {DOLR 4 Old:142} On 4 Oct 1684, Hooker conv. to Michael Wyman, of TA Co., parcels of *Pathomell,* cont. 100 a. and 50 a., on the s. side of Great Choptank River.{DOLR 4 Old:145}

On 8 June 1689, Thomas Hooker, son and heir of Thomas Hooker, dec., conv. to Thomas Tench 660 a. called *Brownton* (except for a small portion already given to the Quakers for a meeting house and burying ground).{AALR IH#1:312} On May 1701, Thomas and Sarah conv. 248 a. *Maiden's Dairy* to John Yeakley.{BALR HW#2:66}

---

[43] On 10 Aug 1691, Benjamin Hooker conv. 210 a. *Hooker's Addition* to John Norris of AA Co.{AALR IH#3:108}

Thomas Hooker, m. 2nd, Eleanor (N) by Sep 1720, when they conv. *Samuel's Hope* to Benjamin Bowen.{BALR TR#DS:277}

Thomas Hooker patented two tracts of land in BA Co.: 500 a. *Samuel's Hope,* on 10 Nov 1695, and 248 a. *Maiden's Dowry,* on 10 March 1696.{MPL 34:139, 40:273, 521} He also patented other tracts of land in BA Co.: 380 a. *Gerar* on 25 April 1717, 100 a. *Bather* on 10 Sep 1717, and 200 a. *Jericho* on 15 Aug 1729.{MPL EE#6:316, FF#7:179, PL#4:289, 293, PL#7:197, and IL#B:44}

On 20 May 1695, Thomas was listed as a creditor in the estate of Nicholas Nicholson, of AA Co.{INAC 13A:313} In Dec 1699, he was listed as a debtor in the estate of Edward and Elizabeth Boothby of BA Co.{INAC 11B:32} On 4 Oct 1701, Thomas Hooker and Robert Hopkins appraised the estate of Eleanor Cotton, widow, of BA Co.{INAC 21:46} On 2 Dec 1706, he was paid out of the estate of Matthew Hawkins. {INAC 26:117}

On 21 April 1718, Thomas Hooker and George Hitchcock appraised the estate of George Pickett of BA Co.{MINV 1:26}

Thomas Hooker and wife Eleanor, on 2 Nov 1726, conv. that part of *Gerar* called *Hooker's Farm* to Samuel Hooker. On 17 June 1730, they conv. 280 a., the residue of *Gerar,* to Penelope Deye.{BALR IS#H:287, IS#K:301}

Thomas Hooker d. in BA Co. leaving a will dated 14 Dec 1743 and proved 7 Nov 1744, naming wife Eleanor (to have *Eleanor's Lookout*), son John (to have the land afsd. tract after mother's death), sons Samuel and Richard (to have one s. and no more), son Benjamin, daus. Ruth and Edith, and the children of Benjamin Carr. Wife Eleanor was to be extx. Nicholas Haile, Moses Merryman, and Elextious Lemon were wits.{BAWB 2:16}

Thomas was the father of: SAMUEL, b. c1686/7; JOHN; RICHARD, b. 24 Sep 1701; BENJAMIN; RUTH; and EDITH.

3.   JACOB HOOKER, son of Thomas and Joane, was b. 12 da., 6 mo., 1665. (He was still living on 3 Nov 1700 when he wit. the will of Eliza Rigby of St. James Parish.{MWB 11:10}) On 16 June 1691, Jacob and Benjamin Hooker, sons of Thomas Hooker, of AA Co., dec., conv. 600 a. *Walnut Ridge* (which their father had bought from John Edmondson and later willed to them) to Job Evans, merchant, of AA Co.{TALR 5:323}

4.   SAMUEL HOOKER, son of Thomas (2) and his first wife Sarah, was b. c1686/7, and d. 1773. He m. Sarah (N). He made several depositions placing his birth as c1686/7 (age 41 in 1727, 44 in 1731, 62 in 1748, 63 in 1749, 67 in 1754, 75 in 1761, 77 in 1763).{Peden, *More Maryland Deponents*:55 cites AA and BA Co. Land Commissions}

Samuel Hooker was accepted into membership of Gunpowder Meeting in 1754, with his four children (whose births were already recorded): Lovely, Richard, Thomas, and Sarah, all four being alive. {QRNM:35}

On 24 April 1756, Samuel Hooker, with consent of wife Sarah, conv. 307 a. *Come By Chance* to Jonathan Hanson.{BALR BB#I:536}

Samuel Hooker, age 77, one of the people called Quakers, affirmed on 27 Aug 1764 mentioning John Martin, dec., who was m. to a sister of the owner of land called *Duck Cove*.{AAEJ:Kelsoe, James, and wife Rebecca}

Samuel Hooker was the father of{QRNM:29, 41}: SAMUEL, b. 8 da., 2 mo., 1724; LOVELY, b. 27 da., 1 mo., 1727; RICHARD, b. 3 da., 8 mo., 1730; THOMAS, b. 17 da., 2 mo., 1733 (he was disowned on 27 da., 3 mo., 1761, for "going out in marriage with a young woman not of this Society"); SARAH, b. 19 da., 6 mo. 1735{QRNM:29}, m. Richard Richards on 14 July 1754; and SOPHIA, m. Arthur Chenoweth.

5.   SAMUEL HOOKER, son of Samuel, was b. 8 da., 2 mo., 1724, and d. 12 Aug 1756.

On 30 March 1748, he surv. 100 a. *Addition*. On 12 Aug 1756, his bro. and heir-at-law, Richard Hooker, conv. the land to John Ensor.{BALR BB#I:580}

THE GERARD HOPKINS FAMILY

Refs.: A: Burke. *American Families with British Ancestry.* B: Walter Lee Hopkins. *Hopkins of Virginia and Related Families.* (Richmond: J. W. Ferguson, 1931). C: Henry Peden. *Early Harford Countians* (Westminster: Family Line Publications). D: *The Thomas Book.* By Lawrence Buckley Thomas. Reprinted Bowie, MD: Heritage Books.

1.   GERARD HOPKINS, progenitor, is stated by Burke to have possibly been b. in Coventry.{A:2749} He d. in AA Co. in 1692.

Walter Lee Hopkins states that Gerard Hopkins settled at the Head of Chesapeake Bay c1640.{B:230} He is almost certainly the "Garrett" Hopkins who was transported into MD between 1658-1661.{MPL 4:625} Research to date has failed to discover any instance of Gerard Hopkins going to VA before his arrival in MD.

He was in AA Co. by 2 Dec 1675, when he was listed as a debtor in the inventory of Thomas Chandler, of AA Co.{INAC 2:36} On 7 April 1683, "Garrett" Hopkins, Francis Greene, Robert Hoakins, and Owen Bradway wit. the will of Francis Holland, Sr.{MWB 4:134}

On 4 July 1684, he purchased 152 a. called *Peake with Additions* from Samuel Heathcote of Derby, County Derby, England, nephew and heir of Nathaniel Heathcote, of AA Co., dec.{AALR WH#4: 24}

Gerard (or "Garrard") Hopkins d. leaving a will dated 12 Oct 1691, naming his wife Thomsen, and children Garrard, Ann, Thomsen, and Mary. William Collier and John Standforth were wits.{INAC 11A:46½}

The inventory of his estate was taken 9 Jan 1692 by Thomas Hughs and John Trundell, and valued at £138.10.0. Sureties were John Trundell and Robert Smith. John Chappell, planter, filed the inventory on 23 July 1692.{INAC 11A:47}

By his wife Thomasine he had several children{A}: GERARD; THOMSEN OR THOMASINE; ANN; and MARY.

2.   GERARD HOPKINS, son of Gerard (1), d. in AA Co. by 1743. He m. in Jan 1700/1, Margaret Johns, dau. of Richard and Elizabeth (Kinsey) Johns.{D:347}

Gerrard Hopkins, of AA Co., d. leaving a will dated 1 Jan 1741/2 and proved 2 Feb 1743. His eldest son Joseph was to have the real and personal estate already given him. Wife Margaret was left *White Hall, The Angles, Arnold's Gray,* and *Rope's Range.* Son Johns was left parts of the above tracts. Son Gerard was to have the residue of the above tracts. Son Philip was to have *Peak* and *Hopkins Fancy.* Sons Samuel and Richard were to have 800 a. *Friends Discovery* in BA Co. Son William was to have 300 a. in BA Co. which the testator bought from Henry Chew. Granddaus. Priscilla and Mary Hill were left personalty. Execs. were wife and son Gerard. The will was wit. by Joshua Warfield, William Wood, and Alex. Galt.{MWB 23:302}

Gerard and Margaret were the parents of{D:347}: MARGARET, m. Aquila Johns; ELIZABETH, b. 17 June 1703, m. on 10 Jan 1723/4, Levin Hill; JOSEPH, b. 6 Nov 1706, m. 17 Aug 1727, Ann Chew; GERARD, b. 7 March 1709; PHILIP, b. 9 Aug 1711, m. 1736, Elizabeth Hall; SAMUEL, b. 16 Jan 1713/4; RICHARD, b. 15 Dec 1715, m. Katherine Todd; WILLIAM, b. 8 da., 6 mo., 1718; and JOHNS, b. 30 Dec 1720.

3.   JOSEPH HOPKINS, son of Gerard (2) and Margaret, was b. 6 Nov 1706. He m. on 17 Aug 1727, Ann Chew, dau. of John and Eliza Chew.{D:347}

Joseph and Ann (Chew) Hopkins were the parents of{D:347}: JOSEPH, m. Elizabeth Gover; SARAH, m. Skipwith Coale; and ELIZABETH, m. on 6 March 1760, Samuel Hill.

4.   GERARD HOPKINS, son of Gerard (2) and Margaret, was b. 17 March 1709, and d. 3 July 1777. He m. on 7 May 1730, Mary Hall, a Roman Catholic who joined the Friends c1733.{D:347}

Gerard and Mary (Hall) Hopkins were the parents of{D:347-348}:
MARGARET, b. 11 Jan 1730/1, m. John Thomas; GERARD, b. 25 Aug
1732; MARY, b. 11 Nov 1734, m. in 1761, Philip Gover; SARAH, b. 20
Sep 1737, m. John Cowman; RICHARD, b. 7 Feb 1739/40;
ELIZABETH, b. 3 Nov 1741, m. Basil Brooke; RACHEL, b. 30 Dec
1742, m. Evan Thomas; JOSEPH, b. 11 Jan 1744/5; RICHARD, b. 20
March 1747/8; HANNAH, b. 29 Aug 1749; and ELISHA, b. 15 Oct
1752, m. 1st, Hannah Howell, and 2nd, Sarah Snowden.

5.   PHILIP HOPKINS, son of Gerard (2) and Margaret, was b. 9 Aug
1711. He m. in 1736, Elizabeth Hall.{D:347}
      Philip Hopkins, of AA Co., d. leaving a will dated 19 March 1757
and proved 29 June 1757. He named his wife Elizabeth and children
Gerrard, Richard, Samuel, Philip, William, Elizabeth, and Margaret
Hopkins. He mentioned the tract *Hopkins Choice*, and the 100 a. of *Peak*
which he had sold to George Neal. Wife Elizabeth was to be extx. The
will was wit. by Joseph Richardson, Edw. Cole, and George Gardiner.
{MWB 30:299}
      Philip and Elizabeth (Hall) Hopkins were the parents of{D:347}:
GERRARD; RICHARD; SAMUEL, m. Mary Gover; PHILIP;
WILLIAM; ELIZABETH; and MARGARET.

6.   SAMUEL HOPKINS, son of Gerard (2) and Margaret, was b. 16
Jan 1713/4. He m. on 2 Sep 1740, Sarah Giles, dau. of John and
Cassandra (Smith) Giles. She d. 15 May 1795.{D:349}
      Samuel and Sarah (Giles) Hopkins were the parents of{D:350}:
GERRARD, b. 26 April 1742, m. 1st (N) Dawes, and 2nd, Rachel
Willson Harris; SAMUEL, b. 9 Dec 1743, moved to NY; JOHN, b. 4 Jan
1745/6, m. Elizabeth Chew; MARGARET, b. 2 Sep 1747, m. Job Hunt;
PHILIP, b. 30 Sep 1749; ELIZABETH, b. 17 Aug 1751, m. Isaac
Webster; JAMES, d. unm.; CASSANDRA, b. 6 Jan 1755, m. John
Ellicott; RICHARD, d. young; JOSEPH, b. 2 Sep 1758; WILLIAM, b.
23 July 1760, m. (N) Twining; NICHOLAS, d. young; and JOHNS, b. 6
June 1764.

7.   RICHARD HOPKINS, son of Gerard (2) and Margaret, was b. 15
Dec 1715. He m. Katherine Todd. Richard and Katherine were the
parents of{D:347}: NICHOLAS, b. 12 May 1747, m. Mary Brian;
RACHEL, b. 31 Jan 1749/50; RICHARD, b. 15 Feb 1750/1; SARAH, b.
20 Sep 1751, m. Charles Rodgers; KATHERINE, b. 1753, d. 1763;
GERRARD, b. 21 Feb 1754, d. 1757; SAMUEL, b. 25 Sep 1756, d.
1757; ELIZABETH, b. 17 Sep 1758, m. Israel Cox of HA Co.; and
JOSEPH, b. 9 April 1761, m. Sarah Hopkins.

8.   WILLIAM HOPKINS, son of Gerard (2) and Margaret (Johns), was b. 8 da., 6 mo., 1718, and was living in 1776.{Peden; *Early Harford Countians:*204} He m. Rachel Orrick (b. c1720, living in 1776:F), by 2 Nov 1742 when they admin. the estate of Charles Daniel. On 2 Aug 1743, William and Rachel conv. part of *Hector's Fancy* to William Jenkins.
        In 1776, William, 58, and Rachel, 56, were living in Deer Creek Lower Hundred, HA Co., with Andrew Thompson, 18, and the children listed below.{1776 Census of HA Co.}
        In 1783, William was listed in Deer Creek Lower Hundred as owning *Arabia Petrea, Bachelor's Good Luck,* and *Jones' Venture.* {HATL 1783}
        William and Rachel were the parents of{C; D:352-3}: GERARD, b. c1743 (age 33 in 1776); ELIZABETH, m. William Husband; RACHEL; SUSANNAH, b. c1749 (age 27 in 1776), m. George Mason; WILLIAM, Jr., b. c1751 (age 25 in 1776), d. unm.; JOHN, b. c1753 (age 23 in 1776); LEVIN, b. c1755 (age 21 in 1776), m. Frances Wallace; HANNAH, b. c1758, (age 18 in 1776); CHARLES, b. c1761 (age 15 in 1776); and SAMUEL, b. c1764 (age 12 in 1776).

9.   JOHNS HOPKINS, son of Gerard (2) and Margaret (Johns), was b. 30 Dec 1720. He m. 1st, Mary Gillis. He m. 2nd, 14 Nov 1749, Mary, dau. of Joseph Richardson, and widow of Col. John Crockett. Johns Hopkins m. 3rd, on 16 Jan 1758, Elizabeth, dau. of Samuel and Mary (Snowden) Thomas.{D:351-352}
        By Mary Gillis, Johns Hopkins was the father of{D:351}: EZEKIEL, b. 11 May 1747.
        By Mary Richardson Crockett, Johns Hopkins was the father of {D:351}: JOHNS, b. 8 July 1751, m. 1st, Elizabeth Harris, and 2nd, on 3 April 1779, Catherine Howell.
        By ELizabeth Thomas, Johns Hopkins was the father of{D:354}; SAMUEL, b. 3 Feb 1759, m. Hannah Janney; PHILIP, b. 24 Sep 1760, m. Mary Boone; RICHARD, b. 2 March 1762, m. Hannah Hammond; MARY, b. 7 Jan 1764, m. Samuel Peach; MARGARET, b. 20 Feb 1766, m. Jesse Tyson; GERARD T., b. 24 Oct 1769, m. Dorothy Brooke; ELIZABETH, m. John Janney; EVAN, b. 30 Nov 1772, m. Elizabeth Hopkins; ANN, b. 26 Feb 1775, m. Thomas Shrieves; RACHEL, b. 7 Sep 1777; and WILLIAM.

10.   JOSEPH HOPKINS, son of Gerrard (4) and Mary (Hall) Hopkins, was b. 11 Jan 1744/5, and d. 11 Sep 1825. He m. Elizabeth Howell, who d. 4 Nov 1810.{D:348}
        Joseph and Elizabeth (Howell) Hopkins were the parents of{D:348}: ISAAC HOWELL, b. 19 Dec 1770; PATIENCE, b. 5 Nov 1771, m. Philip Snowden; GERARD, b. 22 Jan 1775, m. 1st, Henrietta Snowden,

and 2nd, Mary Gover; HANNAH (twin), b. 12 April 1777; MARY (twin), b. 12 April 1777; MARGARET, b. 2 March 1779; JOSEPH (twin), b. 10 March 1781; ELIZABETH (twin), b. 10 March 1781; ISAAC GRAY, b. 26 June 1783; PRISCILLA, b. 24 Oct 1785; MARY, b. 9 April 1785; SAMUEL, b. 9 April 1790, m. Rachel Worthington; and SARAH, b. 3 Sep 1792.

11.   RICHARD HOPKINS, son of Gerrard (4) and Mary (Hall) Hopkins, was b. 20 March 1747/8, and d. 20 Sep 1823. On 23 Dec 1774, he m. Ann, dau. of Samuel and Elizabeth Thomas Snowden. She d. 16 March 1818.{D:349}

Richard and Ann (Snowden) Hopkins were the parents of{D:349}: ELIZABETH, b. 20 Nov 1775, m. (N) Plummer; GERARD R., b. 10 Aug 1777; MARY, b. 1 Sep 1779; SAMUEL SNOWDEN, b. 15 July 1783; HENRIETTA SNOWDEN, b. 20 Jan 1786, m. (N) Plummer; ANN, b. 29 June 1789, d. unm. in 1864; RICHARD, b. 26 Dec 1791, d. 1872; SARAH, b. 16 April 1793, d. unm. in 1874; and MARY JANET, b. 6 Oct 1796.

12.   ELISHA HOPKINS, son of Gerrard (4) and Mary (Hall) Hopkins, was b. 15 Oct 1752, and d. 30 Sep 1809. He m. 1st, on 27 June 1777, Hannah Howell, of Philadelphia. He m. 2nd, on 24 Nov 1796, Sarah, dau. of Samuel and Elizabeth (Thomas) Snowden.{D:348}

Elisha Hopkins was a doctor, and owned part of *White Hall*. At his death, the land descended to his children, some of whom were minors. A bill of complaint was filed in Chancery Court so that a guardian could be appointed to look after the interests of the minor heirs.

The bill stated that Elisha d. intestate leaving a widow, Sarah, who was still alive in 1810, and the following children to whom the land descended{MCHP 2702:Bill of Complaint of Gerard Hopkins et al}: Patience, m. Gerard Hopkins; Isaac H.; Deborah; Elizabeth; Hannah K., minor in 1810; Samuel, minor in 1810; Basil R., minor in 1810; Henrietta S., minor in 1810; Thomas, minor in 1810; Johns, minor in 1810; and Richard, minor in 1810.

By Hannah Howell, Dr. Elisha Hopkins was the father of{D:348}: PATIENCE, m. Gerard Hopkins; ISAAC HOWELL, b. 31 March 1781; DEBORAH, b. 8 July 1782; ELIZABETH HOWELL, b. 2 July 1812, m. Joseph Janney; and HANNAH HOWELL, minor in 1810, m. Joseph Janney.

By Sarah Snowden, Dr. Elisha Hopkins was the father of: SAMUEL SNOWDEN, b. 6 Nov 1797; BASIL BROOKE, b. 6 Nov 1799; HENRIETTA ANN, b. 30 July 1801; THOMAS SNOWDEN, b. 18 June 1803; JOHN SNOWDEN, b. 16 May 1805; and RICHARD SNOWDEN, b. 1 Sep 1807.

13.   RICHARD HOPKINS, son of Philip (5), d. by 29 Aug 1797. His
wife's name has not been determined.
    In 1763, he mortgaged *Hopkins Fancy* to Stephen West.{AALR BB#3,
No. 1:81}

    Richard, bro. of Gerard, Samuel, Philip, William, Elizabeth, and
Margaret Hopkins, was mentioned in the 1768 mortgage of Hopkins'
estate.{AALR IB&SB#1:67}
    Richard Hopkins d. in AA Co. by 29 Aug 1797 when his estate
was dist. by Mrs. (N) Hopkins, the admx. Sureties were Barzilla
Simmons and Benjamin McCeney. The unnamed widow received her
thirds. The remainder was divided into ninths and dist. among his
children.{AAHO:16 cites AADI JG#1:77}
    Richard Hopkins of Philip was the father of: PHILIP;
ELIZABETH; MARGARET; SAMUEL; WILLIAM; JOSEPH;
JOHNSEY; SARAH; and EDWARD.

14.   GERARD HOPKINS, son of William (8) and Rachel, was b.
c1743. In 1776, at age 33, he lived in Deer Creek Lower Hundred, with
his wife Sarah, age 29, and son John Wallis Hopkins, age 8 mos.{1776
Census of HA Co.}

    Gerard and Levin Hill Hopkins were named as nearest of kin in
the inventory of Grace Wallis, filed 11 Sep 1781.{HA Co. Estate File No. 201}
    Gerard Hopkins d. by 4 Dec 1799.{Estate file 770} John W. Hopkins
was admin. Nearest of kin were Frances and Susan Hopkins.{C:570}
    Gerard and Sarah (N) Hopkins were the parents of{Records of Deer Creek
Meeting}: JOHN WALLIS, b. 7 da., 12 mo., 1775; LEVEN, b. 20 da., 12
mo., 1777; FRANCES, b. 8 da., 8 mo., 1779; SUSANNAH, b. 26 da., 8
mo., 1781; WILLIAM, b. 10 da., 3 mo., 1783; GRACE JACOB, b. 15
da., 2 mo., 1785; and AMELIA, b. 9 da., 12 mo., 1787.

15.   LEVIN HILL HOPKINS, son of William (8) and Rachel (Orrick)
Hopkins, was b. c1755.
    In 1775, he was fined as a non-Associator.{C}
    On 31 da., 1 mo., 1778, Levin Hill Hopkins produced a certificate
from Deer Creek Monthly Meeting, dated 4 da., 12 mo., 1777, and was
received into Gunpowder Meeting.{D:71} On 25 da., 7 mo., 1778, he
requested to [re-]join Deer Creek Meeting.{QRNM:72}
    On 2 da., 3 mo., 1780, Levin Hill Hopkins, son of William and
Rachel Hopkins, declared his intention in Deer Creek Meeting to marry
Frances Wallis, dau. of Samuel Wallis, dec., and wife Grace.{D:139}
    Gerard and Levin Hill Hopkins were named as nearest of kin in
the inventory of Grace Wallis, filed 11 Sep 1781.{HA Co. Estate File No 201)

Levin Hill Hopkins d. by 17 Jan 1785.{HA Co. Estate File 314} Admin. was
Gerard Hopkins.

Levin Hill Hopkins d. by 17 Jan 1785{C}, or by 24 Feb 1800.{HA Co.
Estate File 777} Admin. de bonis non was John W. Hopkins. The first admin.
was Gerard Hopkins. A final account of 13 Aug 1802 mentioned his
widow and two heirs. Also mentioned were lands in York County.

John W. Hopkins, admin., dist. the estate of Levin Hill Hopkins in
Aug 1802. Heirs and legatees were Frances Hopkins, widow of the dec.,
and Elizabeth and Joel Hopkins.{Peden; *Heirs and Legatees of HA Co., MD, 1802-1846:*1}

16.   JOHN WALLIS HOPKINS, son of Gerard (14) and Sarah, was b.
7 da., 12 mo., 1775.

On 24 da., 1 mo., 1793, a certificate was requested from Deer
Creek Meeting for John Wallas Hopkins, a minor, to join York Monthly
Meeting.{QRNM:152} On 13 da., 10 mo., 1796, John Wallace Hopkins,
young man, was received into Baltimore Monthly Meeting from York
Monthly Meeting.{QRNM:193}

John Wallis Hopkins m. Susanna Dallam by license dated 9 Oct
1800.{HAML}

THE HOPPER FAMILY

It appears that members of the family sometimes spelled their
name Hooper.

1.   ROBERT HOOPER [*sic*] is listed in Skordas twice: once as a
servant transported in 1650{MPL 1:166}, and once claiming land for service
in 1663.{MPL 7:86}

He may be the father of Robert and Charles "Hopper" listed
below.

Robert Hooper d. in SM Co. by 28 May 1675, when his estate was
admin. by the widow, now wife of Thomas Doxey. An inventory showed
a value of 6,190 lbs. of tob. Henry Pennilane was paid for the
maintenance of Mary Hooper, one of the orphans.{INAC 1:335}

Robert Hooper was the father of: MARY; and at least one other,
possibly ROBERT; and possibly CHARLES.

2.   ROBERT HOOPER or HOPPER, possible son of Robert the
settler of 1650, was bur. 14 Nov 1700 in AA Co. c1701.{AACR:16} He m.
Mary (N).

As Robert Hooper, he was listed as a debtor in the inventory of Andrew Roberts on 22 May 1682. Other names in the inventory place Andrew Roberts as probably living in AA Co.{INAC 7C:145}

As Robert Hooper, of MD, he was appointed attorney by Edward and Thomas Haistwell (or Hashwell) of London, merchants, on 20 Oct 1699.{AALR WT#1:104}

He was first clerk of the first vestry that built All Hallows Church and named the Parish. He was Cryer of the County Court.

Robert Hopper and Walter Phelps appraised the estate of Richard Cheney, Sr., of AA Co., on 16 Aug 1688.{INAC 10:88}

On 28 Sep 1694, he wit. the will of Robert Wade of South River, AA Co.{MWB 7:6} In June 1695, he and Walter Phelps appraised the estate of John Grayes, of AA Co.{INAC 13A:377} Robert Hopper and Leonard Wayman appraised the estate of Gilbert Pattison on 4 July 1699.{INAC 19:113}

A member of All Hallows Parish, he d. leaving a will dated 17 Aug 1700, proved 4 Jan 1700, and wit. by Eliza Duvall, Catherine Howe, and William Warner. In addition to his wife Marey, whom he named extx., and a bro.-in-law David Bell, he named the children listed below, all b. in All Hallows Parish.{MWB 11:2}

His estate was inv. by Walter "Phillips" (almost certainly Phelps) and William Roper, and valued at £96.11.1.{INAC 20:200}

His widow Mary m. 2nd, Isaac Davies, on 12 June 1701.{AACR:16; AALR WT#2:181} In all of the deeds in AALR WT#2, Mary Davis made her mark by three vertical lines.

Robert and Mary were the parents of{AACR:2}: ROSE, b. 12 Jan 1679, m. Ralph Bazil (who was named as son-in-law in Hopper's will); THOMAS, b. 18 Feb 1685; and JAMES, b. 31 Jan 1688.

3. CHARLES HOPPER, possible son of Robert, the settler of 1650, and probably bro. of Robert, m. Anne (N). Ann may have been the Ann Hopper who m. Daniel Pearsy on 10 (?) 16(?) in All Hallows Parish. {AACR:6}

Charles and Ann were the parents of the following children, b. in All Hallows Parish{AACR:1, 7, 18}: ROSE, b. 20 Jan 1683, bapt. 18 Aug 1698, probably the Rose Hopper who m. William Diaper on 11 Feb 1703 in All Hallows Parish; and ROBERT, b. 16 Sep 1689, bapt. 18 Aug 1698.

4. THOMAS HOOPER, son of Robert (2) and Mary (N), was b. 18 Feb 1685.{AACR:2} On 7 April 1705, Mary Davis gave bond, with Charles Harrison and Walter Phelps as sureties, that she would pay Thomas Hopper, orphan of Robert Hopper, the sum of £7.07.02 when he (Thomas) would attain the age of 21.{AALR WT#2:191}

Thomas Hopper and Susanna Nicholson were m. in All Hallows Parish on 21 Oct 1708.{AACR:24} A Susannah Hopper m. Thomas Cheney in All Hallows Parish on 7 June 1716.{A:26}

Thomas and Susannah were the parents of{AACR:30}: JOHN, b. Nov 1711, bapt. 18 April 1712.

5.   JAMES HOPPER, son of Robert (2) and Mary (N) Hopper, was b. 31 Jan 1688.{AACR:2} On 7 April 1705, Mary Davis gave bond, with Charles Harrison and Walter Phelps as sureties, that she would pay James Hopper, orphan of Robert Hopper, the sum of £28.03.06 when he (James) would attain the age of 21.{AALR WT#2:190}

James Hopper m. Elizabeth Pattison on 5 May 1709 in All Hallows Parish.{AACR:25} They were the parents of at least one son, bapt. in All Hallows{AACR:28}: BENJAMIN, bapt. 29 May 1710.

6.   ROBERT HOPPER, son of Charles (3) and Ann, was b. 16 Sep 1689, and bapt. 18 Aug 1698, in All Hallows Parish.{AACR:1, 7} On 16 April 1718, he m. Deborah Lee in All Hallows Parish.{AACR:197}

They were the parents of{AACR:35, 39, 200}: JOHN, bapt. 29 July 1719; ROBERT, bapt. 2 Aug 1721{IGI}, evidently d. young; CHARLES, b. 12 Oct, bapt. 14 Nov 1722; ROBERT, b. 16 March, bapt. 26 March 1724 at All Hallows Parish{IGI}; and EDWARD, b. 17 Jan 1724.

7.   JOHN HOPPER, son of Thomas (4) and Susannah (Nicholson), was b. Nov 1711, and bapt. 18 April 1712.{AACR:30} John Hopper, of AA Co., gave his age as 43 in 1754.{AALC 2:424} On 20 Aug 1730, he m., in All Hallows Parish, Rachel Nicholson.{AACR:44}

On 12 Feb 1742, John Hopper and Lewis Chaney signed the inventory of Susannah Brown as next of kin.{MINV 27:419} John Hopper, grandson of Robert Hopper, was mentioned in a 1757 deposition of Lewis Chaney.{AALC 2:478-480}

John and Rachel were the parents of{AACR:50}: THOMAS, b. 7 Oct 1730; and MARY, b. 10 Feb 1731.

8.   ROBERT HOPPER, son of Robert (6) and Deborah, was b. 16 March{AACR:35}, and bapt. 26 March 1724 at All Hallows Parish.{IGI} He may be the Robert Hopper, schoolmaster, mentioned in a 1757 deposition made by Thomas Ricketts, Sr.{AALC 2:474, 476}

9.   THOMAS HOPPER, son of John (7) and Rachel (Nicholson), was b. 7 Oct 1730. Thomas Hopper gave his age as 35 in 1764.{AALC 2:616} He m. Mary (N). They were the parents of{AACR:54}: RACHEL, b. 15 Feb 1754, in All Hallows Parish.

Unplaced

HOPPER, CHARLES, was transported c1674.{MPL 15:322}

HOPPER, MARY, m. John Jacobs in All Hallows Parish, on 6 Jan 1732.
{AACR:46}

HOPPER, MARY, had an illegitimate son, b. in All Hallows Parish:
BENJAMIN, b. 2 Nov 1769.{AACR:58}

THE JAMES FAMILY

1.   RICHARD JAMES, of AA Co., may be any one of several men
who were listed in Skordas as having come to MD between 1663 and
1679. He d. by April 1685. He m. Elinor (N), who m. 2nd, John Turner.
     On 7 March 1669, Robert Paca sold to Richard James 100 a.
James Chance, adj. land laid out for James Ogden. This deed was re-
recorded at the request of Abraham Simmons.{AALR IH#3:123}
     Nathaniel Smith, of Herring Creek, AA Co., made his will on 10
April 1672, leaving personalty to Richard James (and others).{MWB 1:488}
     On 9 Aug 1677, Richard James was listed as a debtor in the
inventory of Christopher Birckhead of AA Co.{INAC 4:253}
     Richard James, of AA Co., d. leaving a will dated 12 Jan 1684 and
proved 18 April 1685. He left his home plant. to his extx. and wife,
Elinor, for her life. After the death of his wife, the plant. was to descend
in succession to his daus., Mary, Sarah, Martha, Rachel, and Deborah.
Mary Symons and Robert Orme were left personalty. Wm. Symons, Jno.
Milner, Sarah Orme, and John Elsey wit. the will.{MWB 4:95}
     On 2 Aug 1687, his estate was admin. by (N), his widow, now
wife of John Turner. There was an inventory worth 4,189 lbs. of tob.{INAC
9:362} His estate was admin. again on 3 April 1688 by the extx. Ellinor,
wife of John Turner.{INAC 9:474}
     By 1707, John Turner held 100 a. *Dan* (originally surv. 3 July
1663 for Robert Paca), in right of his wife, the relict of Richard James.
{MRR:116}
     Richard and Elinor (N) James were the parents of: MARY, m.
Teague Tracey; SARAH; MARTHA; RACHEL; and DEBORAH.

2.   MARY JAMES, dau. of Richard, m. Teague Tracey. On 26 April
1703, Teague Tracey and wife Mary sold 100 a. *James Chance*, adj. land
laid out for James Ogden, to Abraham Simmons.{AALR WT#2:60}

THE ROBERT JOHNSON FAMILY

1.   ROBERT JOHNSON, d. by Nov 1734. He m. Rebecca Ragg on 13 Jan 1716/7 in St. Anne's Parish.{AACR:78} She also d. by Nov 1734.

The estate of Robert Johnson, barber, of AA Co., was admin. 7 Nov 1734 by Dr. Charles Carroll, admin. of Rebecca Johnson, who was the original admx. of the dec. An inventory of £112.7.3 was mentioned. {MDAD 12:523}

Rebecca Johnson's estate was admin. by Dr. Charles Carroll on 12 Feb 1735. An inventory of £113.16.6. was mentioned. The representatives were a son and a dau.{MDAD 14:147}

Robert and Rebecca were the parents of two children, bapt. in St. Anne's Parish{AACR:83, 90}: GEORGE, b. 11 Oct 1718, bapt. 30 Oct 1718; and SARAH, b. 11 Aug 1722.

2.   GEORGE JOHNSON, son of Robert and Rebecca, was b. 11 Oct 1718.{AACR:83} He m. Mary Harrison on 3 July 1737 in St. Anne's Parish. {AACR:98, 99, 100} They were the parents of: ROBERT, b. 13 Feb, bapt. 13 March 1741 in St. Anne's Parish; JOHN, b. 10 Feb 1744/5, bapt. 19 March 1744/5; and ELIZABETH (named in will of her bro. Robert).

3.   ROBERT JOHNSON, son of George and Mary, was b. 13 Feb 1741, and d. by July 1773. He m. Anne (N).

Robert Johnson, of the City of Annapolis, AA Co., d. leaving a will dated 8 June 1773 and proved 16 July 1773. He named his son George, son Robert (to have the house where his mother lived), son John, sister Elizabeth (to have house and lot in Baltimore Town), and wife Anne, extx. Bro. John was to be co-exec. His sons were not yet of age. Thomas Hewitt, Robert Reynolds, and Robert Lambert were wits.{MWB 39:240}

Robert and Mary were the parents of{AACR:104}: ROBERT, b. 14 Nov 1766; GEORGE, b. 12 April 1768; and JOHN, b. 12 Sep 1770.{C:104}

THE STEPHEN JOHNSON FAMILY

1.   STEPHEN JOHNSON d. in BA Co. by 3 Feb 1701/2.

On 22 Sep 1694, Stephen Johnson conv. a negro boy to his wife Ann.{BALR TR#RA:403}

On 4 Aug 1694, James Todd, of BA Co., conv. part of *Todd's Range* to Stephen Johnson, of AA Co.{BALR RM#HS:398} On 9 Oct 1695, Thomas Todd, of Ware Parish, Gloucester Co., VA, confirmed the sale his bro. James made to Stephen.{BALR RM#HS:479}

Stephen Johnson and William Wilkinson appraised the estate of
Thomas Durbin, of BA Co., on 3 May 1697.{INAC 14:145} He and Henry
Wrothesley appraised the estate of John Slye, of BA Co., on 22 July
1700.{INAC 20:44}

In Jan 1699, Stephen Johnson and wife Ann conv. 250 a.
Johnson's Dock to Robert Johnson, of BA Co., shipwright.{BALR TR#RA:416}

On 24 July 1701, Johnson admin. the estate of Richard Isaacs, of
BA Co.{INAC 21:173}

Stephen Johnson d. leaving a will dated 20 Sep 1700 and proved 3
Feb 1701/2, naming wife Ann (extx.), son Robert, and granddau. Mary,
dau. of Robert Lusby. Henry and Ann Wriothesley and Thomas Cutchin
were wits.{MWB 11:150}

Johnson's estate was appraised on 13 June 1702 by John Owings
and John Rawlings. John Fuller and Henry Mathews were listed as
debtors. The estate was valued at £116.13.8, which included 7,680 lbs. of
tob.{INAC 21:375}

Mrs. Ann Filkes, the relict [widow], admin. his estate on 8 Dec
1703. Edward Felkes, who m. the widow, was mentioned.{MWB 3:366}

His estate was admin. again on 10 Dec 1707 by the widow Anne,
now Anne Filkes. There were two inventories, totalling £148.10.8 and
£164.18.10. Robert Johnson was mentioned in the account.{INAC 28:23}

Stephen and Anne were the parents of: ROBERT; and (N), m.
Robert Lusby.

2.   ROBERT JOHNSON, son of Stephen and Anne, d. by Sep 1722.
He m. Hannah (N) by 29 April 1703 when she joined him in the sale of
250 a. *Johnson's Dock* to George Eager.{BALR HW#2:251} Hannah was
almost certainly a dau. of Jacob Lusby, of AA Co., whose will dated 12
March 1708/9 and proved 19 July, 1709, named dau. Hannah Johnson,
and named Robert Johnson as co-exec. with his own eldest son Jacob
Lusby.{MWB 12 Part 2:121}

On 12 Aug 1700, John Cross and wife Eleanor, of AA Co., conv.
to Robert Johnson, of BA Co., 100 a. part of *The Level.*{AALR WT#1:76} In
1705, John Prindowell, planter, conv. to Robert Johnson 70 a. *Fuller's
Point.*{AALR WT#2:290}

In 1719, the General Assembly gave Robert Johnson permission
to use the Ship Carpenter's Lot (on the n.e. side of the Dock) under the
condition that only the art of shipwright could be practiced on the
grounds. Johnson d. in 1722 and Robert Gordon was given the same
privilege under identical conditions.{Baltz; *The Quays of the City; An Account of the Bustling
Eighteenth Century Port of Annapolis:*7}

Robert Johnson, shipwright, of AA Co., left a will dated 6 Sep
1721 and proved 22 Sep 1722. He named his wife Hannah, extx., eldest
son Stephen (all land in Annapolis), son Jacob (dwell. plant. *Thomas'*

Point), son John (to have £50 at age 21), 5 younger children, Peter, Barbara (at age 18 or marriage), Robert, Thomas, and Samuel (all to have residue of estate equally). Rebecca Ruley, Anthony Ruley, Jr., and Frances Ruley were wits.{MWB 18:121}

The estate of Robert Johnson, of AA Co., was appraised by Anthony Ruley and Henry Hill at £508.13.6. Richard Hill and Samuel Peele signed as creditors. Robert Lusby, Sr., and Thomas Lusby signed as next of kin. Hannah Johnson, the extx., filed the inventory on 21 Nov 1723.{MINV 9:201}

Hannah Johnson admin. the estate on 1 July 1725. No heirs were named in the admininstration account.{MDAD 6:396}

Hannah Johnson, of PG Co., d. leaving a will dated 23 March 1742/3 and proved 1 June 1743, naming sons Robert (exec.), Stephen, and Thomas, and granddau. Anne (not yet 16). William Ross and Jacob Lusby were wits.{MWB 23:260}

The estate of Mrs. Hannah Johnson was appraised on 29 Aug 1743 by Ezekiel Gillis and Thomas Ruley. No value was given. William Chapman and Thomas Lusby signed as creditors, and Thomas Johnson and Stephen Johnson signed as next of kin. Robert Johnson, exec., filed the inventory on 12 March 1743/4.{MINV 29:97}

Robert and Hannah (Lusby) Johnson were the parents of{AACR:83, 84, 89, 90}: STEPHEN (the eldest son), may have d. young; JACOB; JOHN (not yet 21); PETER; BARBARA (at age 18 or marriage);[44] ROBERT, living in 1776; THOMAS; SAMUEL, b. 14 Feb 1718/9, bapt. 23 March 1719; STEPHEN, b. 7 April 1722 in St. Anne's Parish; and SARAH, b. 11 Aug 1722 [sic] in St. Anne's Parish.

3.   SAMUEL JOHNSON, son of Robert and Hannah (Lusby), was b. 14 Feb 1718/9, and bapt. 23 March 1719 in St. Anne's Parish. Samuel m. Susanna Lusby on 21 June 1742 in St. Anne's Parish, AA Co. {AACR:99}

Samuel Johnson, of AA Co., d. leaving a will dated 4 March 1776 and proved 15 May 1776. The will was wit. by Jacob Lusby, John Cross, and Ann Tilly, and named the following children{MWB 40:654}: VACHEL (inherited £1.4.0); STEPHEN (inherited £1.0.0); SAMUEL (inherited £1.0.0); ROBERT (inherited stock and 1/3 of the residue of the estate); PETER (inherited stock and 1/3 of the residue of the estate); and DEBORAH (inherited 1/3 of the residue of the estate).

---

[44] Barbara Johnson, of AA Co., d. leaving a will dated 30 April 1776 and proved 14 May 1776, leaving all her estate to her bro. Robert Johnson, exec. Lewis Duvall, Henry Ridgely, and Priscilla Pinkney were wits.{MWB 40:651}

Unplaced

JOHNSON, SAMUEL, m. Ann Nelson on 17 Feb 1708 in St. Anne's Parish, AA Co.{AACR:67}

JOHNSON, SAMUEL, orphan. On 4 June 1793, William James posted bond he would serve as guardian to Samuel Johnson, orphan under age. {AA Testamentary Papers, Box 26, folder 80, MSA}

On 7 Feb 1795, his property (several negroes) was valued by William Goldsmith and A. Gordon.{AA Testamentary Papers, Box 32, folder 63, MSA}

In 1800, William James, guardian of Samuel Johnson, petitioned the court that he be allowed to sell a negro man.{Index to AA Co. Orphans Court Minutes, MSA}

In 1806, Samuel Johnson's guardian filed his fifth account. This is the last account noted in the card index, so it may be presumed that in 1806 or 1807, Samuel Johnson was an adult.{AA Testamentary Papers, Box 76, fol. 72}

JOHNSON, SAMUEL, d. by 12 Jan 1813, when Ann Johnson posted bond as admx. of Samuel Johnson.{AA Testamentary Papers, Box 198, folder 2, MSA}

Later in 1813, William Carman and wife Ann (formerly Johnson), admx. of Samuel Johnson, formally requested that a sale of property be held.{AA Testamentary Papers, Box 110, folder 60, MSA}

JOHNSON, THOMAS, of AA Co., d. leaving a will dated 7 Nov 1770 and proved 13 Dec 1770, naming dau. Mary Seabourn, and his own father-in-law Thomas Climpse.{MWB 38:152}

THE MORGAN JONES FAMILY

1.   MORGAN JONES, of AA Co., bur. 13 Sep 1718 in St. James Parish{AACR:163}, first appeared in MD when he was listed as a servant in the April 1676 inventory of Jery Sudenant of AA Co.{INAC 2:218} Skordas lists several individuals of the name, but Morgan, of AA Co., is probably the Morgan Jones who was transported by c1674.{MPL 15:431 and 18:121} He m. Jane, dau. of John Whipps, whose will of 10 Dec 1716 named his children, including a dau. Jane Jones.{MWB 14:172; MDTP 38:172} However, a Jane Jones was bur. in St. James Parish on 18 April 1711.{AACR:159}

Morgan Jones may have been illiterate, since, on 26 Jan 1694, he made his mark on a deed.{AALR WH#4:49} Nevertheless, he prospered. On 26 Jan 1694, as Morgan Jones, cooper, he purchased 40 a. *Eagle's Nest,*

158

surv. in 1679 for Nicholas Gross.{AALR WH#4:52; MRR:133} On 10 March 1717, as Morgan Jones, carpenter, he purchased 100 a. from Robert Sollers. {AALR IB#2:504}

By c1707, he had acquired 25 a. *Carter*, a 600 a. tract originally surv. in 1651 for Capt. Edward Carter in Herring Creek Hundred.{MRR:112}

Morgan Jones d. leaving a will dated 18 Feb 1717 (date of probate not given). He left property which had belonged to Jenerate [Jeremiah] Sullivan to his sons William and Morgan. He left *Elgul Island* to his son John, and personalty to his daus. Jane and Blanch. Son Morgan was exec. and residuary legatee. The will was sworn to by his eldest son William, age c23, and John Standforth, age c52.{MWB 15:40}

Robert Wood and John League appraised the estate of Morgan Jones [date not given] and valued it at £143.6.6. John Jones, Dorothy Powell, and Samuel Chew appraised the inventory.{MINV 1:433} A second inventory was appraised on 15 June 1719 and valued at £25.11.8. William Jones, admin., filed the inventory on 4 Sep 1719.{MINV 2:158}

Morgan Jones' estate was admin. by William Jones on 4 Sep 1719 and 7 Sep 1719. Two inventories, worth £143.6.6 and £25.11.8, were mentioned. One of the legatees was the "father-in-law of the dec. to dau. Jane Jones."{MDAD 2:201, 215} Another administration account was filed on 10 Aug 1726.{MDAD 7:486}

Morgan and Jane were the parents of{AACR 148, 151, 153, 155, 156, 158}: SYBIL, b. 15 Dec 1691, may have m. (N) Wells by c1730{MINV 16:25}; WILLIAM, b. 17 Feb 1693, bapt. 14 Aug 1698; DOROTHY, b. 4 May 1696, bapt. 14 Aug 1698, may have m. 1st, by c1718, (N) Powell, and 2nd, by 1746, (N) Wood; JOHN, b. 7 April 1699, bapt. 7 May 1699; JANE, b. 12 Dec 1701, bapt. 5 April 1702; MARGERY, b. 18 April 1704, bur. 18 April 1710; MORGAN, b. 23 Aug 1706, bapt. 22 Sep 1706; and BLANCHE, bapt. 24 April 1709.

2.   WILLIAM JONES, son of Morgan (1) and Jane, was b. 17 Feb 1693, gave his age as c23 in 1717, and d. by May 1730. He is probably the William Jones who m. Hannah Norris (c1715 but date not given) in St. James Parish.{AACR:162} William probably m. 2nd, Mary (N).

The estate of William Jones, of AA Co., was appraised by Thomas Wells and George Henderson and valued at £111.3.7. Sebell Wells and Morgan Jones signed as next of kin. Mary Jones, admx., filed the inventory on 29 May 1730.{MINV 1:25}

William and Hannah were the parents of{AACR:164}: WILLIAM, b. 22 Oct 1718 in St. James Parish.

3.   JOHN JONES, son of Morgan (1) and Jane, was b. 7 April 1699 and bapt. 7 May 1699 in St. James Parish.

He may be the John Jones who m. Mary (N), and had a son {AACR:164}: JOHN, b. 30 July 1719, bapt. 7 June 1720 in St. James Parish.

4.   MORGAN JONES, son of Morgan (1) and Jane, was b. 23 Aug 1706, bapt. 22 Sep 1706, and evidently d. by 1747. By 1733, he had m. Susan (N), who m. 2nd John Dowell.{MDAD 41?:23}

On 6 Oct 1746, Morgan Jones' personal estate was appraised by Joseph Chew, James Tongue (who d.), and John Wood, and valued at £492.13.6. Dorothy Wood signed as next of kin, and Susanna Dowell (lately Susanna Jones), admx., filed the inventory on 14 May 1747.{MINV 34:300}

On 13 Dec 1750, another inventory was taken by Richard Smith and Joseph Chew, and valued at £104.5.9. John Wood and Dorothy Wood were mentioned. Susanna Dowell, wife of John Dowell, admx., filed the inventory on 15 March 1750.{MINV 44:437}

Morgan and Susan were the parents of{AACR:165, 167}: MORGAN, b. 16 Sep 1733, bapt. 14 Oct 1733 in St. James Parish; and SUSANNA, b. 24 Sep 1735.

5.   MORGAN JONES, son of Morgan (4) and Susan, was b. 16 Sep 1733, and bapt. 14 Oct in St. James. He is probably the Morgan Jones who m. Priscilla, dau. of Sarah Wooden.{MDAD 41:135}

In Jan 1759/60, Joseph Hill and wife Elizabeth, and Morgan Jones and wife Priscilla, filed a petition in the Chancery Court. The Bill of Complaint stated that Solomon Wooden had d. leaving three daus.: Elizabeth, wife of Joseph Hill; Priscilla, wife of Morgan Jones; and Sarah, wife of Charles Connant.{MCHR 10:25}

Morgan and Susan had issue, all b. in St. James Parish{AACR:171}: SARAH, b. 3 Nov 1757; PRISCILLA, b. 10 Feb 1760; WILLIAM, b. 10 April 1763; and MORGAN, b. 10 Dec 1767.

THE JOYCE FAMILY

Refs.: A: Register of Queen Anne Parish, PG Co., MSA.

1.   JOHN JOYCE d. by 28 Nov 1699, when his estate was appraised by John Pottenger and Christopher Tompson, and valued at £41.1.8.{INAC 19½B:3} He may have m. Susannah (N), who wit. a deed on 16 March 1700.{PGLR A:61}

John Joyce was in PG Co. by 24 Nov 1696, when he and Christopher Tompson wit. a deed.{PGLR A:24}

John Joyce was probably the father of: JOHN; and THOMAS.

2.   JOHN JOYCE, son of John, d. in St. Margaret's Parish, AA Co., on 12 Jan 1743.{AACR:138} He m. Sarah Brooks in Queen Anne Parish, PG Co., on 3 July 1721.{A: Marriage Register:2}

He was in PG Co. by 30 July 1701, when he and Ann Joyce were listed as debtors in the adminitration account of Jonathan Wilson.{INAC 20:235}

On 19 July 1707, he was again listed as debtor in the administration account of Jonathan Wilson, of PG Co.{INAC 27:31}

On 1 Dec 1721, John Joyce, with consent of his wife Sarah, conv. 150 a. part of *The Exchange,* to James Mackbee. Thomas Joyce was a wit.{PGLR I:195}

The personal estate of John Joyce was appraised on 25 Feb 1744 by Richard Jacob and Thomas Wright. No value was given for the property. John Bailey and Richard Snowden signed as creditors, and Thomas Joyce and Thomas Rowles signed as kin. Sarah Joyce, the admx., filed the inventory on 13 Aug 1746.{MINV 33:140}

John and Sarah were the parents of at least one child b. in Queen Anne Parish, PG Co., and two children b. in St. Margaret's Parish, AA Co.{A:25; AACR:121}: JOHN, b. 13 Dec 1731 in Queen Anne Parish; ELIJAH, b. 22 April 1739; and HENRIETTA, b. 14 Sep 1741.

3.   THOMAS JOYCE, son of John Joyce, of PG Co., settled in AA Co., where he d. by May 1749. He m. 1st, on 22 April 1716, Eliza Cheney, in Queen Anne Parish, PG Co.{A:Marriage Register:1}, and 2nd, Elinor (N), who m. 2nd, Nathan Shaw.

Elizabeth Cheney was the Elizabeth Joyce named as a dau. in the will, made 24 Aug 1737, of Thomas Cheney, planter.{MWB 21:879}

Thomas Joyce d. leaving a will dated 25 Nov 1748 and proved 15 May 1749. He named his wife Elinor, and his children John, China, and Elizabeth. He mentioned his two youngest sons, and the tract *Nickler's Hunting Quarter,* and he appointed his wife Elinor as extx. The will was wit. by Patrick Lynch, John Cretin, and George Brammell.{MWB 26:135}

The personal property of Thomas Joyce was appraised at a value of £290.6.1 on 14 Nov 1749 by William Cromwell and Thomas Wright. Eleanor Shaw, the widow and admx., filed the inventory on 15 Feb 1749. {MINV 43:68}

The estate of Thomas Joyce was dist. on 14 Aug 1753 by the execs. Nathan Shaw and his wife Eleanor. One-third of the balance went to the widow, but the "representatives were not known to the Office."{BFD 1:74}

By Elizabeth Cheney, Thomas Joyce was the father of{A:17, 18}: THOMAS, b. 1 Feb 1718; JOHN, b. 29 Dec 1720; ELIZABETH, b. 27 Sep 1722; and CHENEY, b. 7 July 1724.

4.   THOMAS JOYCE, son of Thomas (3) and Elizabeth (Cheney), was b. 1 Feb 1718. He also m. Elizabeth (N).

Thomas and Elizabeth were the parents of the following children, b. in St. Margaret's Parish{AACR:120}: WILLIAM, b. 10 Dec 1729; LEURANER, b. 1 March 1731; RICHARD, b. 10 Aug 1734; JACOB, b. 23 June 1736; ZACHARIAH, b. 16 Oct 1738; SARAH, b. 6 May 1741; JOSEPH, b. 5 Jan 1742; and THOMAS, b. 22 May 1745.

5.   RICHARD JOYCE, son of Thomas (4) and Elizabeth, was b. 10 Aug 1734, and d. by April 1788. He m. Fanney Shaw in St. Margaret's Parish in May 1759.{AACR:134}

Richard Joyce was listed as a private in Capt. Richard Chew's Co. of Col. John Weems's Battalion, on 5 Oct 1776. On March 1778, he took the Oath of Allegiance before the Hon. Samuel Harrison, Jr.{AARP:110}

The final dist. of Richard Joyce's estate took place on 28 April 1788 by Henry Ashbaw, exec. One-third went to the widow and the rest to Richard, William, and Elijah Joyce.{AARP:110, cites AAHO:11}

Richard and Fanney were the parents of{AACR:126}: ANN, b. 23 Dec 1760 in St. Margaret's Parish; RICHARD, b. by 1777, when he was named in the will of his uncle Thomas Joyce; WILLIAM; and ELIJAH.

6.   ZACHARIAH JOYCE, son of Thomas (4) and Elizabeth, was b. 16 Oct 1738. He m. Rachel (N). They were the parents of the following children, b. in St. Margaret's Parish{AACR:127, 128}; THOMAS, b. 29 Aug 1763; ELINOR, b. 27 Oct 1766; BASIL, b. 9 Aug 1769; ANN, b. 8 Nov 1773; and RACHEL, b. 16 March 1778.

7.   THOMAS JOYCE, son of Thomas (4) and Elizabeth, was b. 22 May 1745, and d. by 16 May 1777. He m. Elizabeth (N).

Thomas Joyce, of AA Co., d. leaving a will dated 7 March 1777 and proved 16 May 1777. He left all of his estate to his son Thomas, then to his wife Elizabeth, and when she d., to Richard Joyce, son of the testator's bro. Richard. James Cary, Henry Ashbaw, and Zachariah Jacob were wits.{MWB 41:433}

Thomas and Elizabeth had two sons{AACR:128}: HENRY, b. 27 May 1774; and THOMAS, named in his father's will.

162

Unplaced

JOYCE, ABEL, m. Anne (N). They were the parents of at least one son, b. in St. James Parish{AACR:173}: RICHARD, b. 8 Feb 1787, bapt. 2 May 1791.

JOYCE, HONOR, m. William Grace on 26 Feb 1750 in St. Anne's Parish.{AACR:102}

JOYCE, JOHN, m. by 9 Nov 1736, Anna Maria Bond, niece of William Powell, of AA Co.{MDAD 15:212}

JOYCE, NATHAN, m. Rebecca (N). They were the parents of the following children, b. in St. Margaret's Parish{AACR:128}: JOSHUA, b. 20 July 1764; THOMAS, b. 4 April 1767; NATHAN, b. 10 March 1769; JOSEPH, b. 15 March 1771; and STEVEN, b. 17 April 1773.

JOYCE, RACHEL, m. Jacob Morrice on 30 Nov 1745 in St. Margaret's Parish.{AACR:133}

JOYCE, SARAH, m. Thomas Rowles on 16 Oct 1740 in St. Margaret's Parish.{AACR:132}

THE KNIGHTON FAMILY

1.   (N) KNIGHTON, of England, was the father of at least four sons {MCHR PC:733}: THOMAS; JAMES; JOHN; and GEORGE.

2.   THOMAS KNIGHTON, son of (N), and bro. of James, John, and George, was b. c1636. He gave his age as 41 in 1677.{ARMD 67:345-346} He m. by 2 Jan 1687, Dinah, sister of Seaborn Battee.{MWB 4:286} She may have m. 2nd, (N) Brewer, for on 21 Dec 1705, Ferdinando Battee made a will naming, among others, his dau. Dinah Brewer, grandson Samuel Brewer, and grandson Thomas Knighton.{MWB 3:744}
    As Thomas Knighton, Attorney of the Provincial Court, he was in MD by 1669.{MPL 12:347, 491}
    On 26 July 1680, he patented 197 a. in AA Co. called *Knighton's Folly*.{MPL 28:37} On 12 June 1683, with the consent of his wife Dinah, he conv. the 197 a. tract to Robert Orme and Robert Wood, of AA Co.{AALR IH#2:230} In the meantime, on 13 June 1681, John Hall (son of John Hall, of AA Co., dec.) conv. 150 a. *Marsh's Seat* and 140 a. *Gad Hills* to Knighton. Sarah Hall released her right of dower.{AALR WH#4:134}

Thomas Knighton, of Herring Creek, AA Co., d. leaving a will dated 12 Aug 1684 and proved 28 April 1693. He named his wife Dinah extx. and residuary legatee. His daus. Mary, Eliza, and Millicent, were to have personalty and to be of age at 18. His eldest son Thomas was to have 150 a. *Marsh's Seat.* Son George was to have *Gad Hill.* The will was wit. by Geo. Parker and William Holland. {MWB 6:12}

On 19 June 1711, Samuel Guishard dep. that he was b. in Geneva, came to MD at age 16, and has been here about 24 years. He served his time with Thomas Knighton, the Elder. He knew the latter's son George, but did not know if he d. under age or not. He knew Sarah Knighton, dau. of Thomas, and that she d. c25 years earlier, age c6 months. {MCHR PC:733}

Thomas and Dinah (Battee) Knighton were the parents of: THOMAS, b. c1685; GEORGE, d. by 1711; SARAH, d. c1686, age 6 months; MARY; ELIZA, m. George Simmons or Simons; and MILLICENT.

2. THOMAS KNIGHTON, son of Thomas and Dinah, was b. c1685. On 19 June 1711, he gave his age as c26 when he dep. he was the son and heir of Thomas Knighton, of Herring Creek, Gent., dec. About 5 years after his father's death, he went to England to inquire of his father's bros., George, James, and John, if they knew anything of his father's will. {MCHR PC:733}

Thomas Knighton m. Dorothy Wood in St. James Parish on 3 Dec 1700. {AACR:151}

Thomas Trott dep. on 19 June 1711 that he had seen a deed for *Marsh's Seat* dated 19 Nov 1701 from Thomas Knighton and wife Dorothy to Christopher Vernon. {MCHR PC:733}

On 9 March 1709, Thomas Knighton, with consent of his wife Dorothy, conv. 100 a. *Knighton's Fancy* to Nicholas Fitzsimmons. {BALR TR#A:46}

On 25 Sep 1718, Thomas Knighton admin. the estate of Samuel Taylor. {BAAD 1:197}

Thomas and Dorothy were probably the parents of: KEYSER.

3. KEYSER KNIGHTON, probably son of Thomas and Dorothy, was living as late as 1736. Keyser and Mary Holliday were m. in All Hallows Parish in 1734. {AACR:48} He m. 2nd, Sarah (N).

In June 1716, having formerly been bound out to John Hall, he was returned to his father. {BACP 21:137}

On 11 April 1734, Kezer Knighton wit. the will of Darby Conner of AA Co. {MWB 21:111}

Keyser and Sarah were the parents of{AACR:166}: SAMUEL, b. 14 Oct 1736 in St. James Parish; and THOMAS.

Unplaced

KNIGHTON, MARY, m. John Sparrow on 3 Sep 1728 in All Hallows Parish.{AACR:43}

KNIGHTON, THOMAS, and Mary Lockwood were m. in All Hallows Parish on 8 Oct 1723.{AACR:37} Mary was a dau. of James Ellis, of AA Co. Samuel Lockwood, of AA Co., had made a will of 1 March 1722, naming his wife Mary as extx.{MWB 17:249}

On 13 June 1733, Mary Knighton, sole dau. and heir of James Ellis, of AA Co., for love and affection she had for her sons Samuel Lockwood and Thomas Knighton, and for her grandsons Samuel Brown (son of James and Cassandra Brown) and Thomas Sparrow (son of Solomon and Charity Sparrow), conv. to them various portions of a tract in BA Co. called *James' Park*, which was patented by her father on 10 May 1685.{PCLR PL#8:193}

Thomas and Mary, as execs., admin. the estate of Samuel Lockwood, of AA Co., on 11 July 1724, 9 March 1724/5, and 10 Nov 1725.{MDAD 6:24, 277, 7:171}

Thomas and Mary were the parents of{AACR:40}: ELIZABETH, bapt. 31 May 1726 in All Hallows Parish.

THE NICHOLAS LAMB FAMILY

1.   NICHOLAS LAMB was transported to MD c1674.{MPL 18:94} He d. in AA Co. by 16 May 1697. He m. Hannah (N).

Nicholas Lamb d. leaving a will dated 19 Oct 1696 and proved 17 May 1697. He named his wife Hannah extx. and residuary legatee, and left all his real estate to his sons James and Nicholas at age 21. William Forman, Jno. Kendall, and Jno. Cooley were wits.{MWB 7:258}

Lamb's personal estate was appraised on 17 May 1697 by Thomas Besson and William Foreman. No value was given.{INAC 15:275}

Nicholas and Hannah were the parents of: JAMES; and NICHOLAS, d. 10 Jan 1707 in St. Margaret's Parish.{AACR:137}

2.   JAMES LAMB, son of Nicholas and Hannah, d. in BA Co. prior to 4 Dec 1710, when his estate was admin. by Nicholas Besson. An inventory of £12.15.11 was mentioned. Payments were made to William Forrest and John Rattenbury.{INAC 32B:6}

THE JOHN LAMB FAMILY (1)

1.   JOHN LAMB, merchant, m. Elizabeth, widow of John Belt in All
Hallows Parish on 25 July 1701.{AACR:13}
        John Lamb, of AA Co., d. leaving a will dated 27 Dec 1714 and proved
14 Jan 1715. He left personalty to his dau. Margaret, son-in-law Jeremiah Belt,
and Sarah Belt, and he named his wife Eliza as extx. and residuary legatee. The
will was wit. by Elinor Mariarte, Jno. Belt, and W. Wootton.{MWB 14:55}
        Elizabeth Lamb, of AA Co., d. leaving a will dated 1 Aug 1737
and proved 14 Dec 1737. She named sons John, Joseph, Benjamin, and
Jeremiah Belt, and daus. Charity Mullikin, Sarah Harwood, and Margaret
Watkins. She also named son-in-law Nicholas Watkins, and
grandchildren Mary Norwood, and Nicholas, Elizabeth, and Anne
Watkins. Her will was wit. by Samuel Smith, George Taylor, and
Edward Scott.{MWB 21:813}
        Elizabeth Lamb's personal estate was inv. by Thomas Stockett and
Ferdinand Battee, and valued at £282.19.4. Jeremiah Belt and Samuel
Chew signed as creditors, and Joseph and Jeremiah Belt signed as next of
kin. Nicholas Watkins, exec., filed the inventory on 5 Aug 1738.{MINV
23:213}
        John and Elizabeth Lamb were the parents of the following child,
b. in All Hallows Parish{AACR:18}: MARGARET, bapt. 14 Dec 1703, m.
Nicholas Watkins.

THE JOHN LAMB FAMILY (2)

1.   JOHN LAMB, no known relationship to any of the above, m.
Katherine Galloway on 16 April 1703 in St. Margaret's Parish.{AACR:129}
        By Katherine, John Lamb was the father of the following children,
b. in St. Margaret's Parish{AACR:108, 110}: MARY, b. 8 Feb 1704; and
JOHN, b. 11 Feb 1711.

2.   JOHN LAMB, son of John and Katherine, was b. 11 Feb 1711. He
gave his age as 22 in 1734, 38 in 1751, and 40 in 1754.{AALR RD#2:135; MCHR
8:933, AALC 2:413} He m. 1st, Elizabeth Hodge, on 1 Oct 1736 in St.
Margaret's Parish.{AACR:132} Elizabeth Lamb d. 19 Dec 1741.{AACR:138}
John Lamb m. Sarah (N), who was b. c1723. Sarah, wife of John Lamb,
of AA Co., ship carpenter, gave her age as 28 in 1751.{MCHR 8:910}
        John and Sarah were the parents of the following children, b. in
St. Margaret's Parish{AACR:120, 124, 125, 134}: NICHOLAS, b. 19 Dec 1742;
JOHN, b. 26 Jan 1744; SARAH, b. 5 March 1745; MARY, b. 3 Nov

1750, probably the Mary who m. James Moss on 20 Jan 1772; JOSHUA, b. 21 Jan 1752; and MARGETT, b. 6 Nov 1757.

3.   JOHN LAMB, son of John and Sarah, was b. 26 Jan 1744. In 1733, as John Lamb, son of John, he gave his age as 33.{AALC 3:262-263}
     John Lamb, of John, is probably the John Lamb who, on 12 Dec 1776, was a private in Capt. Fulford's Co. of Artillery stationed at Annapolis.{AARP cites ARMD 18:562}

THE LOCKWOOD FAMILY

1.   ROBERT LOCKWOOD, of Aberford, Yorkshire, England, m. Eliza and had at least four children{MWB 12, Part 2,:75}: ANN, m. Robert Saws of Aberford; THOMAS; JOHN; and ROBERT, d. 1704 in AA Co.

2.   THOMAS LOCKWOOD, son of Robert and Eliza, was the father of at least two sons, who were devised the estate of their uncle Robert Lockwood in 1709. These sons sold the estate to Samuel Harrison. It is possible that one of Thomas's Lockwood's sons was: SAMUEL.

3.   ROBERT LOCKWOOD, youngest son of Robert and Eliza, was in AA Co. by 29 Dec 1672, when he wit. the will of James White of AA Co.{MWB 1:50}
     On 3 June 1680, Edward Talbott and wife Eliza conv. to Robert Lockwood 82 a. called *Talbott's Timber Neck*.{AALR IT#5:40}
     On 17 April 1686, Robert Phillips, of AA Co., made a will leaving personalty to Robert Lockwood and others.{MWB 6:204}
     On 28 Oct 1687, Robert Lockwood, with consent of wife Eliza, conv. 1,000 a. *Friendship* in BA Co. to John Wilson. The deed stated the tract had been patented by Lockwood on 1 July 1685.{BALR RM#HS:24}
     Christopher Gardiner, of AA Co., planter, on 29 March 1688, conv. to Robert Lockwood 40 a. *Daborne's Hope*.{AALR WH#4:311} Anthony Holland, on 4 May 1691, conv. to Lockwood 100 a. originally called *Bonnerstone*, but later called *Holland's Charge*.{AALR WH#4:315} On 14 March 1692, Nicholas Waterman and wife Anne conv. to Lockwood 120 (perches?; a.?) called *Watertowne*.{AALR WH#4:149}
     Robert Lockwood, of AA Co., d. leaving a will dated 14 Oct 1704 and proved 22 April 1709, naming himself as a son of Robert and Eliza Lockwood of Aberford, Yorkshire, and naming his sister, Ann, wife of Robert Saws, and his bros., Thomas and John, as well as his wife, Eliza, and his son-in-law, Samuel Harrison. He left his estate in MD to the sons of his bro., Thomas.{MWB 6:204}

Robert Lockwood's estate was admin. on 9 Oct 1710 by the widow, Eliza Lockwood. An inventory of £1090.15.0 was listed. {INAC 32A:26}

Sometime after Robert Lockwood's death, and before 30 Dec 1717, Samuel Harrison purchased part of Lockwood's estate from the afsd. sons of Lockwood's bro., Thomas. {AALR IB#2:457}

Eliza Lockwood, widow, of AA Co., d. leaving a will dated 18 Dec 1711 and proved 29 Dec 1711. In her will she named Samuel Lockwood, Thomas Ratclift, his wife Mary, and their dau. Anne, and Edward Parrish. Samuel Galloway, Sr., Richard Jones, Jr., and William Richardson, Sr., were named execs. and residuary legatees. {MWB 13:467}

Eliza Lockwood's estate was inv. on 8 Jan 1711 by Capt. Thomas Larkin and John Blackmore. Personal property was valued £730.12.7. Edward Parish and Samuel Lockwood signed as creditors. {INAC 35A:376}

Another inventory was taken on 21 July 1712 by Thomas Larkin and John Blackmore, who appraised her personal property at £816.4.8. {INAC 34:15}

4. SAMUEL LOCKWOOD, possibly son of Thomas (2), d. by May 1722. He m. Mary Ellis, widow of (N) Tydings, who m. 3rd, Thomas Knighton.

He was named in the will of Eliza Lockwood, widow of Robert (3), and may have been one of the sons of Thomas mentioned in the will of Robert Lockwood.

Samuel Lockwood, of AA Co., d. leaving a will dated 1 March 1722 and proved 22 May 1722, naming wife Mary, extx., sons-in-law Richard Tydings and Laurence, and daus.-in-law Cassandra and Charity Tydings. {MWB 17:249} Samuel Lockwood was bur. in All Hallows Parish on 7 April 1722. {AACR:33}

Lockwood's estate was admin. on 13 June 1723 by extx. Mary Lockwood. An inventory of £234.6.5 was listed. {MDAD 5:144} His estate was admin. again on 11 July 1724, 9 March 1724, and 10 Nov 1725, by the execs. Thomas Knighton and wife Mary. {MDAD 6:24, 277, 7:121}

On 13 June 1733, Mary Knighton, sole dau. and heir of James Ellis, of AA Co., for love and affection she had for her sons Samuel Lockwood and Thomas Knighton, and for grandsons Samuel Brown (son of James and Cassandra Brown) and Thomas Sparrow (son of Solomon and Charity Sparrow), conv. to them various portions of a tract in BA Co. called *James' Park*, which was patented by her father on 10 May 1685. {PCLR PL#8:193}

Samuel and Mary (N) (Tydings) Lockwood were the parents of two sons, bapt. in All Hallows Parish, AA Co. {AACR:200}: SAMUEL, bapt. 17 June 1719, m. Eleanor Chiffen, no record of any children; and JOHN, bapt. 17 June 1719.

5.   SAMUEL LOCKWOOD, son of Samuel and Mary, was bapt. 17 June 1719 in All Hallows Parish, and d. by Nov 1758. He m. Eleanor Chiffen, who m. 2nd, (N) Reed.

On 17 Nov 1743, Samuel Lockwood, with the consent of his wife Elinor, conv. 500 a. *James Park* in BA Co. to John Bond.{BALR TB#C:367}

On 15 Nov 1758, the estate of Samuel Lockwood was dist. by Eleanor, the admx., now wife of William Reed, with Joseph Howard and Thomas Tydings as sureties. The balance of £240.17.5 was dist. among the widow and the two children.{BFD 2:96}

Samuel and Eleanor had two children.

Unplaced

LOCKWOOD, JAMES, was bur. in All Hallows Parish, AA Co., on 13 Sep 1722.{AACR:33}

LOCKWOOD, ROBERT, of AA Co., d. leaving an inventory filed 22 May 1731 by John Nicholson and Godfrey Walters, and valued at £41.19.6. John Rockhold and Sarah Rockhold signed as next of kin, and Rachel Lockwood, admx., filed the inventory on 7 Aug 1731.{MINV 16:337}

LOCKWOOD, RICHARD, Gent., of SO Co., d. leaving a nunc. will dated 12 Nov 1737 and proved 19 Jan 1727/8, naming sons Armel, Benjamin, John, and Samuel, dau. Rachel Evans, and granddau. Elizabeth Russell.{MWB 21:834}

THE MARRIOTT FAMILY

Refs.: A: McIntire. *Annapolis, Maryland, Families.*

1.   JOHN MARRIOTT, progenitor, was b. c1648, and d. in St. Anne's Parish on 16 Feb 1718/9.{AACR:83} He m. Sarah Acton who d. by 10 Nov 1724.

John Marriott was in AA Co. by 13 Jan 1679, when he purchased 200 a. *Hereford* from Charles and Eliza Stevens.{AALR IH#1:33} On 9 Aug 1684, Marriott and his wife conv. 26-1/2 a. of *Hereford* to John Buck, son of John Buck, dec. The grantee was the nephew of John Marriott's wife.{AALR IH#3:73} On 7 Feb 1689, John Marriott, with consent of wife Sarah, conv. 60 a., part of *Brooksby Point,* to Thomas Aldridge.{AALR IH#2:144}

On 4 Sep 1682, John Marriott, of AA Co., patented 300 a. called *Cordwell.*{MPL 24:463, 29:511}

On 3 May 1688, John Acton made a will and named bro.-in-law John Marriott as exec.{MWB 6:1}

John Marriott, planter, of AA Co., d. leaving a will dated 20 Aug 1716 and proved 10 March 1718. To son Joseph, he left *Cawdwell,* where Joseph was living. To son Emanuel, he left 100 a. *Hereford,* where he was seated, and the dwell. plant. Son John was to have the residue of *Hereford,* and 100 a. *Brooksby's Point.* Sons Augustine and Silvanus where to have the residue of *Brooksby's Point* and 250 a. *Shepard's Forest.* John Riggs was to have the residue of *Shepard's Forest.* Henry Sewell and William Stephens were each left 40 s. Dau. Ann Gambrell was to have £5 and personalty. Dau. Sarah was to have £30. The execs. were sons Joseph and Augustine. The will was wit. by Peter Porter, William Stevens, and Edw. Benson.{MWB 15:1}

John Marriott's estate was inv. on 11 May 1719 by Richard and Alexander Warfield, and appraised at £251.8.8. Emanuel and Silvanus Marriott signed that they approved.{MINV 2:28} An additional inventory worth £37.14.11 was also compiled.{MINV 3:229}

Richard and Alexander Warfield also appraised the estate of Mrs. Sarah Marriott, and appraised it at £65.10.4. Joseph and Emanuel Marriott signed of next of kin, and Peter Porter and Augustin Marriott, admins., filed the inventory on 10 Nov 1724.{MINV 10:214}

John and Sarah (Acton) Marriott were the parents of{A:449}: JOSEPH; EMANUEL; JOHN; AUGUSTINE; SYLVANUS; ANN, m. Joshua Gambrill; and SARAH.

2.   JOSEPH MARRIOTT, son of John (1) and Sarah (Acton), d. in AA Co. by 3 Oct 1774, having m. Elizabeth (N).

Joseph Marriott d. leaving a will dated 18 Feb 1773 and proved in AA Co. on 3 Oct 1774. He named his dau. Sarah, who was to have half of *Cordwell,* the rest of which went to his sons Thomas Davis and Emanuel Marriott. He named his daus. Rachel and Mary, and mentioned 6 children. Robert Davis, Sr., William Templeman, James Babbs, and Thomas Warfield were wits.{MWB 40:34}

Joseph and Elizabeth were the parents of the following children, the first two of whom were definitely bapt. in All Hallows Parish{AACR:197, 201}: AUGUSTINE, bapt. 18 May 1718; MARY, bapt. 15 Aug 1720; SARAH; THOMAS DAVIS; EMANUEL; and RACHEL.

3.   EMANUEL MARRIOTT, son of John (1) and Sarah (Acton), joined Sylvanus Marriott in signing the inventory (filed 26 Oct 1730) of Henry Sewell, as next of kin.{MINV 16:30}

4.   JOHN MARRIOTT, son of John (1) and Sarah (Acton), on 12 Nov 1729 patented 15 a. in BA Co. called *Hereford's Addition*.{MPL PL#7:305, IL#A:56}

5.   AUGUSTINE MARRIOTT, son of John (1) and Sarah (Acton), d. 1772. On 1 Jan 1730, he m. Mary Warfield, dau. of John and Ruth. {AACR:95}

Augustine Marriott's will, dated 3 Jan 1771 and proved 17 June 1772, named his wife Mary as extx., and his children Sarah Yealdhall, Mary Sewell, and John Marriott, as well as son-in-law John Hall and his three daus., Mary, Sarah, and Achsah. John Marriott, Joseph Warfield, and Joshua Gambrill wit. the will.{MWB 38:835}

Augustine and Mary were the parents of{A:449}: MARY, b. 1730, m. John Sewell; JOHN, m. Elizabeth Davis; ACHSAH, m. John Hall; and SARAH, m. (N) Yealdhall.

6.   SYLVANUS MARRIOTT, son of John and Sarah (Acton), d. in AA Co. by June 1764, having m. on 8 Dec 1730, Rachel Davis.{A:449; AACR:97}

Sylvanius Marriott, of AA Co., d. leaving a will dated 19 May 1764 and proved 14 June 1764. He named his wife Rachel, and son John (to have the dwell. plant.), son Silvanus (to have 150 a. part *Duvall's Delight*), and dau. Hamutal Warfield. The will was wit. by Joseph and John Sewell, and John Marriott, Jr.{MWB 32:150}

Sylvanus and Rachel were the parents of: JOHN; SYLVANUS; and HAMUTAL, m. (N) Warfield.

7.   JOHN MARRIOTT, son of Augustine (5) and Mary, d. in AA Co., leaving a will dated 27 Feb 1776 and proved 13 Feb 1777. He named John Sewell's son Augustine, his own wife Anne Marriott, mother Mary Marriott, and Thomas Marriott's son Joseph.{MWB 40:652}

THE FRANCIS MEAD FAMILY

Later generations of the Mead Family are traced in BCF.

1.   FRANCIS MEAD, progenitor, d. in AA Co., between 4 Jan 1716 and 6 Aug 1717. He m. as his second wife Anne (N) (who d. in BA Co. in 1725).{BCF}

Francis was in AA Co. by 31 Aug 1678, when he was listed as a debtor in the inventory of James Cox.{INAC 5:457}

On 19 June 1680, he had surv. 225 a. *Bear Neck*. By 1707, 64 a. of this was owned by Thomas Robinson and 161 a. was still held by Mead.{MRR:252; MPL 28:63, 28:152}

By 1707, he owned 100 a. *Pen Lloyd als. Swan Neck* and 130 a. of *Huckleberry Forest.*{MRR:229, 260}

On 7 Nov 1682, he was listed as a debtor in the estate of Robert Franklin.{INAC 8:27} On 25 Nov 1694, his land was mentioned in a deed. {AALR IH#1:94}

On 31 Oct 1694, Francis Mead and Thomas Darsone inv. the estate of Jacob Hallett.{INAC 13A:185} On 3 May 1697, John Meade and Francis Hurst inv. the estate of Thomas Woods.{INAC 15:105}

A deed dated 18 April 1702 mentioned 50 a. of *Swan Neck*, originally surv. as 100 a. for Edward Lloyd. He sold the 100 a. to Christopher Rowles, who, in 1663, sold 50 a. to John Browne, who sold his 50 a. to Henry Catlin. It passed to Abraham Dawson, whose son Thomas Dawson sold it Thomas Rowles, grandson of sd. Christopher. Thomas Rowles sold it to William Taylard.{AALR WT#1:281}

On 29 Oct 1702, Richard Beard, boatwright, sold to Francis Mead, planter, 103 a., part of *Huckleberry Forest.* Beard's wife, Susannah, consented, and Thomas Dawson and William Mead were wits. {AALR WT#1:319} On the same day, Francis Mead, with the consent of his wife Ann, conv. to Thomas Robinson, 64 a. of *Bear Neck*, originally granted to Francis Mead on 24 Sep 1680 for 225 a.{AALR WT#1:61}

Francis Mead d. leaving a will dated 6 Aug 1717, naming sons William, John, and Benjamin, dau. Susanna Long, son-in-law Thomas Dawson, granddau. Hannah Crans, dau.-in-law Mary Wright, and John and James Beard [actually BOARD].{BCF; MWB 14:441}

William and Anne Mead admin. the estate of Francis Mead on 10 June 1719. The inventory totalled £141.4.3. Payments included a mare paid to Thomas Dawson, being a legacy. Balance due the estate was £125.9.6.{MDAD 2:34}

His estate was admin. again by William and Anna Mead on 11 Aug 1719. The previous balance was £141.4.3. Payments included one to Thomas Long, being a legacy left to Thomas Long's wife, Susannah Long.{MDAD 2:203}

An additional inventory was filed 27 Sep 1725, appraised by Philip Jones and Robert Jubb, and filed by Francis Mead, acting exec. {MINV 11:92}

A second additional account was made by William Mead on behalf of himself and Ann Mead, the execs., on 4 Oct 1725. Payment was made to several people, including Mary Wright.{MDAD 7:100-101}

Anna, relict of Francis Mead, d. leaving a will dated 9 Jan 1723 and proved 10 Nov 1725, naming son Benjamin and his dau. Nanney, her dau. Mary Wright, her sons John and James, and grandchildren John and James Boards.{BCF; MWB 18:409}

Administration bond on the estate of Anna Mead was posted 5 Jan 1737 by Benjamin Cadle.

Francis Mead was the father of: SUSANNA, m. 1st, Thomas Long, and 2nd, on 3 April 1722, Stephen Body; BENJAMIN, gave his age as 75 in 1761{AALC 2:561}, d. 1764; JOHN; WILLIAM, d. by 6 May 1735, when his estate was appraised by Robert Boone and John Burle and valued at £12.5.0. John Mead, Benjamin Meade and William Meade were mentioned. Joane Mead, admx., filed the inventory on 31 May 1735.{MINV 20:430}; and JAMES.

THE MEWSHAW FAMILY

Refs.: A: MCHP #9833 (Not Recorded), AA Co., 1848.

1.   JOHN MOONSHAW m. Elizabeth Fisher on 22 May 1727 in St. Anne's Parish, AA Co.{AACR:94}
    Between 1728 and 1729, he mortgaged 60 a. of *Boyde's Chance* to John Worthington.{AALR RD#1:126} In 1733, he sold the land outright to Worthington. Mewshaw's wife Elizabeth Consented.{AALR IH&TI#1:582}
    John Mewshaw patented two tracts in AA Co.: 20 a. *Struggle for Life,* on 4 Sep 1744{MPL PT#2:318}, and 30 a. *Vanely Mount,* on 18 March 1747.{MPL TI#4:390 and BY#1:599}
    John and Elizabeth (Fisher) Moonshaw/Mewshaw may have been the parents of: DAVID.

2.   DAVID MEWSHAW, possibly son of John and Elizabeth, d. in AA Co. He m. Mary, dau. of Ebenezer Pumphrey.
    On 15 Aug 1729, David Mewshaw, Mary Mewshaw, and John Mewshaw were listed as debtors in the inventory of Amos Garrett of AA Co.{MINV 15:46-73}
    In 1757, Pumphrey conv. by deed of gift *Saw Mill Supply* to his dau. Mary Mewshaw.{AALR BB#2, Vol. 1:35}
    Ebenezer Pumphrey d. leaving a will dated 20 Aug 1759 and proved 8 July 1761, naming his dau. Mary "Moonshaw" and the heirs begotten by [her husband] "David Moonshaw," who were to have 24 a. *Saw Mills Supply*. Pumphrey also named a granddau. Margaret Moonshaw.{MWB 31:458}
    David Mewshaw signed the inventory of Ebenezer Pumphrey as one of the next of kin on 5 June 1762.{MINV 78:150}
    David and Mary left the following children{A}: MARGARET, named in grandfather's will; DAVID, Jr,; HAZEL (ASEL); ACHSAH; SARAH; MARY; and JOSEPH.

3.   MARGARET MEWSHAW, dau. of David (2) and Mary, was named in her grandfather's will. She m. Abraham Dicas, both of whom

have d. intestate, leaving four children{A}: ABRAHAM DICAS, d. intestate, without issue; ABSOLOM DICAS, went off in the War of 1812 and was not heard of since, and whom the orators state has departed this life without heirs; ACHSAH DICAS, m. Aaron Thornton; and LAWRENCE DICAS.

4.   DAVID MEWSHAW, son of David (2) and Mary, was living on 16 May 1765 when he wit. the will of Lazarus Pumphrey, of AA Co.{MWB 38:396} He d. intestate before 1848, leaving four children as heirs-at-law (they were among the orators in the Chancery Case){A}: CHARLES; DAVID; JAMES; and LEAH, m. Henry Barker.

5.   HAZEL (ASEL) MEWSHAW, son of David (2) and Mary, d. in AA Co. c1830, unm., and without any children. He owned some 70 a. of land, partly enclosed, which came to him from his mother Mary Mewshaw. His only heirs were his bros. and sisters, or descendants of dec. bros. and sisters.{A}

6.   ACHSAH MEWSHAW, dau. of David (2) and Mary, and sister of Hazel, m. one David Mewshaw, whom she survived, and d. c1842 intestate, leaving three children who were among the orators in the Chancery Case: JOSEPH; HAZEL; and ACHSAH, m. Charles Mewshaw.

7.   SARAH MEWSHAW, dau. of David (2) and Mary, and sister of Hazel, m. Vincent Forrest, whom she survived, and d. c1837, intestate, leaving seven children, who were among the orators{A}: SARAH FORREST, widow of Jonathan Mewshaw; MARY FORREST, m. Richard Wood, both of whom d. intestate, leaving two children (ACHSAH HOLSTEAD, widow, oratrix; and MARGARET WOOD, oratrix); AQUILLA FORREST; ANNE FORREST, m. (N) Forrest, both of whom have d., leaving an only child (JOSHUA FORREST, orator); RACHEL FORREST, one of the defendants; PRISCILLA FORREST, d. unm.; and MERCY FORREST, m. Beale Gaither, orators.

8.   MARY MEWSHAW, dau. of David (20 and Mary, m. Francis Lawrence, whom she survived, and d. intestate about 1836, leaving the following children, who were among the orators{A}: DAVID LAWRENCE; ELIZABETH LAWRENCE, m. James Phelps; WILLIAM LAWRENCE; MARGARET LAWRENCE, m. Ebenezer Phelps; MARY LAWRENCE, m. Samuel Yieldhall; FRANCIS LAWRENCE; and ELLEN LAWRENCE, m. John Vansant.

9.   JOSEPH MEWSHAW, son of David (2) and Mary, and bro. of Hazel, d. intestate before Hazel, leaving a widow, Parthy, one of the

defendants, and the following children, who were among the defendants {A}: WILLIAM; JOSEPH; MARY; ELIZABETH, m. William Baldwin;

HEZEKIAH; DENNIS; CALEB, lives in the w., beyond the jurisdiction of the court; and CHARLES, d. c1845, intestate, without children.

THE MUSGROVE FAMILY

1.   ANTHONY MUSGROVE was in AA Co. by c1684 when he was listed as a debtor in the inventory of Nathan Smith.{INAC 8:202}
    He was listed as "dead and insolvent," in the administration account, filed 22 April 1704, of Lewis Evans, of AA.{MWB 3:411}
    Anthony was probably the father of: ANTHONY, b. c1686.

2.   ANTHONY MUSGROVE, probably son of Anthony, who d. by 1704, was b. c1686 and gave his age as 60 in 1746, when he stated he was an overseer for John Gresham the Elder.{AALC 2:242-243}
    Anthony Musgrove m. Margaret Deaver on 25 Nov 1707 in St. James Parish, AA Co.{AACR:157}
    He seems to have been in BA Co. by 16 May 1721, when he wit. the will of James Barlow, Jr.{MWB 17:50} On 5 Feb 1721, he was listed as having received a payment from the estate of Edward Feall [Teall?] of BA Co.{MDAD 4:129}
    On 7 Aug 1758, Anthony Musgrove joined Robert and Mary Tevis in selling *Addition to Treadway's Quarter* to Abel Browne.{BALR B#G:207}
    Anthony Musgrove wit. the will of William Ridgely, of Charles, of AA Co., on 15 June 1755.{MWB 30:5}
    In 1768, Sarah Nelson, widow of Burgess Nelson, conv. him 93 a. *Inspection*.{AALR IB&JB#1:75}
    In 1770, he conv. property, chattel, and a servant Nicholas Miller, to Samuel Musgrove, Sr., and to John Musgrove.{AALR IB#2:191}
    In 1770, Henry Gaither conv. him 61 a. called P*resly Butted*.{AALR IB#2:224}
    Anthony Musgrove, of AA Co., d. by 7 Sep 1772, when his estate was appraised by Anthony Holland and John Brown. Edward Gaither, Raphael West, and Thomas Gassaway, of Michael, signed as creditors, while Samuel Musgrove, Jr., and Samuel Musgrove, of Anthony, signed as kin. Anthony Musgrove was admin.{MINV 110:199}
    Anthony and Margaret had the following children, b. in All Hallows Parish, AA Co.{AACR:28, 30, 157}: JOANNA, b. 27 May 1708, bapt. 27 June 1708 in St. James Parish; MARY, bapt. 30 April 1710; ANNE, bapt. 20 April 1712; SAMUEL; (possibly) JOHN; and (possibly) ANTHONY.

3.   SAMUEL MUSGROVE, son of Anthony, signed the inventory of Anthony Musgrove on 7 Sep 1772.

As Samuel Musgrove, of AA Co., he patented 100 a. called *Platt* in AA Co. on 15 Nov 1741.{MPL LG#B:388} On 22 Jan 1767, he wit. the will of Miriam Richardson, of FR Co.{MWB 35:572}

In 1743, he conv. a tract called *Platt* to William Spires. Samuel's wife Sarah consented.{AALR RB#1:313} In 1761, Richard Snowden conv. him 40 a. *Hammond's Delight.*{AALR BB#2: Vol. 2:558} In 1771, Samuel Musgrove conv. to John Warfield 220 a. called *Goodwill.*{AALR IB#3:182} Samuel Musgrove and Rachel Musgrove, in 1774, conv. to Nathan Barnes, of Nathan, 15-2/9 a. *Shipley's Discovery.*{AALR IB#5:120}

Samuel Musgrove had at least one son: STEPHEN.

3.   JOHN MUSGROVE, possibly son of Anthony, was in PG Co. in 1761, when he signed a petition as an inhabitant of Prince George's Parish, to build a chapel of ease.{Scharf, *Western Maryland.*745}

John Musgrove wit. the will, dated 10 Dec 1784, of John Crockett Dorsey, of FR Co.{FRWB GM#2:187-188}

John Musgrove d. in MO Co., MD, leaving a will dated 5 June 1785 and proved 8 Aug 1785. In it, he named his son Amos, son Nathan (to be co-exec. with Richard Ijams), and mentioned other children. The will was wit. by Anthony Holland, Benjamin Gaither, and John Scrivener.{MOWB B:207; or 1:172}

A Chancery paper at MSA names the heirs of John Musgrove as sued by Samuel Larkins and wife Sarah: Dorsey Barnes and wife Lydia (living in BA Co.), Richard and Thomas Ijams, Nathan and Zachariah Musgrove, Phenice Stallion and wife Delilah, Joshua Plummer and wife Elizabeth, and Rachel and Amos Musgrove.{MCHP 3178, MSA}

John Musgrove was the father of: LYDIA, m. Dorsey Barnes; NATHAN; ZACHARIAH; AMOS; DELILAH, m. Phenice Stallion; and ELIZABETH, m. Joshua Plummer.

4.   STEPHEN MUSGROVE, son of Samuel, in 1769 was conv. 11 a. *White Oak Bottom* by John Ward.{AALR: NH#1:20}

Unplaced

MUSGROVE, (N), m. by 21 March 1757, Sarah Truman, sister of Notley Goldsmith. In his will of that date, Goldsmith named his sister Sarah Truman Musgrove and her dau. Anne.{MCW 11:164}

MUSGROVE, ABRAHAM, tailor, of BA Co., d. by 9 Dec 1772 when his estate was appraised by Conrad Small and John Stoler. Job Greene and Richard Parker signed as creditors, and John Musgrove signed as next of kin. William Spencer was admin.{MINV 110:363}

MUSGRAVE, BENJAMIN, of CH Co., m. by 24 April 1742, Mary, extx. of Thomas Clark, of CH Co.{MINV 27:49}

Benjamin Musgrove was one of the appraisers of the estate of Anthony Simms, of PG Co. (the inventory was filed 1 Nov 1756).{MINV 62:102} On 10 Nov 1756, he and Luke Marbury appraised the estate of Moses Lenham, of PG Co.{MINV 62:179} As admin. of the estate of Susannah Humphreys, Benjamin filed the inventory of her estate on 29 March 1758.{MINV 65:194} He was one of the appraisers of the estate of Thomas Thomson, of PG Co., on 13 June 1763.{MINV 82:13} On 17 April 1765, he and Zachariah Wade appraised the estate of widow Sarah Rober(t)son.{MINV 90:135}

Benjamin Musgrove m. Mary (N), and had issue: LYDIA MARGARET, bapt. 22 Oct 1752.{King George's Parish, PG Co.}

MUSGROVE, CHARLES, was in CH Co. by 21 March 1716, when he wit. the will of John Posey.{MWB 14:270} On 18 April 1734, as Charles Musgrave, of CH Co., he appraised the estate of John Crain.{MINV 18:304}

Charles Musgrove, of CH Co., d. leaving a will dated 16 Feb 1744 and proved 4 May 1751, naming wife Catherine (to have *Burlius Hills*), son Harrison (to have sd. tract after Catherine's death), son Charles (to have 460 a. *Hog Island*), and mentioning 6 children. Wife Catherine was to be extx. James Keech, Jr., Courts Keech, and Ann Keech were wits. {MWB 28:177}

On 18 May 1751, his estate was appraised by Courts Keech and John Chandler. Elizabeth Larender and Robert Horner signed as creditors, and Charles Musgrave and Harrison Musgrave signed as kin. Katherine Musgrave, accountant, filed the inventory on 27 July 1751. {MINV 47:259}

MUSGROVE, CHARLES, of SM Co., d. by 4 May 1757, when his estate was inv. by Samuel Briscoe and Edward Turner. The inventory was filed by admx. Sarah Farmon [Truman?] Musgrove on 25 July 1757. {MINV 63:404}

MUSGRAVE, ELIZABETH, was named in the will, dated 5 Feb 1725, of Mary Posey, of CH Co.{MWB 18:342}

MUSGROVE, HARRISON, signed the inventory (not dated, but filed 31 May 1757) of William Vinson, of CH Co.{MINV 63:500}

He d. by 22 May (---) when his estate was appraised by Charles Court and George Keech. James Campbell and Andrew Buchanan signed as creditors, and Notley Warren and Henrietta Posey signed as kin. Mary

Musgrave, admx., filed the inventory on 22 May 1760.{MINV 70:192}

MUSGROVE, MARY, signed the inventory (not dated, but filed 6 June 1758) of Capt. Barton Warren, of CH Co., as next of kin.{MINV 64:280}

MUSGRAVE, SUSANNA, was named as a granddau. in the will, signed 19 Aug 1718, of Edward Philpott, of CH Co.{MWB 14:672}

THE NICHOLS FAMILY

Refs.: A: "Better Days: A Nichols Family of Anne Arundel, Prince George's and Howard Counties," by Carson Gibb, *BMGS* 36 (1) 56-60.

1.   SAMUEL NICHELL was transported by Jeremy Swillivan, of AA Co., by 17 Nov 1670.{MPL WT:12} Samuel Nickolls, or Nichell, is listed as a debtor to William Russell in 1679 and to George Skipwith c1685, both of whom lived in the southern part of AA Co.{INAC 6:74, 10LC:33}
      In 1701, Samuel was mentioned in a deed.{AALR WT#1:255} In Aug 1705, he was mentioned in court as a defendant "non est." Evidently he was presented as a defendant, but it was found there was no case against him.{AAJU August 1705:54}
      Samuel was of the right place and time (probably b. c1650) to be father of{A:58}: ROBERT.

2.   ROBERT NICHOLS, possibly son of Samuel, was living as late as 1736.
      In a Judgment of March 1710/11 for £6.19.1, he promised to pay (N) Rumney.{AAJU March Court 1710/11:248-9}
      He appeared in a list of taxables of Mattapany Hundred of PG Co. (a few miles down the Patuxent from Queen Anne) in 1733.{CMSP: The Black Books, Item #276}
      He was living at Queen Anne Town, PG Co., when he was stated to have possessed a shallop of William Metcalf, of Annapolis, in a bill of sale of 15 July 1736.{AALR RD#2:376}
      A judgment of November Court 1736 stated that Robert Nichols was said to have obtained a license to keep Queen Anne's Ferry.{AAJU November Court 1736:69}

      He does not seem to have left a will, inventory, or admin. account. This Robert may have been father of{A:58}: WILLIAM.

3.   WILLIAM NICHOLS, possibly son of Robert, d. by July 1722. He m. Sarah, admx. of Richard Symons, on 23 Oct 1718 in St. James Parish.{AACR:163}

On 6 Oct 1718, he was surety for Sarah Simonds, admnx. of Richard Symonds.{MDTP 23:261} Sarah, wife of William Nicholas, admin. the estate of Richard Symons on 16 Aug 1720.{MDAD 3:194} In 1718, he was exec. of the estate of Robert Moss, of AA Co.{MDTP 23:190}

On 5 May 1722, John Welsh and Richard Duckett appraised the estate of William Nicholls, of AA Co., at £9.10.2. Richard Lancaster and Michael Morris signed as creditors, and Sarah Nichols, Sr., and Matthew Mogbee signed as next of kin.{MINV 7:296} On 26 July 1722, his estate was admin. by Robert Tyler, Gent. The inventory of £9.10.2 was mentioned. {MDAD 4:166}

William, of Robert, may have been the father of: WILLIAM; and SAMUEL.

4.   WILLIAM NICHOLS, possibly son of William, Sr. (3), d. by 28 July 1784.

William Nichols appeared in AA Co. Records in 1744. On 14 July, he wrote to Phillpott and Lee, merchants in London, ordering them to pay 5.10 sterling to William Beall, Jr.{AALR RB#2:164}

In 1759, William Nichols was being sued by Francis King, exec., and Marg't Keene, extx. of Richard Keene, and is identified as William Nicholl, of AA Co., planter, otherwise called William Nicholls of PG Co. The court considered that King recover £0.29.17 from him.{AAJU August Court 1759:115}

He had assets enough to require probate records, which tell us some things about him.

On 28 July 1784, his estate was appraised by Leonard Sellman and John Basford, and appraised at £42.19.6. The inventory was filed on 19 April 1788 by William Nichols, admin. An account of sales was filed 30 July 1784. Items were purchased by William Nichols, Isaac Nichols, and John Nichols. William Nichols was the admin.{AA Testamentary Papers, hereafter cited as AATP, Box 13, folder 22, MSA}

The first account was filed 19 April 1788. It mentioned income from the sales totalling £64.4.11, money due from Isaac Nichols, and a balance due the estate of £28.19.8.{AATP, Box 14, folder 27}

A final account was filed 11 Aug 1788. The account mentioned payments to Dr. Robert Pottinger, John Williams, Tyler and Duckett, and others. John Nichols was mentioned. The account shows the estate overpaid by £1.17.3/4. This financial position is much lower than the social position suggested by the title "Mr." Since the estate was overpaid, there was no balance to be dist.{AATP, Box 14, folder 52}

William Nichols, Jr., was the father of: WILLIAM, admin. of his father's estate. In Sep 1785, William Nichols, admin. of William Nichols,

continued (futilely) a suit for debt against Thomas Gordon, which the
William, now dec., started in PG Co. Court in 1777{PG Co. Court Proceedings
38:533 and EE #2:237}; and ROBERT.

5.   SAMUEL NICHOLS, possibly son of William, Sr. (3), was in FR
Co. in 1770, when he was conv. a negro slave by his father-in-law,
William Reed.{AALR IB#2:228} He was too young to be the father of William,
and was more likely a bro. It should be noted that Robert Nichols who m.
Sarah Robertson had a son Samuel and a son Nelson Reed Nichols.
     Samuel's first appearance in PG Co. records was in 1760, when,
along with John Nicholson, he is fined for turning in four too few squirrel
heads.{PG Levy Book A:689; PG Court Proceedings DD #1:457; PG Court Proceedings DD#2:113, 365;
EE#1:439, 516} In his next appearance, in Aug 1774, he is bound in £400 to
keep "an ordinary house of entertainment at the Town of Queen Anne"
(on the Patuxent) for the following year. There is no record of a renewal
of his license. Instead, in the next session, November Court 1774,
Samuel Nicholls, of Queen Anne, was "presented for assault on the body
of Thomas Perry," and in the next session, March 1775, William Nicholls
was presented for beating Moses Veach. In November Court 1775,
William's case was struck off, he paying fees. Samuel was still being
prosecuted in March Court 1776, when he had been dead for several
months. As William probably was b. by 1730, Samuel is more likely to
have been his bro. rather than his father.
     On 3 Jan 1776, in PG Co., William Nicholls, with Richard
Wooten and Singleton Wooten as sureties in £1,500, was bound as
admin. of Samuell Nicholls. On 17 Dec 1776, the personal estate of Mr.
Samuel Nichols was appraised at £184.7.9-1/4, and William Nicholes
and Jane Nicholes signed as next of kin. The balance of the first and only
extant account of Samuel's estate, including sperate debts of £164.18.10,
was £459.0.5.{PG Original Administration Bonds, Box 19, folder 42; PG Inventories, Box 25, folder 53}

6.   ROBERT NICHOLS, son of William (4), was b. c1755/6, and d.
c1821. He m. Sarah Robertson, by AAML dated 21 July 1787.
     No record has been found for military service in the Revolutionary
War. So far, no record has been found of land ownership in the 1783 or
1798 tax lists.
     On 9 Aug 1790, Robert filed a libel, or complaint, against William
Nichols, of PG Co., admin., and one of the sons of William Nichols, of
AA Co., dec. The complaint is that payment of £45.15.1 shown in the
admin's. account are not justified. A note at the bottom says that the
matter was "agreed before Tryal" and the paper was ordered not to be
recorded. This paper is the earliest evidence of Robert's
impecuniousness,

but more important, it is the one piece of evidence that links Robert to his father, the dec. William.{AATP Box 20, Folder 57, MSA}

Gibb states that, although Robert Nichols, of AA Co., (c1764-1820), did not hold any land, he showed signs of above-average station. For many years he was a constable and a tavern-keeper; at one time he owned at least five slaves. He was often - once seriously - in debt.

About two years after his marriage, Robert was in debt to Lawrence Robinson, to whom, on 2 Feb 1791, he mortgaged personal property to secure payment of a debt, with interest, from 24 Oct 1789. On 23 Feb, three weeks after executing the mortgage, he brought a stray before John Brice, J. P. On the next day he was put in jail for debt. A petition he submitted in March to three justices, Allan Quynn, Robert Condon, and John Brice, says that he had been "a languishing prisoner in AA Co. goal [jail] since the 24th day of Feb last past at the suit of a certain Benja. Marsh and John Ray for debts he is unable to pay with all the property he hath and therefore prays your worships will extend to him the benefit of the Act of Assembly ... for the relief of Insolvent Debtors ..." On 27 March, the three justices set 18 April as the date to consider the petition, and on that date they directed the sheriff to discharge Robert Nichols.{AALR NH#5:73 and NH#5:445; AA Insolvent Debtors 1788-1804:33-34}

In 1790, Robert Nichols was listed in AA Co. with one white male over 16, one white male under 16, and two white females.

He was in court for debt in 1803, 1809, 1810, and 1812. About 1810, however, Robert's affairs seem to have taken a turn for the better. On 8 May 1811, with William Nichols and William Cox as sureties in $800, he was bound as constable of Middle Neck Hundred. According to the AA Co. Levy Lists, he was constable from 1811 to 1817; 1811 is the only year in which his hundred is known and the only year but one, 1815, for which the land records have a bond. In September Court 1813, he was admitted to keep an ordinary, and he was admitted again in 1814, 1817, 1818, and 1819. On 18 Sep 1814, he gave a young slave and a bed to each of his five children: Samuel, Sarah, Martin, Jeremiah, and Rachel. But Robert still had trouble. About a year and a half later, on 28 March 1816, for $200, he sold to his daus., Sarah and Rachel, a negro woman, Sall, about 30 years old; and two and a half years after that, on 12 Sep 1818, for their love of him and $100, they sold him negro woman, Sall, 31 years old, mulatto girl, Rebecca, 4 years old, and one boy, Sam, 18 months old. In effect, his daus. gave him $100 for two little slaves. After 1813, Robert was not in court for debt, but he was there on another charge, assault. He was charged in 1812 by John Thomas Barber, and in 1816 by Benjamin Lusby, and in 1818 he and his son, Martin were

charged by Robert Gafford. We have the approximate date of his death
from the notation of 24 June 1820, "Defendant [in assault case] dead."{AA
Levy Lists 1811-1817; AALR NH#16:494, WSG#3:576, and WSG#4:298; AAJU WSG#7, WSG#9:5,
WSG#14:28, WSG#16:23, and WSG#18:18; WSG#3:217; AALR WSG#4:203, and WSG#6:77; AA Court
Dockets 1813, Sep: Trials #356; 1816; April: Appearances #25; 1818, April: Criminal Appearances #47 & 48;
1820, April: Criminal Continuances #51}

Robert and Sarah were the parents of: SAMUEL, b. c1786/7;
SARAH; MARTIN; JEREMIAH; and RACHEL.

7.   SAMUEL NICHOLS, son of Robert (7), was b. c1786/7, and m.
Susan Hardy, by AAML dated 21 Sep 1815.
About 1807, he was enrolled in a militia company between Severn
and South Rivers. During the War of 1812, he served 13 days, between
13 April and 17 May 1813, in Capt. Henry Woodward's Company. He
served 30 days, between 28 July and 1 Sep 1813, as sergeant in Capt.
Henry Woodward's 1st Company of the 22nd regiment. Between 28 July
and 15 Oct 1814, he served 80 days as a sergeant stationed at the AA Co.
Magazine. Then he served 19 days, between 15 Oct and 3 Nov 1814, in
John Hatherly's Company. Between 4 Nov and 12 Dec 1814, he served
39 days as a sergeant in the same company, and finally he served 79
days, from 13 Dec 1814 and 1 March 1815.{Maryland Militia: War of 1812, Vol. 4: Anne
Arundel and Calvert. By F. Edward Wright. Silver Spring: Family Line Publications: 1981: 6, 33, 37}

He may be the Samuel Nichols named as a bro. in the will, proved
20 Nov 1821, of Martin Nichols.{AAWB 38 1/2:23}
On 26 Oct 1835, Samuel Nichols was security for Ann Jenkins,
admx. of Francis Jenkins.{AADI TH#1:240}
Samuel Nichols was the father of: BENJAMIN FRANKLIN
NICHOLS.

THE GEORGE NORMAN FAMILY

1.   GEORGE NORMAN, of AA Co., d. in AA Co. by Aug 1677. He
was transported to MD c1662.{MPL 5:68, 6:15} George Norman m. Johanna
(N). Johanna Norman was listed as a debtor of Henry Lewis in the latter's
inventory of 28 April 1679.{INAC 6:156} Sometime before 28 May 1701,
John Gadsby and his wife Johannah were appointed admins. of the estate.
{INAC 20:109, 22:66} On 29 March 1708, they sold several tracts of land.{AALR
WT#2:631}

He laid out a 30 a. tract called Graves.{AALR WT#1:191}
He left a will dated 13 Jan 1675 and proved 28 Aug 1677. He
named a son George, who was to have all land at 21 years, and appointed

his wife extx. The will was wit. by William Hopkinson, Thos. Roles, and Jeremiah Berry.{MWB 5:284}

George Norman was the father of: GEORGE.

2.   GEORGE NORMAN, of BA Co., son of George, d. by March 1697/8. He m. Eliza (N). On 14 Oct 1697, Eliza, wife of George Norman, was named as the youngest dau. of James Smith when the latter's estate was admin. by Ann Smith. The other dau. was Mary (Smith), wife of Edward Gibbs.{INAC 15:180}

On 31 Dec 1692, George Norman conv. to Edward Lunn 30 a. of *Graves*, which his father George had laid out.{AALR WT#1:191}

George Norman d. leaving a will dated 28 Feb 1697 and proved 24 March 1697/8. The heirs named were sons George and William, each of whom was to have 150 a. of the *Home Plantation*, and the testator's wife Eliza, who was named extx. The will was wit. by Richard Cromwell, Thomas Reynolds, and Sarah Hopkins.{MWB 7:356}

Eliza Norman probably did not survuve her husband very long, for the joint estate of George and Eliza Norman was appraised c1687/8 by James Mooray and Jacob Jackson. Their personal property was valued at £74.10.0.{INAC 16:46}

The estate of George Norman was admin. on 28 May 1701 by John Gadsby and his wife Johanna [almost certainly George Norman's mother]. An inventory of £74.10.0 was mentioned.{INAC 20:109}

George Norman was the father of: GEORGE; and WILLIAM.

3.   GEORGE NORMAN, son of George and Eliza, is probably the George Norman who m. Mary Wood on 26 Oct 1717 in St. Anne's Parish.{AACR:81}

THE NICHOLAS NORMAN FAMILY

Refs.: A: MCHR 94:377. B: Robert Barnes. *Maryland Marriages, 1778-1800.* Baltimore: Genealogical Publishing Co., 1978. C: Robert Barnes. *Maryland Marriages, 1634-1777.* Baltimore: Genealogical Publishing Co., 1975.

1.   NICHOLAS NORMAN, d. by June 1769. He m. Elizabeth Carr on 24 Dec 1731 in St. James Parish.{AACR:165}

Nicholas Norman, of AA Co., d. leaving a will dated 12 Feb 1768 and proved 26 June 1769. He named his children John, Benjamin, Nicholas, Joseph, William, Thomas, and Elizabeth, wife of Joseph Gott. He also named his grandchildren Rachel, Elizabeth, Mary, Priscilla, and Margaret Chocke, children of John and Margaret Chocke. The execs.

were sons Nicholas and John. The will was wit. by John Duckett, Jr., Richard Gott, and William Journey.{MWB 37:210}

Nicholas and Elizabeth were the parents of{AACR:165, 166, 167, 168, 169, 170}: MARGARET, b. 3 Oct 1732; NICHOLAS, b. 12 March 1733/4, bapt. 1 May 1735, and d. 9 Feb 1815; JOHN, b. 12 Nov 1735 (Neither he or any heirs are mentioned in the Chancery case of 1815, so he probably d. young, without issue.); PRISCILLA, b. 17 Dec 1736; WILLIAM, b. 4 Sep 1739; ELIZA, b. 5 April 1741, bapt. 13 Sep 1741, m. by 1815 Joseph Gott; BENJAMIN, b. 11 July 1744; JOSEPH, b. 1 Dec 1745 (Neither he or any heirs are mentioned in the Chancery case of 1815, so he probably d. young, without issue.); THOMAS, b. 4 June 1748; and RICHARD, b. 4 Jan 1749/50.

2.   MARGARET (PEGGY) NORMAN, dau. of Nicholas and Elizabeth (Carr), was b. 3 Oct 1732,{AACR:165} and d. by 1815. She m. (N) Chalk{AAHO:65}, and left the following children{A}: MARY CHALK; RACHEL CHALK, m. Thomas Dorsett; MARGARET ("PEGGY") CHALK, m. William Simmons on 24 April 1781 in St. James Parish, AA Co.{B}; ELIZABETH, m. William Crandall in 1771 in St. James Parish, AA Co.{C}

3.   NICHOLAS NORMAN, son of Nicholas and Elizabeth, was b. 12 March 1733/4, bapt. 1 May 1735, and d. 9 Feb 1815.{AACR:166} At his death, he owned 400 a. of land. He d. intestate, without issue. He had four bros. and three sisters. They and their children are named in the chancery case of 1815.{A}

On 2 Dec 1823, Robert Franklin, admin. of Nicholas Norman, of AA Co., dist. the estate. William and Robert Norman were sureties, and the balance of the estate was divided into sixths. One-sixth went to each of the following: the heirs of bro. William; the heirs of bro. Benjamin Norman; the heirs of bro. Thomas Norman; the heirs of sister Priscilla Owens; the heirs of sister Margaret Chalk; and the heirs of sister Elizabeth Gott.{AADI TH#1:57}

4.   PRISCILLA NORMAN, dau. of Nicholas and Elizabeth (Carr), was b. 17 Dec 1736.{AACR:167} She m. Isaac Owens, son of Thomas and Anne Owens, b. 9 May 1729{AACR:168}, and d. 21 Sep 1805. During the Revolutionary War, Isaac Owens was a private in the militia, and took the Oath of Fidelity before the Hon. Samuel Lane on 1 March 1778.{AARP:146}

Isaac and Priscilla (Norman) Owens were the parents of{AARP:146}: ELIZABETH OWENS, m. James Owens; ANN OWENS, m. (N) Childs; CHARLES OWENS; PRISCILLA OWENS, m. (N) Welsh; BENJAMIN OWENS; ARTRIDGE OWENS; MARGARET OWENS, m. (N) Lowry; ISAAC OWENS; THOMAS OWENS; JOHN OWENS;

WILLIAM OWENS; NICHOLAS OWENS; and JOSEPH OWENS.

5.   WILLIAM NORMAN, son of Nicholas and Elizabeth, was b. 4
Sep 1739.{AACR:168} He d. by 1815, leaving four children{A}: JOHN;
JOSEPH; ELIZABETH OWENS, m. John Woodfield on 28 Feb 1782 in
St. James Parish{B}; and JANE, m. Abraham Parkerson [sic] on 5 Oct
1783 in St. James Parish.{B}

6.   ELIZA NORMAN, dau. of Nicholas and Elizabeth, was b. 5 April
1741, and bapt. 13 Sep 1741.{AACR:168} She m. by 1815 Joseph Gott.

7.   BENJAMIN NORMAN, son of Nicholas and Elizabeth, was b. 11
July 1744,{AACR:169} and d. by 1815, leaving two children{A}: WALTER;
and ELEANOR, d. by 1815, m. (N) Deale, and had issue.

8.   THOMAS NORMAN, son of Nicholas and Elizabeth, was b. 4
June 1748,{AACR:170} and d. by 1815, leaving five children named in the
chancery suit.{A} He m. Margaret Deale in 1771 in St. James Parish.{C}
His estate was dist. on 14 April 1823 by Theophilus Norman, admin.,
with James Tongue and John Hurst as sureties. The widow, Margaret,
received her thirds, and the residue was divided into fifths and dist. to the
children named below{AADI TH#1:49}: THEOPHILUS; WILLIAM;
SOLOMON; SAMUEL; and RACHEL, m. (N) Weems.

9.   RICHARD NORMAN, son of Nicholas and Elizabeth, was b. 4
Jan 1749/50,{AACR:170} and d. by 1815. He left two "infants" (i.e., children
under 21), but they both may have d. by 1823 as they did not receive a
share of Benjamin Norman's estate{A; B: 65}: JANE; and NICHOLAS.

10.   ELIZABETH CHALK, dau. of (N) and Peggy (Norman) Chalk,
m. William Crandall in 1771 in St. James Parish, AA Co.{C} She d. by
1815, leaving issue{A}: JAMES CRANDALL; ABRAHAM
CRANDALL; JOHN CRANDALL; ADAM CRANDALL; HESTER
CRANDALL, m. (N) Phibbons; ELIZABETH CRANDALL, m. (N)
Stevens; RACHEL CRANDALL; and WILLIE CRANDALL.

11.   ELIZABETH OWENS, dau. of Isaac and Priscilla (Norman)
Owens, m. James Owens, Sr., b. 1748, d. 1797. He was a private in the
MD Line.{C:146} James "Owings" and Elizabeth "Owings" were m. in
1771 in St. James Parish.{C} Elizabeth Owens Owens d. by 1815 leaving
the four children named below.{A} In 1827, her heirs received 1/10 of
Thomas Owens' estate.{AAHO:72} Her children were: JAMES

OWENS; NICHOLAS OWENS; PRISCILLA, m. Abraham Woodward, by FRML dated 5 Oct 1797{B}; and MARY OWENS, m. (N) Sherbert.

12.   CHARLES OWENS, son of Isaac and Priscilla (Norman) Owens, d. by 1815, leaving an infant dau. named below.{A} In 1827, his heirs received 1/10 of Thomas Owens' estate.{AAHO:72} Charles was the father of: ELIZABETH OWENS.

13.   JANE NORMAN, dau. of William, d. by 1815. As Jeane Norman, she m. Abraham Parkerson [sic] on 5 Oct 1783 in St. James Parish. She left two children{A}: WILLIAM PARKINSON; and ABRAHAM PARKINSON.

14.   ELEANOR NORMAN, dau. of Benjamin, d. by 1815. She m. (N) Deale, and had issue{A}: ELIZA DEALE; JOSEPH DEALE; THOMAS DEALE; SAMUEL DEALE; NATHAN DEALE; MARIA DEALE (possibly under 21 in 1815); RACHEL DEALE (possibly under 21 in 1815); and ANN DEALE (possibly under 21 in 1815).

THE PARSONS FAMILY

1.   THOMAS PARSONS was in MD as early as 1649. Skordas lists Thomas Parsons as having been transported c1649.{MPL 5:87 and 12:314} He m. Isabella (N), who m. 2nd, Benjamin Capell, and d. c1717.

On 12 Nov 1659, Parsons and John Shaw surv. 100 a. called *Bipartite,* on the e. side of West River. By 1707, this land was held by Benja. Capell for Matt. Selby's orphans.{MRR:141} On 10 July 1663, Parsons surv. 50 a. *St. Thomas' Neck,* later held by John Norris.{MRR:145} On the following day, he surv. 150 a. on the w. side of West River called *Parsons Hill* or *The Peak,* but he sold this to Peter Allumby.{MRR:144} On 20 June 1673, Parsons and William Andrews surv. 50 a. called *The Friendship,* which was patented only in the name of Parsons who was the survivor. By 1707, the land had passed to Benjamin Capel.{MRR:129}

On 12 June 1677, Thomas Parsons, of AA Co., planter, conv. 80 a. in Herring Creek Swamp to Benja. Capell. Isabell Parsons gave her consent.{AALR WH#4:194}

Thomas Parsons and Thos. Warren wit. the will of Francis Trottin on 7 Jan 1667.{MWB 1:304} On 17 April 1675, he and Edward Price and Thomas Lobia wit. the will of John Meers of AA Co.{MWB 2:72}

Thomas Parsons, of AA Co., d. leaving a will dated 10 Oct 1683 and proved 31 May 1684. He named his dau. Eliza (to have one s.), dau. Isabella and heirs (to have 50 a.), and daus. Mary and Susanna (to have the plant. equally after the death of their mother). If Mary and Susannah should die without issue, sd. plant. was to pass to younger daus. Daus. Sarah and Hannah were to have personalty. Anthony Holland and Benj. Capell were named as execs., and Jas. White, Jno. Mayhew, Nich. Grose, and Rose Grose wit. the will.{MWB 4:28}

The inventory of Thomas Parson was appraised on 20 June 1684 by Richard Gott.{INAC 8:186}

Isabella, widow of Thomas Parsons, m. 2nd (N) Capell. As Isabel Capell, she d. leaving a will dated 10 Sep 1717 and proved 22 Dec 1717, naming grandson Jacob Holland who was to have 50 a. part of *Friendship,* grandchildren Isabella Price and Thomas Tucker who were to have personalty, and dau. Mary Price, extx., who was to have the residue of the estate, real and personal. William Foard and Robert Gott wit. the will.{MWB 14:442}

Isabel Capel's estate was appraised c1717 by John Cheshire and Robert Franklin, and valued at £78.0.6. Thomas Holland signed as next of kin.{INAC 39C:155}

The estate of Isabell Capel was admin. on 9 May 1717 by Edward Parish, atty. for Stephen Price, exec. of Mary Price (dau. of dec.) who was the original extx., and by Thomas Carr. An inventory of £78.6.0 was mentioned. Jacob Holland was named as a legatee.{MDAD 2:399}

Thomas and Isabella (N) Parsons were the parents of:

ELIZABETH; ISABELLA, m. Anthony Holland{Records of West River Monthly Meeting}; MARY, m. Mordecai Price; SUSANNA; SARAH; and

HANNAH.

THE WILLIAM PEARCE FAMILIES

1.   WILLIAM PEARCE, the immigrant of 1665, came to MD in 1665, his way having been paid by Thomas Howell, who claimed and received 50 a. for Pearce's transportation.{MPL Q:62}

In 1662 (seven years later; seven years was the usual term of indenture), William demanded 50 a. for having completed his term of service to Thomas Howell. He and Robert Neave jointly demanded 250 a., and a warrant was issued to the Surveyor General for the 250 a.{MD Warrants 5:55}

He is probably the William Pearce who was in BA Co. by Aug 1668 when he purchased *Neife's Choice* from Robert and Elizabeth Neife.{BALR IR#PP:63} In Nov 1670, he and his wife Isabel conv. the 150 a. to Thomas Weymouth and John Powell.{BALR IR#PP:91}

On 4 Aug 1668, Philip Holleger and wife Mary conv. to Pearce and Timothy Lendall 400 a. of land.{Scisco; *BA Co. Land Records*}

In March 1669/70, he was conv. 200 a. called *Tibbals* by Philip and Mary Holleger.{BALR IR#PP:78}

2.   WILLIAM PEARCE, relationship to the above not definitely established, d. by April 1675. He m. Sarah (N).

On 8 April 1675, Sarah Pearce, of AA Co., with William Burgess as surety, posted bond she would administer the estate of William Pearce. Robert Franklin and Walter Carr signed as wits.{MD Testamentary Papers, Box 3, folder 230, MSA}

On 18 April 1675, the inventory of William Pearce of AA Co. was taken by Walter Carr and John Walters, and appraised at 4,031 (lbs.?) of tob.{INAC 1:356}

3.   WILLIAM PEARCE, relationship to either of the above not definitely established, d. c1705.

He may be the William Pearce who obtained by 1707 100 a. of *Pascall's Chance,* part of 300 a. surv. for George Pascall in 1662.{MRR: 1:5}

This William Pearce seems to have d. by 1705, when Jonathan Tipton petitioned that he was in possession of part of *Pascall's Chance* (originally surv. for George Pascall for 300 a.) in right of his wife Sarah, dau. of William Pearce.{MD Warrants 6:426-427}

William had at least two children: WILLIAM; and SARAH, m. Jonathan Tipton.

4.   WILLIAM PEARCE, son of William (3), d. c1719. He m. Elizabeth Anderson on 5 Sep 1711 at All Hallows Parish, AA Co. {AACR:25}

On 16 Jan 1716, William, of AA Co., patented 100 a. called *Pearce's Folly* in BA Co.{MPL FF#7, 305; PL#4, 392; MRR #18:96, MSA}

William Pearce and Robert Franklin appraised the estate of Richard Simmons, of AA Co., on 8 Oct 1718.{MINV 1:424}

William Pearce, of AA Co., tailor, d. leaving a will dated 12 Sep 1719 and proved 19 Oct 1719. His sons William and John were to share the real estate equally and were to be of age at 16. His wife Elizabeth was to be extx., and his nephews Thomas and William Tipton were to be overseers.{MWB 15:217, and Original Wills, Box P, folder 19, MSA}

On 9 Nov 1719, Elizabeth Pearce, with Robert Franklin and Sam Man...(?) as sureties, posted bond she would administer the estate of William Pearce.{Testamentary Papers, Box 26, folder 8, MSA}

The inventory of William Pearce's estate was appraised by John Norris and John Talbott (no date given). John Giles signed as creditor. The property was appraised at £81.8.2.{MINV 3:230}

Elizabeth Manning, widow of William Pearce, admin. the estate on 12 Feb 1722. She mentioned a prior account filed 16 Aug 1720.{MDAD 5:31}

William Pearce seems to have had a sister Sarah Pearce who m. Jonathan Tipton, and had two sons: THOMAS, b. 8 April 1693, bapt. 25 April 1699, and WILLIAM, b. 27 July 1696, bapt. same day as his bro. {AACR:150}

William and Elizabeth were the parents of the following, b. in St. James Parish{AACR:162}; WILLIAM, bapt. 20 June 1714; and JOHN, b. 10 March 1714, bapt. 11 April 1714.

5.   WILLIAM PEARCE, son of William (4) and Elizabeth (Anderson) Pearce, was bapt. 20 June 1714. He is probably the William Pearce who m. Priscilla West, dau. of Stephen and Elizabeth West, named as an heir in the will and administration account of Robert Wood, of AA Co.{MWB 20:94; MDAD 12:96}

6.   WILLIAM PEARCE, relationship to the above not established, m. Johanna French on 2 May 1768 in All Hallows Parish.{AACR:57} They were the parents of the following children, also b. in All Hallows Parish {AACR:60, 61}: BENJAMIN, b. 5 Dec 1769; EMM, b. 23 June 1771; ELIZABETH, b. 15 Dec 1773; WILLIAM, b. 2 March 1775; ISRAEL, b. 5 Dec 1776; ELIZABETH, b. 1 April 1779; MARTHA, b. 4 Nov 1783; and ANN, b. 27 March 1786.

THE PENNINGTONS OF ANNE ARUNDEL

1.   WILLIAM PENNINGTON, of AA Co., d. by 23 March 1670.
He is probably the William Pennington who claimed land in 1666 for having transported himself into the Province sometime earlier.{MPL 9:28} On 14 Nov 1661, Nathaniel and Mary Utie conv. to William Pennington land which Pennington then conv. to Ralph Williams.{AALR IT#5:68}

At his death, he left two sons, William and Thomas. On 23 March 1670, Samuel Withers, of AA Co., committed them to the care of Capt. William Burgess and Richard Hill.{MWB 1:436}
William was the father of: WILLIAM; and THOMAS.

2.   WILLIAM PENNINGTON, son of William (1), and left an orphan by 1670, may have m. Eliner (N) who d. Nov 1705.{AACR:137}
On 11 Nov 1684, William Pennington purchased 110 a. *Sturton's Rest* from George Sturton, formerly of AA Co., but now of CE Co.{AALR IH#3:43}

William claimed two tracts of land, *Young Richard* and *The Addition*, devised to him by Edmund Duncalf, and also a tract called *The Foothold*, which he purchased from Thomas and his wife Frances Pennington on 8 June 1686.{AALR IH#1:221, IH#2:22}

William was the father of the following children, b. in St. Margaret's Parish{AACR:107}: THOMAS, b. 9 Feb 1680; WILLIAM, b. 20 Dec 1682; TITUS, b. 26 July 1686; SABRAH, b. 19 Dec 1692; SERETAH, b. 2 Nov 1696; DORATHA, dau. of William and Eliner, d. Jan 1703.{AACR:136}

3.   THOMAS PENINGTON, son of William (1), and left an orphan by 1670, probably m. 1st, Frances (N), by 1686. He may have m. 2nd, Ann, who d. Jan 1703 in St. Margaret's Parish{AACR:136}

In 1686, Thomas Pennington and wife Frances conv. to William Pennington 135 a., part of a tract called *Foothold*.{AALR IH#2:22}

Thomas d. and, according to his dau. Hannah Eager, left a will, but no such will has been found to date.

Thomas Pennington was the father of: WILLIAM, b. St. Margaret's Parish on 10 March 1686, and d. young{AACR:107; AALR IB#2:321}; and HANNAH, m. George Eager, who d. by Oct 1716.

4.   THOMAS PENNINGTON, son of William (2), was b. 9 Feb 1680 in St. Margaret's Parish. He may be the Thomas who was the father of: ANN, b. 4 Sep 1708 in St. Margaret's Parish{AACR:109}. She may be the Ann Pennington who m. Thomas Rodwell on 28 Aug 1727 in St. Margaret's Parish.{AACR:131}

5.   WILLIAM PENNINGTON, Jr., son of William (2), was b. 20 Dec 1682 in St. Margaret's Parish. He m. Susanna Smart on 15 Dec 1706 in St. Margaret's Parish{AACR:130}, by whom he had the following children, b. in St. Margaret's{AACR:110, 111, 112, 116}: TITUS, b. 13 Dec 1709/10; WILLIAM, b. 12 Jan 1714; THOMAS, b. 10 Oct 1717; NICHOLAS, b. 4 July 1700 [1720?]; and SUSANNA, b. 9 May 1723.

6.   WILLIAM PENNINGTON, son of Thomas (3), was b. 10 March 1686. On 8 May 1693, Jacob Hollett, of AA Co., made a will, leaving William, of Thomas, personalty.{MWB 7:18}

7.   HANNAH PENNINGTON, dau. of Thomas (3), m. George Eager in St. Anne's Parish on 24 Aug 1705.{AACR:73}

On 5 Jan 1716, Hannah Eager, widow of George Eager, conv. two tracts to Amos Garrett, of Annapolis. One was the tract *Foothold*, which "by the will of her father, Thomas," and the death of her bro. William, became her property; the other tract was *Deep Creek Neck*, which John Worrell conv. to the sd. Hannah Eager.{AALR IB#2:321}

8.   TITUS PENNINGTON, son of William (5), was b. 26 July 1686 in St. Margaret's. He m. 1st, by 20 Feb 1710/11, Eliza, dau. of John Ray {See AALR PK:332}, and 2nd, by 6 April 1715, Martha (N).

On 20 Feb 1710/11, Titus Pennington and wife Elizabeth conv. to Richard Todd several parcels of land.{AALR PK:332}

Titus and Martha were the parents of{AACR:111}: JOHN, b. 6 April 1715.

Unplaced

PENNINGTON, CHARLES, of AA Co., planter, d. leaving a will dated 8 Sep 1772 and proved 16 Oct 1772. He named sons Charles and Nathan Pennington, sons-in-law Richard Morrow (exec.) and Charles Connoway, and grandson Charles Pennington. The will was wit. by Daniel Sowers and Sarah Abbott. Morrow renounced as exec., and desired that William Pennington, son of the dec., serve.{MWB 39:247}

On 19 Oct 1773, his estate was dist. by William Pennington, admin., with Richard Murroe and Charles Pennington sureties. Legatees were Charles, Nathan, and grandson Charles Pennington, and Charles Connoway. The balance was dist. to the widow (unnamed), and the balance to five children and one grandson: Elizabeth, William, Charles, Sarah, Nathan, and grandson Charles Pennington.{BFD 6:294}

PENNINGTON, CHARLES, m. Keziah Abbett on 12 Dec 1772 in St. Margaret's.{AACR:134}

PENNINGTON, JAMES, was bur. in St. Anne's Parish on 25 July 1705. {AACR:75}

PENINGTON, KEZIAH, no parents given, was b. 10 Oct 1701 in St. Margaret's Parish.{AACR:107} She m. Thomas Graham on 18 Sep 1722. {AACR:130}

PENNINGTON, MARGARET, m. John Slater on 11 April 1708 in St. Anne's Parish.{AACR:67}

PENNINGTON, MARY, m. William Haycraft in St. Margaret's on 18 July 1742.{AACR:133}

THE PHELPS FAMILY[45]

First Generation

1. WALTER PHELPS, progenitor, was b. c1639. He gave his age as
67 in 1706 and 79 in 1718.{Henry C. Peden, Jr., *Maryland Deponents, 1634-1799*, Family Line
Publications, 1991:148} Walter Phelps, the immigrant to MD, may be the Walter,
son of Walter Phelps, who was bapt. 16 Oct 1635 at Wells Diocese,
Somersetshire, England.{*Dwelly's Parish Registers*, 2:273; note in Phelps material collected by
Harry Wright Newman, and deposited in the Southern MD Learning Center, CH Co. Community College, La
Plata, MD.}

Walter Phelps m. Elizabeth Benson, sister of George Benson,
sometime before 1681.{MDTP 14:17} He was bur. 5 May 1719, and she was
bur. 18 Aug 1706, both in All Hallows Parish, AA Co.{AACR:21}

He may be the Walter Phelps who, with William Godby, glover,
on 13 Aug 1660, was bound to Edward Hope, grocer, to serve four years
in VA.{Peter Wilson Coldham, *Complete Book of Emigrants, 1607-1660*, GPC, 1987:467}

He was in MD by 7 June 1673, when Hubert Lambert of South
River conv. to him 100 a. of land, part of 500 a. laid out for Ann Covill,
widow.{AALR IH#2:225}

On 18 Sep 1676, he was listed among the debts of Daniel Taylor,
of AA Co.{INAC 2:285} [It is not clear whether Phelps was a creditor or a
debtor.-RWB]

He had Mark Client bound to him on 13 Oct 1679 for five years in
MD.{Coldham, *Complete Book of Emigrants, 1661-1699*, GPC:350}

Walter Phelps, of AA Co., immigrated to MD with his wife
Elizabeth and mother Rebecca and three other persons, and in 1680
Phelps claimed land for their transportation. Mark Clyant was one of the
three persons.{MPL WC#2:178-179}

On 12 Oct 1684, Phelps patented 200 a. *Phelps' Choice.*{MPL
25:144,33:97} On 1 Oct 1700, he patented 34 a. *Elk Thicket.*{MPL DD#5:16, PL#2;3}

On 20 May 1703, Walter Phelps and Sitt.[?] Welsh appraised the
estate of John Gather, Sr.{INAC 1:634}

Walter and Elizabeth (Benson) Phelps were the parents of:
WALTER, b. 17 June 1680; WILLIAM, b. 13 Sep 1682; JOHN, b. 1
June 1684; GEORGE, b. 18 May 1689; ELIZABETH, b. May 1693, bur.
12 April 1703{AACR:15}; BENJAMIN, b. 5 Dec 1695; JOSEPH, b. 9 Aug

[45] See Robert Barnes, "The Phelps Family," *BMGS* 34 (4), 364-378, and Louis F. Giles,
"Further Notes on Phelps," *BMGS* 37 (1) 36-ﬤ

1698, bapt. 15 Aug, and bur. 16 Aug 1698{AACR:5}; and CHARLES, b. 17 Oct 1699.

Second Generation

2. WALTER PHELPS, Jr., son of Walter and Elizabeth, was b. 17 June 1680, and m. 1st, Mary Cheney on 1 Dec 1702.{AACR:17} He m. 2nd, on 2 Jan 1717, Rose Bazil. On 27 March 1728, Ralph Bazel, of AA Co., made a will naming "Ruth, [sic] wife of Walter Phelps, Sr."{MWB 19:527}
On 1 April 1701, he wit. the will of George Eastall, of AA Co. {MWB 11:191}

In 1724, Walter Phelps conv. 100 a. *Phelps's Choice* to Charles Phelps and Susanna (Meek) Phelps, widow of John Phelps.{AALR SY#1:48}
In June 1740, Walter Phelps testified in a land commission, giving his age as 61. He was evidently still living in March 1760/1 when, as "Walter Phelps, Sr.," he gave his age as c80.{AALC, 1724-1767:141,552}
Walter Phelps and his first wife Mary (Cheney) were the parents of{AACR:20, 21, 29, 199}: WALTER, b. 14 Sep 1703, bapt. 20 Aug 1704, m. 9 Jan 1727, Mary Bazil; RICHARD, b. 13 April 1706, bapt. 12 Sep 1711; JOHN (twin), bapt. 12 Sep 1711, m. by banns 15 Sep 1730, Sarah Bazil; MARY (twin), bapt. 12 Sep 1711, m. Richard Poole on 24 Feb 1730; ELIZABETH, bapt. 18 May 1719 [If she were a dau. of Walter by his first wife, she could have been b. any time prior to 1717, and bapt. in 1719.].
Walter and Rose/Ruth (Bazil) were the parents of{AACR:33, 38, 45, 199}: BAZIL, son of Walter and Rose [sic], bapt. 18 May 1719; RUTH, bapt. 15 May 1722; WILLIAM, b. 13 July 172-(?), bapt. 21 Oct 1724; and GEORGE, b. 4 July 1730.

3. WILLIAM PHELPS, son of Walter and Elizabeth, was b. 13 Sep 1682, and m. Elizabeth Cheney on 8 Aug 1706. Elizabeth, wife of William, was bur. 12 Sep 1711, and William m. 2nd, Rachel (N) on 11 Dec 1718.{AACR:22, 31, 198}
In Aug 1738, he dep. in a land commission, giving his age as 56. In Feb 1738/9, he again dep., naming himself "son of Walter."{AALC, 1724-1767:113, 116}

William Phelps d. leaving a will dated 12 July 1748 and proved 20 Aug 1748, appointing his wife extx., and naming his sons Richard, John, Benjamin, Zachariah, and William. His will named tracts *Phelps' Adventure* on Flat Creek Branch, and the *Upper Part*. Samuel Day, Clark Cromwell, and Elizabeth Cheney were wits.{MWB 25:389}
On 26 Dec 1748, his estate was inv. by Samuel Day and Joseph Coward, and valued at £112.18.1. Walter Phelps and John Phelps signed

as kin, and Mrs. Rachel Phelps, extx., filed the inventory on 12 April 1748. Another inventory was taken on 13 July 1749 by the same appraisers and valued at £23.2.7. Rachel Phelps filed the second inventory on 9 Sep 1749.{MINV 37:441; 40:140}

William had at least two children by his first wife. His others were almost certainly by his second wife. His children were{AACR:23, 29}: (N), b. (date of birth not given); and WILLIAM, bapt. 12 Sep 1711.

William and Rachel were the parents of: RICHARD, d. intestate and without issue c1 Sep 1795. A chancery case names the children of his bros. William, John, and Zachariah{AALC, 1791-1805:14}: JOHN, b. c1720; BENJAMIN, may have s.p. as he is not mentioned in the 1795 chancery case involving his bros. Richard, William, John, and Zachariah (He may be the Benjamin Phelps who took the Oath of Fidelity to the State of MD on 1 March 1778 before Richard Harwood, Jr.){AARP:151}; and ZACHARIAH, b. 8 Oct 1729.{AACR:45}

4.   JOHN PHELPS, son of Walter and Elizabeth, was b. 1 June 1684, and d. 1725. He m. Susan Meek on 16 Oct 1718 in All Hallows Parish. After John Phelps' death, she m. 2nd, William Anderson.
{Giles:40}

On 7 March 1708, John Phelps wit. a deed in AA Co.{AALR PK:22}

John Phelps, of AA Co., d. by 25 Sep 1724 when his admx., Susannah Phelps, filed the inventory of his estate,, which had been made by Benjamin Gaither and Joseph Williams. They appraised the personal property at £49.3.9. William and Charles Phelps signed as next of kin. J. Mouatt and Joseph Burton signed as creditors.{MINV 10:199}

Susannah Phelps, admx., admin. the estate of John Phelps on 14 Sep 1725. Payments and disbursements equalled £19.19.2.{MDAD 7:85}

Susanna Phelps was still living on 11 Sep 1733 when she and John, James, Samuel, Christopher, and Ruth Meek were named as the representatives of Mary Boyce, widow, of AA Co.{MDAD 12:28}

Susanna (Meek) (Phelps) Anderson d. in AA Co. leaving a will dated 8 Sep 1758 and proved 30 Dec 1766. She named her children John Phelps, James, William, and Absolom Anderson, dau. Mary Stewart, and dau. Jane Waters. The will was wit. by Jeremiah Mullikin, William Nichols, and Joshua Clarke.{MWB 35:253}

John and Susanna were the parents of{Giles:41}: JOHN, m. Priscilla (N), and moved to FR Co.; and MARY, m. (N) Howard.

5.   CHARLES PHELPS, son of Walter and Elizabeth, was b. on 17 Oct 1699, and may have d. between Jan 1770 and March 1772. He m. 1st, Susanna Stephens, on 19 Dec 1723.{AACR:37} Susanna was probably dead by 1739. He m. 2nd, by 12 Aug 1747, Margaret Charnock.

In 1739, Charles Phelps, carpenter, conv. 60 a. *Phelps' Choice* to William Anderson. No wife joined him, so Susanna was probably dead. {AALR RD#3:150}

On 12 Aug 1747, Charles Phelps and wife Margaret, of AA Co., deeded to Charles Carroll their right to 250 a. of land in BA Co. called *Brother's Unity* or *Expectation*. The tract had descended to Margaret from her parents Anthony Charnox and his wife Hannah, who was a dau. of George Hollingsworth. Geo. Hollingsworth d. leaving the tract to his children George, Otho, Charles, James, and Hannah. George, Otho, and Charles s.p., and Hannah m. Anthony Charnox on 14 May 1717 in St. Anne's Parish, AA Co.{PCLR EI#8:339; AACR:80} Margaret Charnock, age 12 in Sep 1737, had been bound the preceding June to William Robinson of Spesutia until she attained the age of 16 (which would be about 1741).{BA Co. Court Proceedings, HWS#1-A}

On 26 Feb 1748, Charles Phelps patented 50 a. *Phelps' Fancy.* {MPL TI#4:60, BY#1:599}

Charles Phelps, "being very poor," was provided with £30 in Jan 1770 by the Vestry of St. Anne's Parish. Margaret Phelps was given £30 in March 1772, so Charles may have d.{St. Anne's Vestry Proceedings, Vol. 2, 1767-1818:36, 43}

Charles and Susannah were the parents of{AACR:45}: ZEBULON, b. 25 May 1731. By Margaret, Charles was the father of at least one son: WALTER, b. c1750.

Third Generation

6.   WALTER PHELPS, son of Walter and Mary (Cheney), was b. on 14 Sep 1703, and d. by March 1764. He m. Mary Bazil on 9 Jan 1727 in All Hallows Parish.{AACR:42} On 27 March 1728, Ralph Bazel made a will mentioning Mary, wife of Walter Phelps, Jr.{MWB 19:526}

In 1760, Walter Phelps conv. 103 a. of *Phelps' Luck* and *Devil's (Covell's?) Folly* to Basil Phelps.{AALR BB#2:325}

Walter Phelps d. leaving a will dated (8?) Oct 1760 and proved March 1764, naming sons John, George, and Joseph. He stated they were not to hinder Richard Poole and wife Mary from living where they were. Joseph Bazil, Richard Phelps and Joseph Poole were wits.{MWB 32:60}

On 18 June 1764, his estate was inv. by Robert Welsh and Gassaway Watkins, and valued at £12.15.0. John Phelps and Mary Poole signed as kin, and George Phelps and Joseph Phelps, execs., filed the inventory on 23 Feb 1765.{MINV 86:145}

It would appear that Walter Phelps was the father of{AACR:43, 44}: ISAIAH, bapt. 23 March 1728 (he was not in his father's will); ELIZABETH, bapt. 13 Dec 1730 (she was not in her father's will); JOHN; GEORGE (in 1767 he and his bros. Isaiah and Joseph conv. 50 a.

Covell's Folly, 50 a. *Phelps' Luck,* and part of *Elk Neck* to Nicholas Maccubbin){AALR BB#3:332}; and JOSEPH; he was still living in 1767 when he and his bros. conv. land to Nicholas Maccubbin.

7.   JOHN PHELPS, son of Walter and Mary Cheney, was b. by 1711, and m. Sarah Bazill on 9 Aug 1730.{AACR:44}
    He is probably the "John Phelps, Sr.," who gave his age as 52 in March 1760/1.{AALC 1724-1767:552}
    John and Sarah (Bazil) were the parents of{AACR:45}: JOHN, b. 8 April 1731.

8.   BAZIL PHELPS, son of Walter and Rose [sic], was bapt. on 18 May 1719.{AACR:199} He d. by Oct 1760. His wife Leah was probably a dau. of Edward and Rachel Gaither, and seems to have m. 2nd, (N) Kirkland.
    In 1760, Walter Phelps conv. to Basil Phelps 103 a. of *Phelps' Luck* and *Devil's (Covell's?) Folly.*{AALR BB#2:335}
    Bazil Phelps left a will dated 12 Aug 1760 and proved 18 Oct 1760, naming his wife Leah, his three sons Edward, Bazil, and Gather, and mentioning an unborn child. His wife was named extx., and the will was wit. by Richard Poole, George Phelps, and William Beard.{MWB 31:87}
    On 5 May 1761, his estate was appraised by Joseph Kenard and Benjamin Williams, and valued at £153.19.10. Walter Phelps and George Phelps signed as next of kin, and Leach (Leah?) Phelps, extx., filed the inventory on 7 May 1761.{MINV 74:26}
    A second inventory was taken by the same appraisers (but Joseph Kenard was Joseph Howard), and valued at £16.17.0. George and Joseph Phelps signed as kin, and Leah Kirkland, admx., filed the inventory on 12 Nov 1766.{MINV 89:201}
    Bazil Phelps was the father of: EDWARD; BAZIL; GAITHER; and (N), (child unb. in Aug 1760; almost certainly ABSOLUTE PHELPS).

9.   WILLIAM PHELPS, son of William and Elizabeth, was bapt. 12 Sep 1711, and d. by 30 Oct 1765. He m. Susanna (N). [Some sources say she was Susanna Meek, dau. of John and Mary (N) Meeks, but proof has not been found; see John Phelps #4 above.]
    In a letter dated 23 Dec 1993 to the compiler, John H. Pearce, Jr., of Butler, MD, stated that Susanna may have m. 1st, on 23 July 1726, William Anderson, who d. 1741 in AA Co., and had by him five children: William; James, b. c1725 [sic]; Absolom, b. 17 Feb 1737; Jane, m. (N) Waters; and Mary, m. (N) Stewart. Louis Giles points out that William Anderson m. c1725, Susanna, widow of John Phelps. However, that Susanna was an Anderson at the time of her death.{Giles:40}

In March 1760/1, William Phelps, son of William, dep., giving his age as c50.{AALC, 1724-1767:551}

William Phelps d. leaving a will dated 24 April 1765 and proved 30 Oct 1765. In his will, he named his wife Susanna extx., and children William, John, Richard, Joseph, Joshua, Jacob, Elizabeth Holbrook, and Susanna Cheney. He mentioned *Duvall's Range.* Francis Belmear, John Belmear, and Thomas Oliver were wits.{MWB 33:507}

Susanna Phelps appeared in the 1776 census of All Hallows Parish with five white males, three white females, and three white children.{1776 Census of MD, in Brumbaugh, *Maryland Records*} In 1782/3, she was listed in South River Hundred, AA Co., owning part *Duvall's Range.*{1782/3 Assessment List of AA Co.} She is probably the widow of William (9) Phelps.

William Phelps' children are mentioned in a chancery case found with a petition dated 1796.{AALC, 1791-1805:14; W. H. and Maxine Swango, *Phelps Family from Zachariah to Ann Virginia*}

William and Susanna were the parents of{AACR:49, 50, 51, 52, 54, 57}: ELIZABETH, b. 31 March 1739, m. (N) Holbrook; WILLIAM, b. 17 Dec 1740; SUSANNAH, b. 10 Sep 1742, m. (N) Cheney (another source says she m. Nathaniel Hall on 28 Feb 1778); JOHN, b. 13 Jan 1744 (or 31 March 1745); THOMAS, b. 14 Feb 1746/7, m. Sarah Forsten in 1779; REBECCA, b. 18 Sep 1750; RICHARD, b. 18 Aug 1753; JOSEPH, b. 24 Dec 1754; JOSHUA, b. 22 Feb 1758; and JACOB, b. 29 March 1761.

10.   RICHARD PHELPS, son of William, d. intestate and without issue c1 Sep 1795.

In 1764, James Bryan conv. to Richard Phelps 300 a. of *Cheney's Rest.*{Card Index to AALR; MSA}

In 1776, Richard Phelps was listed in the 1776 census of All Hallows Parish, AA Co., with one white male and one white female. {Brumbaugh, *Maryland Records,* 1:409} He took the Oath of Fidelity to the State of MD on 1 March 1778 before Richard Harwood, Jr. {AARP:152}

Richard Phelps is listed in South River Hundred, AA Co., as owning part *Cheney's Rest* and part *Phelps Adventure.*{Assessment List of 1782/3 for AA Co.}

Richard Phelps signed the inventory of Deborah Phelps (q.v.) as a creditor on 13 Nov 1789. He also purchased some of her property on 11 Nov 1789.

Richard Phelps d. by 18 Nov 1795 when his estate was inv. by Vachel Gaither and John Jacobs. His property was valued at £19.18.1. James Maccubbin and Stephen Beard signed as creditors, and John Phelps and Joshua Phelps signed as kin. The inventory was filed 5 Jan

1798 by William Phelps, admin.{AA Co. Inv. and Accounts of Sales, JG#4:55}

At the sale of Richard Phelps' property, purchases were made by George Phelps, Jacob Phelps, Jno. Phelps, Margaret Phelps, William Phelps, and Zachariah Phelps{Ibid.:100}

A chancery case names the children of his bros. William, John, and Zachariah.{AALC 1791-1805:14}

11.   JOHN PHELPS, son of William by his second wife, Rachel, was b. c1720, giving his age as 40 in March 1760/1.{AALC 1724-1767:552}

A chancery case petition dated 1796 states that he d. before his bro. Richard and left the following children{AALC 1791-1805:14}: WILLIAM; MARY, m. (N) Lang; RACHEL, m. Joseph Clewly by 25 Aug 1803, when they conv. to Zachariah Phelps their claim, right, and interest in their 1/8 part of *Cheney's Rest* by the death of Richard Phelps{AALR NII#12:213}; and HESTER.

12.   ZACHARIAH PHELPS, son of William and Rachel, was b. 8 Oct 1729.{AACR:45} He d. before 1795, and a chancery case named his children.{AALC 1791-1805:14} William Harald Swango compiled *The Phelps Family from "Z" to "A" Zachariah to Ann Virginia* (Charleston: Jalamap Publications, 1986), and suggested that Zachariah may have been the father of William, Isaac, and Samuel. Unfortunately, the facts do not bear his theories out.

Zachariah, of William and Rachel, is probably the Zachariah Phelps who purchased some of the property of Deborah Phelps (q.v.) on 11 Nov 1789. He purchased some of Richard Phelps' (q.v.) property c1795.

In 1798, Zachariah Phelps was listed in Roade River Hundred as owning 180 a. *Cheney's Rest* and 25 a. *Phelps' Adventure.*{Index to Federal Assessment List of AA Co., 1798}

Zachariah Phelps was the father of: ZACHARIAH; MARY, m. (N) Theckerell; MARGARET, m. (N) Pearce, who d. by 25 Aug 1803 when Margaret Peerce, widow, conv. to Zachariah Phelps, her right, claim and interest in 1/8 part of *Cheney's Rest*, which she inherited by the death of Richard Phelps{AALR NH#13:212}; and ELIZABETH Phelps, m. Sparrow Carter, by AAML.

13.   WALTER PHELPS is placed by Giles as a son of Charles. He was b. c1750, and d. c1828. He m. Margaret Chaney by AAML 10 March 1781. In the 1820 census, he was listed as Walter, "son of Charles."

In 1783, he was living near or with Greenbury Pumphrey on *Mistake in Friendship*, in Severn Hundred.{Assessment List of 1783, AA Co.}

In 1799, Walter Phelps purchased 200 a. *Bachelor's Chance* on Long Bridge Branch.{AALR NH#9:656} Walter Phelps and wife Margaret sold *Phelps' Fancy* in 1787.{AALR NH#2:542}

In 1811, Walter and Margaret sold *Bachelor's Chance,* and moved with their sons to an adj. tract called *Addition to Timber Ridge.*{AALR NH#16:594}

Margaret Chaney Phelps gave her age as between 80 and 90 in the 1830 Census of AA Co., and she must have d. soon thereafter.

Walter and Margaret were the parents of{Giles:38}: RICHARD, b. c1783; JAMES, b. c1785; and possibly PRISCILLA, b. c1794, possibly the Priscilla who m. Dennis Griffith, 28 Oct 1810.

Fourth Generation

14.   ISAIAH PHELPS, son of Walter, was bapt. 23 March 1728. {AACR:43} He was not in his father's will, but he was living in May 1756 when he advertised there was a stray mare at his plant. at the head of South River.{AMG 13 May 1756}

In June 1740, Isaiah Phelps, grandson of Walter Phelps, was bound to Richard Goodman, carpenter.{AAJU June 1740 Court:470}

In March 1748/9, Isaiah Phelps was charged with begetting a baseborn child on the body of Hester Chaney.{AAJU March 1748/9 Court:198} Research to date has failed to reveal the identity of Hester Chaney.

On 18 July 1757, he wit. the will of Richard Taylor, of AA Co. {MWB 30:514}

Giles suggests that Isaiah may have been named in his father's will as John, because in 1760 he joined his bros. in conveying land. {Giles:41}

In 1760, Isaiah, George, and Joseph Phelps conv. to Nicholas Maccubbin parts of three tracts: 50 a. *Covell's Folly*, 50 a. *Phelps' Luck,* and part of *Elk Neck.*{AALR BB#3:332}

Isaiah Phelps was listed in the 1776 Census of All Hallows Parish with one white male, three white females, and three white children. {Brumbaugh, *op. cit.,* 1:408}

Isaiah Phelps took the Oath of Fidelity in March 1778 before the Hon. Nicholas Worthington.{AARP:151}

He is placed as the father of Ezekiel Phelps because he is the only Phelps listed in the 1776 Census of AA Co. having children not accounted for, and because Ezekiel named one of his children Walter Watkins Phelps. The Walter could have been for Ezekiel's grandfather, Walter.

He was possibly the father of: EZEKIEL.

15.   JOHN PHELPS, son of John, was b. 8 April 1731.{AACR:45} In Sep 1756 as John Phelps, Jr., he advertised there was a stray horse at his plant. near *The Land of Ease.* {AMG Sep 1756}

16.   EDWARD PHELPS, son of Bazil and Leah, is probably the same Edward who was listed in South River Hundred, AA Co., as a pauper. {Assessment List of AA Co., 1783}

17.   BAZIL PHELPS, son of Bazil and Leah, m. Barbara Davis by AAML dated 21 April 1791.
        Basil Phelps took the Oath of Fidelity to the State of MD on 1 March 1778 before Richard Harwood, Jr.{AARP:151}
        Basil Phelps is listed in 1783 as living in South River Hundred, AA Co., owning part of *Phelps Luck.*{Assessment List of AA Co., 1783}
        Basil Phelps signed the inventory of Deborah Phelps (q.v.) as kin on 13 Nov 1789.
        On 13 July 1793, he dist. the estate of George Stalker. Richard Phelps was a surety.{AADI JG#1:43}
        He may have d. by 1799, when Barbara Phelps m. William Ward by AAML dated 20 March 1799. On 13 June 1799, the AA Co. Orphans Court ordered that if Barbara Phelps, now Barbara Ward, did not take out letters of administration, Absolute Phelps, bro. of Basil, should take them out.{AA Co. Orphans Court Minutes MdHR #4802:58}
        MD Chancery Paper #4053, filed in AA Co., 1815, Nicholas Brewer, Trustee, recorded in Chancery Liber 92:28, contains a bill of complaint (filed 23 Nov 1815) of Sarah Phelps, of AA Co., stating that a certain Basil Phelps of AA Co., dec., in his lifetime owned a tract of land (name not given) between 50 and 60 a. He d. intestate leaving only two children: Sarah (the complainant) and Ann Phelps. The petition stated that the land should be sold, but sd. Ann is under 21. John Brewer was appointed her guardian; Nicholas Brewer was trustee for the sale of the land. Nicholas Brewer reported on the sale of the tract, which was *Covel's Folly.* Each of the two heirs received $263.66- 1/2.{MCHP #4053}
        Basil and Barbara were the parents of: EDWARD GAITHER, b. 25 Dec 1791, d. 31 Jan 1794; SARAH, b. 12 Dec 1793; and ANNE, b. 16 Jan 1796.

18.   ABSOLUTE PHELPS, son of Basil and Leah, was no doubt the unborn child his father mentioned in 1768. Absolute Phelps signed the inventory of Deborah Phelps (q.v.) as kin on 13 Nov 1789. On 13 June 1799, Absolute Phelps, bro. of Basil Phelps, was to be given letters of administration if Barbara Phelps, now Barbara Ward, did not take them out.{AA Co. Orphans Court Minutes, MdHR #4802:58}

He or another Absolute Phelps m. Ann Poole by AAML dated 31 Jan 1809.

19.   JOSEPH PHELPS, son of William and Susanna, was listed in 1776 in South River Hundred, AA Co., as a bachelor.{Brumbaugh, *op. cit.*} He m. 1st, Sophia Taylor, by AAML dated 1 April 1791. He m. 2nd, Catherine Thompson, by AAML dated 8 Aug 1801.

Joseph Phelps, of Annapolis, d. leaving a will dated ... 1833 and proved ..., in which he named his wife Catherine and mentioned their children.{AAWB TTS#1:166}

Catherine Phelps (possibly the widow of Joseph), d. leaving a will dated 11 Dec 1838 and proved 1 Jan 1839. In her will, she named her son-in-law Richard R. Goodwin, granddau. Catherine Ann Goodwin, and daus.{AAWB}

Joseph and Catherine were the parents of: ANN CATHERINE; MARY; and JULIA.

20.   JOSHUA PHELPS, son of William and Susanna, was b. 22 Feb 1758, and on 16 April 1816 was m. by Rev. Morainviller [Pastor of St. Patrick's Roman Catholic Church] to Alicia M. Inglesby.{*Baltimore Federal Gazette*, 24 April 1816} She was the widow of William Inglesby. On 9 Dec 1833, Moses Baines, who had m. Cecilia Inglesby, noted in his diary that he had received word of "Mr. Phelps' death."{Data contained in letter dated 25 May 1994 to Robert Barnes from Mrs. David Howard Peterson of Hitchcock, Texas}

Joshua and Alicia (MacKiernan) (Inglesby) Phelps were the parents of: PARTHENIA, m. Leonard Passano; and JANE.

21.   JACOB PHELPS, son of William and Susanna, was b. 29 March 1761, and m. Parthena (N).

Jacob Phelps purchased some of Richard Phelps' (q.v.) property c1795.

Jacob and Parthenia had issue{AACR:64}: RICHARD DENOONE TAYLOR, b. 23 Aug 1798, bapt. 10 Nov 1801.

22.   ZACHARIAH PHELPS, son of Zachariah, in 1798 was listed in Roade River Hundred as owning 180 a. *Cheney's Rest* and 25 a. *Phelps' Adventure*.{Index to Federal Assessment List of AA Co., 1798}

Zachariah m. 1st, Sarah Davis, by AAML dated 11 Oct 1797, and m. 2nd, Esther Gwinn, by AAML dated 20 Jan 1804. She was a dau. of Francis Gwinn, of AA Co.{AADI JG#2:103, 104}

On 17 Oct 1803, Zachariah Phelps, of AA Co., mortgaged to James Mackubin 180 a. of *Cheney's Rest,* which Zachariah Cheney conv. to Zachariah Phelps, father of the present grantor.{AALR NH#13:170}

Esther Gwinn, now Phelps, received her share of the estate of her father, Francis Gwinn, of AA Co., when it was dist. by Henry Purdy, exec., on 10 April 1807.{AADI JG#2:103} She received a share of the estate of Elizabeth Gwinn when it was dist. on 31 Jan 1809 by Henry Purdy.{AADI JG#2:132}

Zachariah Phelps d. c1821 owning 150 a. *Cheney's Rest*. He left four children, named in the distribution of his estate by Mrs. Hester Phelps, admx., on 19 Sep 1825{MCHP #6045; AADI TH#1:78}: WALTER POOL (who came of age on 11 Oct 1825); SARAH, m. George Allen by 1825; ZACHARIAH; and JOSEPH HENRY.

23.   RICHARD PHELPS, son of Walter and Margaret, was b. c1783, d. 7 Sep 1855, and m. Charlotte Stewart by BAML dated 1 Jan 1806. Charlotte d. 29 April 1851.{Giles:39}

Richard and Charlotte (or Charity) (Stewart) Phelps were the parents of{AA Co. Circuit Court Equity Records, NIIG#5:205}: NELSON, b. c1812, d. 1898, m. 1st, Ellen Benson, and 2nd, Elizabeth Shipley; ANDREW J., b. c1818, m. Mary Ann Benson; RICHARD D., b. c1825, m. 1st, Martha Benson, and 2nd, Julia Chaney; MARGARET, m. Edward Anderson; SUSAN, m. Joshua Anderson; ANN, m. John Hawkins; and MARY, m. Eden Benson.

24.   JAMES PHELPS, son of Walter and Margaret, was b. c1785, and d. 1847 owning 700 a. of land. He m. 1st, Susanna Stewart, by BAML dated 7 Jan 1806. Susanna d. c1817, and James m. 2nd, by BAML 6 Jan 1818, Elizabeth Lawrenson.

In 1817, James conv. 140 a. *Addition to Timber Ridge* to his parents for their lifetimes, and after they d. the property would revert to his sons Walter, Ebenezer, and Joshua.{AALR WSG#4:472}

James and Susanna (Stewart) Phelps were the parents of{Giles:39, cites 17 MD 120, MD Court of Appeals}: WALTER, b. 1810, d. c1831; EBENEZER, b. c1813, m. Margaret Mewshaw; and JOSHUA, b. c1815, d. c1841.

James and Elizabeth were the parents of{Giles:40, cites 17 MD 120, MD Court of Appeals}: JAMES, b. c1819, d. 1893; HANNAH, b. c1821; NELSON, b. c1823; RICHARD, b. c1825, m. Harriet Sappington; ELIZABETH, b. c1826; ELLEN, b. c1827; CHARLES, b. c1828, d. 1879; WILLIAM, b. c1830, d. 1865; AUSTIN, b. c1833; and ANN, b. c1835.

Fifth Generation

25.   EZEKIEL PHELPS, possibly son of Isaiah Phelps, is so placed for the reasons stated above. He was probably b. no later than c1760 as he took the Oath of Fidelity to the State of MD on 1 March 1778 before

Richard Harwood, Jr.{AARP:151} However, he was not listed as head of a household in the 1790 Census. On 19 April 1793, Ezekiel was in SM Co. making a business deal with Mordecai Barry. The agreement was recorded in AA Co. on 22 April 1794.{Geneva M. Phelps. *An Annal Begins*}

In 1798, Ezekiel Phelps was listed in Roade River Hundred as owning two slaves, one exempt from taxation and one taxable. He was a tenant of Edward Hall. The only other Phelps listed in Roade River Hundred was Zachariah Phelps.{Index to Federal Assessment List of 1798, AA Co.}

Ezekiel Phelps, on 25 May 1802, was co-security for William Cheney who was guardian to Charles Cheney, and also guardian to Francis, Richard, Hezekiah, and Sarah Donalson.{AA Co. Orphans Court Minutes, May 1802:170}

The estate of Ezekiel Phelps was dist. by Nelson Phelps, one of the admins. Margaret Phelps received her widow's thirds and the balance was dist. among Nelson, Walter, and Middleton Phelps, and Mary Ann Scott.{AADI H#1:82}

According to Geneva M. Phelps in *An Annal Begins*, Ezekiel and Margaret (Watkins) Phelps were the parents of four children: NELSON, b. c1797; MARY ANN, b. c1798, m. (N) Scott; MIDDLETON, b. 1800, d. 1837, unm. (On 16 Dec 1837, Margaret Phelps renounced her right to administer the estate of Middleton B. Phelps, and recommended Nelson Phelps, bro. of Middleton, as the best person to administer the estate.) {AAWB TTS#1:326}; and WALTER WATKINS, b. 1 May 1801, m. 28 Feb 1832 Catherine Haynes.

Sixth Generation

26.   NELSON PHELPS, son of Ezekiel and Margaret (Watkins) Phelps, was b. c1797, and was living in 1850 when he was listed in the Census of Howard District as a 53 year old farmer. With him was his wife Ann, age 52.{1850 Census of Howard District, AA Co., dwelling 876, family 886}

Nelson and Ann Phelps were the parents of{1850 Census of Howard District, AA Co., dwelling 876, family 886}: EZEKIEL, b. c1822, age 28 in 1850, m. Martha, b. c1830, age 20 in 1850 (They were living with his parents in 1850.); RACHEL, b. c1823, age 27 in 1850, m. (N) Stewart; JAMES S., b. c1828, age 22 in 1850; ELIZABETH, b. c1832, age 18 in 1850; MIDDLETON BELT, b. c1833, age 17 in 1850; and RICHARD F., b. c1839, age 11 in 1850.

27.   MARY ANN PHELPS, dau. of Ezekiel and Margaret (Watkins) Phelps, was b. c1798, and m. (N) Scott.

28.   WALTER WATKINS PHELPS, son of Ezekiel and Margaret (Watkins) Phelps, was b. 1 May 1801 and m. on 28 Feb 1832, Catherine Haynes. Catherine Haynes Phelps d. 4 Dec 1897.{Geneva M. Phelps, *An Annal Begins*:vii}

Walter and Catherine were the parents of: MARGARET, b. c1833, d. unm.; FRANCIS ASBURY, b. 1834, d. 1921; GEORGE AUSTIN, b. 1838, d. 1920; MARY E., b. c1842, d. unm.; JULIET, b. c1845, d. unm.; and WILLIAM H., b. 1851, d. 1896.

Unplaced

PHELPS, (N), widow, was listed in 1783 as a pauper in Middle Neck Hundred.{Assessment List of AA Co. of 1783, MSA}

PHELPS, ALEXANDER, m. 31 Jan 1809, Anne Poole of Anne Arundel, MD.{The IGI}

PHELPS, ANN, m. Edward Disney by AAML dated 4 Nov 1778.

PHELPS, ARCHIBALD, illegitimate son of Rebecca, was b. 25 April 1762.{AARC:57}

Archibald Phelps, son of Rebecca, was mentioned in the will, written 19 March 1765 and proved 5 April 1765, of George Newman, of Annapolis.{MWB 33:141}

Archibald Phelps d. by 3 May 1784 when John Phelps posted bond with Benjamin Howard and Zachariah Duvall as sureties.{AA Co. Bonds, 1780-1785:137}

PHELPS, BENJAMIN, m. Priscilla Wheat by PGML dated 10 Dec 1795.

PHELPS, CHARLES, gave his age as 35 in April 1760.{AALC 1724-1767:518}

PHELPS, CHARLES EDWARD, m. Martha E. Woodman. They were the parents of:{The IGI} ALMIRA, b. 28 March 1876 in Baltimore, MD.

PHELPS, DEBORAH, was listed in 1776 in the Census of All Hallows Parish with one white male, three white females and two white children. {Brumbaugh, *op. cit.*, 1:409} In 1783, she was listed in South River Hundred, AA Co.{1782/3 Assessment List of AA Co.}

Deborah Phelps d. leaving a will dated 1789 and proved 20 May 1789. She named her two sons Robert and George, her dau. Deborah's children, and dau. Mary. Edward Kirkland, Basel Phelps, and Zachariah Phelps were wits.{AAWB JG#1, 1788-1797:95}

Deborah Phelps' estate was inv. on 13 Nov 1789 by Benj. Welch and Stephen Beard, appraisers. Property was appraised at £65.9.0. Richard Beard and Richard Phelps signed as creditors, and Basil Phelps and Absolute Phelps signed as kin. The inventory was filed 16 Jan 1789 by Robert Phelps.{AA Co. Inventory and Accounts of Sales, JG#1:385}

Her property was sold 11 Nov 1789. Purchasers included Richard Phelps and Zachariah Phelps.{Ibid.:389}

When Deborah's estate was dist. on 20 Oct 1792 by her execs., Robert and George Phelps, her children were listed as follows{AADI JG #1: 36}: ROBERT; GEORGE; DEBORAH, m. (?), and had children, whose children received a legacy; and MARY, m. Henry Purdy by AAML dated 30 Sep 1782.

PHELPS, DINAH, m. Benjamin Brown by AAML dated 26 Feb 1783.

PHELPS, ELIJAH, m. Mary Disney by AAML dated 20 Jan 1818. Elijah Phelps, age 63, appeared in April 1855 and applied for a pension, stating that he had been a drummer in the War of 1812 under Capt. Bealmear. Owen Disney was one of the wits. On 13 Dec 1856, John Biggs and Richard Disney stated they were acquainted with Elijah Phelps, and that he served under Capt. Bealmer.{Bounty Land Warrant Application 5-160-65412}

PHELPS, ELISHA, b. c1788, age 62 in 1850, blackmsith, and Mary, b. c1797 (age 53 in 1850) were listed in the 1850 Census of AA Co., Howard District. With them were: BENJAMIN F., b. c1829 (age 21); CHRISTIANA, b. c1831 (age 19); ELISHA H., b. c1833 (age 17); MARY E., b. c1835 (age 15); SUSAN A., b. c1837 (age 13); and SARAH M., b. c1839 (age 11).{1850 Census, AA Co., Howard District, dwelling 389, family 392}

PHELPS, ELIZABETH, of AA Co., d. leaving a will dated 18 Nov 1759 and proved 10 Dec 1762, naming daus. Rachel Phelps and Rebecca Phelps, and sons Daniel, Nicholas, William, and Joseph Pearce. John Jacob wit the will. On 8 Oct 1762, Daniel and Nicholas Pearce, sons of Elizabeth, renounced their right of administration.{MWB 31:800}

PHELPS, GEORGE, probably son of Deborah, purchased some of Richard Phelps' (q.v.) property c1795. He m. Emma Pierce by AAML dated 6 Jan 1795.

PHELPS, GEORGE, b. c1797, was living at age 53, as a laborer in the 1850 Census, Howard District, AA Co. He m. Martha, age 44. In their household were: TABITHA, b. c1833; SARAH A., b. c1835; MARIAN, b. c1838; JAMES, b. c1840; WILLIAM, b. c1843; and MARGARET

WALKER, b. c1832.{1850 Census of AA Co., Howard District, dwelling 328, family 331}

PHELPS, JAMES, was listed in the 1776 Census of All Hallows Parish with one white male, one white female, and five white children. {Brumbaugh, *op. cit.*, 1:407}

PHELPS, JESSE, m. Sarah Pumphrey by PGML dated 2 Sep 1795.

PHELPS, JOHANNA, m. John Coats by AAML dated 14 Nov 1783.

PHELPS, JOHN, m. Love (N). They were the parents of: MARY, bapt. 3 April 1720, in All Hallows Parish.{AACR:201}

PHELPS, JOHN, took the Oath of Fidelity in March 1778. Another John Phelps took the Oath of Fidelity in March 1778.{AARP}
John Phelps posted bond as admin. of Archibald Phelps (q.v.) on 3 May 1784. Jno. Phelps purchased some of Richard Phelps' (q.v.) property c1795.

PHELPS, JOSHUA, b. c1815 (age 35), and Emily, b. c1821 (age 29), were listed in the 1850 Census of AA Co., Howard District. With them was: JOSEPH, 5 mos.{1850 Census, AA Co., Howard District, dwelling 876, family 886}

PHELPS, JOSIAH, on 13 Aug 1773 conv. personal property to Thomas and William Hall.{AALR IB#4:113} He took the Oath of Fidelity to the State of MD on 2 March 1778 before Reuben Meriweather.{AARP}

PHELPS, MARGARET, purchased some of Richard Phelps' (q.v.) property c1795. She may be the Margaret Phelps who m. Benjamin Pearce by AAML dated 12 Jan 1796.

PHELPS, MARY, m. Robert Long by AAML dated 24 June 1780.

PHELPS, MARY, m. Josh Crutchley by AAML dated 2 Aug 1814.

PHELPS, REBECCA, had an illegitimate son: ARCHIBALD, b. 25 April 1762.{AACR:57}

PHELPS, REBECCA, m. Samuel Chaney by AAML dated 13 Feb 1809.

PHELPS, RICHARD, was b. c1800, m. Sarah Anderson, b. c1804. They were the parents of{Richard Phelps Descendancy Chart, LDS Family History Library}:
EDWARD JACKSON, b. 8 June 1826 at Odenton, AA Co.

PHELPS, ROBERT, took the Oath of Fidelity to the State of MD on 1 March 1778 before Richard Harwood, Jr.{AARP}

Robert Phelps, of AA Co., d. leaving a will dated 7 March 1799 and proved 9 May 1799. He left his entire estate to his bro. George Phelps. Nehemiah Younger and Samuel Crane wit. the will.{AAWB JG#2:80}

The inventory of Robert Phelps was filed 31 July 1799 by George Phelps, of FR Co. The property was valued at £29.19.4. No one signed as kin.{AA Co. Inventory and Accounts of Sales, JG#4:564}

PHELPS, RUTH, m. David Bangs by AAML dated 18 June 1789.

PHELPS, SARAH, m. William Richardson by AAML dated 22 Jan 1787. Sarah Phelps m. William Smallwood by AAML dated 14 Oct 1792.

PHELPS, SUSANNA, m. Nathaniel Hall by AAML dated 28 Feb 1778. Another Susanna m. Simon Retullick, Jr., by AAML dated 8 June 1798. Another Susanna Phelps m. George Hardy by AAML dated 24 Dec 1806. Still another Susanna m. Charles W. Eaton by AAML dated 10 Feb 1790.

PHELPS, WILLIAM, d. 13 March 1721/2 in St. Anne's Parish, Annapolis, MD.{AACR:89}

Several marriages for William Phelps have been found. It is not clear whether the references are all to the same William or to several different ones. William m. Sarah Fowler by AAML dated 18 Dec 1778. A William m. Eliz. Morgan by AAML dated 18 June 1785. He or another William m. Ann Dannison by AAML dated 15 Dec 1815.

William Phelps took the Oath of Fidelity to the State of MD on 1 March 1778 before Richard Harwood, Jr. Another William Phelps took the Oath of Fidelity in March 1778.{AARP}

William Phelps purchased some of Richard Phelps' (q.v.) property c1795.

William Phelps, of Annapolis, d. leaving a will dated 1 Nov 1803 and proved 16 March 1804. He named his wife Elizabeth his sole heir and extx. John Sands, Edward Holland, and James Hunter wit. the will. {AAWB JG#2:261}

William Phelps m., by 23 June 1817, Ann, one of the coheirs of Hannah [Norwood] Hobbs, who was a dau. of John Norwood and a sister of Henry Norwood.{MCHP #3743}

THE POOLE FAMILY

Refs.: A: Harry Wright Newman. *Mareen Duvall of Middle Plantation.*
Washington: The Author, 1952.

The Richard Poole Family

1.   RICHARD POOLE, the first known Poole of AA Co., d. after Dec
1726. He m., on 12 Aug 1703, Johanna Duvall, dau. of Mareen Duvall.
Johanna Duvall Poole was bur. 19 March 1711 in All Hallows Parish,
AA. Co.{AACR:17}
    A Richard Poole was transported to MD c1675.{MPL 15:314} He was
in AA Co. by 2 Dec 1675, when he was listed as a debtor in the inventory
of Thomas Chandler, innholder of AA Co.{INAC 2:36} On 13 Sep 1703, he
was listed as a creditor in the account of John Fairbrother, of AA Co.
{INAC 24.181}
    In 1713, Richard Poole was judged to be a debtor. He was still
living on 1 Dec 1726, when he proved the will of John Jacob, Sr.{A:458}
    Newman suggests that Richard and his wife Johanna had three
sons{A:459-460}: BENJAMIN, b. 8 Feb 1705, bur. 7 Jan 1708 (All Hallows),
d. young; ROBERT, b. 31 Jan 1708, bapt. 26 April 1709 (All Hallows);
and (probably) RICHARD, b. c1709/10, sent to England with his bro.
Robert to be educated.[46]

2.   ROBERT POOLE, son of Richard and Johanna (Duvall) Pool,
was b. 31 Jan 1708. He was a physician and moved back to England,
where he lived at Goodman's Fields, Middlesex. On 9 Sep 1742, he m.
Anne, dau. of Sir Samuel Gower, Kt., of the Parish of St. Mary White
Chapel, Middlesex.
    On 31 Dec 1731, Mr. Robert Poole of Islington, Middlesex,
England, granted power of attorney to Benjamin Hewit, of London, to
claim any estate due him in MD.{A:460} On 4 March 1741/2, Robert Poole,
of St. Mary's Parish, Islington, Dr. of Physic, appointed Capt. William
Carpenter, of Annapolis, his attorney with the same responsibilities given
to Hewit.{A:460}
    Madam Anna Poole, in England, in 1754 gave a letter of attorney.
{AALR RB#3, Vol. 2:676}
    Robert d. leaving a will dated 13 Sep 1748 and executed in 1753,
naming his wife, Anne, his father, and three young children.{AALR RB#3:676}

---

[46] Newman places him as a son of Richard and Johanna, even though no record of his
birth or baptism has been found.

Robert and Anne (Gower) Poole were the parents of{A:461}:
SARAH, b. 14 Sep 1743; ANNE, b. 2 Jan 1745; and SAMUEL
GOWER, b. 26 July 1748. He was still living on 30 Dec 1774, when he
sold to Thomas Harwood land in AA Co.{AALR IB#5:213}

3.   RICHARD POOLE is stated by Newman to have been a son of
Richard and Johanna (Duvall) Poole, to have been b. c1709/10, and to
have been sent to England with his bro. Robert to be educated. Newman
places him as a son of Richard and Johanna, even though no record of his
birth or baptism has been found.
      Richard m. Mary Phelps, dau. of Walter and Mary (Cheney)
Phelps, on 24 Feb 1730.{AACR:45}
      In 1750, Richard Poole was listed in the AA Co. Debt Book as
owning 336 a. *Larkin's Choice* and 200 a. *Duvall's Range.* This property
was later claimed by his elder bro. Robert and eventually sold by
Robert's son, Samuel Gower Poole.
      Mary Poole is named as next of kin in the inventory, appraised 18
June 1764, of Walter Phelps, of AA Co.{MINV 86:145}
      Richard and Mary (Phelps) Poole were the parents of{A:463-464}:
RICHARD, b. 15 Nov 1731, living in 1758; JOHN, b. 21 March 1733,
m. Sarah Collier; SARAH, b. 4 July 1736, bapt. 1 Aug 1736; JOSEPH, b.
6 April 1738, bapt. 17 Sep 1738; MARY, b. 24 June 1741, bur. 31 Dec
1741; ELIZABETH, b. 3 March 1742; RACHEL, b. 18 July 1744;
SAMUEL, b. 10 Nov 1747;[47] WALTER, b. 4 Oct 1751, bapt. 9 Feb
1752; and HENRY, placed by Newman as a theoretical son of Richard
and Mary.

4.   SAMUEL GOWER POOLE, son of Robert, on 30 Dec 1774, was
a sugar refiner living at Queen Street, London (formerly of College Hill,
London), when he executed a deed.{AALR IB#5:213}
      Samuel Gower Poole, of the City of London, was conv. 311 a.
Larkin's Choice by Mareen Duvall.{AALR IB#4:44}
      Samuel Gower Poole, of London, was the son and heir of Dr.
Richard Poole, who was a son of Richard and Johanna (Duvall) Poole. In
1775, he conv., to Thomas Harwood, 200 a. *Duvall's Range* and 311 a.
Larkin's Choice.{AALR IB#5:212}

5.   JOHN POOLE, son of Richard and Mary (Phelps) Poole, was b.
c1733, and d. 1816. He m. Sarah Collier, and took the Oath of Fidelity to
the State of MD in 1778. He and his wife were the parents of{A:464}:
JOHN, b. 1768, m. Priscilla Sprigg; ELIZABETH, b. 1769, m.

------

[47] He was living in 1773 when he mortgaged property to Stephen West.

Hanbury Jones; ANNE, b. 1771, m. Francis Pile, by MOML dated 10 Feb 1798; SARAH, b. 1774; PRISCILLA; and REBECCA, m. Henry Young.

6.   JOSEPH POOL, son of Richard and Mary (Phelps) Pool, was b. 6 Aug 1738 in All Hallows Parish. He moved with his bro. John to FR Co. He m. 1st, Mary McCauley, and 2nd, by FRML 9 June 1792, Eleanor Glaze.

Joseph was the father of nine children by Mary McCauley, and one child by Eleanor Glaze. His children were: JOSEPH, b. 11 Dec 1764, d. unm.; MARY, b. 14 May 1770, d. unm.; BENJAMIN, m. Ann Willet Manly; RACHEL; ELIZABETH, b. 5 Feb 1777; SAMUEL, b. 28 Feb 1783, s.p., 1860; WALTER, b. 28 Feb 1779; SARAH, b. 25 Dec 1784; WILLIAM, b. 20 Jan 1788, m. Harriet Hempstone; and (possibly) REBECCA, b. 13 July 1795, m. Jacob Heffner.

7.   HENRY POOLE, theoretical son of Richard and Mary (Phelps) Poole, d. in 1815, having m., on 22 Dec 1775, Elizabeth Mercer. They had children.{A:467}

8.   JOHN POOLE is placed as a son of John and Sarah (Collier) Pool in W. M. Sellman's *John Sellman of Maryland and Descendants.*

He m., in Jan 1800, Priscilla Woodward Sprigg, dau. of Major Frederick and Deborah (Woodward) Sprigg. John and Priscilla were the parents of: ANN PRISCILLA WOODWARD, m. William Oliver Sellman; and others.

The Basil Pool Family

1.   BASIL POOL m. Lois, dau. of Adam and Lois (N) Shipley, on 24 Nov 1724.{AACR:92}

On 1 Jan 1728, he was mentioned in the inventory of James Crouch, of AA Co.{MINV 15:248}

John Worthington, merchant, c1728/9 conv. to Basil Poole, tailor, 60 a. *Vine's Fancy.*{AALR RD#1:24} In 1744, Basil Poole conv. this land to Charles Porter. His wife Lois consented.{AALR RB#1:429-430}

On 9 Nov 1729, Basil Poole wit. the will of Thomas Wainwright, of AA Co.{MWB 20:90} On 6 Nov 1730, he was listed as a creditor in Wainwright's estate.{MDAD 10:530}

In 1746, Poole mortgaged 79 a. *Poole's Chance* to Philip Hammond.{AALR RB#2:21}

On 13 June 1753, Basil Poole gave bond he would keep Eliza Poole's bastard from being a charge on the county.{AAJU ISB#2:596}

In 1764, he mortgaged his goods and chattels to Samuel Mansell. {AALR BB#3, Vol. 1:101}

Basil Poole, tailor, of AA Co., d. leaving a will dated 17 April 1769 and proved 6 Aug 1770, naming his wife Lois and sons Samuel and Charles. The will was wit. by James Barnes, of Peter, Francis Mercier, and Thomas Hobbs.{MWB 38:29}

On 15 April 1773, Lois Pool, for the love she bore her son Samuel, conv. him all her interest in 200 a. *Poole's Chance*.{AALR IB#I:39}

Basil and Lois (Shipley) Poole had at least two sons: CHARLES; and SAMUEL.

2.   CHARLES POOLE, planter, son of Basil and Lois, of AA Co., in 1771 sold a crop of tob. to Stephen West.{AALR IB#3:163}

3.   SAMUEL POOLE, son of Basil and Lois, was living as late as 1774.

In 1773, he mortgaged his tob. and white servants, John Pittman, James Dohity, and Ann Butterworth, to Stephen West.{AALR IB#4:34}

In 1774, he conv. *Poole's Chance* to John Hood.{AALR IB#4:37} In 1775, he conv. 200 a. *Poole's Chance* to John Hood. His wife Mary relinquished her right to the land.{AALR IB#5:201-202}

The Peter Poole Family

1.   PETER POOL, of AA Co., was living in 1778, and may have d. before 1790, since he is not listed in the 1790 Census. He m. Ruth Whips, b. 13 Feb 1749, dau. of John and Sarah Lucrese (N) Whips.{"Whips Family Bible," in *BMGS* 17:165}

On 9 May 1774, Peter was conv. *Avery's Desire,* 21-1/2 a., and *Worth Nothing*, 25 a., by John Avery.{AALR IN#4:402}

On 22 Aug 1776, Peter Poole mortgaged 96-1/2 a. in AA Co., and a lease from John Hood of 197 a. in BA and AA Cos., to Stephen West. {PCLR DD#6:209}

On 4 June 1778, Peter Pool and wife Ruth of BA Co. conv. 71-1/2 a. of *Overy's Desire* and 25 a. *Worth Nothing* to Adam Porter of AA Co. {AALR IB#5: 573}

Peter Poole, of BA Co., took the Oath of Allegiance before Hon. Reuben Meriwether on 2 March 1778.{AARP:155}

On 13 Aug 1779, Peter Poole mortgaged his corn crop and a negro boy named Toby to Edward Gaither, Jr., for £1,500.{AALR WG#D:263}

Peter and Charles Poole wit. a mortgage on 10 Feb 1787 from Samuel Poole to Matthias Poole.{AALR NH#2:542}

Peter and Ruth (Whips) Poole were the parents of at least two children: JOHN WHIPS; and (probably) LLOYD POOLE.

2.   JOHN WHIPS POOL, son of Peter and Ruth (Whips) Poole, was living as late as April 1813. He m. Rebecca (N).

John Whips Pool, of Peter, was named as a grandson in the will, dated 1 Jan 1781, of Sarah Lucresia Whips.{AAWB 3:52} He was also named as an heir in the distribution of Sarah Lucresia's estate on 14 Oct 1794.
{AADI JG#1:55}

On 23 March 1805, George Whips and wife Susanna conv. to John Whips Pool and to Lloyd Pool 21 a. part of *First Choice,* 6 a. *Hood's Friendship,* and part of *Whips Hill Resurveyed.*{AALR NH#14:25}

On 23 March 1807, John Whips and Lloyd Poole stated they were indebted to George Whips, who was about to move to KY.{AALR NH#13:655}

On 13 April 1813, John Whips Pool was conv. part of *Whips Hill* by Edward Dorsey. On the same day, John and his wife Rebecca conv. 16-1/4 a. *Whips Hill.*{AALR WSG#2:440, 402}

John W. Pool, of Ross Co., OH, on 13 Sep 1815 deeded *Whips Hills* to Charles Alexander Warfield.{AALR WSG#4:160}

3.   LLOYD POOL, son of Peter and Ruth (Whips) Pool, was b. c1781, and d. 22 Feb 1863, aged 81 years, 11 months, 8 days. Because he was b. in 1781, he was probably not b. when his grandmother Sarah Lucresia Whips made her will.

He m. Naomi Barnes, dau. of Adam and Ruth (Shipley) Barnes, by BAML dated 17 March 1805. Naomi was b. 10 June 1785, and d. 12 May 1873.

Between 13 and 26 May 1813, Lloyd Pool was a private in Capt. Thomas Owings' Company of the 32nd Regiment, stationed at Annapolis.{Wright; *MD Militia, War of 1812, Vol. 4: AA and CV Cos.,* p. 41}

According to information given the compiler by the late Dr. Caleb Dorsey, Naomi was an excellent horsewoman, and was also trained in the art of healing. She once rode after dark into a part of CR Co. known as Wolf Bottom to rescue a little girl believed to have wandered into a wolf-infested forest.

Lloyd Poole d. in CR Co., leaving a will dated 23 Jan 1863 and proved 10 Feb ---, naming wife Naomi, and the children listed below.{CR Co. Wills, 3:117}

Lloyd and Naomi (Barnes) Poole were the parents of: HENRY; JOSEPH; REUBEN; ASENATH, m. Amon Shipley, by BAML of 14 Dec 1830; KETURA, m. Frederick Shipley, by BAML dated 14 Dec 1832; SARAH ANN, m. (N) Grimes; HAMMUTAL, m. (N) Wilson; MARY ANN, m. (N) Creswell; and MARTHA ANN.

Unplaced

POOLE, DAVID, Liverpool merchant, and father of Josias Poole, in 1743 was so mentioned in a deed from Capt. John Tunstall to Eleanor Simpson.{AALR RB#1:308}

POOL, JOSEPH, of Baltimore, comb-maker, advertised for the return of his runaway son Joseph, aged 13.{Baltimore *Telegraphe*, 28 July 1795} He was the father of: JOSEPH, b. c1782.

POOLE, WILLIAM, in 1768 was conv. 160 a. *Additional Defense* and 73 a. part of *Wiseman's Folly,* by Samuel Mansell.{AALR IB#JB#1:172} In 1771, he mortgaged 160 a. *Additional Defense* to John Hood.{AALR IB#3:181}

POOL, WILLIAM, advertised in the *MD Journal and Baltimore Advertiser* of 10 Feb 1786 he would not pay the debts of his wife Anne.

THE PORTER FAMILY

Refs.: A: "Porter" in Ancestral Files of Church of Jesus Christ of Latter Day Saints. B: James Wade Emison. *Supplement (1962) to the Emison Families, Revised (1954).* Vincennes: The Author, 1962.

1.   PETER PORTER, was b. 1605 in England, and m. Frances (possibly Dorsey), who was b. c1605.{A}
        Porter sailed from England in the *Tiger* on 21 Sep 1621, and settled on the Eastern Shore of VA. He held 100 a. of land in Lower Norfolk Co., and c1623/4 served in Capt. Epes' Co. of Indian Fighters. {B:166}
        He was among the 100 families of Puritans who migrated c1649/50 from VA to AA Co., MD.{B:166} Peter Porter transported himself and his wife Frances into the Province, and on 19 Sep 1659, Cecil, Lord Baltimore, granted him a patent for 200 a. called *Porter's Hill.*{AALR WH#4:150} Porter conv. this land to Samuel Howard on 14 Aug 1666. No wife is mentioned, so Frances may have d.{AALR WH#4:151} Porter also took up *The Ridge.*{B:166}
        Peter and Frances were the parents of{A}: PETER, b. c1652.

2.   PETER PORTER, son of Peter (1) and Frances (Dorsey) Porter, was b. c1652 in AA Co., MD [Emison gives 1645 as the birth date], and probably d. by 12 Nov 1679.{AALR} The inventory of Peter Porter, of AA Co., was appraised by Andrew Norwood and Edward Dorsey at 8,814 lbs. of tob.{INAC 3:87}

Peter Porter m. Sarah Ruth Howard, b. c1650. They were the parents of{A}: PETER, b. 1675.

3.   PETER PORTER, son of Peter (2) and Sarah Ruth (Howard), was b. c1675 in AA Co., MD, and d. c1755.{B:166} He gave his age as 41 in 1716.{AALC 1:6, 8} He m. Lois Shipley, b. c1675.

On 12 Nov 1679, Cornelius Howard, of AA Co., Gent., conv. 333 a. *Howard and Porter's Fancy,* to Peter Porter, orphan and heir apparent of Peter Porter, late of Severn River, dec.{AALR IH#1:40}

Peter Porter and Augustine Marriott, admins., filed the inventory of Mrs. Sarah Marriott on 10 Nov 1724.{MINV 10:214}

Peter and Lois (Shipley) Porter were the parents of{A; AACR:70, 77}: PETER, b. 1704; PHILIP, b. c1706; LOIS, b. c1708; CHARLES, b. 1711; MARY, bapt. 12 March 1713 in St. Anne's Parish; JOHN, b. 6 Feb 1715/6, bapt. 24 June 1716 in St. Anne's Parish; SARAH, bapt. 15 June 1718; CATHERINE D., b. by 21 May 1721, m. David Todd; and SYLVANIUS, b. by 10 June 1723.

4.   PETER PORTER, son of Peter (3) and Lois (Shipley), was b. c1704 in AA Co., MD. He m. (N) Shipley. They were the parents of{A; B:166}: PETER, b. c1738, m. (N) Dorsey; ADAM, b. 1742, m. Delilah Tivis; KEZIA, b. c1744, m. John SHIPLEY, b. c1744; and JAMES, b. c1746, d. c1802, m. Anne Barnes.

5.   PHILIP PORTER, son of Peter (3) and Lois (Shipley), was b. c1706 in AA Co., MD. He m. Keturah Barnes, b. c1706.{A} Philip Porter d. by 17 Aug 1758 when his estate was inv. by Robert Davis and John Hatherly, Jr., who appraised the estate at £144.17.3. P. Hammond and William Hall of Ek. signed as creditors, and Peter Porter, Sr., and Charles Porter signed as next of kin. Keturah Porter signed as admx. or extx.{MINV 67:531}

6.   CHARLES PORTER, son of Peter (3) and Lois (Shipley), was b. in 1711. In 1761, he conv. to Charles Hammond 100 a. of *Bachelor's Vineyard,* part of *Adam The First.*{AALR BB#2, Vol. 2:525} In 1761, with the consent of his wife Susanna, he conv. 400 a. *Porter's Care* to Charles, John, Philip, Denton, and Rezin and Matthew Hammond, devisees of the will of Philip Hammond.{AALR BB#2, Vol. 2:529}

7.   LOIS PORTER, dau. of Peter (3) and Lois (Shipley), was b. c1708 in AA Co., MD. She m. Robert BARNES, son of James and Keturah (Shipley) Barnes, on 11 Feb 1728 in St. Anne's Parish.{A; AACR:95}

8.   JOHN PORTER, son of Peter (3) and Lois (Shipley), was b. 6 Feb 1715/6 and bapt. 24 June 1716 in St. Anne's Parish.{AACR:77}

9.   ADAM PORTER, son of Peter (4) and (N) (Shipley), was b. c1742 in AA Co., MD. He m. Delilah Tevis.{A}
       In 1774, Peter Porter conv. 57-1/2 a. of *Robert's Advantage* to him.{AALR IB#4:436}

10.   JAMES PORTER, son of Peter (4) and (N) (Shipley), was b. c1746 in AA Co., MD, and m. Ann BARNES, b. c1746.{A}
       In 1774, Peter Porter conv. him 110 a. of *Porter's Lot*.{AALR IB#4:439}

THE WILLIAM POWELL FAMILY

1.   WILLIAM POWELL, of AA Co., d. after June 1698.
       On 22 July 1678, Patrick Hall, of AA Co., and wife Mary, conv. to William Powell 300 a. *Gowry Banks*.{AALR WH#4:119}
       William Powell left a will dated 30 June 1698 (date of probate not given). He left his sons Richard and Thomas *Little Plantation* and 100 a. adj. Benjamin Chew's. Son John was to have 50 a. of the same tract. Son William was to have the afsd. plant. if Richard and Thomas d. without heirs. His wife (unnamed) was to be extx. Daus. Margaret and Ann, not yet 16, were also mentioned.{MWB 6:110}
       The personal estate of William Powell was appraised 28 Nov 1696 [sic] at £144.4.3 by John Denner and Thomas Hughes.{INAC 19:137}
       Anna Mary Powell admin. the estate c1699. No heirs were named. {INAC 19-1/2 A:119} Ann Powell admin. the estate of William Powell on 16 Sep 1703.{INAC 24:208}
       William was the father of: RICHARD; THOMAS; JOHN; WILLIAM; MARGARET; and ANN.

2.   JOHN POWELL, of West River, AA Co., probably son of William, d. leaving a will dated 28 May 1745 and proved 8 July 1745. He named his dau. Elizabeth, who was to have the land possessed by his bro. William Powell and the land he possessed, and the plant. rented to James Trott named *Gory Banks*. His wife was mentioned but not named. The will was wit. by James Trott, William Stone, and Abraham Tanqueray.{MWB 24:197}
       The inventory of John Powell's estate was taken on 11 Oct 1745 and filed 21 Nov 1745 by Rebecca Powell, the extx. Thomas Weller and William Wilson appraised the estate at £132.2.4. William Ludwig and John Trott signed as next of kin.{MINV 31:401}

John and Rebecca Powell had at least one dau.: ELIZABETH.

THE JOHN POWELL FAMILY

1. JOHN POWELL d. by 7 Nov 1715. He m. Elizabeth (N) by 29 Sep 1694. She m. 2nd, (N) Jacks.
   John and Elizabeth were the parents of the following children, b. at All Hallows Parish, AA Co.{AACR 1, 3}: JOHN, b. 29 Sep 1694, bapt. 13 Oct 1706; and JOSEPH, b. 10 May 1696, bapt. 15 Aug 1698.{A:3}

2. JOHN POWELL, son of John and Elizabeth, was b. 29 Sep 1694, bapt. 13 Oct 1706.{AACR:1, 23} He d. leaving a will dated 7 Nov 1715 and proved 6 April 1716, mentioning the tract *Powell's Inheritance,* and naming his father John, dec., his mother Elizabeth Jacks, and bro. Joseph Powell. He also named bros. Christopher Walters and Thomas Jacks, Jr., son and heir of Thomas Jacks, Sr., Eliza, dau. of Thomas Jacks, and Barbara Jacks.{MWB 14:227}

Unplaced

POWELL, BENJAMIN, of AA Co., d. by May 1716. He m. Larthy [Juliatha?] (N).
   On 14 May 1716, his estate was appraised at £10.10.0 by Robert Sollers and Thomas Holland. John Powell signed the inventory.{INAC 27A:197} His estate was admin. on 13 June 1717 by Samuel Maccubbin and Samuel Chew, Jr.{INAC 38A:77}
   Benjamin and Larthy were the parents of: WILLIAM, b. 3 Aug 1712, bapt. 12 Oct 1712 in St. James Parish.{AACR:160}

POWELL, JOHN, and JAMES POWELL were living in AA Co. by 8 Oct 1672 when Robert Wilson conv. to them 200 a. of land called *Wilson's Grove,* laid out for sd. Wilson in 1671.{AALR IH#1:58} On 4 Nov 1674, they conv. this land to William Jones. No wives came to give consent.{AALR IH#1:62}

POWELL, JOHN, m. Mary Dunstone (or Dunstan) in All Hallows Parish on 27 April 1703.{AACR:19}
   John and Mary were the parents of{AACR:20, 21, 23, 27, 32, 37, 40, 48, 195, 198}: ELIZABETH, b. 12 Aug(?) 1704, bapt. 8 Oct 1704, and bur. 22 Aug 1705 at All Hallows Parish; MARY, b. 25 Sep 1706, bapt. 11 April 1707; DORCAS, b. 8 Feb 1708, bapt. 27 April 1709; JOHN, b. 31 March 1712, bapt. 3 Dec 1712; THOMAS, b. 27 June 1715, bapt. 21 Aug 1715; ANNE, b. 3 Aug 1718, bapt. 8 Oct 1718, m. Benjamin Sellman on 16

April 1733; JOSEPH, b. 23 June 1721; and ELIZABETH, bur. 16 Jan 1723.

POWELL, JOHN, m. Elizabeth Purner in St. Anne's Parish, AA Co., on 21 April 1707.{AACR:65} They may be the John and Elizabeth Powell whose children were b. in St. James Parish, AA Co.{AACR:158}: JOHN, b. 25 Sep 1707; HENRY, b. 9 Nov 1709, bapt. 8 Dec 1709, and bur. 12 Dec 1709.

POWELL, JOHN, m. Elizabeth Pierce in All Hallows Parish on 21 July 1720.{AACR:201}

POWELL, JOHN, m. Mary Carvil on 14 Jan 1722 in All Hallows Parish. {AACR:35}

THE PUDDINGTON FAMILY

1.   GEORGE PUDDINGTON, d. c1674 in AA Co. He immigrated to MD in 1649 and is styled "Mr. George Puddington." With him were Jane, Mary, and Comfort Puddington.{MPL 2:614 and ABH:40}
    He m. Jane "sister-in-law" of Richard Robins.{BDML} According to a deposition by her granddau. (see below), she was the widow of Capt. Edward Robins.
    Puddington was a delegate to the Lower House of the Assembly from AA Co., 1650-55.{BDML}
    His will, dated 15 Aug 1674 and proved 24 Sep 1674, names son-in-law Robert Franklin, kinsmen James Chilsott and Augustine Skinner, and mentions the children of his "son" Richard Beard, and of his "grandson" Neale Clarke, and names George, William, Edward and Susanna Burgess, children of Capt. William Burgess. His wife Jane is to have certain moneys in lieu of her interest in the estate. The will was wit. by Nathaniel Heathcote, Charity Stone, William Broome, William Laus, and William Burgess.{MWB 2:6}
    The estate of George Puddington was appraised at 116,734 lbs. tob. on 6 Oct 1674 by Robert Framlin [Franklin?], Nathaniel Heathcote, and Thomas Francis.{INAC 1:92}
    About 1727 (or 1707?), Rachel Freeborn, of AA Co., age c80 years, stated that about 56 years earlier, there came into this province Alice Skinner of the County of Devon and a near relation Mary Skinner. They came to her at the instance and request of the deponent's grandmother, a certain Jane Puddington, who before her marriage to sd. Puddington, was the widow and relict of a certain Edward Roberts [or Robins].{Proceedings of the Chancery Court, c1727, made available to the compiler by Richard T. Foose}

George Puddington was the father of{BDML}: MARY; and
COMFORT.

THE REED FAMILY

1.   WILLIAM REED, of *Clarke's Inheritance,* d. in AA Co. in 1772.
The name of his first wife has not been determined, but between 4 Sep
1750 and 15 Nov 1758 he m. Eleanor, widow of Samuel Lockwood.
    Eleanor Chiffin, dau. of William and Rachel, was b. 2 May 1720
in All Hallows Parish.{AACR:34} She m. 1st, Samuel Lockwood, and 2nd,
William Reed.
    In 1750, James J. Mackall conv. to William Reed the tract *Clark's
Inheritance.*{AALR RB#3:326}
    The estate of Samuel Lockwood was appraised 12 June 1750 by
Richard Moore and John Burgess, and valued at £34.2.5. Thomas
Knighton and Richard Tydings signed as next of kin, and Eleanor
Lockwood, widow and admx., filed the inventory on 4 Sep 1750.{MINV
43:322}
    On 15 Nov 1758, William Reed and wife Eleanor, widow of
Samuel Lockwood, conv. to his son John, Eleanor's dower rights in *West
Puddington,* in possession of William Chiffin.{AALR BB#3:300}
    In 1759, John Bond conv. to William Reed, husband of Eleanor
Lockwood Reed, widow of Samuel Lockwood, title to 500 a. of *James
Park.*{AALR BB#2:301}
    In 1770, Reed conv. a negro, Rachel, to his son-in-law Samuel
Nichols.{AALR IB#2:228}
    In 1771, William Reed conv. various negroes to William Davis,
Jr., son-in-law of Reed's wife.{AALR IB#3:34}
    In his will dated 1 July 1771 and proved 6 Oct 1772, he named his
wife Eleanor, his sons Nelson and William, and granddaus. Eleanor and
Amelia, daus. of his dec. son John Reed; also his daus. Martha Hill, Mary
Griffin, and Priscilla Nicols. He may have had a dau. Jeane by his second
wife.{MWB 38:834}
    The estate of William Reed was appraised by Thomas N. Stockett
and Thomas Watkins on 4 Nov 1772, and valued at £277.0.8. James
Reed and William Reed, Jr., signed as next of kin, and Eleanor Reed,
extx., filed the inventory on 8 Sep 1773.{MINV 113:103}
    In 1781, Eleanor Reed conv. *Clark's Inheritance* to Nelson Reed.
{AALR NH#1:189}
    The children of William and his first wife were: WILLIAM;
NELSON, d. 1798 in Fairfax Co., VA, m. Rebecca Sanders; MARTHA,
m. (N) Hill; MARY, m. (N) Griffin; JOHN, d. 1770; PRISCILLA, m.

Samuel Nichols of FR Co., who in 1770 was conv. a negro slave by his father-in-law William Reed.[48]{AALR IB#2:228}

2.   WILLIAM REED, son of William (1) by his unidentified first wife, was conv. 100 a. of *Clark's Inheritance* by Thomas Wilson.{AALR NH#1:64}'
        William was the father of the following children, b. in All Hallows Parish{AACR:61}: REBECCA, b. 28 Nov 1769; ELIZABETH, b. 8 Aug 1772; MARY, b. 28 Jan 1773; ISABEL (twin), b. 18 Aug 1776; ELENOR (twin), b. 18 Aug 1776; and RACHEL, b. 21 Aug 1778.

3.   NELSON READ, son of William (1) by his unidentified first wife, d. 1798 in Fairfax Co., VA. He m. Rebecca Sanders.
        Nelson and Rebecca were the parents of the following children, b. in All Hallows Parish{AACR:53, 54, 55}: JAMES, b. 31 Jan 1752, bapt. 19 April 1752; NELSON, b. 28 Nov 1753; (N) (son), b. 8 Jan 1756, bapt. 8 Feb 1756; ELIZABETH, b. 23 Dec 1757, bapt. 12 Feb 1757; REBECCA ANN, b. 7 Oct 1759; and ROBERT SANDERS, b. 6 June 1761.

4.   JOHN REED, son of William (1) by his unidentified first wife, d. in AA Co. in 1770.
        His estate was inv. on 15 May 1770, appraised by Benjamin Williams and Gassaway Watkins, and valued at £237.16.1. The inventory was signed by his father William and bro. William Reed as next of kin, and filed by William Lockwood, admin., on 13 June 1770. {MINV 103:183}
        John had two daus.: ELEANOR; and AMELIA, b. 27 Aug 1766, in AA Co., d. 9 Sep 1838, m. James Davidson. (See The Davidson Family)

Unplaced

REED, WILLIAM, of AA Co., was charged in Jan 1703 with being the father of an illegitimate child.{AA Judgements January 1703:10}

THE ROBINS FAMILY

Refs.: A: Frederick V. Saunders. "Edward Robins: Corrections to His English Ancestry and Identification of His Wife Jane Skinner," *BMGS* 37

---

[48] This couple is probably the parents of Robert Nichols who had two sons: Samuel Nichols and Nelson Reed Nichols.

(2) 169-186. B: Thomas Robins. *Outline of Robins Family History in England and America.* New York City: The Author, 1939, GS film 0599461, item 3, and Thomas Robins, *Robyn 1377 to Robins 1939,* GS film 0532048, item 3. (Saunders notes that both sources, though titled differently and done on different typewriters, are essentially the same manuscript). C: Robins Pedigree Chart. By Alice Granbery Walter (GS Pedigree File no. 1192, copyright 1971, also on GS film 1231524, item 3). D: R. L. Greenall, ed. *The Parish Register of Long Buckby, Northamptonshire, 1558-1689.* (Leicester: The University of Leicester, Dept. of Adult Education, Leicester, 1971, GS film 0990138, item 4).

1.   THOMAS ROBYNS, m. Joan (N). Thomas Robyns, husbandman, wrote a will in Jan 1651, but it was evidently never filed for probate.{A: cites *Archdeaconry Court of Northampton Wills and Administrations, 1st Ser., Book D:397,* GS film 0187576} He made bequests to son John Robyns, dau. Joane Robyns, son Henrie Robyns, son Thomas Robyns, son Edward Robyns, Margerye Tymcok, Esabell Tymcok, wife Johanne, and son William Robyns, execs. No probate date.

Joan (N) Robyns wrote a will in 1635, but it was evidently never filed for probate.{A:186: cites *Archdeaconry Court of Northampton Wills and Administrations, 1st Ser., Book E:* 170, GS film 0187577} She made bequests to son Henry Robyns who was the residuary heir, son Thomas Robyns, son Edward Robyns, son William Robyns of Upton, Margery Tymcok, Isabell Tymcok, Thomas Hoggies' two children (unnamed), Richard Robins' two children (unnamed), and dau. Joys Hoggies. Execs. were William Robyns and "Richard my son." James Tanfilde was supervisor. Wits. were Edward Hughston, and John (N).

Robins in his manuscripts{B} stated that Richard Robins was the son of Edward Robyns who wrote his will at Upton in 1546, and that Edward was the son of Thomas Robins whose will was written in 1531 at Holdenby, and of Joane Robins who wrote her will in 1535 at Holdenby. {A:185} Robins did qualify this stating, "Although the genealogist who made the search for my cousin, R. P. Robins, seems to have been satisfied that Edward was the father of the Richard from whom we are descended, Mr. Humphries is not sure that Edward and Richard were not bros. instead of Father and Son. I am, however, accepting for the present the findings of Major Robins."

A pedigree chart compiled by Alice Granbery Walter shows Richard as a son of Thomas and Joan of Holdenby, and bro. to Edward Robyns of Upton. {C}

Saunders states that the combined wills of Thomas, Edward, Henry, and Joan make it appear that Richard is the son of Thomas and Joan, and bro. to Edward.{A:186}

Thomas and Joane (N) Robyns were the parents of: RICHARD; JOHN; JOANE; HENRY; THOMAS; EDWARD; AND WILLIAM.

2. RICHARD ROBINS, probably son of Thomas (1) and Joan, evidently d. by Nov 1584, before either of his parents. His wife's name is not known.

Richard Robyns of "Long Bugby," d. leaving a will dated 20 Oct 1582 and proved 4 Nov 1584.{A:183: cites *Prerogative Court of Canterbury*, 35 Watson, GS film 0091966} He made bequests to the children of his son Thomas, the bequests to be paid at age 21 or marriage. The grandchildren named were Richard, William, Edward, Thomas, Jone, and John. He also named his dau. Elizabeth, every one of the children that William Wylles had by Richard's dau. Alice, the children that Henry Alman of Mares Ashby had by the testator's dau. Jone, all servants (unnamed), dau. Alice Willes, and dau. Creaton [sic: no first name given]. Son Thomas Robyns was named residuary legatee and exec., and William Willes and John Creaton were named overseers. The will was wit. by John Woodworth, John Andrewe, and Henry Collman.

Richard Robyns was the father of: THOMAS; ELIZABETH; ALICE, m. William Wylles; JOAN, m. Henry Alman; and (N), dau., m. (N) Creaton.

3. HENRY ROBYNS, son of Thomas (1), d. leaving a will dated 8 Oct 1569 at "Holdenbye," and proved March 1569.{A:185 cites *Archdeaconry Court of Northampton Wills and Adm., 1st Ser., Book S:*100, GS film 0187586} He made bequests to son Frannces, dau. Margret, servant Elizabeth Dunckley, son William, son-in-law Edward Marryat's two children John and William Marryott, Robt. Robyns, son of his son William, John Norman's three children Margret, Mary and Dorothye, Thomas Golbye, the "poore of Holdenbye," wife Ales, and son "Xpofer" (Christopher), who were residuary heirs and execs., overseers "my bro. Richard Robyns and my bro.-in-law Robt. Butlyn," wits. John Norman and Edmunde (N).

Henry was the father of: FRANCIS; WILLIAM (father of Robert); son Christopher; and possibly a dau., (N), who m. Edward Marriott.

4. EDWARD ROBYNS, son of Thomas (1), d. leaving a will dated 8 Oct 1546 at Upton.{A:185 cites *Archdeaconry Court of Northampton Wills and Administrations, 1st Ser., Book I:*202, GS film 0187579} He named his bro. Hary Robyns (unnamed), Rycd Robyns' children (unnamed), son William at age 18, wife Margret, Thomas Hoggs' children (unnamed), wife Margret residual heir and extx., and William Robyns exec. Supervisor was John (N).

By his wife Margaret, Edward was the father of at least one son: WILLIAM.

5.   THOMAS ROBINS, son of Richard (2), was bur. 8 Aug 1606. He
m. Elizabeth Pamer in 1563.{D}

Thomas was the father of the following children, who were named
in the will of their grandfather Richard as not yet being 21, or who were
named in the Long Buckby Parish Register{D}: RICHARD; WILLIAM;
EDWARD; THOMAS; JONE, may have m. William Wills on 11 March
1594 at St. Sepulchre's, Northampton, Northamptonshire, England{IGI};
JOHN; HENRY, bapt. Dec 1584, bur. 7 Dec 1584; and SAMUEL, bapt.
20 June 1587.

6.   RICHARD ROBINS, son of Thomas (5) and Elizabeth (Pamer),
was not yet 21 when his grandfather Richard wrote his will in 1582.
Richard Robins, Gent., was bur. at Long Buckby on 19 May 1634. He m.
Dorothy Goodman, who was bur. 20 Feb 1640/1. She was a dau. of
Edward and Mary (Bushall) Goodman, and a granddau. of Margey
Bushall, widow.{D}

As Richard Robins of Buckby, yeoman, he d. leaving a will dated
1 March 1633. No probate date was given. {A:178: cites *Archdeaconry Court of
Northampton Wills and Administrations, 1st. Ser., Book EV*:91, GS film 0187596; also recorded *2nd ser., Book
G:*163, GS film 0187602} He made bequests to the poor inhabitants of Buckby,
his wife Dorothie, sons Obedience, Edward, John, and Thomas, his two
youngest daus. Lemuell and Mary at marriage or age 20, dau. Sara, dau.
Contenew, all grandchildren (unnamed), three bros. (unnamed), friends
John Thornton and William Cartwright, and servants (unnamed). Son
Richard was residuary legatee and exec. Loving friends John Thornton
and William Cartwright and bro. William Wills wew appointed
overseers. The will was wit. by Wm. Cartwright, Richard Carvell, and
Valentine Robinson.

Richard and Dorothy (Goodman) Robins were the parents of{D}:
CONTINUE (dau.), bapt. 2 April 1598; RICHARD, bapt. 10 Dec 1599;
OBEDIENCE, bapt. 16 April 1601; JOHN, bapt. 25 Sep 1692;
EDWARD, bapt. 26 Aug 1604; SARAH, bapt. 1 Sep 1606; THOMAS,
bapt. 3 April 1608; DOROTHY, bapt. 23 Dec 1610, bur. 1 Nov 1624;
LEMUELL (dau.); and MARY.

7.   EDWARD ROBINS, son of Richard (6) and Dorothy (Goodman)
was bapt. at 26 Aug 1604 at Long Buckby, and d. by 1646 in
Northampton Co., VA. He m. Jane Skinner, who m. 2nd, George
Puddington, who came to AA Co., MD, with his family in c1649. Mr.
George Puddington immigrated c1649 and transported Jane [his wife],
and Comfort and Mary Puddington.{MPL 2:614 and ABH:40}

Edward Robins, age 33, was transported to VA on the *Thomas* by
Mr. Henry Taverner, on 21 Aug 1635.{CBE1:164}

Edward Robins was in Accomac Co., VA, by 1 May 1637 when he was ordered to pay a debt to Thomas Nuton.{Fleet, *VA Col. Abstracts,* 1:37} He still had not paid the debt by October 1637.{Fleet 1:56} In May 1638, he was ordered to be paid a half share for his work from James Barnaby who would deduct for diet and house rent.{Fleet 1:66}

On 4 June 1646, Elizabeth and Rachel Robins, orphans of Edward Robins, were granted 350 a. in Northampton Co. for the transportation of seven persons (including Edward Robins and others).{Nugent, *Cavaliers and Pioneers,* 1:167} Evidently, Edward Robins had never claimed land for his own transportation.

Edward and Jane (N) Robins were the parents of: RACHEL, m. Richard Beard, who was a Quaker and made the first map of Annapolis. {Wise, *Ye Kingdom of Accawmacke,* GPC:362} Richard and Rachel were m. by 1650 when Richard and Rachel Beard claimed land for immigrating to MD{MPL 5:585}; and ELIZABETH, m. William Burgess.

THE ROWLES FAMILY[49]

1.   CHRISTOPHER ROWLES was transported to MD c1649, and was probably still living in 1662.{MPL 6:43} In Dec 1653, Jno. Browne and John Clarke conv. him 60 a. of land. In Aug 1662, Edward Lloyd conv. him 100 a. of land, which in 1701 Christopher's grandson, Thomas Rowles, sold William Taylard.{AALR WH#4:46, WT#1:224, 388}

Either this Christopher or his son was the Christopher Rowles, debtor, listed on 4 Jan 1675 in the inventory of James Rawbone of AA Co.{INAC 3:88}

Christopher was the father of{BCF:558}: CHRISTOPHER.

2.   CHRISTOPHER ROWLES, son of Christopher (1), d. c1691 in AA Co., having m. Elizabeth, possibly dau. of Benjamin Richand. Benjamin Richand d. leaving a will dated 24 Jan 1684, naming among others, his dau. Elizabeth Rowles.{MWB 4:80} Elizabeth (Richand) Rowles m. 2nd, Joseph Hawkins.{BCF:558}

He may have been the Christopher Rowles called cousin in the May 1674 will of Thomas Meares.{MWB 2:3} In Aug 1681, he surv. 11 a. *Rowles' Chance,* which was later held by his orphans.{MRR}

Christopher Rowles d. by 2 June 1691, when his estate was inv. by Maurice Baker and Mathew Howard, who set a value of £88.5.3 on his personal property. Sureties were John Rowles and William Sutton, and Elizabeth Rowles was the admx.{INAC 11A; 6-1/2}

---

[49] See also Robert Barnes. *Baltimore County Families, 1659-1759.* Baltimore: Genealogical Publishing Co., 1989.

His estate was admin. on 14 Feb 1695 by Elizabeth Roles and Joseph Hopkins [*sic*]. Distribution was to his widow and orphans (unnamed).{INAC 10:483} An additional account was filed on 30 May 1699 by Elizabeth, wife of Joseph Hawkins.{INAC 18:194}

Christopher and Elizabeth were the parents of{BCF:528}: THOMAS, b. c1670; JOHN, b. c1675; MARY, b. c1677, m. Philip Jones on 3 Jan 1700; MARTHA, b. c1679; and WILLIAM, b. 9 July 1682.

3.   THOMAS ROWLES, son of Christopher (2) and Elizabeth, was b. c1670, and d. c1743 in AA Co. He m. Sarah, dau. of William and Elizabeth (Scott) Fisher, who d. 1756.

Thomas Rowles was in BA Co. by May 1705 when he patented *The Stones*.{MPL CD#4:268}

On 15 Feb 1701, Joseph Hawkins, who had m. the "widow and relict" of Christopher Rowles, conv. 40 a. *Burton's Hope* to Thomas Rowles. The same day Thomas conv. part of the tract to Charles Stevens.{AALR WT#1:201, 202} In Dec 1701, he sold to William Taylard land which had been conv. to his grandfather, Christopher Rowles.{AALR WT#1:224} On 12 Sep 1704, he and his wife Sarah conv. 40 a. *Burton's Hope* to Edward Hall.{AALR WT#2:168}

By Nov 1720, he was living in BA Co., when he and his wife sold to John Mills various lands in DO Co., which had been devised to Sarah Fisher Rowles by Philip Griffin, second husband of her mother.{BCF:558}

Thomas Rowles d. leaving a will dated 20 Oct 1738 and proved in AA Co. on 18 May 1743, naming wife Sarah, children Thomas, John, Elizabeth Bell, and Ruth Witham, and the tracts *Gray's Luck, The Stones,* and *Solomon's Hills*.{MWB 23:258}

Rowles' estate was inv. by Law. Hammond and James Walker, and valued at £409.14.6. Thomas and John Rowles signed as next of kin, and Sarah Rowles, extx., filed the inventory on 17 Nov 1743.{MINV 28:218} His estate was admin. on 8 June 1751.{BCF}

Sarah Fisher Rowles d. leaving a will dated 17 Sep 1754 and proved 13 Sep 1756. She named her children Elizabeth Graham, Sarah Smith, Rachel Kitten, Susannah Stewart, Mary Cheney, Ruth Graham, Constant Yieldhall, Thomas and John Rowles, and Comfort Robinson. She also named grandchildren Sarah Kitten, Sarah Cheney, and Thomas Kitten. John Rowles was the exec. The will was wit. by James Walker, John Dorsey, and Robert Caples.{MWB 30:294}

The estate of Sarah Rowles was appraised by Nathan Hughes and Henry Gillis at £256.13.0. John Rowles, exec., filed the inventory on 1 Feb 1757.{MINV 63:208}

Thomas and Sarah (Fisher) Rowles were the parents of{BCF:558}: THOMAS, b. c1696; JOHN, b. c1698; ELIZABETH, b. c1710, m. 1st, on 18 Feb 1727, Jacob Bell, and 2nd, (N) Graham; RUTH, b. c1712, m.

1st, (N) Witham, and 2nd, (N) Graham; MARY, b. c1712; COMFORT, b. c1716, m. 13 Nov 1740, O'Neal Robinson; RACHEL, b. c1718, m. Edward Kitten; CONSTANT, b. c1720, m. Robert Yieldhall; SARAH, m. 3 Aug 1736, John Smith; and SUSANNAH, b. c1724, m. (N) Stewart.

4.   JOHN ROWLES, son of Christopher (2), was b. c1675 in AA Co., MD, and d. by Dec 1702. He m. Mary Hill, b. 1678 in MD, widow of James Crouch. After Rowles' death, she m. 3rd, Philip Jones.

On 21 Dec 1702, Philip Jones admin. the estate of John Rolls of AA Co. Inventories totalling £94.10.8 and 21,468 lbs. of tob. were mentioned. Payments made included one to the orphans of James Crouch.{INAC 23:118}

On 10 May 1713, Philip Jones and wife Mary (dau. and surviving heir-at-law of William Hill) conv. to James Crouch and John Rolls, sons of the sd. Mary by her former husbands James Crouch and John Rolls, 300 a. *North Crouchfield.*{AALR IB#2:93}

John and Mary (Hill) Rowles were the parents of one son{AACR:109} : JOHN, b. 25 May 1698 in St. Margaret's Parish, AA Co.

5.   WILLIAM ROWLES, son of Christopher (2), was b. 9 July 1682 in AA Co., MD. He m. 1st, Martha Baker, 2nd, Eliza, dau. of John Davis {AALR CW#1:293}, and 3rd, Ann (N), who was named in his will.

William Rowles, of BA Co., d. leaving a will dated 31 Jan 1748/9, and proved 1 Dec 1750. He named sons Jacob (exec.), David, John, and William, and wife Ann. In his will, he mentioned *Jacob's Delight, James Adventure, William the Conqueror, Rowles,* and *Jacob's Adventure.* The will was wit. by William Robert Davis, of Thomas, John Sellman, Jr., and Jason Frizell.{MWB 27:427}

The estate of William Rowles, of BA Co., was dist. on 24 Sep 1765 by Jacob Rowles, exec., with David Rowles and Stephen Wilkinson as sureties. There was a balance of £262.17.7. Legatees were the dec.'s children, John and William, and the balance went to the widow for the rest of her life.{BFD 4:136}

By his wife Martha Baker, b. by 1700, William was the father of {BCF:558}: CHRISTOPHER, b. 9 May 1708 in AA Co., MD;[50] WILLIAM, b. 1 Aug 1710; MARY, b. 1 Aug 1710; JACOB, b. c1710/1715 in AA Co., MD, m. 1st Ann Lynch, b. c1710, 2nd, Constance Sampson,[51] b.

---

[50] He was the father of{BCF:558}: JOHN, b. 11 April 1734.

[51] By his 2nd wife, Jacob Rowles was the father of{BCF:558-559}: RICHARD, b. 25 Sep 1728, Baltimore, MD, m. Anne Gostwick, b. 1728; WILLIAM, b. 1730/1740, Baltimore, MD; CHRISTOPHER, b. c1730/1740, Baltimore, MD; and RUTH, b. 1743 in AA Co., MD.

1718, 3rd, Mary Scarf, b. c1710, and 4th, by 14 Jan 1772, Patience, b. 1732, widow of Nathaniel Stinchcomb{BALR AL#D:257}; DAVID, b. c1712; and JOHN, b. c1714.

6.   ELIZABETH ROWLES, dau. of Thomas (3) and Sarah (Fisher), was b. c1710; m. 1st, on 18 Feb 1727, Jacob Bell, and 2nd, (N) Graham.
     Jacob and Elizabeth (Rowles) Bell were the parents of: HENRY, b. 8 Sep 1730, Baltimore, MD; THOMAS, b. 14 July 1732, Baltimore, MD; and RACHEL, b. 9 March 1734, Baltimore, MD.

THE SCRIVENER FAMILY

Refs.: A: Coldham. *Lord Mayor's Court of London Depositions Relating to Americans, 1641-1736* (Washington: National Genealogical Society, 1980). B: Withington. "Maryland Gleanings in England," *MHM* 2:185-186.

1.   BENJAMIN SCRIVENER, of St. Botolph Aldgate, cutler, d. by May 1681 leaving a widow and extx. Elizabeth, who m. 2nd, Edward Williams. On 10 May 1681, Edward and Elizabeth Williams appointed Thomas Barrett, then bound for New England, as their attorney.{A:6}

2.   BENJAMIN SCRIVENER, also of St. Botolph without Aldgate, possibly related to Benjamin (1), first appeared in MD about 1684 as a servant in the inventory of Nathan Smith.{INAC 8:202} He m. by March 1688, Grace, dau. of John Burrage.{AALR IH#3:76-78}
     Scrivener was a free man by 19 Jan 1687, when he appraised the estates of Francis and Sarah Holland.{INAC 9:479} On 5 March 1688, Benjamin Scrivener, of AA Co., Gent., and wife Grace gave bond to Thomas Tench.{AALR IH#3:77} In 1693, as Mr. Benjamin Scrivener, he was a debtor in the inventory of John Atkins, of AA Co.{INAC 12:71} On 6 Aug 1695, he was listed as a creditor of Luke Gregory, of AA Co.{INAC 10:442}
     Benjamin Scrivener, of St. Botolph without Aldgate, County Middlesex, merchant, drew up his will on 22 Dec 1686; it was proved 26 June 1699. He gave 1/3 of his estate in the parish of Hartley Wintney, County Southampton, and in MD and elsewhere, to his wife Grace. If he s.p., the other 2/3s were to go to his kinswoman Frances Freeman, dau. of

his bro.-in-law Thomas Freeman, and to Benjamin Kinsley, son of his sister Rhoda. If they d. before age 21, or unm., the residue was to go to Elizabeth Freeman, another dau. of his bro.-in-law Thomas Freeman. His wife Grace was to be residuary legatee and extx. The will was wit. by Rhoda Kinsley, Thomas Freeman, Mary Hounson, and William Jones Scrivener.{B: cites PCC Pett 107}

On 25 June 1699, his estate was inv. by Nicholas Rhodes and Thomas Hughs, and appraised at £19.0.0.{INAC 19½A:85}

On 2 Oct 1707, Thelma Smith dep. that she had heard Benj. and Grace acknowledge sale of land to Thomas Tench.{AALR IH#3:77}

Benjamin and Grace may have been the parents of: RICHARD; and JOHN.

3.   RICHARD SCRIVENER, possibly son of Benjamin (2) and Grace, d. by May 1762, and m. 1 Sep 1709 in St. James Parish, Mary Burck, age 23, b. Sep 1687, bapt. 1 Sep 1709.{AACR:158} [It is not clear if this entry refers to Richard or Mary.]

On 2 Sep 1746, Richard Scrivener and John Dew signed the inventory of James Mackdannan as next of kin.{MINV 33:280}

Richard Scrivener, of AA Co., d. by May 1762 when William Child and Cephas Child appraised his personal estate at £159.2.5. Richard Scrivener and Mary Simmons were mentioned, and Samuel Scrivener, admin., filed the inventory on 15 May 1762.{MINV 78:137}

Richard and Mary were the parents of the following children, b. in St. James Parish{AACR:158, 161}: JOHN, "son of Richard and Mary age 22 years, b. Sep 1687, bapt. 1 Sep 1709,"[52] RICHARD, b. Jan 1710 [probably 1710/11]; and WILLIAM, b. Sep 1713.

4.   JOHN SCRIVENER, possibly son of Benjamin (2) and Grace, d. by Oct 1727. He m. Eliza Gott on 8 Nov 1713 in St. James Parish. {AACR:183}.

He is probably the John "Scriven" who wit. the will of Samuel Chew, merchant, on 16 July 1717.{MWB 14:699}

John Scrivener d. in CV Co. prior to 27 Feb 1726 when his estate was appraised at £26.6.3 by Isaac Smith and Josias Sunderland. Richard and John Scrivener signed as next of kin, and Elizabeth Scrivener, admx., filed the inventory on 8 May 1727.{MINV 12:98} Scrivener's estate was admin. on 30 Oct 1727 by the admx. Elizabeth Scrivener. An inventory of £26.6.3 was mentioned.{MDAD 8:458}

John and Eliza were the parents of{AACR:163}: BENJAMIN, b. 17 Feb 1717.

---

[52] His line is traced in Elise Jourdan's *Early Families of Southern Maryland* (Westminster: Family Line Publications, 1993) 2:117-118.

5.   JOHN SCRIVENER, son of Richard (3) and Mary, was b. Sep 1687, bapt. 1 Sep 1709, age 22, and d. in AA Co. by Sep 1757. About 1732 he m. Mary Lewin.

Robert Ward and John Birckhead took the inventory of John Scrivener's estate and appraised the value at £617.12.6. Lewis and Richard Lewin signed as next of kin. Mrs. Mary Scrivener filed the inventory on 21 Sep 1757.{MINV 64:517}

John and Mary were the parents of{AACR:166}: RICHARD, b. 26 Jan 1733; JOHN, b. 22 Dec 1735, bapt. 23 May 1736; and others.

6.   WILLIAM SCRIVENER, son of Richard (3) and Mary, was b. Sep 1713.

He is probably the William Scrivener who wit. the will of Sarah Harrison, of AA Co., on 25 Nov 1741.{MWB 22:421}[53]

7.   BENJAMIN SCRIVENER, son of John (4) and Eliza (Gott), was b. 17 Feb 1717. In 1745, he wit. the will of James Chappell, of CV Co. {MWB 24:129}

Unplaced

SCRIVENER, (N), m. by 2 June 1745, Mary, granddau. of James Macdannan, of AA Co.{MWB 24:438}.

SCRIVENER, FRANCIS, in 1770 purchased 254 a. *Carter Bennett* from Francis Holland.{AALR IB&JB#1:536} Sometime between 1771 and 1773, he conv. 127 a. of land to his mother Mary Scrivener. His bro. William Scrivener was to live rent free on the land.{AALR IB#3:289}

SCRIVENER, JOHN, schoolmaster, of AA Co., in 1764 conv. to Anthony Holland 39 a. *Disappointment* (part of *Brown's Enlargement*) and 4 a. of *Brown's Enlargement*.{AALR BB#3:278} In 1764, his wife Rebecca joined him, and Anthony Holland and wife Mary, in selling 264 a. *Harness' Range* to John Wilmot.{AALR BB#3:335}

SCRIVENER, LEWIS, m. Kisriah [sic] Trott on 16 Jan 1781 in St. James Parish.{AACR:179}

SCRIVENER, MARY, m. Joseph Cambden on 19 --- 1772 in St. James Parish.{AACR:175}

---

[53] His line is traced in Elise Jourdan's *Early Families of Southern Maryland* (Westminster: Family Line Publications, 1993) 2:213-214.

SCRIVENER, MARY, m. William Brown on 12 Feb 1775 in St. James Parish.{AACR:176}

SCRIVENER, SARAH, m. Henry Childs in St. James Parish in 1770. {AACR:174}

SCRIVENER, WILLIAM, and ELIZABETH SCRIVENER, on 22 Dec 1746 were named as son-in-law and dau.-in-law of William Thornbury, of AA Co.{MWB 27:277}

SCRIVENER, WILLIAM, m. Henrietta Dixon on 31 Oct 1779 in St. James Parish.{AACR:178}

THE SEWELL FAMILY

Refs.: A: Warfield. *Founders of Anne Arundel and Howard Counties,* pp. 137-140.

1.   HENRY SEWELL, of AA Co., d. by 5 Dec 1700. He m. Johanna Warner, dau. of James and Anne Warner. They were m. before 13 Feb 1673, when James Warner made his will naming his dau. Johanna Sewell and son Henry Sewell{MWB 1:618}.

Henry Sewell patented *Sewell's Increase.*{AALR WT#2:53}

On 21 April 1670, Sewell, with John Rockhold, appraised the estate of Dorothy Bruton, of AA Co.{INAC 1:270}

Sewell d. leaving a will dated 29 Sep 1691 and proved 5 Dec 1700, naming wife Eliza [a second wife?] and children James, Henry, Philip, Joshua, Sarah, and Ann. Abraham Child and Jno. Merritt were appointed guardians of children during their minority.{MWB 11:16, 81}

In 1700, Eliza Sewell was mentioned in a deed when her son James sold to Philip Howard 120 a. *Warner's Neck,* which had passed to Johanna on the death of her mother Elizabeth [sic], and from Johanna to her son James.{AALR WT#1:172}

Henry Sewell was the father of: JAMES; HENRY; PHILIP, b. c1684; JOSHUA; SARAH; and ANN (possibly the Ann Sewell who m. Richard Acton in St. Anne's Parish on 11 Dec 1707).

2.   JAMES SEWELL, son of Henry (1), was living in 1702. He m. Rebecca (N), who joined him, his bro. Henry, and Henry's wife Mary in selling 150 a., part of *Sewell's Increase,* to Amos Garrett of Annapolis. {AALR WT#2:75}

3.   HENRY SEWELL, son of Henry (1) Sewell, d. 1726. He m. Mary Marriott.

On 20 Aug 1716, John Marriott, of AA Co., made his will and left among other bequests 40 s. to Henry Sewell.{MWB 15:1}

Henry Sewell d. leaving a will dated 29 April 1726 and proved 21 May 1726, naming his children Samuel, Mary, Henry, Joseph, Philip, and John. He appointed his wife (unnamed) and sons Henry and Samuel to be execs.{MWB 18:496}

The estate of Henry Sewell was admin. on 2 Sep 1729 by the execs. Mary, Henry, and Samuel Sewell. An inventory of £128.9.11 was listed.{MDAD 9:458}

The estate of Henry Sewell, of AA Co., was appraised again by Richard and Alexander Warfield, who valued his personal property at £5.13.7. Silvanus and Samuel Marriott signed as next of kin. Mary, Henry, and Samuel Sewell, execs., filed the inventory on 26 Oct 1730. {MINV 16:30}

Henry and Mary (Marriott) Sewell were the parents of{AACR:34}: JOHN; SAMUEL; HENRY; JOSEPH; PHILIP; and MARY, bapt. 3 June 1722 in All Hallows Parish.

4.   PHILIP SEWELL, son of Henry (1), was b. c1684. He is almost certainly the Philip Sewell, of AA Co., who made several depositions, giving his age as 74 in 1758, age 82 in 1766 (when he mentioned a bro. James Sewell living 60 years earlier, but now dec.).{AALC IB#1:463, 489, 667} Philip Sewell m. Sarah Floud on 10 Feb 1708 in St. Anne's Parish. {AACR:67}

In 1710, Philip Sewell and wife Sarah, and Joshua Sewell, sold part of *Sewell's Increase* to Amos Garrett.{AALR PK:212}

5.   JOHN SEWELL, son of Henry (3) and Mary (Marriott), was probably much older than some of his bros. and sisters. He m. on 30 May 1721, Hannah Carroll, dau. of Daniel and Hannah (N) Carroll. Hannah Carroll and Daniel Carroll, children of Daniel, were baptized on 12 March 1713 in St. Anne's Parish.{AACR:70}

John and Hannah were the parents of{AACR:36, 41}: HENRY, bapt. 2 May 1723, All Hallows Parish; and JOHN, b. 9 March 1725, bapt. 4 July 1726 in All Hallows Parish.

6.   JOHN SEWELL, son of John (5) and Hannah (Carroll) Sewell, was b. 9 March 1725, and d. 1805.{AARP:179 gives his date of birth as 1740} He m. Mary Marriott, dau. of Augustine and Mary (Warfield) Marriott.

In 1776, John Sewell and wife Mary sold 3 a., pt. of *Brookesby's Point,* to John Hammond.{AALR IB#5:231}

John Sewell took the Oath of Fidelity before the Hon. Nicholas Worthington in March 1778.{AARP}

John and Mary (Marriott) had: JOHN, b. 1761; ACHSAH, b. 1768, d. 1833, m. in 1791, Leonard Mallonnee, b. c1763, d. 1854; SARAH; and MARY.

Unplaced

SEWELL, JOSEPH, m. by 1770, Jemima (N), who joined him in seeking 30 a. *Howard and Porters's Fancy.*{AALR IB&JB#1:513}

SEWELL, PHILIP, m. by 1768, Jane (N), who joined him in a deed. {AALR IB&JB#1:153}

THE SIMPSON FAMILY

1.   THOMAS SIMPSON, of AA Co., was bur. 14 May 1709 in All Hallows Parish.{AACR:30} He m. Elizabeth, dau. of Henry and Elizabeth Pierpoint{BCF:50754} who was bapt. 8 July 1700 in All Hallows Parish. {AACR:10}

On 15 Nov 1699, Philip Griffin conv. a black mare and her increase to Amos Simpson, son of Thomas.{AALR WT#1:11}

Simpson's estate was inv. on 11 Aug 1709 by Walter Phelps and William Dorsey. James Pierpoint and Amos Pierpoint signed as next of kin. The value of the personal property was valued £51.16.0.{INAC 30:114}

The estate of Thomas Simpson was admin. on 5 Aug 1710 by Elizabeth Simpson, the admx. An inventory of £59.16.8 was mentioned. {INAC 31:342}

On 15 Aug 1711, Elizabeth Simpson, widow, and Amos Pierpoint gave bond that they would pay Amos, Richard, Rachel, Mary, Sarah, and John Simpson, orphans of Thomas Simpson, their share of £38.8.3 as they came of age.{AALR PK:414}

Thomas and Elizabeth (N) Simpson were the parents of the following children, all bapt. 8 July 1700 in All Hallows Parish (unless otherwise noted){AACR:10, 11, 15, 19}: JOHN, bur. 30 April 1700; AMOS THOMAS; RICHARD; RACHEL; MARY, b. 26 Dec 1700, bapt. 26 July 1702; SARAH, b. 12 March 1703, bapt. 5 June 1704; and JOHN.

2.   AMOS (THOMAS) SIMPSON, son of Thomas (1) and Elizabeth, was bapt. 8 July 1700 in All Hallows Parish.

---

[54] BCF cites an undocumented chart of the Pierpoint Family at the MHS, done by a Mr. Stickney.

On 24 April 1716, he m. Elizabeth Duvall.{AACR:26}

3.   RICHARD SIMPSON, son of Thomas (1) and Elizabeth, was bapt. 8 July 1700 in All Hallows Parish.

On 20 Oct 1717, Richard Simpson, with consent of wife Rebecca, conv. land to Samuel Galloway and Gerard Hopkins.{AALR IB#2:441}

On 14 July 1730, Richard Simpson patented 375 a. in AA Co. called *What You Will*.{MPL PL#7:468, IL#B:476}

As "Richardson" Simpson, he and wife Rebecca had issue {AACR:197}: THOMAS, b. 13 Feb 1717.

Unplaced

SIMPSON, JOHN, m. Elizabeth (N). They were the parents of{AACR:122}: THOMAS, b. 1 Jan 1747 in St. Margaret's Parish.

THE SISSON FAMILY

1.   JOHN SISSON immigrated to MD by 1659.{MPL 5:484, 516} He d. in AA Co. leaving an undated will which was proved 16 March 1663.

On 10 Nov 1662, John Norwood conv. 420 a. called *Norwood's Fancy* to John Sisson. One moiety of the land descended to one of Sisson's coheirs, Jane, who by Oct 1710 was m. to Edward Hall.{AALR PK:305}

In his will, John Sisson left his plant. to his wife Frances, whom he named extx., personalty to his eldest dau. Jane, and land bought from Edward Lloyd to Eliza Sisson. He also named his bros. Benjamin Sisson and Cornelius Howard (who was named overseer with Richard Higgins). The will was wit. by William Wilson and William Grymes.{MWB 1:197}

John was the father of: JANE, m. William Yieldhall; and (probably) ELIZABETH, m. Thomas Brown, Jr.

2.   JANE SISSON, dau. of John (1) Sisson, d. by Oct 1710. She m. 1st, William Yieldhall, and 2nd, Edward Hall.

William Yieldhall, of Severn River, AA Co., d. leaving a will dated 18 Oct 1683 and proved 26 July 1684. He left personalty to Edward Hall, named his wife Jane his extx., and also named children William and Eliza, both under age. The will was wit. by Nich. Shepard and Jas. Williams.{MWB 4:44}

On 11 Oct 1710, Edward Hall and wife Dorcas, and John Hall, son of Edward Hall by his former wife Jane, conv. to Amos Garrett 210 a., being one-half of *Norwood's Fancy*.{AALR PK:305}

By William Yieldhall, Jane Sisson was the mother of: WILLIAM; and ELIZA.

By Edward Hall, Jane Sisson had at least one son: JOHN.

3.   ELIZABETH SISSON, probably dau. of John (1), m. by Sep 1710, Thomas Browne, Jr.

On 21 May 1666, a certificate of survey called for some 271 a. (200 a. of which are called *Orphans Inheritance*) to be laid out for Elizabeth Sisson, the orphan of John Sisson. Elizabeth and her husband, Thomas Brown, Jr., assigned their rights to Amos Garrett. {AALR PK:267} Amos Garrett patented the 200 a. assigned to him as *Providence*. However the patent states the land was assigned to him by Elizabeth, widow of John Sisson, and now wife of Thomas Brown. {MPL DD#5:633, PL#3:173}

4.   WILLIAM YIELDHALL, son of William and Jane (2) (Sisson), was living in AA Co. as late as Dec 1711. He m. Mary (N).

On 12 Dec 1711, Andrew Norwood, son of Andrew Norwood, and grandson and heir-at-law of John Norwood, conv. to William Yieldhall, son of William and Jane, one-half of *Norwood's Fancy*. {AALR PK:422} The next day, William and his wife Mary conv. *Norwood's Fancy* to John Brice. {AALR PK:424}

THE STEWART FAMILY

Refs.: A: "David Stewart of Anne Arundel County, Maryland," *Stewart Clan Magazine,* 9 201-202, 207-209 (Nov-Dec 1930-1931). B: Chart of Stewart Family, in collections of Mrs. Henry Clay Smith; MSA SC 675. C: Stewart Notes in Mrs. Albert Aiken Collection (MSA G-823).

First Generation

1.   DAVID STEWART, progenitor, was b. c1616, probably in Scotland. He came to MD c1660, and m. Margaret (N). On 10 Dec 1661 he was commissioned a Lieutenant under Capt. Thomas Besson, commander-in-chief of AA Co. {A:201}

On 6 Oct 1674, he was listed as a debtor in the inventory of George Puddington, Gent. {INAC 1:92}

He was bur. 30 Oct 1696, age 80, and his widow Margaret was bur. 8 Nov 1700. He d. leaving a will dated 11 Oct 1696 and proved 21 May 1697, naming wife Margaret as extx., and his sons David, Robert, Charles, and James. He did not name any daus., but the will of his son David in 1703 named two sisters. {A:201; MWB 7:281}

The estate of David Steward was appraised on 21 May 1697 by Edward Carter and Stephen Warman, and valued at £46.8.8.{INAC 15:107} Margaret Steward admin. the estate on 30 Aug 1698. The balance was paid to her as extx.{INAC 16:129}

David and Margaret were the parents of{B}: ELIZABETH, m. John Frizell (and had two children: Priscilla and John); DAVID, b. c1673; ROBERT, b. c1675; MARY, m. (N) Davis; CHARLES, b. c1680; JAMES, b. c1682.

Second Generation

2.   DAVID STEWART, son of David and Margaret, was b. c1673, and was bur. 5 Oct 1703, evidently unm., leaving a will dated 2 Oct 1703 and proved 30 Oct 1703, naming bros. Charles, James, and Robert Stewart, bro. John Frizell, sister Elizabeth Frizell, and nephew and niece Priscilla and John Frizell. He also named a sister Mary Davis. {A:201; MWB 11:396}

David Stewart's estate was appraised at £78.2.0 by Edward Carter and Stephen Warman.{MDTP 9B:16}

The estate of David Stewart was admin. on 30 June 1704 by Charles Stewart, exec.{MWB 3:166}

3.   ROBERT STEWART, son of David and Margaret, was b. c1675 in All Hallows Parish, and d. 1739/40. He m. Susanna Watts on 26 Jan 1699. Susanna was bur. 16 Nov 1733.{A:201}

Robert Stewart d. leaving a will dated 18 Feb 1739 and proved 1 April 1740, naming the following children{A:202}: STEPHEN, b. 28 Dec 1699, m. twice; DAVID, b. 24 Aug 1703; VINCENT, b. 15 April 1706; CHARLES, bapt. 29 May 1710;[55] JOHN, b. 23 May 171(2?), was living in 1749 when he was named exec. of his bro. David; SUSANNAH, b. 15 April 171(4?); DINAH, b. 30 April 1718; ROBERT, b. 10 Aug 172(0?), was living at 1739; and CALEB, b. c1724.

4.   CHARLES STEWART, son of David and Margaret, was b. c1680, and was bur. 18 Nov 1717. He m. Elizabeth (N), who m. 2nd, in 1718, Samuel Jacobs. Charles and Elizabeth were the parents of the following children, all b. in All Hallows Parish{B; A:202, 208}: ROBERT, b. 6 Aug 1712; DAVID, b. 23 July 1714; and EDWARD, b. 25 June 1716.

---

[55] He was living in 1739 when his father made his will, and he may be the Charles Stewart, named in the *Providence (Rhode Island) Gazette* of 8 Nov 1763, as having been killed by Indians at Frederick Town, MD.

5.   JAMES STEWART, son of David and Margaret, was b. c1682 in All Hallows Parish and may be the James "Stuard" who with Walter Pardoe was baptized in All Hallows Parish as "young men."{AACR:12} He m. Rachel Wicholl on 21 July 1710 in All Hallows Parish.{AACR:25}

In 1709, his request for re-recording a deed was granted.{AALR WH#4:110} In 1712, James Stewart, with wife Rachel, conv. 30 a. *Neglect* to Joseph Hill.{AALR IB#2:8-9} In 1747, James Steward conv. 100 a. *Steward's Chance* to James Stewart, of James.{AALR RB#3:1}

He is probably the James Stewart bur. 1 July 1752.

James and Rachel were the parents of the following children, b. in All Hallows Parish{B; AACR:196, 197}: (possibly) SOPHIA, bapt. 29 May 1713; DAVID, bapt. 18 Oct 1717; MARGARET, bapt. 18 Oct 1717, m. Ebenezer Pumphrey; JAMES, bapt. 18 Aug 1723; and EZEKIEL, named in the 1761 will of his bro. James.[56]

Third Generation

6.   STEPHEN STEWART, son of Robert and Susanna, was b. 28 Dec 1699 in All Hallows Parish, and d. leaving a will dated 28 Jan 1742 and proved 25 Feb 1742. He m. 1st, on 12 Jan 1730, Elizabeth Rutland, dau. of Thomas and Jane (Linthicum) Rutland. In Dec 1734, he m. 2nd, Elizabeth Ward.{A:207}

Stephen Stewart was the father of{A:207}: ELIZABETH; AVIS; STEPHEN, b. after 1734, m. c1778, Elizabeth Thomas; and EDWARD, m. Mary (N).

7.   DAVID STEWART, son of Robert and Susanna, was b. 24 Aug 1703 in All Hallows Parish, and d. leaving a will dated 14 March 1748/9 and proved 20 May 1749. He m. Mary (N).

David and Mary were the parents of{A:207}: DAVID, d. leaving a will dated 13 Aug 1792; SUSANNA; MARY; and ELIZABETH.

8.   VINCENT STEWART, son of Robert and Susanna, was b. 15 April 1706, and m. Ann (N). Vincent and Ann were the parents of {AACR:45, 53}: SUSANNAH, b. 28 Sep 1735; ELIZABETH, b. 3 June 1737; MARY, b. 15 Sep 1739; SARAH, b. 1 April 1743; DAVID, b. 27 Aug 1747;[57] and ANNE, b. 20 Sep 1748.

---

[56] He may be the Ezekiel Stewart listed in the 1783 Assessment of Patapsco Hundred, AA Co., as owning 200 a. part *Piney Grove*.

[57] David Stewart, son of Vincent, in 1768 conveyed 50 a. *Younger Benson [Besson?]* to Alexander Ferguson, tailor.{AALR IB&JB#1:542}

9.   CALEB STEWART, son of Robert and Susanna, was b. c1724 in All Hallows Parish, and was last heard from in 1752. Circa 1747 he m. Catherine (N).

Caleb was the father of{A:208; AACR:52, 54}: ROBERT, b. 4 Feb 1748;[58] JAMES, b. 10 March 1749; DAVID, b. 29 Aug 1752; (possibly) CALEB, b. 1756, Revolutionary Soldier; and (possibly) EDMUND.

10.   JAMES STEWART, son of James and Rachel, was bapt. 18 Aug 1723, but must have been b. much earlier.

As James Stewart (sometimes Sheart), he was listed in the AA Co. Debt Books as owning *Stewarts Chance* from 1753 to 1774.{AADB, at MSA}

A James Steward, living near the head of Severn, advertised in the *MD Gazette* of 5 June 1760 that he would not pay the debts of his wife, Sarah, "who had behaved very ill, and run him into debt."

James Stewart's will, dated 6 Oct 1761 and proved 17 Nov 1761, named bros. Ezekiel and David, and sister Margaret wife of Ebenezer Pumphrey. He named his own children Rebecca (to be raised by Margaret and Ebenezer as their own), Joshua, Mary, Ann, Rachel, Dinah and Charles.{MWB 31:462}

James Stewart was the father of: REBECCA; JOSHUA; MARY; ANN; RACHEL; DINAH; and CHARLES.

11.   EZEKIEL STEWART, son of James and Rachel, was named in the 1761 will of his bro. James. He may be the Ezekiel Stewart listed in the 1783 Assessment of Patapsco Hundred, AA Co., as owning 200 a. part *Piney Grove*.

Fourth Generation

12.   DAVID STEWART, son of David and Mary, in 1768 was conv. by Nicholas Maccubbin 160 a. *Gray's Luck*.{AALR IB&JB#1:156} In 1774, he was conv. another 60 a. of *Gray's Luck* by William Marsh.{AALR IB#4:407}

He d. in AA Co. leaving a will dated 13 Aug 1792 and proved 22 Sep 1795.{AAWB JG#1:516} In his will, he left his son Charles the tract *Gray Luck* and two negro boys named Jacob and Caleb. Also named were his

---

[58] He may be the Robert Stewart who owned quite a bit of property. He d. intestate c1810, leaving four bros. as his only heirs-at-law: James; Caleb; David; and Edmund. Bro. David Stewart, on 20 April 1811, took out letters of administration. Bro. James, on 16 Nov 1824, assigned his share of his bro. Robert's estate to his own son: JOHN, orator of this petition (Maryland Chancery Paper 11135).

dau. Sarah Pumphrey, sons David and Ezekiel Stewart who were to have the residue of *Gray's Luck*, dau. Rachel Jacob's two daus. Ann and Charity, and his dau. Susanna Waters. Son David to be sole exec. Test: Francis Cromwell, Paul Phillips, and Joshua Cromwell.

David was the father of: CHARLES; SARAH, m. (N) Pumphrey; DAVID; EZEKIEL; RACHEL, m. (N) Jacobs; and SUSANNA, m. (N) Waters.

13.   JOSHUA STEWART is stated by Mrs. Albert Aiken to have been b. 1714 [but he was almost certainly b. much later], d. 1800, and to have m. Deborah (N). Joshua Stewart, son of James, was probably b. c1729. This would fit provided his father was b. much earlier than 1723. Joshua's wife has not been determined.

Joshua Stewart, sometime between 1740 and 1744, was conv. 100 a. *Best Intent* from William Beasman, of BA Co., and his mother Elizabeth Beasman. {AALR RB#1:30}

In June 1749, Joshua served on the AA Grand Jury. {AAJU June 1749 Court:231}

In 1753, as Joshua Steward, he registered his cattle mark of brand. On the same day, David Steward registered his cattle mark. {AALR RB#3, Vol. 2:582}

On 13 June 1753, Joshua Stewart and Nathan Pumphrey, Jr., gave bond they would keep Ruth Hawkins' bastard child from being a charge on the county. {AAJR ISB#2:596}

On 17 Nov 1770, Joshua Stewart, of AA Co., planter, for love and affection, conv. to his son Ebenezer Stewart the tract *Intent*. Ebenezer Stewart was to take possession of the tract after Joshua's decease. No wife joined him. {AALR IB#2:233}

In 1790, a Joshua Stewart was listed as head of a family which consisted of one white male over 16 and one white female. Next to him were listed Ebenezer Stewart (see below) and James Stewart (one white male over 16 and five white females). {1790 Census of MD, p. 15, col. 1} These may have been sons of Joshua.

Joshua Stewart was the father of: EBENEZER, b. c1753; and (probably) JOSHUA, Jr.;[59] and JAMES.

Fifth Generation

14.   DAVID STEWART, son of David, m. by 1797 Ann, dau. of Syranus [Sylvanus] Pumphrey. {MCHP #288}

---

[59] In 1783, Joshua Stewart, Jr., was listed in the Assessment of Patapsco Hundred as owning 100 a. *Stewart's Chance*.

He d. in AA Co. leaving a will dated 18 Jan 1804 and proved 25 Oct 1810. His son David was to have dwell. plant. *Grays Luck*, and 100 a. called *Stone* agreeable to the deed the testator had from Joshua Pumphrey. The residue of the estate was to be divided among five children: David, Rachel, Mary, Ann, and Susannah Stewart. No exec. was named. Test: Christian Kneass, Elijah Johnson, Leander Johnson, and Stephen Gambrill. David Stewart's widow, Ann, renounces the will and elects to taker her dower. {AAWB JG#2 (37):519}

David and Ann (Pumphrey) were the parents of the following children, named in his will: DAVID, b. c1796; ANNE, b. 5 Nov 1798; JOSEPH, b. 25 Sep 1800 (not named in his father's will); RACHEL; MARY; and SUSANNAH.

15.   EBENEZER STEWART is stated by Mrs. Albert Aiken to have been a son of Joshua and Deborah, b. 1754, and d. 28 April 1814. He m. on 20 March 1777, Susannah Caples, b. 15 Oct 1774, d. 31 Dec 1826, age 72 years, 2 months, and 16 days, a dau. of Robert Caples.{C} She may have been a relative of William Caples listed in AA Co. in 1790 as head of a family consisting of three white males over 16, three white males under 16, and five white females. {1790 Census of MD, p. 15, col. 1}

In 1783, Ebenezer Stewart was listed in the Tax List for Patapsco Hundred as owning 60 a. part of *Interest*. James Stewart, Jr., owned 40 a. of the same tract.{AATL 1783}

In 1790, Ebenezer Stewart was listed in AA Co., next to Joshua and James Stewart (see above), as head of a family which consisted of one white male over 16, five white males under 16, and four white females. {1790 Census of MD, p. 15}

Ebenezer and Susannah were the parents of{C}: THOMAS, b. 14 Feb 1778, d. 16 May 1835, m. Elizabeth Benson who d. 16 June 1819; ROBERT, b. 2 Sep 1779; STEPHEN C., b. 2 Jan 1782, d. 2 Aug 1832; ANN C., b. 30 Nov 1783, m. Richard Cromwell on 14 Jan 1816; MARGARET, b. 7 May 1785; ABRAHAM C., b. 14 Aug 1788, d. 20 Sep 1835 (m. Louisa Cromwell, b. 3 Aug 1794, d. 24 April 1839); JOSHUA, b. 25 Dec 1790; and EBENEZER, b. 1 Dec 1792, m. Mary Ann (Edwards?)

Sixth Generation

16.   DAVID STEWART, b. c1796, is tentatively placed as a son of David and Anne. He was living in 1850 in Elk Ridge Landing, now HO Co. With him were his wife Sarah, age 52, and the children listed below. {B}

During the War of 1812, he was a private in Capt. Andrew Slicer's Company with whom he marched to Baltimore. On 7 Aug 1823, he m. Sarah Cole in AA Co. He d. in AA Co. on 28 Aug 1850. On 19 May 1855, Sarah Cole Stewart was living in Washington, DC, when she applied for a pension, and recited the preceding facts. Sylvester Clarke and Benjamin Whittle resided in Washington, DC, and stated they were acquainted with her. {Pension/Bounty Land Application 55-160-85473}

David and Sarah Stewart were the parents of{B}: CALEB, b. c1832; ELIZABETH, b. c1839; SARAH, b. c1841; and LOUISA, b. c1843.

17.   THOMAS STEWART, son of Ebenezer and Susannah, was b. 14 Feb 1778, and d. 16 May 1835, age 57 years, 3 months, 1 day. He m. 1st, Elizabeth Benson, who d. 16 June 1819. She was a dau. of Thomas Benson who d. in 1795.{C} He evidently m. 2nd, Elizabeth (probably Cole, by BAML dated 1 July 1820), who survived him. {MCHR 154:386ff}

On 17 July 1835, Ebenezer Stewart, Joseph B. Stewart, of Baltimore City, and Benson Stewart, Elizabeth Stewart, Susan Stewart, and Margaret Ann Stewart, of AA Co., filed a petition in the Court of Chancery stating that their father, Thomas Stewart, d. 17 May 1835, having made a will, devising all his property to be divided among all his children. He named his two eldest sons Ebenezer and Joseph B. Stewart as execs. Joseph B. Stewart renounced the executorship. The dec. left a widow Elizabeth, the children named making the petition, and also the following children who are infants under the age of 21: Richard, Abraham, Maren [Mareen?], Rachel, Margery, Nancy, Thomas S., and Mordecai Stewart. {MCHR 154:386ff}

Thomas Stewart was the father of the following children{C}: (by his first wife): EBENEZER, b. 1 April 1804; THOMAS, b. 1 Aug 1807; JOSEPH BENSON, b. 23 March 1809; BENSON, b. 15 Aug 1810; DEBORAH, b. 23 March 1812; ELIZABETH BENSON, b. 5 Oct 1813, m. Randolph Smith Cromwell (b. 7 July 1803, d. 2 July 1865); SUSANNA CAPLES, b. 19 Aug 1815; MARGARET ANN, b. 11 Aug 1817; RICHARD BENSON, b. 6 April 1819; (by his second wife): ABRAHAM GARDNER, b. 22 April 1821; MAREN [MAREEN?] DUVALL, b. 21 Nov 1822; ANN, b. 27 March 1824; RACHEL CAPLES, b. 10 Dec 1825; MARGERY SCISSELL, b. 15 Oct 1827; THOMAS WESLEY, b. 8 Feb 1830; and CHARLES MORDECAI, b. 24 May 1834.

18.   ABRAHAM C. STEWART, son of Ebenezer and Susanna (Caples) Stewart, was b. 14 Aug 1788, and d. 20 Sep 1834 or 1835. If he d. in BA Co., he d. intestate. He m. 4 Aug 1814 (by Rev. [Hagerty?]) Miss Louisa Cromwell. Louisa Stewart, wife of Abraham C. Stewart, d. 24 April 1839, age 45 years, 8 months, and 21 days.{C}

19.   JOSHUA STEWART, son of Ebenezer and Susanna (Caples), was b. 25 Dec 1790, and m. on 24 Dec 1816, Caroline Cromwell, b. 2 May 1796, d. 2 Feb 1879.[60]

On the back pages of the Bible, Joshua Stewart wrote the following account: "1816: Removed to the country from BC. Commenced work at blacksmithing on the first day of Nov and worked one year and five years in partnership with Abraham C. Stewart.

April 27 1818: The lawsuit between James Pitcher and Thomas Benson was settled in favor of Benson. The will was upset of Basil Smith which was wrote by John G. Cromwell about three years before it was upset.

1818: Removed to the New House on the last day of March and commenced working my own fostten? on first day of April."

On another page: "In the year of Our Lord 1819, the plague was very thick in Baltimore, and very destructive to the Inhabitants. Hundreds, it's said, d. of this dreadful complaint and many removed to the country to Chinquapin and Loudenslager's Hills and encamped in tents and were supported by the Higher classes of citizens. The streets of Fells Point were also strewed with Lime to prevent the infection but it was in vain. It still continued until the weather got cold which was about the 1st of Dec 1819 at which time that dreadful disease left the City of Baltimore. /s/ Joshua Stewart."

Joshua and Caroline (Cromwell) Stewart were the parents of: JOHN THOMAS, b. 18 Oct 1817; LEROY STEPHEN, b. 27 July 1819; JOSHUA CROMWELL, b. 2 Aug 1821; SEDWICK MARION, b. 20 July 1823; CAROLINE MIRANDA, b. 18 May 1825; FRANKLIN, b. 25 July 1827; and EBENEZER JAMES, b. --- 1830.

Unplaced

STEWART, CHARLES, d. leaving a will dated 17 Feb 1781 and proved 15 March 1781. His eldest son Mordecai Stewart was to have land in *Poplar Neck* and *Mitchell's Addition*. Son Charles was to have the new dwelling house. He named daus. Mary Burgess, Eleanor Smith, Susannah Griffin, and Sarah Stewart. Sons Mordecai and Charles were to be execs. The will was wit. by Jos. Howard, Stephen Rawlings, and Jas. McCulloch.{AAWB TG#1 (34):16}

Charles Stewart was the father of: MORDECAI; CHARLES; MARY, m. (N) Burgess; ELEANOR, m. (N) Smith; SUSANNAH, m. (N) Griffin; and SARAH.

---

[60] Much of the information on his family comes from the Stewart Bible Records, copied in *Entick's New Spelling Dictionary;* MSA G-834.

STEUART, Capt. DAVID, (sometimes spelled STEWART), late of AA Co., dec., was in his lifetime possessed of considerable real estate, and conv. some of this property in trust to Caleb Steuart who was to pay David Stewart's debts. David Stewart d. intestate sometime in the year 1826 leaving issue{1}: JOHN; HENRY H.; HAMMOND; CATHERINE; MARGARET; ELIZABETH; MARTHA; ANN, of AA Co.; and DAVID STEUART, of BC.

STEWART, DAVID, m. Thurs., 20 Oct 1825, by Rev. Mr. Nevins, Mary Adelaide, only dau. of late Nathaniel Morton. {*Baltimore Federal Gazette*, 21 Oct 1825}

STEWART, EDWARD, Sr., of AA Co., d. leaving a will dated 13 Nov 1794 and proved 18 Dec 1794. He named his dau. Sarah Basford to have 203-3/4 a. *Duvall's Range*, younger son William Stewart 182-3/4 a. land in PG Co.; widow Mary; son Stephen; execs. to be son William and wife Mary. Test: Henry Woodward, William Maccubbin, and George Murphy. {AAWB JG#1:453}

Edward Stewart was the father of: STEPHEN; WILLIAM; and SARAH, m. (N) Basford.

STEWART, ROBERT, d. 16 Dec 1863 in AA Co., in his 67th year. {*The [Baltimore] Sun*, 18 Dec 1863}

THE SEABORN TUCKER FAMILY

1.   SEABORNE TUCKER was b. c1672, and was bapt. 25 da., 7 mo., 1698, in All Hallows Parish. {AACR:150} In 1738, he stated he was age 66, and in 1739 he gave his age as 67. He stated he had been an overseer to Col. William Holland. {AALC 2:104, 122} He d. in AA Co. by March 1753.

He m. c1694/5, Dorothy (N), admx. of Charles Harrington, of CV Co. {INAC 10:447}

Tucker was in AA Co. by 11 Nov 1699 when he wit. the will of Robert Gover, of AA Co. {MWB 6:364}

On 2 Aug 1718, Seaborn Tucker and Robert Wood appraised the estate of Mary Watkins, of AA Co. {MINV 1:232} Sometime prior to 17 March 1728, Tucker and Thomas Wells appraised the estate of John Walters, of AA Co. {MINV 15:235}

Seaborn Tucker, of AA Co., d. leaving a will dated 22 June 1752 and proved 12 March 1753. He left his dwell. plant. to his dau. Ann Birckhead. Money in John Boshman's hand was left to the testator's son John and grandson Seaborn Tucker. Son Jacob was left a slave girl. Granddau. Ann Birckhead was also left a slave girl. The remaining part of his estate was to go to John Tucker, Mary Carr, and Ann Birckhead. Son-in-law Samuel Birckhead was named exec. The will was wit. by Nehemiah Birckhead, Alexander Frazier, and Elender Fowler. {MWB 28:434}

Seaborn Tucker's estate was appraised at £605.2.9 on 20 May 1753 by Robert Ward and Lewis Lewin. John Tucker and Jacob Tucker signed as next of kin. Samuel Birckhead, Quaker, filed the inventory on 18 June 1753.{MINV 54:38}

Seaborn and Dorothy were the parents of the following children, b. in St. James Parish{AACR:146, 149, 152, 155, 157, 183}: ANN, b. 12 Feb 1695, bur. 17 Aug 1699; JOHN (twin), b. 17 Aug 1698, bapt. 25 Sep 1698; JACOB (twin), b. 17 Aug 1698, bapt. 25 Sep 1698; ROBERT (twin), b. 4 Dec 1700; ANN (twin), b. 4 Dec 1700; SEABORN, b. 2 Oct 1704, bapt. 24 May 1713; SUSANNAH, 19 June 1707; and MARGARET, bapt. 24 May 1713.

2.   JOHN TUCKER, twin son of Seaborn (1) and Dorothy, was b. 17 Aug 1698, bapt. 25 Sep 1698 in St. James Parish, and may be the John Tucker who d. in CV Co. by June 1757.

John Tucker, of AA Co., planter, d. leaving a will dated 4 Feb 1757 and proved 14 June 1757, naming children John (to have land in CV Co. called *Hamleton's Park*), Seborne (to have *Edmonton's Range*), Mary, Ann, Jacob, and Charles Tucker. John Tucker was to be exec. {MWB 30:300}

On 18 Oct 1758, his exec., John Tucker, filed the inventory. Robert Ward and Lewis Lewin had appraised the estate at £118.9.4. Seaborn and Isaac Tucker signed as next of kin.{MINV 64:506}

The estate of John Tucker was dist. on 25 May 1758 by the exec. The balance of £118.19.4 was dist. equally among his children Ann, Jacob, Charles, Isaac, and Mary.{BFD 2:104}

Another distribution was made 6 Nov 1760 by the exec. A balance of £42.16.5 was dist. to the same five children.{BFD 3:82}

John Tucker was the father of: JOHN; SEABORN; MARY; ANN; JACOB; CHARLES; and ISAAC.

3.   JACOB TUCKER, twin son of Seaborn (1) and Dorothy, was b. 17 Aug 1698, and bapt. 25 Sep 1698.

No doubt he is the Jacob Tucker, of CV Co., who d. leaving a will dated 15 Dec 1762 and proved 9 Feb 1764. He named his son Benjamin Tucker, grandchildren Jacob and Elizabeth Tucker, and appointed his wife (unnamed) as extx. Daniel Tibbens, Wm. Hickman, and Francis Woolfe wit. the will.{MWB 32:49}

Jacob Tucker was the father of: BENJAMIN.

4.   SEABORN TUCKER, son of Seaborn (1) and Dorothy, was b. 2 Oct 1704 and bapt. 24 May 1713 at All Hallows Parish, AA Co. He d. in BA Co. by 8 Aug 1740. He m. Margaret Cobb, dau. of James Cobb, on 2 April 1730. She m. 2nd, Thomas Litton.{BCF}

An administration bond on his estate was posted 8 Aug 1740 by Margaret Tucker with Francis Jenkins and Thomas Bradley. The inventory of Seaborn Tucker's personal estate was taken on 6 Oct 1740 by Richard Dallam and Thomas Litten, who valued his property at £99.5.3. Jacob Giles and Nat. Rigbie signed as creditors, and Gregory Farmer, Sr., and Charles Jones signed as next of kin. Margaret Tucker filed the inventory on 7 Nov 1740.{MINV 25:332}

Seaborn and Margaret Tucker were the parents of{BCF}: JACOB, b. 22 May 1731; SUSANNA, b. 15 April 1734, m. Mordecai Crawford on 16 Sep 1750; and MARGARET, b. 28 Aug 1736.

Unplaced

TUCKER, JOHN, of CV Co., d. by 22 Aug 1721, when his estate was appraised by Sabritt Sollers and Samuel Lyle and valued at £34.16.10. Richard Tucker signed as next of kin.{MINV 7:58}

The estate of John Tucker, of CV Co., was admin. on 18 March 1722 by Jannat Tucker. No heirs were named.{MDAD 4:71} By 20 Aug 1722, Jannat had m. 2nd, John Kent, when she again admin. John Tucker's estate.{MDAD 4:220}

TUCKER, JOHN, of Elk Ridge, AA Co., advertised that his wife Sarah had eloped.{MD Journal and Baltimore Advertiser, 24 Feb 1784}

TUCKER, JOHN, took the Oath of Allegiance before the Hon. Samuel Harrison in March 1778. He d. by 14 Aug 1799, when the final distribution of his estate was made to his widow Ann (who received her thirds), and the balance to the heirs listed below.{AARP:201; AA District Book JG#2:55, 56}

John Tucker's widow, Ann, b. c1766, m. 2nd, Benjamin Winterson.

John and Ann were the parents of: THOMAS; JOHN; JAMES; SUSAN; and WILLIAM, probably the William who d. by 12 Aug 1806 when his estate was dist. by Benjamin Winterson. The estate was divided among his mother, Ann Winterson, and his siblings Thomas, John, James, and Susanna [sic] Tucker.{AADI JG#2:94-95}

TUCKER, JOHN, of AA Co., d. leaving a will dated 13 May 1801 and proved 19 May 1801. He named his wife Susannah, who was sole legatee and sole extx. Thomas Beard, Stephen Beard, and Richard B. Watts were execs.{AAWB 37:167}

TUCKER, RICHARD, of AA Co., d. leaving a will dated 22 Jan 1755 and proved 12 March 1755, naming son-in-law John Clavey, and four children including John, Marthey and Margaret Tucker; he also left a legacy to Robert Ward.{MWB 29:331}

TUCKER, THOMAS, of AA Co., d. leaving a will dated 2 July 1748 and proved 19 Oct 1748, leaving 1/3 of his personal estate to his wife, and naming his dec. father Richard Tucker, and his own sons Richard and Thomas Tucker, as well as Sarah Pane, Susannah Rawling, Mary Beard, Elizabeth White, Sealy Tucker, and Easter Hill. Joseph Cowman was to see that the will was carried out.{MWB 25:441}
On 25 Nov 1748, his estate was appraised at £80.11.7 by James Deale and Richard Franklin. Joseph Cowman and Thomas Caton signed as creditors. Elizabeth and Richard Tucker signed as next of kin. Thomas Tucker, exec., filed the inventory on 18 Jan 1748.{MINV 39:154}

TUCKER, THOMAS, of AA Co., d. by 18 Oct 1802, when William Tucker, admin., divided his estate into tenths for William, John, Abel, Nancy, Francis, James, Enoch, Samuel, Joseph, and Seley.{AADI JG#2:25}
Francis Tucker, son of Thomas, d. by 30 August 1816, when his estate was dist. by William Duvall. The balance was divided into eighths for William, Abel, Nancy, James, Enoch, Samuel, Joseph, and Seley Tucker.{(AADI JG#3:44}

TUCKER, WILLIAM, of AA Co., d. by 16 April 1752, when his estate was appraised at £49.15.8 by John Hall and Zachariah Maccubbin. Joseph Ward, admin., filed the inventory on 26 June 1754.{MINV 57:205}

TUCKER, WILLIAM, of PG Co., d. by 25 Nov 1718, when his estate was appraised at £95.14.9 by William Keny and William Kidd.{MINV 1:77}

TUCKER, WILLIAM, m. Sarah (N). As Mr. William Tucker, he was listed as a debtor in the inventory of Henry Loftus, of AA Co.{INAC 19-1/2 A:80}
William and Sarah were the parents of{AACR:78}: SARAH, b. 9 July 1715; and JOHN, b. 15 Feb 1716/7.

TUCKER, WILLIAM, probably son of Thomas, may be the William who m. Sarah Gardiner on 27 Feb 1770 in St. James Parish, AA Co. {AACR:174}
On 6 March 1776, he was one of the residents of Herring Creek who petitioned the Convention of MD for permission to form a militia company. He later served in Capt. Richard Weems' Co.{AARP:202}

William Tucker, of AA Co., d. by 17 Dec 1819, when his estate was dist. by Abel Tucker. The six heirs were Mary Ann Tucker, Rachel Tucker, Thomas Tucker, Nancy Tucker, Jane Tucker, and Sarah Tucker. {AADI JG#3:90}

William Tucker was the father of: MARY ANN; RACHEL (may be the Rachel who m. Peregrine Pickett); THOMAS; NANCY; JANE; and SARAH.

THE TYDINGS FAMILY

1.   RICHARD TYDINGS, progenitor, claimed land for service in 1659 and again in 1667.{MPL 4:68, 10:600} On 1 Jan 1674, he wit. the will of Thomas Sparrow, of AA Co.{MWB 2:76}

He m. Charity (N).{AACR:204} A search of the MD Calendar of Wills and Skordas revealed several women, one of whom might have been Charity, wife of Richard Tydings. Charity Adams, on 29 May 1662, was named in the will of William Battin, of SM Co.{MWB 1:162} Charity Adams had been transported c1653.{MPL Q:431}

Another Charity was mentioned as having been transported c1666. {MPL 10:433} Charity Bagbie, on 29 April 1670, was named as a dau. in the will of John Bagbie, of CV Co.{MWB 1:409}

Charity Stone, on 15 Aug 1674, wit. the will of George Puddington, of AA Co.{MWB 2:6}

On 15 June 1676, Tydings and John Watkins appraised the estate of John Shaw, of AA Co.{INAC 2:172}

On 29 April 1679, Richard Tydings and James Sanders appraised the estate of Thomas Besson, the Elder, of AA Co.{INAC 6:105} On 17 June 1684, he appraised the estate of Edmond Townhill, of AA Co.{INAC 8:178}

On 13 June 1680, Tydings had resurv. a 200 a. tract in AA Co. known as *Haslenut Ridge*, originally surv. in 1663 for John Gray; the tract was found to contain actually only 166 a. It was later held by John Tydings. On 25 Feb 1684, Tydings had surv. 500 a. in BA Co. called *New Years' Purchase.*{MRR:42, 166}

On 2 Oct 1685, George Thompson, of SM Co., conv. 375 a. in BA Co., called *Nanjemoy,* to Richard Tydings.{BALR RM#HS:164}

Richard Tydings d. leaving a will dated 2 Feb 1687. In it, he left to his son John (at age 21) the tract *Haslenut Ridge*; if John were to s.p., the land was to go to his daus. Charity, Eliza, Preti(o)tia, and Mary. Daus. Preti(o)tia and Mary were to have *New Year's Gift,* also in BA Co. Solomon Sparrow, John Belt, and John Jordaine were to be overseers. The will was wit. by Eliza Chesell, Eliza Butler, Charity Chesell, and John Elsey.{MWB 6:40}

An account of his estate was filed 14 May 1697 by his extx., dau. Charity, wife of John Jordain, of KE Co. Inventories of £166.1.3.4 and £9.3.8 were mentioned, and payments from John Taylor, merchant in London, and Joseph Owens. Payments were made to Col. Darnall. Legatees were his wife (unnamed) and five children (unnamed).{INAC 14:143}

Richard and Charity (N) Tydings were the parents of: JOHN, under 21 in 1687; CHARITY, m. 1st, by 1689, John Jordain{MDTP 6:156; INAC 13B:1; MDAD 14:143}, m. 2nd, by 27 Dec 1726, Michael Pasquinet, of Bath Co., NC; ELIZABETH, probably m. John Belt; PRETI(O)TIA, m. by 15 Jan 1708/9, Dutton Lane; and MARY, m. Philip Dowell on 11 June 1702 in St. James Parish, AA Co.{BALR TR#A: 436, IS#G: 68}

2.   JOHN TYDINGS, son of Richard and Charity, was under 21 in 1687; as "John, son of Richard and Charity Tydings, of AA Co., dec.," he m. Mary, dau. of James and Mary Ellis, of AA Co., at West River Meeting, Society of Friends, on 16 da., 6 mo., 1705.{AACR:204} She m. 2nd, Samuel Lockwood, and 3rd, Thomas Knighton.

On 11 Oct 1721, John Tydings and wife Mary conv. 201 a. *Ellis' Choice* to Richard Colegate, of BA Co.{BALR TR#A:200}

John Tydings probably d. at a relatively young age, and his widow seems to have m. 2nd, Samuel Lockwood. In addition to the Tydings "children-in-law" mentioned below, the Lockwoods seem to have had the three youngest Tydings children baptized in All Hallows Parish on the same day as their own sons Samuel and John.{AACR:200} Mary Ellis Tydings Lockwood m. as her 3rd husband Thomas Knighton, on 8 Oct 1723, in All Hallows Parish.{AACR:37}

Samuel Lockwood, of AA Co., d. leaving a will dated 1 March 1722 in which he named his wife Mary as extx., and his sons-in-law and daus.-in-law Richard, Laurence, Cassandra, and Charity Tydings. The will was wit. by Thomas Stockett, Jr., and William Sellman.{MWB 17:249}

Mary Knighton, sole dau. and heir of James Ellis, of AA Co., for love and affection she had for her sons Samuel Lockwood and Thomas Knighton, and for my grandsons Samuel Brown (son of James and Cassandra Brown), Thomas Sparrow (son of Solomon and Charity Sparrow), on 13 June 1733 conv. to them various portions of a tract in BA Co. called *James' Park,* which was patented by her father on 10 May 1685.{PCLR PL#8:193}

John and Mary were the parents of{AACR:46, 198, 199, 200}: CASSANDRA, bapt. 26 Oct 1718, m. (N) Brown; RICHARD, bapt. 17 June 1719; LURINA (LAURENCE?), bapt. 17 June 1719, bur. 23 Oct 1732; and CHARITY, bapt. 17 June 1719, m. Solomon Sparrow.

3.   CHARITY TYDINGS, son of Richard and Charity, m. 1st, by 1689, John Jordain.{MDTP 6:156; INAC 13B:1; MDAD 14:143} She m. 2nd, by 27 Dec

1726, Michael Pasquinet, of Bath Co., NC, for on that date Michael and Charity gave a power of attorney to John Belt, "their loving cousin," to sell *Nanjemoy*. On 12 Feb 1727, Michael Pasquinet and wife Charity, dau. and devisee of Richard Tydings, by John Belt, Sr., their attorney, conv. 375 a. *Nanjemoy* to John Belt, Jr.{BALR IS#I: 36, 61}

4.   ELIZABETH TYDINGS, dau. of Richard and Charity, m. John Belt. (See The Belt Family)

5.   PRETI(O)TIA TYDINGS, dau. of Richard and Charity, m. by 15 Jan 1708/9, Dutton Lane.{MWB 6:40; AA Co. Rent Roll B#2:423; and BALR RM#HS:634, IS#G:68}

6.   MARY TYDINGS, dau. of Richard and Charity, m. Philip Dowell on 11 June 1702 in St. James Parish, AA Co.{BALR TR#A:436, IS#G:68} They were the parents of{AACR:155, 157, 158, 159, 161, 164}: PHILIP DOWELL, b. 5 Oct 1703, bapt. 20 Aug 1704; ANNE DOWELL, b. 23 Feb 1704, bapt. 22 April 1705; JOHN DOWELL, b. 2 Dec 1706, bapt. 13 April 1707; MARY DOWELL, b. 7 Feb 1708, bapt. 10 April 1709; CHARITY DOWELL, b. 4 April 1711, bapt. 6 May 1711; PETER DOWELL, bapt. 4 April 1714; and BUSCARA VILE DOWELL, b. 11 April 1718.

Unplaced

DOWELL, JOHN, m. by 1711, Mary, dau. of John Tydings.{MWB 6:40; AA Co. Rent Roll B#2:423}

THE WADE FAMILY

1.   ROBERT WADE, of South River, was in AA Co. by 9 June 1675, when he received a payment from the estate of James White.{INAC 1:353} One Robert Wade was transported to MD by 1662{MPL 6:48} and another by 1667.{MPL 1:104, 170} It is not known whether or not these are one and the same person.
        On 9 June 1676, he received a payment from the estate of James White, of AA Co.{INAC 1:353} About the same time, he received payment from the estate of Neal Clarke, of AA Co.{INAC 4:249}
        On 26 March 1679, he and Richard Tydings appraised the estate of Enoch Boulton.{INAC 6:612}
        On 6 Aug 1678, Robert Wade had surv. 75 a. called *Wade's Increase* on the s. side of the river at a bounded white oak of Johns Cabin

Branch. By 1707, this was held by the Widow Davis for Robert Hopper's orphans.{MRR:182}

Robert Wade d. leaving a will dated 28 Sep 1694 and proved 13 Nov 1694. He left personalty to his grandchild Jane Westall, and named his "son" George Westall as one of the overseers. He also named his son Robert, dau. Jane, dau. Temperance, dau. Perseverance Bayly, wife of Thomas Bayly, and their son Robert Bayly. Robert Hopper, William Bateman, and George and Sarah Westall were wits.{MWB 7:6}

No record of an inventory or administration account has been found. No identification of Robert Wade's wife has been made.

Robert Wade was the father: ROBERT; JANE; TEMPERANCE, m. Joseph Holbrook in All Hallows Parish on 4 Feb 1696/7{AACR:7}; PERSEVERANCE, m. Thomas Bayly; and SARAH, m. George Westall.

2.   ROBERT WADE, "son of Robert and wife," was bur. in All Hallows Parish on 4 July 1706.{AACR:21}

Unplaced

WADE, GEORGE, m. Hannah (N), who d. 27 Dec 1744.{AACR:139}

George and Hannah were the parents of the following children, b. in St. Margaret's Parish{AACR:121}: JOHN, b. 5 Aug 1733; JOSEPH, b. 25 Dec 1734; MARGARET, b. 12 Oct 1737; GEORGE, b. 28 Sep 1740; and WALTER, b. 6 March 1743.

THE WARNER FAMILY

Refs.: A: Harry Wright Newman. *Anne Arundel Gentry, Volume Two*. (Annapolis: The Author, 1971). B: J. Reaney Kelly. *Quakers in the Founding of Anne Arundel County, Maryland* (Baltimore: Maryland Historical Society, 1963).

1.   JAMES WARNER, d. testate in 1673. Before his settlement in AA Co., he was church warden of Elizabeth River Parish, Lower Norfolk Co., VA, as late as 15 Aug 1649.{A:231}

James m. 1st, Anne (N), by whom he was had two daus., Catherine and Johanna.{B:22} Sometime after the death of William Harris, of AA Co., in 1670, Warner m. as his second wife, Harris' widow, Elizabeth.{A:231} Kelley states (erroneously in the opinion of this researcher), that Catherine was b. to Elizabeth Harris Warner after the death of James Warner, but it is known that Warner in his will referred to his "sons" [i.e., sons-in-law] Samuel Howard and Henry Sewell, so his daus. must have been b. before his marriage to Elizabeth Harris.{B:81}

Anne Warner is mentioned in a letter of Robert Clarkson, dated 14 da., 11 mo., 1657, as being an early convert to the Society of Friends. {B:22}

Just when James Warner arrived in MD is not clear, because he is not listed in Skordas. However, we know he was in AA Co. by 20 Nov 1651 when he had surv. 320 a. called *Warner's Neck.* By 1707, 200 a. of this were held by one Lolly, by [right of his] marriage with Katherine, widow of Samuel Howard, and 120 a. were held by Henry Pinkney for the orphans of Philip Howard, son of the sd. Samuel. {MRR:193}

On 20 Feb 1661, James Warner and Henry Ridgely surv. 600 a. called *Wardridge* on the s. side of Severn River. By 1707, the property had passed to members of the Ridgely family.{MRR:197} On 20 Feb 1661, Warner also had surv. 200 a. called *Wardrap.* {B:197}

James Warner d. in AA Co. leaving a will dated 13 Feb 1673 and proved 25 May 1673, naming wife Elizabeth, extx., dau. Johanna Sewell, sons Samuel Howard, Philip Warner, and Henry Sewell. The will was wit. by Abraham Child and John Jacob.{MWB 1:614-619}

On 22 Sep 1674, Cornelius Howard and Richard Hill appraised the estate of James Warner. His assets, including two servants, John Husk and Alice Drape, were valued at 46,667 lbs. tob.{INAC 1:100} William Crouch and Abraham Dawson appraised his estate on 10 Jan 1674 and valued his property at 44,637 lbs. tob.{INAC 1:169}

On 4 Aug 1674, Elizabeth Warner, of AA Co., widow and relict of James Warner, late dec., conv. to John Sumerland, of AA Co., 100 a. called *Harris' Mount,* originally granted to William Harris.{AALR IH#1:191}

James Warner and his first wife were the parents of two daus. {A:233}: CATHERINE, m. Samuel Howard; and JOHANNA, m. Henry Sewell.

2.   JOHANNA WARNER, dau. of James, m. Henry Sewell. She and her husband sold *Warner's Neck* to Samuel Howard. The sale was later contested by the Sewell heirs, but the court upheld the sale. {A:233}

THE WATKINS FAMILY[61]

1.   JOHN WATKINS, d. by Oct 1649. He m. Frances (N), who m. 2nd, by 6 Aug 1655 as his second wife, Edward Lloyd. {Johnston, "Lloyd Family," in *MD Genealogies*, II, 171}

Watkins was in Lower Norfolk Co., VA, by 25 May 1640, when he and others agreed to pay £36 for themselves and the other inhabitants of Daniel Tanner's Creek. {FOUW:5}

John Watkins d. leaving a will dated 26 Feb 1648 and proved 31 Oct 1649, leaving his plant. to his wife Frances until their son John came of age, and naming Edward Lloyd as one of the overseers. {See McIntosh, *Lower Norfolk and Norfolk Co. Wills, 1637-1710*, I, 5}

In 1655, Frances, wife of Edward Lloyd, formerly wife of John Watkins, dec., surrendered her dower to Edward Lloyd if he would pay a certain sum to her son John Watkins. {FOUW:7}

John and Frances were the parents of at least one son: JOHN, d. c1682.

2.   JOHN WATKINS, son of John (1) and Frances, may have d. c1682. He was transported to MD prior to 1658 by his step-father, Edward Lloyd, who, on 22 July 1658, assigned 100 a. to his "son-in-law," John Watkins. {MPL Q:70}

On 12 March 1665, John Watkins, acting as attorney (agent) for William Taylor, signed a deed on behalf of Taylor. {AALR WH#4:294}

On 22 Feb 1674, John Watkins had a grant of 300 a. on the n. side of West River, called *Watkins Hope*. On 10 May 1677, he conv. the entire land to William Richardson. {AALR WH#4:21} William Richardson, claimer of the land, requested that the deed be re-recorded.

On 21 Aug 1674, Watkins was listed as a debtor in the inventory of John Shaw, of AA Co. {INAC 1:244} On 15 June 1676, he and Richard Tydings appraised the estate of Sarah Francis, formerly Sarah Shaw, admx. of John Shaw. {INAC 2:171}

On 4 Dec 1675, John Gross, of AA Co., made a will naming John Watkins his exec. {MWB 5:30} On 16 Sep 1677, Watkins, as exec. of John Gross, filed the administration account. {INAC 4:300}

An undated inventory of John Watkins worth of £97.6.6 and 149,881 lbs. tob. was appraised by John Welsh and Thomas Francis. Although there is no date, the preceding and following inventories are dated 1682. {INAC 8:14}

John Watkins was almost certainly the father of: JOHN, d. 1696.

---

[61] See also Elise Jourdan's *Early Families of Southern Maryland* (Westminster: Family Line Publications, 1995), 4:55-68.

3.   JOHN WATKINS, son of John and grandson of John and Frances, d. by July 1697. He m., prior to 10 Jan 1691, Anne Gassaway, dau. of Nicholas Gassaway (who was b. c1634 in London). After the death of Watkins, Anne m. 2nd, William Burgess, on 13 Aug 1697 (he d. 28 June 1698), and she m. 3rd, Richard Jones, by 27 Jan 1700, when their dau. Ann was b. in All Hallows Parish{AACR:7; MWB 2:228}

John Watkins, member of the parish vestry, was bur. 27 Feb 1696. {AACR:7}

On 21 April 1688, John Watkins and Daniel Longman appraised the estate of Benjamin Lawrence.{INAC 10:8}

The inventory of John Watkins, Gent., of AA Co., was appraised 12 July 1697 by Henry Hanslap and John Chappell. No value was set on the inventory. James Sanders, Ferdinando Battee, and Samuel Galloway signed the inventory as approval.{INAC 15:276}

On 28 June 1698, William Burgess made a will leaving 1,000 a. in BA Co. to the two eldest children of John Watkins, former husband of Burgess' wife.{MWB 6:101} On 30 Sep 1704, Richard Jones, Jr., of AA Co., made his will naming his sons-in-law and dau.-in-law John, Nicholas, Gassaway, and Elizabeth Watkins.{MWB 13:684}

Ann Jones, widow, age 67, d. in AA Co., leaving a will dated 29 June 1737 and proved 30 March 1742, naming dau.-in-law Mary Watkins and granddau. Margaret Watkins, also children Gassaway, Nicholas and John Watkins, and Elizabeth Smith. Steven and Mary Warman and John Watkins were wits.{MWB 22:435}

John and Anne (Gassaway) Watkins were the parents of{AACR:1, 26}: JOHN, b. 15 Aug 1689, d. 1734; NICHOLAS, b. March 1691, m. Margaret Lamb; ELIZABETH, b. 11 April 1693, m. Samuel Smith on 27 Jan 1714; GASSAWAY, b. 31 March 1695,[62] m. Elizabeth Rawlings; and ANN.

4.   JOHN WATKINS, son of John (3) and Anne (Gassaway) Watkins, was b. 1689, and d. in 1734. He m. Mary, dau. of Stephen Warman, in All Hallows Parish. The date is not given in the Parish Register, but the marriages are recorded in roughly chronological order and the Watkins-Warman marriage is listed between 18 Dec 1715 and 14 Feb 1715/6.{AACR:26}

John Watkins recorded his cattle mark on 14 Feb 1706.{AALR: WT#2:457}

On 15 May 1740, Stephen Warman, age c70, made a will naming his dau. Mary, wife of John Watkins, and his grandchildren John, Stephen, Mary, and Hester Watkins.{MWB 22:532}

---

[62] His descendants are traced in Elise Jourdan's *Early Families of Southern Maryland* (Westminster: Family Line Publications, 1993), 2:34ff.

On 26 Aug 1743, John and Mary Watkins signed the inventory of Francis Warman, of AA Co., as next of kin.{MINV 28:396}

The inventory of John Watkins was made on 29 Dec 1743 by Richard Harwood and Ferdinando Battee, who found that the personal property was worth £2088.10.2. Caleb Dorsey and Jeremiah Belt signed as creditors, and John Hammond Dorsey and Mary Watkins, Jr., signed as next of kin. Mary Watkins, admx., filed the inventory on 22 May 1744.{MINV 29:118} Mary Watkins filed an additional list of debts due the estate worth £160.12.10.{MINV 30:221}

Mary (Warman) Watkins d. testate in 1768.{MWB 36:307} Her estate was inv. on 6 May 1768 by Richard Richardson and Joseph Cowman, who valued her personal property at £513.10.3. Samuel Watkins and B. Thompson signed as creditors, and Nicholas Watkins and Elizabeth Smith signed as next of kin. The inventory was filed on 17 March 1769 by Stephen Watkins, exec.{MINV 99:327}

John and Mary were the parents of{AACR:32, 34, 38, 42, 47, 48, 172, 197}: ELIZABETH, b. 8 March 1715[/6], bapt. 15 April 1716, bur. 3 March 1733; SARAH, b. 3 July 1718, bapt. 6 Aug 1718; ANN, b. 4 Jan 1720, bapt. 17 Sep 1722; FRANCES, b. 1 May 1723, bapt. 25 July 1724, m. John Hammond Dorsey; MARY, b. 10 May 1725; JOHN, b. 7 Sep 1727, bapt. 31 Oct 1727; HESTER, b. 26 Jan 1729; JANE, b. 22 June 1732; STEPHEN, b. 27 June 1735, m. Eleanor Boyd on 1 Feb 1757 in St. James Parish; and (possibly) NICHOLAS, m. Peggy Boyd.

5.   JOHN WATKINS, son of John (4) and Mary (Warman) Watkins, was b. 1727, and m. Esther Belt.

They were the parents of{AACR:54, 55, 57}: JOHN, b. 6 Nov 1753; MARY ANN, b. 6 May 1756; STEPHEN, b. 28 Feb 1758; ELIZABETH, b. 4 June 1760; MARGARET, b. 5 June 1767, she is almost certainly the Margaret who m. Ezekiel Phelps in 1794.

THE WATTS FAMILY

1.   FRANCIS WATTS was transported to MD c1651.{MPL 4: 66} He m. Sarah (N), who survived him. Alecia Tipton, of Redding, CA, in a letter to the compiler, suggests she m. 2nd, William Disney (his first wife).

On 10 Aug 1680, Thomas Besson, of the Ridge, AA Co., conv. to Francis Watts, planter, 50 a. of *Bessonton*, which was originally granted to Capt. Thomas Besson for 350 a., and deeded by Capt. Thomas Besson and his wife Hester to Thomas Besson, Jr., on 7 June 1663.{AALR IH#3:110} Stephen Warman requested that the deed from Besson to Watts be recorded.{AALR IH#3:109}

Francis Watts d. in AA Co. leaving a will dated 2 Dec 1684. In his will, he named his wife Sarah, daus. Sarah, Eliza, and Susan, and sons Francis and John. The latter two were to share equally 100 a. *Bachelor's Delight* on the Wye River.{MWB 4:195}

The estate of Francis Watts, of AA Co., was inv. on 2 March 1685 by Richard Alding and Robert Ward. Legatees included his daus. Sarah, Elizabeth, and Susanna. James Murrin, John Rastricke, John Sanders, and John Purdy were debtors.{INAC 8:450}

On 31 Oct 1685, John Greene, of AA Co., planter, conv. to Francis and John Watts, sons of Francis Watts, of AA Co., dec., 100 a. on Wye River in TA Co. called *Batchelor's Delight,* which was granted to William Snaggs and conv. by him to Richard Snowden, and by Snowden to sd. Greene.{TALR 5:58}

Francis and his wife Sarah (N) were the parents of: FRANCIS; JOHN; SARAH (She is probably the Sarah Warman, wife of Stephen, and dau. of Francis and Sarah Watts, bapt. 25 Sep 1698 as an adult in All Hallows Parish.){AACR:8}; ELIZA, may have m. George Miller; and SUSAN(NA), dau. of Francis and Sarah, bapt. 21 Aug 1698 in All Hallows Parish.{AACR:8}

2.   FRANCIS WATTS, son of Francis (1) and Sarah, was living on 11 Oct 1696 when he and Stephen Warman wit. the will of David Steward, 80 years old, of AA Co.{MWB 7:281} He d. in AA Co. by 1711. He m. Margaret (N), who m. as her second husband, John Hardin.

Francis Watts' personal estate was appraised in 1711 by James Mouat and William Brewer and valued at £92.0.9. John Warman signed as one of the approvers, and Stephen Warman signed as next of kin. {INAC 33A:66}

The estate of Francis Watts was admin. on 1 Aug 1713 by the admx., Margaret Hardin, wife of John Hardin. An inventory of £92.0.9 was mentioned.{INAC 34:28}

On 14 Nov 1716, John Hardin, William Brewer, and William Purdy, of AA Co., posted bond they would pay Sarah Watts, John Watts, Francis Watts, Richard Watts, and William Watts the balance of £80.18.4 due them from the estate of their father, Francis Watts.{AALR IB#2:349}

Francis and Margaret had the following children, all b. in All Hallows Parish{AACR:4, 8, 13, 14, 15, 17, 23, 40, 195}: SARAH, b. 20 Dec 1696; JOHN, b. 23 Aug 1699; FRANCIS, b. 23 May 1702, bur. 8 Oct 1702; FRANCIS, bapt. 6 Sep 1702, probably d. young; FRANCIS, b. 7 Dec 1703; RICHARD, b. 24 Nov 1706, bapt. 19 Aug 1712; and WILLIAM, bapt. 3 Nov and bur. 9 Nov 1712.

3.   JOHN WATTS, son of Francis (1) and Sarah, is probably the John who m. Mary Moss, als. Kattrick, on 31 Oct 1700.{AACR:13} She may be

the Mary Watts, wife of John, who was bur. 25 April 1712.{AACR:31}

4.   JOHN WATTS, son of Francis (2) and Margaret, was b. 23 Aug
1699, and d. in AA Co. by Jan 1747. He m. Elizabeth Disney on 5 June
1723 in All Hallows Parish.{AACR:36}
    John Watts, of AA Co., planter, d. leaving a will dated 3 May
1747 and proved 13 Jan 1747. He left his personal estate to his sons
Richard and John, and dau. Margaret Perkins. John Cowman was
appointed guardian to Richard and John and was to put them to some
good trade. His son-in-law, John Perkins, was named exec.{MWB 25:314}
    John and Elizabeth were the parents of the following children, b.
in All Hallows Parish{AACR:40, 43, 46, 48}: MARGARET, m. John Perkins, b.
21 March 1724; SARAH, b. 31 May 1726; ELIZABETH, bapt. Feb
1728; FRANCIS, b. 8 Oct 1731, bur. 19 Sep 1734; RICHARD; and
JOHN.

5.   RICHARD WATTS, son of Francis (2) and Margaret, was b. 24
Nov 1706, and bapt. 19 Aug 1712. He is probably the Richard Watts who
m. Susanna Norcraft on 14 Feb 1731 in All Hallows Parish.{AACR:46}
    Richard and Susan were the parents of{AACR:48}: ELIZABETH, b. 6
Aug 1733.

Unplaced

WATTS, JOHN, m. Anne Jollett on 24 Dec 1703 in All Hallows Parish.
{AACR;18} He is probably the John Watts who d. in AA Co. leaving a will
dated 29 Oct 1714 and proved 5 Jan 1714, leaving all his estate in
England and MD to his wife Anne, extx. Thomas Moore and Constance
Young wit. the will.{MWB 13:740}

WATTS, JOHN, m. Love Meek on 3 Feb 1714/5 in St. Anne's Parish.
{B:74}

WATTS, JOHN, m. Jane Aldridge. They were the parents of{AACR:38}:
JOHN, b. 15 Oct 1723, bapt. 3 June 1724 in All Hallows Parish.

WATTS, JOHN, was bur. in All Hallows Parish on 24 Aug 1730.
{AACR:44}

WATTS, JOHN, m. Mary (N). They were the parents of{AACR:56}:
RICHARD, b. 22 Aug 1765 in All Hallows Parish.

WATTS, JOHN, d. in AA Co. leaving a will dated Nov 1772 and proved 7 Dec 1775, leaving personalty to his wife, a looking glass to Rachel Pickett, and mentioning his children, who were to have the residue of his estate. Abraham Johnson and Greenbury Ridgely were execs.{MWB 40:568}

WATTS, JOSHUA, was in AA Co. by 29 June 1759 when he purchased *Trusty Friend* from Charles Carroll. He also owned *Worthington's Beginning* and *Bold Venture*. He d. in 1782 leaving a wife Rachel and children{Query in *Baltimore Sun,* 12 April 1908}: SAMUEL; BETSY; ANNE; MARY; SUSANNA; RACHEL; HENRY; and NATHAN.

THE WESTALL FAMILY

Refs.: A. Julian Hurst Jacob. *Jacob and Allied Families.* (Philadelphia: 1945).

1.　GEORGE WESTALL came to MD by 1659, and d. by March 1673. His wife's name has not been discovered.
　　He is not listed in Skordas, but on 2 May 1659 he was granted 800 a. called *Scorton.* Westall d. by 10 March 1673.{AALR WT#1:270}
　　No will, inventory, or administration account has been found.
　　He was the father of at least one son{A}: GEORGE.

2.　GEORGE WESTALL, son of George, was b. by 1659, and, as "Housekeeper of All Hallows Parish," was bur. 17 March 1701.{AACR:14} Circa 1678/9 he m. Sarah Wade, dau. of Robert Wade.{A}
　　On 10 March 1673, George Westall sold to William Burgess the tract *Scorton,* 800 a., which had been granted George's father, George Westall, Sr.{AALR WT#1:270}
　　On 12 Dec 1676, Edward Mariarte and wife Honour conv. to John Sellman and George Westall 175 a. called *Covill's Folly.* Sometime later, both Sellman and Westall were dead, and Elizabeth Sellman, widow and extx. of John Sellman, was asked to bring the deed into court so it could be re-recorded for the purpose of confirming the estate of John Westall, orphan of George Westall.{AALR IH#3:79}
　　Robert Wade, of South River, AA Co., d. leaving a will dated 28 Sep 1694 and proved 13 Nov 1694. He left personalty to his grandchild, Jane Westall, and named his "son" George Westall as one of the overseers. George and Sarah Westall wit. the will.{MWB 7:6}
　　George Westall, of AA Co., d. leaving a will dated 1 April 1701 and proved 14 May 1702. He left his dwell. plant. to his wife Sarah, extx., for life, and then to his youngest son John, and if he d. to the testator's daus. Alice and Rachel. Sons Richard and George and heirs

were to have 350 a. *Jackson's Venture* on Coppot's Creek in BA Co. Dau.
Sarah, wife of Thomas Cheney, and their children Eliza and Thomas
were left personalty. The residue of his estate was to go to wife Sarah,
and children Jane, Richard, George, Alice, Rachel, and John. Overseers
were to be Leonard Wayman and son-in-law Thomas Cheney. The will
was wit. by Richard Duckett, Chris. Waters, and Walter Phelps, Jr.{MWB
11:191}

George Westall's property was appraised on 13 June 1701 by
Leonard Wayman and Walter Phelps.{INAC 21:389}

By c1707, his orphans still held 350 a. *Jackson's Delight*,
originally surv. 3 June 1685 for John Prindewell.{MRR:76}

George and Sarah were the parents of{A; AACR:2, 5, 7, 12, 17}: SARAH,
b. 31 Aug 1680, m. 19 Aug 1697, Thomas Cheney; JANE, b. 8 Sep 1682,
d. 1748, m. William Ridgely on 4 March 1701; RICHARD, b. 24 April
1689; GEORGE, b. 1 March 1690, m. 1711, Anne Jacob; ALICE, b. 21
Sep 1693, m. 1711, Benjamin Jacob; RACHEL, b. 20 Jan 1695; JOHN,
b. 14 June 1699; and JOSHUA, b. 7 Nov 1701, bapt. 7 Dec 1701, bur. 4
Nov 1702.

3.   GEORGE WESTALL, son of George (2) and Sarah, was b. 1
March 1690, and d. in BA Co. by Oct 1718. He m. Anne Jacob in 1711.
She m. 2nd, by 1720, Hugh Merriken.{A}

George Westall, of BA Co., d. leaving a will dated 23 June 1718
and proved 6 Oct 1718. He left the 365 a. plant. *Jackson's Venture* to his
sons George and Richard. George was to have first choice, but neither
son was to disturb his wife Ann on the plant. Cousin Thomas Bayly and
son John were to have personalty. Wife Ann, extx., was to have the
residue of the estate and the children were to be of age and receive their
portions at age 18. The will was wit. by Joseph Bourton, John Westall,
and John Risteau.{MWB 14:718}

The estate of George Westall was admin. by Ann Merriken, wife
of Hugh Merriken, on 4 May 1720. After all payments were made, the
residue was dist. among the children Ann, George, Richard, and Sarah.
{MDAD 3:18}

George and Ann (Jacob) Westall were the parents of: GEORGE;
RICHARD; JOHN; SARAH, who m. William Fish; and (possibly) ANN.

4.   RICHARD WESTALL, son of George (3) and Anne, was b. 24
April 1689, and d. s.p. by March 1757.

Richard Westall, of AA Co., d. leaving a will dated 17 Jan 1757
and proved 24 March 1757. He named his sister Sarah Fish and her
children Benjamin, William, and Richard Fish. His friends Richard
Jacob, Sr., and Hugh Marchen [Merriken?], Jr., were named execs. The
will was wit. by David Stansbury, of Thomas, Jacob Merriken, and
Sylvanus Pumphrey.{MWB 30:296}

On 8 Aug 1758, the estate of Richard Westall, with a balance of £89.16.9, was dist. by the execs. to Benjamin, Richard, and William Fish, after the death of Sarah Fish.{BFD 2:105}

5.   SARAH WESTALL, dau. of George (3) and Ann, m. William Fish. They were the parents of the following children, b. in St. Margaret's Westminster Parish, AA Co.{AACR:128}: BENJAMIN; RICHARD, b. 17 Sep 1752; and WILLIAM.

THE WOODWARD FAMILY

Refs.: A. McIntire. *Annapolis, Maryland Families.* B: Newman. *Anne Arundel Gentry, Vol. Three.*

1.   WILLIAM WOODWARD, of London, was the father of three sons, who came to MD{FOUW:123}: HENRY; WILLIAM; and ABRAHAM.

2.   HENRY WOODWARD, son of William (1), on 13 Oct 1689, m. at St. Olave's, Southwark, Surrey{IGI} Mary Garrett, dau. of James and Sarah Garrett, late of St. Olave's Street, Southwark, London, and sister of Amos Garrett, b. 1661, first Mayor of Annapolis.
    Henry and Mary settled on the Patuxent, in MD, and they were the parents of{FOUW; MWB 19: 335}: WILLIAM, "the Goldsmith;" MARY, m. Mr. Holmes, of England; ELIZABETH, m. Benjamin Bacon; SARAH, m. C. Calhon, of England; and AMOS.

3.   WILLIAM WOODWARD, son of William (1), of London, m. and had three children{FOUW:123}: ELIZABETH; HANNAH; and WILLIAM.

4.   ABRAHAM WOODWARD, son of William (1), was b. c1685 and d. between 26 Jan and 1 March 1744. He m. 1st, on 3 Dec 1707, Elizabeth Finloes, and 2nd, on 25 Aug 1715, Priscilla (Ruly) Orrick, b. 1690, d. 1773.{A}
    He d. leaving a will signed on 16 Jan 1744 and proved 1 March 1744, naming his wife Priscilla and dau. Rebecca as execs. He left to his son William any interest he had in a dependency in Great Britain which he (the testator) inherited from his own father, William. He named his children Rebecca, Martha, Abraham, Thomas and Priscilla.
{MWB 24:7}
    The estate of Abraham Woodward was appraised on 20 June 1745 by Thomas Davis and Gerard Hopkins who valued his personal property at £350.3.3. William and Rebecca Woodward and Philip Hammond and William Ridgely were mentioned. Priscilla Woodward, extx., filed the inventory on 20 July 1745.{MINV 31:211}

Another inventory valued at £46.1.6 was appraised on 18 Feb 1745 and filed 3 June 1746.{MINV 32:197}

Abraham and Priscilla were the parents of{A; AACR}: WILLIAM, bapt. 6 Dec 1716 at St. Anne's Parish; MARTHA, bapt. 21 March 1718 at All Hallows Parish; REBECCA, bapt. 15 Jan 1722/3 at All Hallows or St. Anne's Parish; MARTHA, bapt. 8 Dec 1726 at St. Anne's Parish; ABRAHAM, bapt. 16 Jan 1729/30 at St. Anne's Parish; THOMAS, bapt. 10 March 1731/2; PRISCILLA, bapt. 16 Feb 1735 at St. Anne's Parish; PRISCILLA, b. 27 Feb 1739, m. William Faris; HENRY; ELIZABETH; and ELEANOR.

5.   WILLIAM WOODWARD, son of Henry (2) and Mary, called "the Goldsmith," "formerly of London," but now of Annapolis, on 28 April 1767 stated that he was the admin. of Elizabeth Guin, of London, widow, who survived a certain Mary Woodward, late of Newington Butts, widow, and he was also bro. and heir-at-law of Elizabeth Bacon, one of the devisees of sd. Elizabeth Guin; on this day he conv. to James Hood, of AA Co., the tract *Baker's Delight*. His wife Jane consented. {PCLR DD#4:190}

William m. Jane (N). They were the parents of{A:126}: WILLIAM, m. Dinah Warfield; and MARIA G., m. Mr. Edmiston, of London.

6.   AMOS WOODWARD, of Henry (2) and Mary, d. 16 March 1734. He m. Achsah Dorsey, dau. of Caleb and Elinor (Warfield) Dorsey, who m. 2nd, Edward Fottrell. Achsah d. intetsate by 12 Feb 1742.{MCHR 8:157}

Amos and Achsah (Dorsey) Woodward were the parents of {FOUW:123}: HENRY; MARY, age 14 in 1742; ELINOR, age 12 in 1742; and ELIZABETH age 8 in 1742.

7.   WILLIAM WOODWARD, son of Abraham (4) and Priscilla, was b. 6 Dec 1716, and d. 1790. He m. Alice Ridgely, dau. of William and Jane (Westall) Ridgely. She m. 1st, Samuel Meek, and 2nd, William Woodward.{B:153}

William and Alice (Ridgely) Woodward were the parents of {FOUW:123; AACR}: JANE, b. 1740, m. 1785, William (or Nelson) Waters, widower; HENRY, m. Mary White; ABRAHAM, bapt. 22 Jan 1744 at St. Anne's Parish, killed in the Revolutionary War; and WILLIAM, Jr., m. Jane Ridgely, dau. of William and Mary (Orrick) Ridgely.

8.   ABRAHAM WOODWARD, son of Abraham (4) and Priscilla, was b. 16 Jan 1730, and is almost certainly the Abraham Woodward who d. in PG Co. leaving a will dated 25 Jan 1774 and proved 26 April 1781.

In his will he named his wife Margaret and children{PG Co. Wills, Box 13, folder 67, MSA}: THOMAS; HENRY; ABRAHAM BOYD; DEBORAH, named co-extx. with her mother; PRISCILLA; SARAH; and MARGARET.

9.   THOMAS WOODWARD, son of Abraham (4) and Priscilla, was bapt. 10 March 1731/2 at St. Anne's Parish.{AACR} He m. Margaret (Waters) Ijams in AA Co. by license dated 21 May 1778.

Thomas and Margaret had{FOUW:126}: NICHOLAS R., b. 1781; ABRAHAM, b. 1783; and PRISCILLA.

10.   WILLIAM WOODWARD, Jr., son of William (7) and Alice (Ridgely), m. Jane Ridgely, dau. of William and Mary (Orrick) Ridgely.

They were the parents of{FOUW:123}: WILLIAM, m. Mary Jacobs and went w.; HENRY, b. 1770; ALICE, m. Stephen Watkins, by AAML 9 Sep 1793; ANNE, m. William Ridgely, by AAML dated 8 Feb 1803; and SARAH, m. Mr. Connand.

11.   ABRAHAM BOYD WOODWARD, son of Abraham (8), m. Priscilla Owens in 1797, so probably cannot be the Abraham b. 1783.

Abraham B. Woodward was surety for the administration of the estate of James Owens, of AA Co., on 13 April 1808. The heirs of Owens were Priscilla Woodward, Polly Shepherd, Nicholas Owens, and James Owens.{AADI JG#2:123}

12.   ABRAHAM WOODWARD, almost certainly son of Thomas (9) and Margaret (Waters), was b. 4 April 1783, and d. 10 Sep 1832. He m. Ann D. Jones on 10 Dec 1807 in PG Co.

On 19 July 1832, A. Woodward and Nicholas R. Woodward wit. the will of Eliza Goodwin.{BAWB 15:54}

Abraham and Ann were the parents of: GEORGE POWELL, b. 4 or 20 Sep 1808; NICHOLAS RIDGELY, b. 26 June 1810; ANN, b. 11 Jan 1813; WILLIAM, b. 24 Aug 1815, d. 26 Oct 1816; ELIZABETH JONES, b. 5 Aug 1817, m. Archibald Russell; JOHN HENRY, b. 29 March 1823; EMILY, b. 27 June 1826, d. 10 Sep 1845; THOMAS, b. 14 March 1829, d. 23 March 1829.

13.   HENRY WOODWARD, son of William (10) and Jane (Ridgely), b. 1770, m. widow Eleanor Turner, dau. of Col. Thomas and Rachel (Duckett) Williams, by AAML dated 13 Feb 1797.

Henry and Eleanor were the parents of{FOUW:123}: JANE MARIA, m. Judge William Henry Baldwin, by AAML dated 6 Oct 1817; WILLIAM, m. Virginia Burneston; HENRY WILLIAMS; and RIGNAL DUCKETT.

14.   GEORGE POWELL WOODWARD, son of Abraham (12) and
Ann (Jones) Woodward, was b. 20 Sep 1808 and d. 5 Nov 1872. On 2
Oct 1833 he m. Elizabeth Gelbach.
    On 12 Sep 1851, Mr. G. P. Woodward and Mrs. Elizabeth
Woodward were admitted members of Second Presbyterian Church, by
certificate from Aisquith St. Presbyterian Church. {Session Minutes of Second
Presbyterian Church, 1846-1874:55}
    On 20 Jan 1855, three children of G. P. and Eliza Woodward were
baptized{Ibid.:87}: ELLA BLANCH; SARAH ANN; and CARRIE
STEWART.

THE WRIGHT FAMILY

1.   HENRY WRIGHT, was b. c1657 and d. in St. Margaret's Parish
on 4 Nov 1742. He gave his age as 74 in 1731.{AALC 2:247} He m. Mary
(N)., who d. in St. Margaret's Parish on 6 Sep 1734.{AACR:138}
    On 9 Aug 1687, Henry Wright purchased from Paul and Elizabeth
Dorrell 100 a. *Asketon*, which had originally been surv. for 230 a.{AALR
IH#2;136} On 14 March 1708, Wright purchased 80 a. *Baker's Increase* and
50 a. *Greenbury* from Thomas and Sarah Reynolds.{AALR PK:35}
    Henry and Mary Wright wit. the will of Maurice Baker, of AA
Co., on 10 Nov 1709.{MWB 11:22}
    On 20 March 1711, John Couzen, formerly of AA Co., and now
of Bucks Co., PA, and wife Rebecca, appointed Henry Wright, yeoman,
as their attorney.{AALR IB#2:28}
    Henry Wright d. in AA Co. leaving a will dated 17 Sep 1742 and
proved 3 March 1742. Son Thomas was to have *Merriken's Purchase,
Point Look Out* and *Huntington Quarter.* Son Dawson was to have 100 a.
Brushy Neck. Son William was to have 60 a. *Summerland's Lot,* 30 a.
Woodcock Nest (at his death to pass to his bro. Dawson). Son John was to
have 225 a. *Maiden's Choice.* Son Benjamin as to have residue of land in
AA Co. Son Henry was to have land on the Eastern Shore of the
Chesapeake Bay. He also named daus. Elizabeth Rockhold, Susannah
Gosnet [Gosnell?], Mary Talbot, Anne Maynard, and Hannah Green, and
granddau. Ruth Gosnet [Gosnell?].{MWB 23:249}
    The estate of Henry Wright, of AA Co., was appraised on 16 July
1743 by Philip Jones and N. Hammond at a value of £243.5.3. Thomas
and Henry Wright signed as next of kin.{MINV 28:268}
    Henry and Mary were the parents of the following children, b. in
St. Margaret's Westminster Parish, AA Co.{AACR:109, 110, 111}: WILLIAM,
b. 20 Nov 1686; ELIZABETH, b. 22 Aug 1694, m. (N) Rockhold;
HENRY, b. Feb 1697; SUSANNA, b. 20 Dec 1699, m. (N) Gosnet
[Gosnell?]; MARY, b. 23 June 1702, m. (N) Talbot; JOHN (twin?), b. 23
Dec 1704;

THOMAS (twin), b. 23 Dec 1704; ANN, b. 6 Feb 1706, m. (N) Maynard; DAWSON, b. 22 June 1709; BENJAMIN, b. 24 Feb 1711; and HANNAH, b. 6 Sep 1714, m. (N) Green.

2.   HENRY WRIGHT, son of Henry (1) and Mary, was b. in Feb 1697, and m. Sarah Hopkins on 23 June 1723 in St. Margaret's Parish, AA Co.{AACR:130}

Henry Wright, Jr., of AA Co., d. leaving a will dated 31 March 1745(?) and proved 14 Feb 1746. In his will, he named his son Person (?) Wright, son Reason, dau. Ann Stinchcomb, and son-in-law Lewis Stinchcom (or Lencom?).{MWB 24:515}

Lewis Stinchcomb, exec., filed the inventory of Henry Wright on 11 May 1747. Peter Jones and Oneal Robosson appraised the personal property at £318.2.3. Doson [i.e., Dawson] and Benjamin Wright signed as next of kin.{MINV 34:282}

Henry and Sarah were the parents of the following children, b. in St. Margaret's Westminster Parish, AA Co.: ANNA, b. 14 Aug 1724 {AACR:113}; PERSON and REASON{MWB 24:515}.

3.   JOHN WRIGHT, son of Henry (1) and Mary, was b. 23 Dec 1704 (twin?), d. in BA Co. by Jan 1744/5.

He left a will dated 29 Nov 1744 and proved 3 Jan 1744/5, leaving 225 a. of *Maiden's Choice* to his cousin John Oram, and named his bro. Cooper Oram as exec.{BAWB 2:20}

On 13 May 1745, his estate was inv. by Thomas Wright. Benjamin Wright signed as next of kin. Cooper Oram was the exec. {MINV 34:3}

4.   THOMAS WRIGHT, son of Henry (1) and Mary, was b. 23 Dec 1704, and d. by Oct 1753. He m. Katherine (N).

Thomas Wright, of AA Co., d. leaving a will dated 21 Aug 1753 and proved 15 Oct 1753. In his will, he named his son Thomas, to have all land except 100 a. left to son Benjamin, but Benjamin was to be under the care of his bro. Thomas. He also named daus. Hannah Jacob, and Constant, Patience, and Mary Wright. Wife Katherine was to be extx. {MWB 28:531}

The estate of Thomas Wright was appraised by John Howard and J. Walker at £784.19.4. Patience Wright and Mary Wright signed as next of kin. Catherine Wright, extx., filed the inventory on 18 Oct 1754.{MINV 57:367}

Catherine Wright, of AA Co., d. leaving a will dated 22 Nov 1761 and proved 6 April 1762. She named her grandsons John Wright and John Boon, son Thomas (exec.), dau.-in-law Mary Wright, dau. Hannah Jacobs, and son Benjamin. The will was wit. by Aaron and Joseph Hawkins and Henry Dorsey, Jr.{MWB 31:676}

Thomas and Katherine were the parents of the following children, b. in St. Margaret's Westminster Parish, AA Co.{AACR:113, 118,120}: HANNAH, b. 11 June 1723, m. (N) Jacob; CONSTANCE, b. 8 Nov 1727 [sic]; WILLIAM, b. 16 April 1727 [sic]; PATIENCE, b. 18 Jan 1731; MARY, b. 19 Jan 1735; and THOMAS, b. 19 June 1740.

5.   DAWSON WRIGHT, son of Henry (1) and Mary, was b. 22 June 1709, and d. by Nov 1755. He m. Elizabeth (N).

Dawson Wright left a will dated 6 Sep 1755 and proved 11 Nov 1755, in which he named his wife Elizabeth. She and his cousin Thomas Wright were to be execs. The will was wit. by Reason Wright and Hamton Robosson.{MWB 30:4}

On 23 Jan 1762, the estate of Dawson Wright was dist. by the widow and admx., who was now the wife of Thomas Rockhold. She was to have the balance of the estate, £69.11.6 for her lifetime, and then it was to pass to his cousin Thomas Wright.{BFD 3:119}

6.   BENJAMIN WRIGHT, son of Henry (1) and Mary, was b. 24 Feb 1711, and d. by Sep 1758. He m. Elizabeth Ledore on 4 March 1735 in St. Margaret's Parish{AACR:131}

Benjamin Wright, of AA Co., d. leaving a will dated 20 April 1758 and proved 5 Sep 1758. He named his children Elizabeth Brown, Mary, Henry, and Benjamin. The extx. was Elizabeth Wright. The will was wit. by Humphrey Boone, Henry Robinson, and Thomas Rockhold. {MWB 30:682}

Benjamin Wright's estate was dist. on 10 Aug 1762 by the extx. Elizabeth Wright, with Philip Pettybone and George Page as sureties. The balance of £438.7.7 was dist. to the widow and the two sons, Henry and Benjamin.{BFD 3:121}

Benjamin and Elizabeth were the parents of the following children, b. in St. Margaret's Westminster Parish, AA Co.{AACR: 116, 117, 119, 120, 123, 138}: THOMAS, d. 19 April 1729; ELIZABETH, b. 13 Dec 1737; THOMAS, b. 11 April 1739; MARY, b. 7 June 1740;[63] REBECCA, b. 20 Dec 1742, d. 11 Sep 1743; and HENRY, b. 5 April 1746.

Unplaced

WRIGHT, THOMAS, m. Diana Evans on 15 July 1708 in St. Anne's Parish, AA Co.{AACR:67} Thomas and Diana were the parents of the

---

[63] She may be the Mary Wright, of Benjamin, who m. Robert Reynolds, of William, on 8 Sep 1763 in St. Anne's Parish.{AACR:104}

following child, b. in All Hallows Parish, AA Co.{AACR:28}: SARAH, b. 23 Nov 1709, bapt. 21 Dec 1709.

WRIGHT, THOMAS, m. Mary (N), who d. 16 Aug 1774 in St. Margaret's.{AACR:140} Thomas and Mary were the parents of the following children, b. in St. Margaret's Westminster Parish, AA Co.{AACR:129}: ELIZABETH, b. 17 May 1768; CATHERINE, b. 17 April 1771; THOMAS, b. 16 Nov 1774 [sic]; and MARY, b. 16 Aug 1774 [sic].

THE WYVIL FAMILY
A Royal Descent and a Lost Baronetcy

Refs.: A: *The Plantagenet Roll of the Blood Royal: The Anne of Exeter Volume.* By the Marquis of Ruvigny and Raineval. (London: 1907) (Reprinted Baltimore: Genealogical Publishing Co., Inc., 1994).

1.   EDWARD III, King of England, was b. 1312, and d. 1377. In 1328, he m. Philippa of Hainault, b. c1309, d. 1369. Among their six children was{A:Table I}: LIONEL.

2.   LIONEL, of Antwerp, Duke of Clarence, K. G., son of Edward III (1) and Philippa of Hainault, was b. 1338, and d. 1368. He m. Lady Elizabeth de Burgh, d. 1363. They were the parents of{A:Table I}: PHILIPPA.

3.   PHILIPPA, of Clarence, dau. of Lionel (2) and Elizabeth (de Burgh), was b. 1355, and d. 1382. In 1368, she m. Edmund de Mortimer, 3rd Earl of March, b. 1352, d. 1381. They were the parents of{A:Table I}: ROGER.

4.   ROGER, 4th Earl of March, son of Edmund Mortimer and Philippa (3), of Clarence, was b. 1374, and d. 1398. He was declared to be heir to the throne of England. He m. Lady Eleanor Holland. They were the parents of{A:Table I}: ANNE.

5.   Lady ANNE MORTIMER, dau. of Roger (4) Mortimer and Eleanor (Holland), m. Richard, Earl of Cambridge (himself a descendant of Edward III), b. c1375, d. 1415. They were the parents of{A:Table I}: RICHARD.

6.   RICHARD, Duke of York, K. G., son of Richard and Anne (5) (Mortimer), was b. 1412, and d. 1460. He m. Lady Cecily Neville, b. 1415, d. 1495. They were the parents of{A:Table I}: King EDWARD IV

(from whom descends the present House of Windsor); King RICHARD III, GEORGE, Duke of Clarence; and ANNE.

7.   Lady ANNE PLANTAGANET, dau. of Richard (6) and Cecily (Neville), of York, was b. 1439, d. 1476. She m. 1st, Henry Holland, Duke of Exeter, who d. 1473, s.p. She m. 2nd, Sir Thomas St. Leger, by whom she had one dau.{A:Table II}: Lady ANNE.

8.   Lady ANNE ST. LEGER, dau. and heiress of Lady Anne (7) Plantaganet and her 2nd husband, Sir Thomas St. Leger, d. 1526. She m. Sir GEORGE MANNERS, 12th Lord Roos, d. 1513. They were the parents of{A:Table II}: Hon. KATHERINE, m. Sir Robert Constable.

9.   Hon. KATHERINE MANNERS m. Sir Robert Constable, of Evringham, who d. 1558. They were the parents of{A:Table XLVII}: Sir MARMADUKE.

10.   Sir MARMADUKE CONSTABLE, of Evringham, son of Sir Robert and Katherine (9) (Manners), d. 1574. He m. The Hon. Jane Conyers and had issue{A:Table XLVII}: KATHERINE.

11.   KATHERINE CONSTABLE, dau. of Sir Marmaduke (10) and Jane (Conyers), d. 1580. She m. Sir Robert Stapylton of Wighill, M. P., b. 1548, d. 1606. They were the parents of{A:Table XLIX}: JANE.

12.   JANE STAPYLTON, dau. of Sir Robert and Katherine (11) (Constable), d. 1656. She m. Christopher Wyvill of Constable Burton, d. 1656. They were the parents of{A:Table LII}: Sir MARMADUKE.

13.   Sir MARMADUKE WYVILL of Constable Burton, 2nd Baronet, son of Christopher and Jane (12) (Stapylton), d. 1648. In 1611, he m. Isabel Gascoigne. Their children included{A:Table LII}: Sir CHRIS-TOPHER; and MARY, m. Arthur Beckwith of Aldboro, York (They were the grandparents of Sir Marmaduke Beckwith, a merchant in VA.).

14.   Sir CHRISTOPHER WYVILL, of Constable Burton, 3rd Baronet, and M. P., son of Sir Marmaduke (13) and Isabel (Gascoigne), was b. 1614, and d. 1681. He m. Lady Ursula D'Arcy, and had{A:Table LII, and p. 549}: Sir WILLIAM.

15.   Sir WILLIAM WYVILL, of Constable Burton, and 4th Baronet, son of Sir Christopher and Ursula (14) (D'Arcy), was b. 1645, and d. c1684. He m. Anne, dau. of James Brooke, of Ellinthorpe, County York. They were the parents of three children including{A:549-550}: D'ARCY.

16.   D'ARCY WYVILL, second son of Sir William (15) and Anne (Brooke), d. 4 Jan 1735, leaving 2 sons{A:550}: WILLIAM; and EDWARD (General Supervisor of Excise at Edinburgh), d. 1791.

17.   WILLIAM WYVILL, son of D'Arcy (16), was b. c1706, and was age 13 on 14 June 1719. He settled in MD, but planned to return to England and is said to have d. on his passage c1750.{A:550}

He actually d. in FR Co. by 1 Aug 1754 when his estate was appraised by Nathan Magruder and Henry Wright Sewell, and valued at £109.15.8. Benjamin Boyd and John Boyd signed as creditors, and Marmaduke and Jane Wyvill signed as next of kin. John Boyd, admin., filed the inventory on 30 March 1754.{MINV 58:95}

After all his debts were paid, there was a balance of £109.15.8 to be dist. among his heirs. On 25 Nov 1756, shares were paid to Jane, Duke [Marmaduke], William, Mary, Elizabeth, and Edward Wyvill, and to John Bewsford, who m. the widow.{BFD 2:44}

Jane Wyvil patented 37 a. called *Sugar Bottom* in PG Co. on 17 Nov 1739.{MPL EI#6:145, LG#C:26}

William m. Elinor Boyd on 14 Feb 1736 in Queen Anne's Parish, PG Co.{Marriage Register:6}

William and Elinor were the parents of{A:550; Register of Queen Anne's Parish:34}: MARMADUKE, b. 19 May ---; EDWARD HALE;

ELIZABETH, b. -- Nov ---; JANE, b. 26 Dec 174-; MARY, b. 27 July 17--; and WILLIAM.

18.   MARMADUKE WYVILL, son of William (17) and Elinor (Boyd), is stated by Ruvigny to have d. 1784 in AA Co.{A:550:but this date appears to be incorrect} Because his cousin, the 7th Baronet, d. unm., he would have been known as the 8th Baronet.

Marmaduke Wyvill m. 1st, at St. James Parish, on 15 March 1764, Harriet Rate, and 2nd, on 15 Oct 1775, Susanna Burgess. {AACR:171,172} He had two sons and three daus. by his first wife, and two sons and three daus. by his second wife. His children included {A:550; AACR:172} (by Harriet): DARCY, b. 16 April 1766; ELINOR, b. 29 April 1768; MARMADUKE, b. 5 Feb 1771, d. 1808; ANN, b. 7 May 1773; JANE, 12 March 1776; (by Susanna): ELIZABETH, b. 12 Oct 1776; SUSANNA, b. 20 Oct 1778; WALTER, b. 4 Feb 1781, bur. Herring Creek Church; MARY, b. 12 May 1782; MATILDA, b. 4 Feb 1784; SARAH, b. 2 March 1787; WILLIAM, b. 5 March, d. 6 March 1789; BENJAMIN, b. 5 March, d. 20 March 1789; HAIL, b. 4 Sep 1790; and PRISCILLA, b. 17 Dec 1792.

11.   EDWARD HALE WYVILL, son of William and Elinor (Boyd) Wyvill, m. Susannah (N).

They were the parents of{AACR:172}: WILLIAM CAMDEN, b. 27 Jan 1771; HENRY, b. 23 Dec 1773; and HALE, b. 3 March 1776.

12.   WILLIAM WYVILL, son of William and Elinor (Boyd) Wyvill, m. Sarah Burgess on 22 June 1777.{AACR:172}

They were the parents of the following children, whose births are recorded in St. James Parish{AACR:142}: JOHN BURGESS, b. 20 May 1778; WILLIAM BOYD, b. 21 Sep 1779; SARAH, b. 12 July 1781; and MARMADUKE, b. 24 Jan 1784, bur. 7 Sep 178-(?).

Unplaced

WYVILL, WILLIAM, d. in CE Co. by 14 July 1710, when his estate was admin. by Col. Richard Tilghman, admin. of Michel Earle, original admin. of the dec. An inventory of £106.13.10 was mentioned.{INAC 31:274}

INDEX

268

James, 195
Jane, 195
Joseph, 124
Joshua, 201
Margaret, 201
Mary, 195
Samuel, 110
Sarah, 120, 205
Sarah Ann, 110, 112
Susan, 193, 201
Susanna, 195
Susannah, 120
William, 120, 193, 194, 195
ANDREW, John, 88
ANDREWE, John, 220
ANDREWS, William, 185
ANGLES, THE, 145
ANN'S DOWRY, 134
ANYTHING, 20, 34
AQUILA'S RESERVE, 67, 72
ARABIA PETREA, 147
ARCHER HAYS, 99
ARDES, George, 92
ARMSTRONG, John, 83
 Mary, 78
ARNOLD, George, 51
 Mary Ann, 35, 50
 Miss, 51
 Sarah, 41
 Sarah Ann, 50, 51
ARNOLD'S GRAY, 145
ARTHUR, Henry, 91
ARUNDEL, Lady Anne, v
ASHBAW, Henry, 161
ASHBY, 133
ASHBY'S ADDITION, 133
ASHER, Anthony, 134
ASIZ, Ambrose, 134
ASKETON, 259
ATKINS, John, 225
ATTLEE, James C., 36
ATWOOD, Ann, 97
 Henry, 97
 Jane, 97
 Mary, xiii
AUCHER, Elizabeth, xxii
 Sir Edward, xxiii

AULD, Dawson, 111
 Elenor Ellen, 111
AUSTIN, Henry, 99, 130
AVERY, John, 210
AVERY'S DESIRE, 210

-B-
BABBS, James, 169
BACHELOR'S CHANCE, 198
BACHELOR'S DELIGHT, 252
BACHELOR'S GOOD LUCK, 147
BACHELOR'S INHERITANCE, 139
BACHELOR'S REFUGE, 37
BACHELOR'S VINEYARD, 213
BACON, Benjamin, 256
 Elizabeth, 256, 257
BADGER, Matilda P., 118
BAGBIE, Charity, 244
 John, 244
BAGLEY, Elizabeth, xx
BAHN, Frederick, xiv
 John, xii
 Julian, xi
BAILE, Sarah, 51
BAILEY, Betty, 28, 40
 Elizabeth, 28, 40
 George, 2
 John, 160
 Robert, 28, 40
 Samantha Jane, 28, 40
 Susan, 40, xvi
BAINES, Cecilia, 200
 Moses, 200
BAKER, Ann, 1
 Catherine, 53
 Elizabeth, 36
 Marcella, 36, 53
 Maria, xii
 Martha, 224
 Maurice, 122, 123, 222, 259
 Nicholas, 86
 Samuel, 36, 53
 Sarah, xiii
 Thomas, 1
BAKER'S DELIGHT, 257

Cordelia, 15, 16, 32, 48
Cynthia, 25, 39
Daniel, 38
David, 18, 33
David Thomas, 46
Dawson, 33, 50
Delila, 25
Delilah, 25
Dennis, 23, 36, 37
Dora, 47
Dorothy Elizabeth, ix
Dorsey, 15, 30, 44, 45, xv, 175
Eamaline, 45
Edward S., 32
Eleanor, 14, 20, 34
Elenora, 34
Eli, 34
Elias, 14
Elijah, 9, 14, 22, 23, 24, 34, 37
Elisha, 16, 22, 32, 36, 48
Elivira, 48
Eliza, 30, 37, 46
Eliza A., 41
Eliza E., 46
Elizabeth, 9, 16, 22, 24, 30, 31,
  32, 33, 35, 36, 39, 42, 43, 45,
  46, 48, 49, 51, 52, 53, xi
Elizabeth A., 41
Elizabeth Ann, 39, 45
Elizabeth Eleanor, 40
Ellen, 52
Ellen I., 46
Ellis, 9, 22, 23, 24
Elmer Francis, ix
Elvira, 35, 53
Elvira A., 48
Emily Lain, 46
Emma E., 46
Emmaline, 43
Emory, 46
Ephraim, 27, 38, 39
Euphemia, 32, 48
Eurith, 42, 45
Ezekial, 11
Ezekiel, 4, 5, 11, 14, 29
F. Washington, 52
Fanceanna, 49

Fanny, 28
Florence, 46
Franceanna, 49
Frances, 53
Francina, 48
Francis A., 48
Francis M., 46
Frederick Mortimer, 40
G. F., 38
Garland Bradford, 39
Gates, 14
Gathers, 13, 28
George, 47, 16, 32, 42, 44
George F., 38
George W., 47, 49
George Washington, 49
Hammutal, 8, 14, 15, 29, 30
Hamutal, 30
Hannah, 5, 6, 14, 15, 16, 17, 22,
  29, 30, 31, 33
Hannah C., 46
Harriet, 16, 27, 31, 40, 47, 48
Harrison, 39
Helen, 27
Henrietta, 25
Henry, 5, 6, 11, 14, 29, 30, 31, 43
Honor, 33, 50, xvii
Honora, 50
J., 19
Jabez, 44
Jabez Nelson, x
James, 2, 3, 4, 5, 6, 7, 8, 9, 10, 16,
  17, 18, 19, 20, 21, 23, 29, 31,
  32, 33, 36, 38, 210, 213, xvii
James A., 30, 46, 47
James Albert, 46
James F. Asbury, 53
James Francis Asbury, 36
James G., 39
James H., 46
James Peter, 35, 51
James W., 49
Jane, 13, 26, 27, 51
Jemima, 43
Jesse H., 48
JoAnne, viii

GAILE, Edward, xxix
Ruth, xxix
GAITHER, Beale, 173
Benjamin, 175, 193
Dennis, 110
Edward, 174, 195, 210
Elizabeth, 110
Henry, 174
John, 61
Leah, 195
Mercy, 173
Rachel, 107, 110, 195
Ruth, 61
Vachel, 196
GALE, Martina, xxviii
GALLOP EMMA, Horace J., x
GALLOWAY, Katherine, 165
Samuel, 167, 231, 250
GALT, Alexander, 145
GAMBRELL, Ann, 169
GAMBRILL, Joshua, 170
GANTT, Priscilla, 72
GARDINER, Christopher, 166
George, 146
GARDNER, Ann, 117
Ann M., 112
Emily Malaily, 112
John, 112, 124
S. Norman, 49
GARLAND, Samuel, 142
GARRETT, Amos, 135, 172, 189,
228, 229, 231, 232, 256
Barbara, xxii
Dennis, xxii
James, 256
Joanna, xx
Mary, 256
Sarah, 256
GARRISON, Elizabeth, 121
Frenetta, 131
GARTRELL, John, 93
GASCOIGNE, Isabel, 263
GASSAWAY, Ann, 250, xxix
Anna, xxvii
Anne, 80, 250, xxviii
Hester, 133

John, 79
Michael, 174
Nicholas, 80, 81, 105, 133, 134,
250, xxviii
Thomas, 11, 79, 174, xxix
GATER, John, 83
GATHER, John, 191
GATRIL, Mary, 73
GELBACH, Elizabeth, 259
GEORGE, DUKE OF
CLARENCE, 263
GEORGE'S PARK, 91
GERAR, 143
GERINGER, Adam, xviii
Elizabeth, xvi
GERLICK, Mary, 13, 28
GERRARD, Anne, xxiii
GHISELIN, Cesar, 61
GIBB, Carson, 177
GIBBONS, Martha A., 112
GIBBS, Edward, 65
Henry, 65
Mary, 182
GILCHRIST, Robert, 9
GILES, Cassandra, 146
Jacob, 131, 242
John, 129, 146, 187
Louis, 195
Louis F., 191
Rachel, 129
Sarah, 146
GILLESPIE, Elenora, 34
Robert, 34
GILLIS, Ezekiel, 156
Hamlet, 37
Henry, 223
Mary, 147
Pantus, 37
GIST, Joshua, 36
GITTINGS, Benjamin, 68
Kinsey, 68
GLAZE, Eleanor, 209
William, 68
GLOVER, Anna, 24
Asa, 24
Azel, 24

William H., 41
HUGHS, Mathias, 135
  Thomas, 123, 145, 226
HUGHSTON, Edward, 219
HUISH, Catherine, 31
HUMPHREYS, Mary, 117
  Susannah, 176
HUNT, Job, 146
  Margaret, 146
  William, 91
HUNTER, Fanny, 77
  James, 206
HUNTING WORTH, 87
HUNTINGTON QUARTER, 259
HUNTSMAN, John, 34
  Matilda, 34
HURST, Francis, 171
  John, 184
HUSBAND, Elizabeth, 147
  William, 147
HUSK, John, 248
HUTCHINS, Elizabeth, 90
  Francis, 90
HUTTON, Mary, 74, 82
  Samuel, 17, 33
  Thomas, 74, 81
  William, 82
HYDE, Col., 18
HYNEMAN, Ann, 26, 37
HYSELL, Betty, 28, 40
  Elizabeth, 28, 40

-I-
IGLEHART, Ann, 136, 138
  Ann Eliza, 138
  Anne, 136, 137
  Cornelius, 136
  Edward, 136
  Frances, 138
  John Wilson, 103
  Matilda, 103
  Nancy, 137
  Sarah T., 138
  Sophia, 136
  T., 137
  Tilghman, 136, 137

  Tilghman H., 138
  Trueman, 137
  William A., 138
  William Augustus, 138
IJAMS, Ann, 117
  Elizabeth, 117
  John, 92, 108
  Margaret, 258
  Mary, 120
  Plummer, 117
  Richard, 175
  Ruth, 117
  Thomas, 175
INDIAN RANGE, 60
INGHAMBRIXON, Hans, 122
INGLESBY, Alicia M., 200
  Cecilia, 200
  William, 200
INGRAM, John, 141
  Mary, 141
INTENT, 236
INTEREST, 237
INVASION, THE, 6, 14, 15, 20,
  29, 34
INVASIONS, THE, 34
ISAAC, Edward, xxx
  Joseph, xxix
  Margaret, xxix
  Richard, xxix, xxxi, xxviii
  Sarah, xxvii
ISAACKE, Elizabeth, xxx
  Richard, xxx
ISAACS, Richard, 155
IVY, Daniel, 91

-J-
JACKS, Barbara, 215
  Eliza, 215
  Elizabeth, 215
  Thomas, 215
JACKSON, Jacob, 182
  James, 81
  John, 81
  Melvina, 38
  Sarah, 81, xi
JACKSON'S CHANCE, 81

Anne, 250
Benjamin, 118
Blanch, 158
Blanche, 158
Charles, 242
Dorothy, 158
Elizabeth, 60, 73, 77, 208, 209
Emily, 118
Hanbury, 209
Hannah, 158
Jane, 94, 157, 158, 159
John, 158, 159
Jonathan, 125
Lewis, 130
Margery, 158
Mary, 62, 63, 158, 159, 223, 224
Mary Ann, 112
Morgan, 157, 158, 159
Peter, 260
Philip, 171, 223, 224, 259
Priscilla, 159
Richard, 167, 250, xxvii
Sarah, 126, 130, 159
Susan, 159
Susanna, 159
Sybil, 158
Thomas, 81
William, 62, 63, 94, 158, 159,
215
JONES' VENTURE, 147
JONHSON, Abraham, 254
JORDAIN, Charity, 245
John, 245
JORDAINE, John, 244
JOSEPH, 212
JOSHUA'A REFUGE, 7
JOSHUA'S REFUGE, 8
JOURDAN, Elise, 226, 227, 250
Elise Greenup, 63, vi
JOURNEY, William, 183
JOY, Edmund, 128
JOYCE, Abel, 162
Ann, 160, 161
Anna Maria, 162
Anne, 162
Basil, 161

Cheney, 161
China, 160
Elijah, 160, 161
Elinor, 160, 161
Eliza, 160
Elizabeth, 160, 161
Fanney, 161
Henrietta, 160
Henry, 161
Honor, 162
Jacob, 161
John, 159, 160, 162
Joseph, 162
Joshua, 162
Leuraner, 161
Nathan, 162
Rachel, 161, 162
Rebecca, 162
Richard, 161, 162
Sarah, 160, 162
Steven, 162
Susannah, 159
Thomas, 160, 161, 162
William, 161
Zachariah, 161
JUBB, Robert, 88, 171
JUDD, Jane, 83
Michael, 83

-K-
KATTRICK, Mary, 252
KEECH, Ann, 176
Courts, 176
George, 176
James, 176
KEELY, John, 58
Mary, 58
KEENE, Marg't, 178
Richard, 178
KEITH, Isaiah, 25
KELLAR, Isaac, 44
Susan, 44
KELLER, Maria Barbara, xvii
KELLY, J. Reaney, 247
KENARD, Joseph, 195
KENDALL, John, 164

309

Pretiotia, 245, 246
Pretitia, 245
Samuel, 90, 117
Sarah, 90
Thomas, 90
LANG, Mary, 197
LANGFILL, Francis, 13
LANGFITT, Francis, 27
Jane, 13, 27
Mary, 13, 27
LANHAM, Archy, 71
Dorothy, xxviii
Elizabeth, xxvi
John, xxvii
Richard, xxvii
LARENDER, Elizabeth, 176
LARKIN, Thomas, 57, 167
LARKINS, Samuel, 175
Sarah, 175
LARKIN'S CHOICE, 208
LASHLEY, John, 66
LAURENCE, John, 6
LAUS, William, 216
LAWRENCE, Benjamin, 65, 142,
250
David, 173
Elizabeth, 173
Ellen, 173
Frances, 173
Francis, 173
Leaven, 17
Levin, 7
Lucy, 65, 67, 68
Margaret, 173
Mary, 173
Sarah, 68
William, 173
LAWRENCE'S PLEASANT
VALLEYS, 36
LAWRENSON, Elizabeth, 201
LAWSON, John, 82
LEAGUE, John, 158
LEATHERWOOD, Elizabeth, 37
LECKE, Joseph, 108
LEDORE, Elizabeth, 261
LEE, Deborah, 152

Edward, 92
James, 131
Lewis, 92
LEEK, Henry, 105, 107
LEEKE, Henry, 108
LEFFELS, Ann, 106
LEISURE, Eliza, 110
LEMON, Elextious, 143
LENCOM, Lewis, 260
LENDALL, Pearce, 186
Timothy, 186
LENHAM, Moses, 176
LENHART, Anna Maria, xxvi
Johan Peter, xxvii
Maria Margaretha, xxvii
Susanna, xxv
Wilhelm, xxvi
LESCALEET, Susan, 41
LESTER, Ann, xxvii, xxviii
Mary, xxvi
Peter, xxvii
LESURE, Nancy, 14
Nancy Pearre, 14, 29
LEVEL, THE, 155
LEWIN, Lewis, 227, 241
Mary, 227
Richard, 227
LEWIS,
Anne, xxiii
Catherine, 119
Henry, 83, 181
James, 105, 135
Job, 1
Keely, 59
Thomas, 105
LEWUR, James, 105
LIGHTFOOT, Rebecca, 64
Thomas, 64
LIGON, Mary Tolley, 49
Sarah Anne, 49
Thomas Watkins, 49
LINDSAY, Amelia, 52
Elizabeth, 35
Hamilton, 52
Hammutal, 14
John, 14, 35, 51

MCCOLLUM, James, 135
MCCORMICK, Anna Maria, 76
MACCUBBIN, James, 196
 Nicholas, 195, 198, 235
 Samuel, 215
 William, 240
 Zachariah, 243, 126
MCCULLOCH, James, 239
MACDANNAN, James, 227
MCDONALD, Harriet, 27, 40
 Samuel, 27, 40
MCDONNELL, Za., 135
MCDOUGAL, Charity, 34
MACGILL, Rev., 24
 Sarah Eleanor, 77
MCGLOCKLIN, Jonathan, 81
MCINTIRE, Elizabeth, 39
MCINTYRE, Elizabeth, 39
 James, 39
MACK, Noreen, 105
MACKALL, James J., 217
MACKBEE, James, 160
MACKDANNAN, James, 226
 John, 96
 Sophia, 96
MACKIERNAN, Alicia, 200
MACKILWAIN, Robert, 82
MCKINSEY, Folger, 35
MACKUBIN, James, 200
MCLOCKLAND, Jonathan, 81
MCMECHEN, David, 15
MACNEMARA, Michael, 91
MADDOX, Samuel, 63
MADDY, Emily, xii
MAGILL, Elizabeth, 70
 John, 70
MAGRUDER, Jeremiah, 85
 Joseph, 73
 Lloyd Belt, 73
 Mary, 73
 Nathan, 264
 Susan, 72
MAHONEY, Mary, xxiv
MAIDEN'S CHOICE, 259, 260
MAIDEN'S DAIRY, 142
MAIDEN'S DOWRY, 143

MALLONEE, Edith, 113
MALLONNEE, Achsah, 230
 Leonard, 230
MALLS, Mary, 77
MALONE, Lucy, 67
MANLY, Ann Willet, 209
MANNERS, Anne, 263
 Honorable Katherine, 263
 Sir George, 263
MANNING, Elizabeth, 188
MANSELL, Samuel, 209, 212
MAN___, Sam, 187
MARBURY, Luke, 176
MARCHEN, Hugh, 255
MARHS'S SEAT, 162
MARIARTE, Edward, 92, 254
 Elinor, 165
 Honour, 254
 John, 92
 Rachel, 92
MARRIOTT, Ann, 169
 Anne, 170
 Augustin, 169
 Augustine, 169, 170, 213, 229
 Edward, 220
 Elizabeth, 169, 170
 Emanuel, 169
 Hamutal, 170
 John, 1, 168, 169, 170, 229
 Joseph, 169, 170
 Mary, 169, 170, 228, 229, 230
 Rachel, 169, 170
 Samuel, 229
 Sarah, 1, 168, 169, 170, 213
 Silvanus, 169, 170, 229
 Sylvanus, 169, 170
 Thomas, 170
 Thomas Davis, 169
MARRYAT, Edward, 220
MARRYOTT, John, 220
 William, 220
MARSH, Benjamin, 180
 Thomas, 87
 William, 235
MARSH HUNDRED, 74
MARSHAL, Rachel, xiv

314

Mary, 166, 252
Robert, 178
MOUAT, James, 57, 252
Sarah, 57
MOUATT, J., 193
MOUNT PLEASANT, 9
MOXEY, Debbie, xxxiii
MUENCH, Johann Peter, xviii
Johann Philip, xx
Maria Christina Barbara, xviii
MUIRRAY, James, xix
MULLICAN, Thomas, 69
MULLIKEN, Charity, 65
MULLIKIN, Charity, 65, 165
James, 65
MUMFORD, Ann, xxii
Edward, xxii
Joseph, 124
Sarah, xxii
MURDOCK, Ann, 70
John, 70
MURPHY, George, 240
MURRAY, Jabex, xvii
Jabez, xiii
John, xv
Kezia, xi
MURRIN, James, 252
MURROE, Richard, 190
MUSBROVE, Benjamin, 176
MUSGRAVE, Benjamin, 176
Charles, 176
Elizabeth, 176
Harrison, 176
Katherine, 176
Mary, 176, 177
Susanna, 177
MUSGROVE, Abraham, 175
Amos, 175
Anne, 174, 175
Anthony, 174, 175
Catherine, 176
Charles, 176
Delilah, 175
Elizabeth, 175
Harrison, 176
Joanna, 174
John, 30, 174, 175, xvii

Lycia Margaret, 176
Lydia, 30, 44, 45, xv
Margaret, 174
Mary, 174, 177
Nathan, 175
Rachel, 9, 22, 175
Samuel, 9, 22, 174, 175
Sarah, 175
Sophia, 31
Stephen, 31, 175
Zachariah, 175
___, 175

-N-
NANJEMOY, 66, 246, 244
NANJEMY, 67
NATHAN'S MORSEL, 23
NEADE, John, 171
NEAL, George, 146
NEALE, Jacob, 87
James, 27
NEAL'S DELIGHT, 94
NEAVE, Robert, 186
NEGLECT STEWARD'S
 CHANCE, 234
NEIFE, Elizabeth, 186
Robert, 186
NEIFE'S CHOICE, 186
NELSON, Ann, 157
Burgess, 174
Dorcas, 101
Hancelip, 101
Sarah, 174
NEVILLE, Lady Cecily, 262
NEW YEAR'S GIFT, 5
NEW YEARS' PURCHASE, 244
NEWMAN, Alexander, xi
Anne, xi
George, 203
Harry Wright, vi, 115, 118, 191,
 207, 247, xxxii
John, xiii
Mary Anne, x
NICHELL, Robert, 177
Samuel, 177
NICHOLAS, Sarah, 178
William, 178

NICHOLES, Jane, 179
 William, 179
NICHOLL, William, 178
NICHOLLS, Samuel, 179
 Samuell, 179
 William, 178, 179
NICHOLS, Ann, 26, 37
 Benjamin Franklin, 138, 181,
  xxiv
 Isaac, 178
 Jeremiah, 180, 181
 John, 26, 37, 178
 Martin, 180, 181
 Mary Jane, 138
 Nelson Reed, 179, 218
 Priscilla, 217, 218
 Rachel, 180, 181
 Robert, 177, 178, 179, 180, 181,
  218, xxv, xxvii
 Rosalie, xxiv
 Samuel, 177, 178, 179, 180, 181,
  217, 218, xxv
 Sarah, 178, 179, 180, 181, xxvi
 Susan, 181
 William, 177, 178, 179, 180,
  xxvi
NICHOLSON, Benjamin, 109
 Elizabeth, 109
 John, 61, 168, 179
 Nicholas, 143
 Rachel, 152
 Rebecca, 61
 Susanna, 152
NICKLER'S HUNTING
  QUARTER, 160
NICKOLLS, Samuel, 177
NICOLS, Priscilla, 217
NISWONGER, Ellen, 52
 Samuel, 52
 Sarah, 52
NIXON, Elizabeth, 71
NOBLE, Susannah, 84
NORCRAFT, Susanna, 253
NORMAN, Benjamin, 182, 183,
  184, 185
 Dorothye, 220

Eleanor, 184, 185
Eliza, 67, 182, 183, 184
Elizabeth, 100, 182, 183, 184
Elizabeth Owens, 184
George, 122, 123, 181, 182
Jane, 184, 185
Jeane, 185
Johanna, 181
John, 182, 183, 184, 220
Joseph, 182, 183, 184
Margaret, 74, 183, 184
Margret, 220
Mary, 182, 220
Nicholas, 98, 182, 183, 184
Peggy, 183, 184
Priscilla, 183, 184, 185
Rachel, 184
Richard, 183, 184
Robert, 183
Samuel, 184
Solomon, 184
Theophilus, 184
Thomas, 182, 183, 184
Walter, 184
William, 182, 183, 184, 185
 ___, 97
NORMAN'S FANCY, 122
NORRIS, Ellen, xi
 Hannah, 158
 John, 54, 142, 185, 187
 Thomas, 98
NORTH CROUCHFIELD, 224
NORWOOD, Andrew, 93, 120,
  212, 232
 Edward, 1, 16
 Elizabeth, 16, 17
 Hannah, 17, 206
 Henry, 16, 206
 Jemima, 16
 John, 6, 16, 87, 206, 231, 232
 Mary, 16, 65, 165
 Patience, 6, 16
 Samuel, 1, 16
 Susanna, xxi
NORWOOD'S ANGLES, 120,
  121

327

ST. LEGER, Lady Anne, 263
Sir Thomas, 263
ST. THOMAS' NECK, 54, 185
SALL, 180
SALT, Ann, xiii
SAM, 180
SAMPSON, Constance, 225
Elizabeth, 33, 49, xi
Sarah, 121
SAMUEL, Catherine, 147
SAMUEL'S HOPE, 143
SANDERS, James, 58, 60, 61, 80,
244, 250
John, 252
Joseph, 83
Rebecca, 217, 218
SANDS, John, 206
SANDYS, Anne, xxii
Edwin, xxiii
SAPPPINGTON, Harriet, 201
SARRI, Nancy Louise, viii
Ronald, viii
SATER, Henry, xviii
Mary, xviii
SAUGHIER, George, 80
Margaret, 80
SAUNDERS, Frederick V., 218
SAW MILL SUPPLY, 172
SAWS, Ann, 166
Robert, 166
SCARF, Mary, 225
SCHAFER, Anna Magdalena, xvi
SCHIEBELHUTH, Anna
Catherine, xv
SCHILLING, Johann Heinrich,
xv
Juliana, xiii
SCHMIDT, Catherine, xix
Henry, xix
John George, xvii
SCHREINER, Anna Catherine,
xviii
SCHWARTZ, Andrew, xviii
Anna Margaret, xviii
Henry, xiv, xvi

SCORTON, 254
SCOTT,
Edward, 165
Elizabeth, 223
Mary Ann, 202
Nancy, xvi
Roger, 132
William, 116
SCRIVEN, John, 226
SCRIVENER, Benjamin, 90, 225,
226, 227
Elisha, 127
Eliza, 226
Elizabeth, 127, 225, 226, 228
Francis, 227
Grace, 90, 226
Henrietta, 228
John, 127, 175, 226, 227
Kisriah, 227
Lewis, 227
Mary, 226, 227, 228
Rebecca, 227
Richard, 226, 227
Samuel, 226
Sarah, 228
William, 127, 226, 227, 228
William Jones, 226
SCUDAMORE, Abigail, xx
Thomas, xx
SEABOURN, Mary, 157
SECOND ADDITION TO
SNOWDEN'S MANOR, 136,
137
SECOND DISCOVERY, 136
SEE, Jesse, 13
SELBY, Enoch, 138
Esther, 116
Mary, xix, xxi
Matthew, 185
Nathan, 116
William, xxi
SELLMAN, Althea, 68
Ann Priscilla Woodward, 209
Anne, 215, 216
Anne Elizabeth, 77
Benjamin, 134, 216

Lois, 2, 4, 8, 209, 210, 213, xix, xxi
Margaret, 47
Patience, 17, 31, 33, xiv
Priscilla, 112
Rebecca, xvi
Richard, 2, 3, 8, xxi
Robert, 2, 3, 7, 8, 9, 29, xvii
Ruth, 15, 29, 41, 42, 43, 44, xv, 211, xix
Susan, 8
Talbot, 31
Ursula, 23
Usley, 23
William, 17, xvi
SHIPLEY'S CHOICE, 2, 5, 10, 18
SHIPLEY'S DISCOVERY, 9, 22, 23, 24, 30, 45, 175
SHIPLEY'S SEARCH, 3, 7, 8
SHOOP, George, 44
Sarah, 44
SHRIEVES, Ann, 147
Thomas, 147
SICKKEY, Prudence, 128
SIDEBOTTOM, Richard, 92
SIMMONDS, Abraham, 125
SIMMONS, Abraham, 59, 153
Barzilla, 149
Eliza, 163
Elizabeth, 57
George, 163
Isaac, 59
Margaret, 183
Mary, 226
Peggy, 183
Richard, 187, xxvi
Sarah, xxvi
William, 117, 125, 183
SIMMS, Anthony, 176
SIMON, Anna Catherine, xviii
Nicholas, xx
SIMONDS, Sarah, 178
SIMONS, Eliza, 163
George, 163
SIMPSON, Amos, 230
Amos Thomas, 230

Comfort, 93
Eleanor, 212
Elizabeth, 230, 231
John, 230, 231
Mary, 230
Rachel, 230
Rebecca, 231
Richard, 230, 231
Richardson, 231
Sarah, 230
Simon, 13
Thomas, 230, 231
SINCLAIR, Elizabeth, xxvi, xxvii
James, xxvi
Ruth, 77
Samuel, 77
William, xxvii
SINDELL, Ann Eliza, 77
SINGLER, Frances, 53
Westminster, 53
SINKLER, Elizabeth, xxvii
William, xxvii
SIPE, Mary Elizabeth, xi
SIPES, John T., xiii
SISSON, Benjamin, 231
Eliza, 231
Elizabeth, 232
Frances, 231
Jane, 231, 232
John, 231, 232
SKINNER, Adderton, 119
Alice, 93, 216
Andrew, 57
Anne, 127, 130
Augustine, 216
Clarke, 127, 130
Eliza, 72
Jane, 218, 221
Mary, 93, 216
Vernon L., vii, xxxiii
SKIPWITH, George, 177
SLACK, Hannah, 22
SLADE, William, 81
SLAGLE, Eleanor, 74
SLATER, John, 190
Margaret, 190

George, 42
James, 231
Jarred, 25
John, 25, 44, 178
Joseph, 93, 193
Katherine, 82
Laurence, 25
Margaret, 54
Mary, 42
Naomi, 42
Priscilla, 37
Rachel, 258
Ralph, 188
Richard, 62
Ruth, 93
Shadrach, 12
T. J. C., 35
Thomas, 25, 66, 67, 82, 258
Zadock, 25
WILLIAMSON'S HOPE, 131
WILLS, Jone, 221
  William, 221
WILLSON, John, 141
WILMOT, John, 56, 227
WILSFORD, Cecily, xxiii
WILSON, Benkid, 128
  Hammutal, 42, 211
  John, 166
  Jonathan, 160
  Mary, 16, 32
  Nancy, 50
  Robert, 215
  Thomas, 218
  William, 214, 231
WILSON'S GROVE, 215
WINDSOR, Basil, 73
WINTERSELL, William, 56
WINTERSON, Ann, 242
  Benjamin, 242
WINTNEY, Hartley, 225
WISEMAN'S FOLLY, 212
WITHAM, Ruth, 223, 224
WITHERS, Samuel, 188
WOLFE, George, 37
  James, 128
  Letitia, 37

Sarah, 128
WOOD, Dorothy, 158, 159, 163
  John, 9, 159
  Margaret, 173
  Mary, 173, 182
  Richard, 173
  Robert, 158, 162, 188, 240
  William, 145
WOODCOCK NEST, 259
WOODEN, Elizabeth, 59, 159
  Priscilla, 159
  Sarah, 96, 159
  Solomon, 96, 159
WOODFIELD, Elizabeth Owens, 184
  John, 184
WOODFORD, 20
WOODLEA, Mary, 142
WOODMAN, Martha E., 203
WOODS, Thomas, 171
WOODS CLOSE, 132
WOODWARD, A., 258
  Abraham, 85, 185, 256, 257, 258, 259
  Abraham Boyd, 258
  Achsah, 257
  Alice, 257, 258
  Amos, 257
  Ann, 258, 259
  Ann D., 258
  Anne, 258
  Carrie Stewart, 259
  Deborah, 209, 258
  Dinah, 257
  Eleanor, 257, 258
  Elizabeth, 256, 257, 259
  Elizabeth Jones, 258
  Ella Blanch, 259
  Ellinor, 257
  Emily, 258
  George Powell, 258, 259
  Hannah, 256
  Henry, 181, 240, 256, 257, 258
  Henry Williams, 258
  Jane, 257, 258
  Jane Maria, 258

Benjamin, 264
Christopher, 263
D'Arcy, 263, 264
Darcy, 264
Duke, 264
Edward, 264
Edward Hale, 264
Elinor, 264, 265
Elizabeth, 264
Hail, 264
Hale, 265
Harriet, 264
Henry, 265
Isabel, 263
Jane, 263, 264
John Burgess, 265
Marmaduke, 264, 265
Mary, 263, 264
Matilda, 264
Priscilla, 264
Sarah, 264, 265
Sir Christopher, 263
Sir Marmaduke, 263
Sir William, 263, 264
Susanna, 264
Susannah, 264
Ursula, 263
Walter, 264
William, 264, 265
William Boyd, 265
William Camden, 265

-Y-
YATE, George, 91, 135
YEAKLEY, John, 142
YEALDHALL, Sarah, 170
YEATES, Andrew, 38
YIELDHALL, Constant, 223, 224
Eliza, 231, 232; Jane, 231, 232
Mary, 173, 232; Robert, 224
Samuel, 173; William, 231, 232
YOUNG, Constance, 253;
Hannah, 30; Henry, 1, 209;
Horace J., x; Joshua, 30;
Margaret, 2; Mayme Noble, x;

Rebecca, 209; Richard, 1, 120;
Sewell, 2
YOUNG RICHARD, 189
YOUNGER, Nehemiah, 206
YOUNGER BENSON, 234
YOUNGER BESSON, 80, 234

-Z-
ZECH, Anna Maria, xiv
Jacob, xviii, Michael, xvi
ZEPP, George, 53
Josephine, 53
ZIMMERMAN, Eliza, 15, 31